The Therapeutics of Activity.

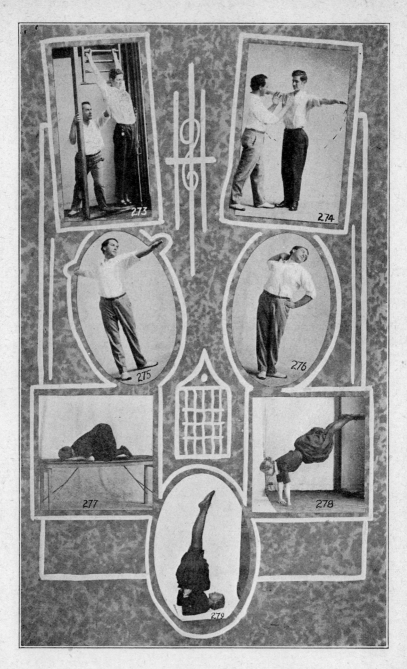

ILLUSTRATING APPLICATION OF OSTEOPATHY

THE
THERAPEUTICS
OF ACTIVITY

By

ANDREW A. GOUR, M.G., D.O.

Professor of Osteopathic Gymnastics and Orthopedics of the
Chicago College of Osteopathy; formerly instructor
of Medical Gymnastics at the Young Men's
Christian Association College
Chicago, Illinois

1923
COVICI-McGEE
CHICAGO

Press of
Printing Service
Company,
Chicago

INTRODUCTION

This book is not a plea for practical gymnastics. It is assumed at the outset that the reader at least believes in exercise, although he may not practice it. Our problem is not to consider in detail how, when, and why exercise should be performed. Such questions concern the philosophy of exercise, and that subject alone would fill several volumes. The chief purpose of this book is to explain the health side of every type of activity, and only enough is said about each topic to give the reader a working principle.

This book will serve as a guide to anyone who desires safe, though not exhaustive, information on the subjects of medical and hygienic gymnastics, and games, sports and dances. The writer does not claim to have developed a new system. Considering the abundance of literature available on the subject, anyone who should claim, at this late date, to have invented a new system of physical culture, would prove himself a charlatan or so ignorant of the subject as to deserve no one's respect. With the exception of a few ideas developed by the writer, this book claims to be, for the most part, simply a new presentation of the best material on the subject.

The foundation principles of all the subjects discussed in this book are drawn from the Ling system. In the writer's opinion the Ling system of gymnastics is certainly the best ever developed and the only one that can be called "scientific." Of course many things have been claimed for the Ling system that have no foundation in fact. But, allowing for the exaggerations of eager enthusiasts, no other method of gymnastics accords with

[I]

the established laws of anatomy, physiology and psychology.

In some ways the stories and claims hovering around the memory of Ling would place him as a demi-god, if all were to accept them. One of his countrymen, Kleen, in a recent book on Medical Gymnastics, is led by his disgust at some of Ling's admirers, to say a number of exaggerated and disparaging things about him. Although some of his points are well taken, his own copious volume has very little to add in any essential sense to the great work of the predecessor whom he would belittle.

The various encyclopedias include brief histories of gymnastics in which they attempt to deal impartially with all so-called systems, but the writers of these articles say things about the Ling system which prove that they had more of an axe to grind than a wish to adhere to the simple truth. Then we have in our country a number of men, prominent in the world of sports, whose reputations among posterity would be better had they left unsaid certain statements about the Ling system. As a notable example consider Walter Camp, who is an expert on "eastern" football. When he writes, as he has, in support of his little "Daily Dozen," that an army officer told him that the Swedish system was unpopular in the American army because the men said the daily drill left them tired out, he lays himself open to such criticism as one dislikes to administer. In the first place, none of the Swedish system was ever given in the American army. As a setting-up drill which is part of the daily routine was arranged by advocates of the German system of gymnastics, there could have been no such experience to report. Moreover, the officer whom Mr. Camp quotes, or refers to, has a name that is as Prussian as "Kaiser."

It is really pitiful that Mr. Camp should have to bolster up his limited collection of movements by saying things against a system concerning which his very state-

[II]

ments prove his ignorance. Of course his fame in the football world has given him enough prestige to sell his little haphazard collection of movements by the hundreds of thousands, and if success is measured in terms of money, he is successful. However, when one realizes that Mr. Camp's "Daily Dozen" is about as poor a collection of movements as any enterprising imposter might collect together, the facts cannot add luster to his fame.

We now find the "Daily Dozen" served up as canned gymnastics on phonograph records in imitation of one whose commercial instinct has always surpassed his ethics and science. When one understands the fallacy of teaching or practicing gymnastics to music, of repeating movements which have been memorized, of the erroneous arrangements of the movements from the standpoint of gymnastic sequence, as well as the worthlessness of the movements themselves, the impelling power of constructive criticism and of public duty compel him to speak out, in spite of one's charity of heart.

Measured by scientific gymnastic standards nearly all phonograph gymnastics and systemettes offered so far should be scrapped. From the basis of proven gymnastic laws we know that fifty percent of the "Daily Dozen" are useless. We know that a larger percentage of Muller's "My System" is bad. As for Wallace's original phonograph records for reducing weight, the writer analyzed the first disk and found six of eight movements wrong. This means that they are on the average seventy-five percent bad.

In this country we have heard several men whom the public consider authorities in the world of sports and gymnastics. Few of these will admit that the Ling system is worthy of any more consideration than any other arrangement of activities. Most of them have accepted Hough's essay as sufficient support for their opinions. This essay, explained in Chapter I, to many is the alpha and omega of gymnastic criticism. Because it saved them the trouble of a little thinking, these critics have hung their judgment caps on Hough's pegs and it would fill many pages to quote their wise saws. Dr. Sargent, for instance, who has introduced more useless apparati for gymnasiums than all others put together, said that the day's order of the Swedish system is of no more importance than the arrangement of food in a menu. Dr. R. T. McKenzie, who is a much better sculptor than a gymnastic authority, in his book, "Exercise in Education and Medicine," attempts to score a point in favor of the American system by quoting from Hough's essay. We might fill this page with names of men and women, notably among the leaders in the German system, who have allowed Hough to do their investigating and thinking for them, but to what purpose?

The statements of such men cannot hurt the Ling system, but they mislead many and delay the popularity and support in this country which this system deserves. Indeed, here in Chicago, a few years ago, when a number of men and women were interested in testing out the merits of the Ling in comparison with the German system, instead of facing the issue squarely and upon its merits, the leaders of the German singing and gymnastic societies all over the city banded themselves together and wrote at least two letters, of which I have copies, to Mayor Harrison, belittled the Ling system, and then threatened to swing over 240,000 votes away from the mayor.

In several of the leading countries of the world, after considering and carefully analyzing the various so-called systems, the Ling was officially accepted as the best in connection with physical upbuilding. This is true of Japan, England, Greece, Holland, and all Scandinavian countries. Even Germany, just before the World War broke out, was revamping its system with Ling ideas. It was in Germany, of course, that the Ling system was conceived.

[IV]

When comparing the Swedish and the German systems we should keep in mind what their founders intended. Guts-Muth, the real father of modern gymnastics, in the latter part of the eighteenth century, had Jahn, the founder of German, and Ling, the founder of Swedish gymnastics as pupils. Guts-Muth stated in his writings that he had two aims in his work: "(1) Work in the garb of youthful play, and (2) a system of exercise having bodily perfection as the aim." The first applied to Jahn and the second to Ling. Jahn founded the modern German system which is particularly noted for its variety of stunts and amusing features, but which does not aim primarily to correct the defects and promote the health of its adherents. Ling developed his system with the primary object of promoting bodily perfection in all who practiced it. So that while amusement and skill are the aims of the German system, health, control and bodily perfection are the aims of the Swedish. The German system does not try so much to build up the weak as to polish the strong into circus performers. The Swedish tries to build the weak up to average or above it and is not so concerned about the strong because it regards the latter as well able to care for himself if he remains active. The German system contains more gymnastic drills with wands, dumbbells, clubs and free standing set to music. In the Swedish system, no music is employed as a general thing and pupils are compelled by the type of work done to keep their minds concentrated upon it, thus establishing the type of mental control that renders the body a servant to the brain. Of course, both systems promote good health.

In this country we were fortunate to have had such men as Baron Nils Posse and Jacob Bolin. Posse surely carried out the ideas of Ling beyond the dreams and concepts of any other exponent of the Swedish system. Posse had also begun to fit the Swedish system to typical

[V]

American needs when his untimely death from accident cut short his work. This book is an attempt to continue the work of Posse. Jacob Bolin performed work which supplements much of Posse's. His book on "Gymnastic Problems" explains why so many popular types of activity do not produce the results intended by those who teach them and until one is acquainted with the work of Bolin and Posse he is not equipped to judge and denounce the Swedish system. The so-called Danish system which is now being introduced in this country in a few localities is nothing but the Ling system mixed up with Danish folk plays and dances and rendered more amusing. While it adds variety it does not essentially improve on the Ling foundations.

While this book has been used as a text in some schools it is a slight departure from the usual text book on gymnastic instruction. The primary aim is to equip the reader with the necessary understanding and material to care for himself. There are no commands given with the exercises except for little children and as an appendix at the end of the volume.

The writer has tried to explain everything in plain enough language to enable the average reader to understand all. The descriptions of movements and their underlying principles and applications are presented. As one reads on he will see how vast a subject this gymnastic question is. It will take away any desire to claim a new system.

It seems strange how most persons who become interested in gymnastics immediately dream of launching a new system. One can invoke the gods of activity and churn out a new method, but the days are past when a new system which owes nothing to the works of predecessors can be evolved.

There are many systemettes and tabloid systems possible, but there are really only two great systems that should be understood in order to know which one to avoid and which one to foster. We have in this country the so-called American system, which is made up of whatever the instructor feels like giving provided there is enough play to suit the fancy of its advocates. But such an arrangement of activities is not determined by any known laws of the exact sciences. What we do need is a better understanding of the Ling system to which we should add such competitive and play activities as are favored most generally by our growing population. Certainly more of the corrective types of activities are imperative. During the drafting and examining before we took part in the World War it was found out that over one-third of the men rejected for physical weaknesses were afflicted with conditions which could have been prevented, and in most cases overcome, by physical activity, especially of the medical gymnastic type. It makes one wonder how long it will take for our country to learn its lesson.

Many who are for America first, right or wrong, and want nothing to do with other nations' ideas, like to hold up the records of our boys on the track fields as a proof of our physical superiority. There is no question as to the superiority of the American athletes, but there is a question as to what gives them this superiority. They have to possess superior physiques to withstand the grind and strain of the athletic field, and their prowess is not so much the result of such work as that they possess their physiques in spite of it. The stock from which Americans descend was the peasant and working stock of Europe of a generation or two back. Because their fathers possessed strong bodies when they came here it requires little training to qualify their descendants as successful athletic competitors. But it is interesting to note the appearance of an athlete who has specialized in some single sport to the exclusion of all other activities. No matter how strong a physique one has inherited, to specialize for a few years in one type of activity is to

[VII]

produce such unbalanced development as to often amount to deformity. What we need more than winning athletic teams is the best possible physical foundations in all our youths, male and female, and we should never allow competitive sports to enter into their lives until they have reached the highest state of health that it is possible for them to attain. In outlining a course of training that will assure perfect physiques we can include all kinds of games and sports, but the foundations must be gymnastic. All such points as these are discussed and made clear throughout this book.

That there is a need for corrective and hygienic gymnastics ought to be plain to all. It does not require a very keen appreciation of the ideal physique to enable one to understand the advantages of such an endowment. Everything else in life is rendered easier and better by a good physique. It requires no great perceptive faculty to become conscious of the fact that very few normal physiques are to be found today. The very fat or very thin, the awkward, loose-jointed or rigid and muscle-bound, the drooping-head, round-shouldered, flat-chested, scrawny, muddy complexioned are everywhere seen. Indeed, these defects are so common as to be often overlooked. Dr. Sargent, in a moment of mental aberration, said that the common occurrence of spinal curvatures and other anatomical defects was perhaps a new step in the physical evolution of man. If such were true we ought to delay this kind of evolution for a while by preventive and corrective gymnastics. The fact of the matter is that such statements are made to please those who are lazy and thus find reasons for not exerting themselves, and they may be a proof that the one who makes them does not fully understand the laws and applications of corrective gymnastics. All the above facts, considered together, are a strong plea for systematic exercise.

No system of healing is complete without including

exercise as an adjunct and no school except the Swedish gymnastic school has made a thorough enough study of this subject. There are laws governing gymnastics which have been discovered after many years of experiment and earnest research. Exercises have been arranged according to these laws, and it will repay anyone to try to understand them before summarily condemning them. There are many conditions which will succumb to nothing but exercise, but the exercises must be specific and not haphazard. Orthopedics may correct certain defects, but it cannot strengthen any part of the body without the employment of proper activity. Osteopathy may correct or adjust various lesions, but in most cases, unless proper exercises are employed, there will be recurring lesions or little relief. A real state of perfection and health cannot be maintained without regularly practiced activity of a type to suit individual needs. It is an important thing to know that particular exercises are best in each case. This book, rightly understood, will settle the question of specific activities for everyone.

CHAPTER I.

BASIC PRINCIPLES OF GYMNASTICS.

Principal sources of material—General Kinesiology, its meaning and scope—Special Kinesiology, its meaning and scope—Mechanics of exercise; application of physics—viz: laws of penetrating energy—reciprocating motion—centrifugal force—laws of leverage—gravity and length of base—line and centre of gravity in human body—Exercise to counteract gravity—Posture correct and incorrect. In daily life flexors used most—in gymnastics aim to exercise extensors—value of gymnastics of muscular contraction from origin to insertion—typical balance movement, heel elevation —example of balance movements and their value to antagonize gravity. Gymnastic Osteology—shape and structure of bone to fit function—Spine as typical long bone with specialized functions—function may change structure even of bone—Relation of exercise to development and shape of bone. Arthrology—study of articulations—possibilities and limitations of motion—voluntary and involuntary limitations—exercise and mobility of joints—Myology—in gymnastics a study of muscular function—guide of progression in strength of movement—movements voluntary and involuntary—under volition predominant—relation of contractility and extensibility—resultant elasticity synergy and antagonism—"slow-leg movement" or vascular expansion, generally misunderstood, explained and illustrated. Respiratory and "slow-leg movement" differentiated and applied—General rule governing effects of exercise. Forms of contraction excentric, concentric and static—their application. Effects of continued pressure on muscular tissue—Exercise and muscular tissue—Need of oxygen to activity—fatigue—overwork or strain and the heart—value of progressive exercise for heart leakage—exercise and muscular growth—co-ordination voluntary and involuntary—active repose—Grace and its significance—Health first aim of exercise—next control—Dynamics; bodily heat—relation to exercise—weather and athletics—Heat, oxidation and health—conduction, convection and radiation—how perspiration cools—importance of cleanliness. Physiology of exercise—exercise and respiration—necessity of oxygen—relation of rest and various degrees of activity to respiration—Vital capacity—Correct type of respiration, how acquired—Respiration and metabolism—Importance of thoracic suppleness—Importance of correct posture—relation of head and chest—Exercise and circulation—Forces that keep the blood flowing—helps and hindrances—The muscle-cell and its function—Exercise and the pulse—Regurgitation—Compensation—gymnastic treatment—Extension vs. contraction and circulation—Respiration and circulation—Exercise and metabolism—Proper exercise promotes metabolism—excessive exercise—Exercise and quality of blood—Evil effects of inactivity—Abdominal and lateral trunk movements and their relation to obesity—Nature's corset—Exercise and neurition—Importance of proximity between brain and muscle—Ideal of physical education—Efficiency and health not merely mental nor physical—Perfect physique a tool and support to the brain—Importance of concentration on exercise—Progression in gymnastics—useful vs. spectacular—Exercise and dramatic interpretation—"Posture produces feeling"—Periodicity—regularity of short doses vs. occasional strain—Exercise through life—Individuality—Exercise to be effective must fit one's needs. Philosophy of exercise—How to supplement or counteract other activities by gymnastics—Methods of progression.

CHAPTER II.

HOME GYMNASTICS.

Arranged after Baron Nils Posse's interpretation—progressive—meet needs of average—How to practice them—Brief explanation of Ling's system—its aim—Day's order—Explanation of each division of exercise in the day's order—Fundamental standing positions—its importance—Twenty-seven lessons explained and illustrated.

CHAPTER III.

GAMES AND SPORTS: THEIR ACTIVE PRINCIPLES AND CORRECTIVE APPLICATIONS.

Methodical Gymnastics "too dry" for most people—games and sports most popular activity—one-sided; this fact taken advantage of in selecting—Value of play—Age as factor in selecting games—keeping in condition—Danger of indulging in one sport at exclusion of others—Classification, active principle and therapeutic value of combative exercises—fencing, foil, broadsword or rapier—single stick—boxing—bag punching—hand-wrestling—tug-of-war—jiu-jitsu—Running and other ball games—basketball—baseball—football—Rugby—lacrosse—tennis—handball. Other games and sports—field hockey—ice-hockey—hurling—ice-polo—golf—croquet—bowling—swimming—rowing—archery—canoeing—skating on ice—roller-skating—skiing—snow-shoeing—walking—bicycling—horseback riding—athletics—Gymnastic games and children's games—medicine ball—dodge ball—straddle ball—volley ball—hill dill—hangtag—Indian club wrestling—chicken fight—stick wrestling—bull-in-the-ring—tournament—arch-ball—Dancing—leg work—ballroom dancing—old and new styles compared—folk dancing—esthetic dancing—classic and interpretive dancing—Russian dancers—Eurhythmics of Dalcroze—Value and comparison of various styles of dancing—Conclusion: therapeutic application of typical play activities.

CHAPTER IV.

MEDICAL GYMNASTICS.

Definition—difference between medical and hygienic gymnastics—Subdivisions of the subject—Value of massage—origin and brief history—Experiments of Mosso and Maggiora of Turin to prove value of massage—Value of massage as introductory to muscular exertion—as a restorative—aid to circulation—as passive exercise—Friction—little value—Kneading—most valuable—correct method—its effects on circulation, heart and nerves—Abdominal kneading to relieve constipation and bowel impaction—Circumduction, how given—effects—indications—Nerve pressure compared to stimulation and inhibition—Percussion of some value as nerve stimulant—methods of application—Vibration of great service when properly applied—especially helpful in adhesions—Active movements—kinds and applications—passive—assistive—single—resistive—applied according to patient's powers and strength—Respiratory exercises—effects and use.

CHAPTER V.

APPLICATION OF MEDICAL GYMNASTICS IN OSTEOPATHY.

Only such procedures as may aid osteopathic treatment—Disorders of circulation—General procedures in Endocarditis—Myocarditis—typical outline in valvular leakage—Fatty infiltration—Arterio-sclerosis—Varicose veins—How to flush or drain a part of blood—Disorders of respiration—Typical respiratory exercises for therapeutic use—Adjuncts to osteopathy in rhinitis—laryngitis—pharyngitis—tonsilitis — pleurisy — bronchitis — corrective of thoracic defects from pleurisy—emphysema—tuberculosis—Disorders of digestion—enteralgia—constipation—prolapsus of rectum—hemorrhoids—Disorders of neurition—neurasthenia—sciatica—neuritis—paralysis—chorea—epilepsy—infantile paralysis—locomotor ataxia—occupation neuroses—hysteria—cephalgia—After treatment of fracture—Sprains—strain—synovitis—bursitis—rheumatism—arthritis deformans—gout—ptoses and treatment.

CHAPTER VI.

CORRECTIVE GYMNASTICS; PRINCIPLES AND APPLICATIONS.

Explanation of laws underlying corrective gymnastics—Application of corrective gymnastics, with typical exercises, done singly, against resistance or with apparatus in—drooping-head—round-shoulders—drooping-shoulders—posterior dorsal—shallow chest—narrow chest and shoulders—anterior dorsal one-sided chest defect—pigeon breast—lordosis—posterior lumbar—knock-knees—bow-legs—flat-foot—adhesive plaster in flat-foot treatment—Correcting foot deformities—pigeon toes—externally rotated feet.

CHAPTER VII.

THE GYMNASTIC TREATMENT OF INGUINAL HERNIA.

"Rupture"—origin of the term—definition of hernia—named according to location—contents of sac—clinically divided into reducible and irreducible—incarcerated, inflamed and strangulated—explanation and importance of each—Hernia also named according to contents—enterocele—epiplocele—Causes of hernia—first symptoms—test for coming hernia—Palliative treatment—proper truss—Philosophy of gymnastic treatment—Application of treatment—

patient's position—reduction of hernia—Osteopathic and other procedures—preceding exercise—Exercise according to patient's strength—twelve typical exercises given in progressive order.

CHAPTER VIII.

LATERAL CURVATURE OF THE SPINE.

History of scoliosis—Definition of scoliosis—common defect—most common in women—causes—muscular—osseous—Value of exercise in correcting—combined with osteopathy and brace—explanation of gymnastic treatment—Structural changes in vertebrae and ribs—Infantile paralysis and organic lesions as causes of scoliosis—Innominate lesions—C curvature—S curvature—Tests for primary curve—age of patient as factor—prognosis—Precautions to be observed—heart conditions, etc.—removable plaster jacket—how utilized—Abbott method—how applied—value and limitations—Osteopathic procedures—Principles of gymnastic treatment—Three typical programs of nine exercises each explained, for single dorsal, double, and single lumbar curvatures.

CHAPTER IX.

INDIVIDUAL PROGRAMS.

How to outline program to fit individual needs—Types of blank forms—Outlines of progressive programs, with explanations and precautions for their applications in—Heart disturbances—Pulmonary consumption—Locomotor Ataxia—Infantile paralysis—After treatment in Apoplexy—Restoring function after fracture—Treatment for Obesity—How to add to your weight—Reducing weight thighs—How to have a beautiful throat—Exercise while travelling—Stretching and relaxing exercises for the muscle-bound—Antagonistic exercises for the flabby-muscled and loose-jointed—Applying corrective procedures in conjunction with hygienic exercises—Exercises to articulate and limber the spine—Occupational Gymnastics.

The Therapeutics of Activity.

Miss. Klipfel
San Francisco

235

CHAPTER I.

BASIC PRINCIPLES OF GYMNASTICS.

The fundamental laws of gymnastics have been most clearly expounded in this country by Baron Nils Posse and Jacob Bolin. Most of the important points in this chapter have been based upon notes taken at the Posse Gymnasium or suggested by the writings of these two men.

There are so many movements possible to the human body that any system worthy of the name should include only those that are useful and beneficial. All useless, doubtful or injurious movements should be eliminated. The experiences of years of observation and experimentation have been carefully recorded and such information is available for reference in selecting and arranging gymnastics.

Baron Posse has applied the term General Kinesiology to the study of all forms of movement, gymnastic or otherwise. For our purpose only bodily movements shall be considered.

In various parts of the world, for a very long time, men interested in physical development have experimented with various types of bodily movements. The results upon those performing them were noted and the movements have been classified and adopted according to their true gymnastic value or rejected with good reason. The gymnastic school founded by P. H. Ling, in Sweden, in 1809, has done most in this respect and the results of its work will always influence good gymnastic teaching.

The purpose of General Kinesiology as a science is to purify gymnastics by suppressing all useless or injurious movements, games or sports; to sift gymnastics by choosing only the beneficial from all possible bodily movements; to enrich gymnastics by adding useful, interesting and beneficial movements; and to make known new discoveries by bringing them before the public through lectures and publications.

General Kinesiology applies to all systems of gymnastics but each system has a special kinesiology of its own which considers the mechanics, effects, limitations and classifications of all movements. For a complete consideration of the special kinesiology of the Ling system one should read Baron Nils Posse's "Special Kinesiology of Educational Gymnastics." For our purpose a brief consideration of some of the laws of General Kinesiology will serve.

In the mechanics of exercise (under the subject of physics) there are important gymnastic laws based upon various forms of energy. To understand these thoroughly is to clarify many important reasons for the way in which gymnastic movements and also athletic feats should be performed.

Penetrating energy is an important force whose governing law applies in gymnastics. The power of penetration increases as the square of the rate at which the velocity increases. For example, given a train of cars travelling at thirty miles an hour, when all power is shut off it will, of its own momentum, travel a certain distance. Let the same train of cars, under similar conditions, travel sixty miles an hour and when the power is shut off it will, of its own momentum, travel four times as far as in the first case, allowing for friction and the power of gravity. If the speed of travel is trebled the train will travel, of its own momentum, nine times as far as in the first case, and so on. Applying this law to gymnastics, in arm extension sideways, for instance, the more speed is put into the extension the greater the expansive and broadening effect on the chest and shoulders. Increasing the speed in trunk sideways flexion increases the difficulty of the movement and thus makes for progression. It is also clear why speed in the run means so much in such a feat as the running broad jump.

Reciprocating motion must be considered in conjunction with penetrating energy. If a rubber ball is thrown on the floor at a certain speed it will rebound a given height. If the speed at which it is thrown is doubled the ball will, allowing for gravity, tend to rebound four times as high as in the first instance, and so on. The rule is similar to that of penetrating energy. The best application of this law is in connection with the high jump. The more force is put into the final contact with the ground at the take-off the higher will be the jump. Combining these two laws in the running broad jump, the more speed is put into the run and the stronger the spring in the final take-off the longer the jump will be. Expert coaches often place a string at a height of four or five feet, a few feet beyond the take-off board, and drill their pupils in clearing this string after the speediest run possible. With this kind of practice record breakers are made.

Centrifugal force, the tendency of a body to fly off at a tangent when swung in a circle, is an important power to consider in gymnastics. The law of increase in centrifugal force corresponds to that of penetrating energy or reciprocating motion. The common practice among country boys of poking a stick into an apple and by a long upward sweep of the stick to cause the apple to fly off at great speed is an example of centrifugal force. Another example is to tie a horse chestnut or stone to a string and swing it rapidly in a circle and then let go of the string. The object thus swung travels a much greater distance than one could throw it. The story of David and Goliath is a mythological application of the law of centrifugal force, in so far as the stone and the sling are concerned. And, I would say, David made a lucky shot.

Through centrifugal force we may affect the circulation of the blood. Swinging the arms rapidly in a circle will make the fingers tingle because of the great amount of blood forced into them. The familiar sight of a teamster or truck driver striking his hands across his chest to warm them in the winter time is an application of centrifugal force. If he only knew it, it is not the force with which he strikes himself so much as the speed of the sweep of the arm that warms the hands. His purpose would be more quickly achieved if he merely swung the arms in a circle. To stand with the feet apart and the arms out from the shoulders and twist the trunk rapidly from side to side will drive blood into the arms and hands. Rapid trunk flexion sideways will cause blood to rush to the head.

It is because of centrifugal force that one develops dizziness or headache from rapid trunk bending backward and forward alternately, as is so commonly done by those who do not know, or do not care to observe the natural laws which influence the body. A movement which is commonly practiced is that of describing a wide circle with the head by bending forward, sideways, backward and to the other side and then forward again, several times. In many public gymnasiums and even in gymnastic school classes, I have witnessed this performance and when the pupils complained that they were dizzy the instructor invariably said that in time they would get used to these movements without such results. As if repeated violation could offset a natural law!

As an example of how the law of centrifugal force is counteracted, witness how circus riders incline inwardly to keep their balance. In running around a corner one must lean inwardly or decrease his speed because of this force. The saucer or bowl race track is built with this force in mind.

The law of centrifugal force is strongly manifested in certain medical gymnastic procedures. Rapid circumduction of a limb will draw more than a normal amount of blood to it. This is useful in cases where we wish to congest a part or drain a distal part of the body and will be fully explained in another chapter.

In relation to the laws of leverage and gravity, progression in gymnastics is made by lessening the base, or lengthening the lever, or by both. By lessening the base we mean shortening the base in the direction of action. The base means the position of the feet. As an example let us consider trunk bending sideways. The easiest way to perform this type of movement is with the feet apart. Up to a certain point, the farther apart the feet the easier the movement. The closer the feet are to each other the shorter the base in the direction of action and the more difficult the movement becomes.

Lengthening the lever, or raising the center of gravity, is accomplished by changing the arms. If we take the same movement mentioned above, that is, trunk bending sideways, it is done, first with the arms hanging straight down, then the hands on the hips; later the hands are on the shoulders and still later they are behind the head or extended upward. It is obvious that bending the trunk sideways with the arms extended upward must be more difficult than with the hands on the hips. The higher the arms the longer the lever from the center of motion and, because raising the arms means raising the mass of weight, it also means raising the center of gravity so that the combination of a longer lever and a higher center of gravity tends to lessen the stability of the body in motion. If we combine the increase in the length of lever with the raising of the center of gravity and the shortening of the base in the direction of action, we have a threefold means of increasing the difficulty of a movement and thus make for progression.

The stability of a body standing on end depends upon the size of its base and the height of its center of gravity. The human body is subject to the same laws as an inanimate body and may be considered from the same standpoint. In normal standing position the base of a man is bounded by the balls of the feet and the heels and the line joining these. Given healthy muscles, the longer the feet and, up to a certain point, the farther apart they spread, the more stable the body. The shorter the feet and the closer they are held together the less stable the body. To preserve stability the line of gravity must be kept within the boundary of the base. If one carries a heavy burden he must incline the body in a direction opposite to the burden in order to keep the line of gravity within the boundary of the base; otherwise he could not stand up. It is utterly impossible for anyone, no matter how skillful, to defy the law of gravitation. We sometimes see pictures of expert dancers, so posed as to be out of the line of gravity, but this is merely a trick of photography. When such pictures are taken the subject is supported by an assistant or by a fixed support, and when the cut is made the support is taken out.

The bony skeleton of the body is so constructed as to render it more stable in the transverse direction but, through lack of normal activity and muscular development, the masses of muscles that are essential to everyday life are at the front and back of the body and so we find it stronger and more stable in the sagittal direction. Regardless of the strength and arrangement of muscles, however, the rule prevails that stability depends principally upon the relation between the base and the altitude of its center of gravity; increasing as the base increases and decreasing as the altitude of the center of gravity increases. So, to make movements easy, we make the base broader and keep the center of gravity low. To make a movement more difficult, we increase the effort to preserve equilibrium by decreasing the base and raising the center of gravity.

When in good standing position with the head erect, chin in, chest forward over the balls of the feet and the head held with a sense of upward reaching, the line of gravity in the body passes in front of the cervical and upper dorsal vertebrae, thus causing the need of stronger muscles at the back than the front of the spine to stand erect. These muscles, called the erectors of the spine, keep the body from falling forward. The line of gravity passes behind the hips and knee joints, which fact explains why we find stronger muscles at the front than the back of the thighs. It then crosses the legs through the tibia, passes in front of the ankle and through the arch of the foot.

The line of gravity thus considered represents the path of the downward pull on the body and the erectors of the spine. The extensors of the thighs and the calf muscles constitute a force sufficiently strong to counteract this downward pull of gravity as well as to oppose successfully the flexors of the body which work with gravity. The constant downward pull of gravity tends to exhaust the erectors of the body and these muscles tend to gradually succumb to this pull, unless kept in perfect tone. The flexors of the body, which means the muscles which work against the erectors just considered, work with gravity so as to render the normal function of the erectors much more difficult. In time these downward pulling forces become triumphant, as is shown in what is known as "old man's stoop," in which the head is bowed, the shoulders drooped and the knees partly bent, while the person walks with a shuffling gait.

"Old man's stoop" is the bodily posture into which everyone is drifting unless his occupation or gymnastic activity is such as to counteract it. In the Ling system of gymnastics special effort is always made to extend the flexors of the body and to practice strengthening movements to tone up the erector muscles generally.

In muscular contraction the extremities of the muscles are drawn nearer together. The more movable end usually moves toward the fixed end. The fixed end of a muscle is usually the end nearer the central framework of the body and is called the origin. The movable end is usually the distal end from the central framework and is called the insertion. Therefore it is a fact that muscles usually contract from the insertion to the origin, bringing with them the movable members to which they are attached.

The muscles that elevate the ribs have their origin along the cervical vertebrae and back of the head. Each internal intercostal elevates the next lower rib when the ribs are fixed from the top. From the spine, neck, back of head and collar bone originate the muscles which are inserted into the upper arm and around the shoulder. From the upper arm originate the muscles which are inserted into the forearm bones and move them. From the forearm most of the muscles originate which are inserted into the wrist and fingers and which move them. Thus, at every muscular contraction the looser end moves toward the fixed end. But, besides the downward pull of gravity, through this very force of the muscles that causes its ends to draw together, there is a constant, though slight, tendency for the fixed end to give way a little and move toward the insertion end. The most firmly knit body is but flesh and bone and every action by it leaves its reaction upon it. We therefore find that the tendency of the body to give up to gravity and to this downward pull toward the movable end requires special attention. To counteract this tendency it is found advisable in gymnastics to practice movements in which the insertion end of the muscles is made the fixed end during their performance. This of course necessitates the use of apparatus. If in the ordinary flexing of the

arm the shoulder is caused to move downward, by pulling the body up to bent arm on a horizontal bar we establish a situation in which the insertion ends of all the
muscles of the arms, shoulders and ribs, become the fixed
ends and the origin ends are made to move toward them.
The effect of such an exercise is to elevate the ribs and
shoulders and thus facilitate the work of the erectors of
the spine.

Movements the chief effect of which is to counteract
the force of gravity by strengthening the erectors and
stretching the flexors of the body are valuable as corrective and preventive forces.   To extend the flexors of the
spine and the entire trunk, backward bending, especially
of the upper spine, is valuable.   To cultivate contractility
of the muscles which counteract gravity, no class of
movements surpasses the balance movements of the Ling
system.   Every one of this class of movements requires good general control of the muscles whose function it is to keep the body in erect posture.   Every balance movement is performed with one or both feet on the
ground; the body itself, and various positions of the
arms, legs and trunk, form the means of progression.
There is no need of external apparatus for balance movements, although dumbbells may sometimes be used to increase the difficulty of some of them.

One of the first and most commonly practiced of
balance movements is heel elevation.   As one rises on the
toes the center of gravity moves forward slightly and the
muscles of the back have to contract harder to keep the
body from falling forward.   Standing on the balls of the
feet with the trunk erect and the head kept as tall as
possible requires a high degree of control in itself, but
the movement or position is rendered more difficult and
its effect is felt more powerfully the more speed one puts
into the heel lifting.   The more speed one puts into the
rise the more the body tends to fall forward, because of

penetrating energy, and thus the more corrective the movement becomes.

In coming down from toe standing position the heels should be lowered slowly, because a quick drop from the toes onto the heels will jar the spine and perhaps counteract all the good effects of the heel lifting. Therefore the rule is to rise on the toes quickly, the quicker the better, and then lower the heels slowly. This rule always obtains in any gymnastic movement, whether balance or jumping, in which the heels are lifted and lowered at any portion of the movement.

The value of toe balancing and toe walking has been found so beneficial by a French physician that he has advocated what he calls a new system of physical development which is so simple that anyone may learn it and so valuable that all will derive benefit from the very start. His system consists of nothing more than merely rising on the toes and holding the head as high as possible while balancing in this position or while walking forward or backward. There is no question as to the great benefits to be derived from the simple but regular practice of heel elevation. But there is a question about a physician's integrity and character who claims, at this late date, to have discovered a new system which is made up of nothing more than the simplest and most commonly practiced of balance movements of the Ling system.

Another group of physicians have recently created a stir over their statement that all that there is of value in physical training may be derived from nothing more than standing erect and holding the head as high as possible ten or twelve times per day, and that this is to be practiced until such a time as holding the head high becomes second nature. The ample support for this theory is based upon the idea that when primitive man descended from the tree and began to balance upon his nether ends his entire attention was absorbed in per-

forming the balance feat and that this established an unconscious neuro-muscular control which has since been
lost or perverted through conscious physical training.
The earnest advocates of conscious erect standing to
re-establish unconscious neuro-muscular control affirm
that the daily practice of standing with the head held
high, as high as possible, without paying any attention to
the posture of the chest and shoulders or any other portion of the body, will so tax the intrinsic muscles of the
spine, or the central areas of the nerves and muscles,
that no other form of activity will prove necessary for
complete development.

This is so absurd on the face of it that one should
hardly dignify the proposition by discussing it. But its
advocates include so many of our leading physicians and
others who ought to know better that one cannot close
this phase of our subject without a few words upon this
new development. The affirmation that to merely hold
the head as high as possible will tend to properly align
the spine, ribs and all their attachments is excellent.
But to state that this alone will suffice to keep the general musculature in healthy condition is simply absurd.
Of course the advocates of this simple method of physical
development advise indulgence in games of various sorts,
but when one understands the one-sidedness of all games
and sports he also understands the limitations of any
such one-idea system.

One of the chief advocates of the neuro-muscular
development idea states that he is opposed to the Ling
system because this system makes for conscious development and control. There is a slight difference between
the Ling system and the neuro-muscular development
system in that the Ling system properly begins where
this unconscious control development system would end.

Briefly put, every kind of physical development
which is scientific in its concept goes through the conscious period of effort until the movement or position

practiced becomes easy, when it grows into an automatic or unconscious power. This is true of educational gymnastics, of games, of eurhythmics and also of dancing of every kind. Nearly all of the modern discussions by learned lecturers and writers go into activities from a more or less scientific psychological angle which usually lands them back to first principles of the type the Ling system includes when thoroughly understood.

As a second step in advance of the chief stock in trade of the unconscious neuro-muscular development advocate, to further elucidate the effects of balance movements upon the extensors of the body and thus more quickly restore the power of erect posture such as our forebears of the stone age came by with such difficulty, place the hands on the hips, rise on the toes, or, to be specific, on the balls of the feet, and hold this position without disturbing the good posture of any part of the body. While holding this position, keeping the head as tall as possible, twist it to the left and to the right a number of times. This movement requires a higher degree of equilibrium control than the simple one of simply holding the head as high as possible and will, after it has become automatic, assure a higher degree of unconscious neuro-muscular control than the simpler example already cited.

Before dismissing the topic of standing and posture, it might be appropriate to say a few words about the latest theory advanced. A certain shoe firm advocates standing with the feet pointing straight forward and the toes slightly inward, with the heels far enough apart so that the feet will rest exactly below the articulations of the ilia and the femurs. This position not only looks unnatural and strained, but it is absolutely unanatomical. The graceful bend in the shaft of the femur is perfectly adapted to having the knees and the heels together in standing erect, no matter how the toes are pointing. If one continued to stand or walk with the feet apart there would of necessity develop a change in the shape of the femur which, though adapted to this arbitrary and commercialized position, would not add to the femur's strength, elasticity or efficiency. Of course, such a change in the structure of the femur would require many generations for accomplishment, if persisted in by father and mother and child down the centuries. Until such a change in the femur is achieved this awkward position will prove strained and useless.

There is another new theory which is gaining vogue among a small group who know more about the theory than they seem to know about the body's anatomy and physiology. The position is one in which the feet and legs are in the position just explained and the lumbar spine is forced back into straight or slightly posterior position, so as to allow the viscera to settle into the pelvic basket! as explained by its advocates. In this position the aim is to keep the shoulder joint directly above the anterior crest of the ilium, the head with the chin in, so as to force the forehead anterior to the chin. It is claimed that this position will equalize the work of all the muscles of the spine, of the pelvis and legs, whatever that may mean and to whatever great advantage it may be claimed. The fact is that there is nothing to this posture that equals that of the Ling system for the reasons explained above.

The normal curves of the spine in perfect health are anterior at the cervical, posterior at the dorsal, and anterior at the lumbar regions. The most serious blunder ever committed by the Ling school, one that has been overlooked by all its critics, was that they advocated movements and efforts to straighten the dorsal spine. This is all right where there is a pronounced posterior exaggeration at this region, but in the average spine no effort of this sort is necessary or advisable because it has been proven that a straight or anterior dorsal spine predisposes to lung, heart and digestive disturbances. To make an effort to hold the lumbar spine straight or posterior means to compel a straightening or posterior bending in the dorsal spine because the bottom of the spine determines the posture of the upper regions. Posterior lumbar always predisposes to or causes constipation, general visceral ptoses, and, as a consequence, pelvic disturbances. It seems so illogical to advocate conscious development of so unphysiological a bodily posture, that one would be inclined to pass it by with scorn were it not advocated by people who hold responsible positions in the educational world.

It must not be understood by this discussion that the writer advocates or approves of lordosis. What is desirable, always, is the normal anterior lumbar and posterior dorsal curves. These curves are best adapted to efficient function and normal position of the internal organs. A fact that should never be forgotten, when one decides to change the world's standing posture, is that the internal organs are all attached from the posterior walls of the chest and abdominal cavities. These attachments are adapted to the anatomy of the four-footed creature. The human body in upright posture allows gravity to drag down these organs. Any such position as the last one described, which favors, as its chief advocate asserts, a settling down of the viscera into the pelvic basket, will work for general ptoses of all the organs and a physician needs no argument beyond this fact to prove its undesirability. To advocate this straight lumbar position for the reason that it will allow the diaphragm to descend even lower than normal into the abdominal cavity and thus massage the intestines is not only fallacious but injurious. Instead of trying to devise some way to relieve the work of some of the muscles of the spine and produce a planned descent of the abdominal viscera, every effort should be made to counteract the downward pull of gravity and produce a lifting of the internal organs. The ideal gymnastic position described in relation to the line of gravity is most favorable to this end. More will be said about the diaphragm in our discussion of respiration. The ways of assuring correct posture of the spine will be taken up in Chapters VI and VIII.

GYMNASTIC ANATOMY.

To all students of anatomy the old statement: "Dry as bones," is full of meaning. There is no romance in the study of anatomy. So far as anatomy is concerned one either knows or he does not know, because whether you dissect one or a million cadavers you will find the same structures in the same place and relation to the rest of the anatomy. Because fancy plays no part in the study or knowledge of anatomy, this subject is usually the least popular in any medical student's life. In most topics one can bluff through and make a fair case in answering examination questions, but in an anatomy examination only fact and memory play a part.

Of all divisions of the study of anatomy that of bones is least interesting. However, from a gymnastic angle the mechanics of anatomy are interesting, for one will find the shape and structure of the bones perfectly adapted to their purpose. The composition of the bones, through the arrangement of the gelatinous and mineral matter, gives them great tenacity. All long bones are built on the hollow tube principle, thus combining strength, elasticity and lightness. The short bones which have to sustain great weight, as the bones of the feet, and the epiphises of long bones where weight is to be sustained from varying angles, are constructed on the oblique beam principle, as in steel bridge structures which combine the greatest strength with the least amount of material.

There are several regions of the body the peculiar bony framework of which might prove interesting but none surpass in interest the bones in the arches of the foot. In the longitudinal arch, articulating one with an-

other, are a series of bones which are in themselves short
arches. They are individually concave underneath and
convex on top and shaped like slight wedges so as to fit
together like a Roman arch from the rear to the front
end of the foot. Beginning with the heel there are
really five longitudinal arches, from the outer to the inner, each slightly higher than the other. These five
arches are so adjusted as to produce a concavity from
side to side as well as from back to front; this arrangement gives what is known as the anterior or metatarsal
arch. The structure of each bone in these arches is of
the oblique beam type with the addition of the combination of oblique beam and hollow tube structure in the
metatarsal bones.

A point of interest here is that these bones alone,
even with such appropriate structure, would be helpless
to retain the arches normal unless the ligaments, knitting
them together, and the tendons of the muscles of the leg
were in tonic state. The tendons of the muscles of the
leg are attached in four strong layers to the bottom of
the bones of the arch and they act as the steel cables of
a bow string arch bridge do. As long as these tendons
are at normal tension the arches are flexible and strong
and free of pain. When there is pain in the arch it
means that some of the bones composing it are slightly
out of place, slipped downward, because the tendons or
bow strings are slightly lax. To replace these displaced
bones by pressure or thrust, or by wearing an arch support, will never offer relief of itself. A complete restoration of the arches can only come after the slipped bones
have been replaced and the tendons of the muscles have
been restored to normal tonicity through exercises and
adjustments of the lumbar and innominate bones. What
is true of the arches of the feet is true of any region of
the body. The bones, wherever they are and whatever
their function, are helpless except for the muscles which
move them and preserve their positions one to the other.

The ligaments simply hold their articulating surfaces together, but it is the tendons of the muscles that have most to do with the normal position of the bones making up the arches of the feet. It is the tendons of the muscles that determine the position and limitations of motion of every movable bone in the body.

The spinal column may be regarded as a long bone with a shaft and two extremities. The series of central foramina may be regarded as the medullary canal found in all long bones. The shape, viewed from the side, is like the letter S. This, combined with the intervertebral cartilages and the mobility and flexibility afforded by the segmentation, allows the greatest elasticity, strength and protection against falls. The head and the sacrum may be regarded as the extremities. The transverse and spinous processes of the vertebrae serve as a net-work of protection and as a means of muscular attachments. The normal curves of the spine should be very slight. Where these curves are abnormally marked, or where there is a lateral curvature, special exercises are necessary.

In the young the shape of any limb or long bone may be changed, in time, by special exercises. The shape of the legs changes from time to time in growing children and also in adults according to occupation. A person who has to carry great weights frequently and for a long time is apt to become knock-kneed, from constantly bringing the knees together for a steadier base. One who has ridden horseback from childhood shows an outward curve from the hips to the feet, involving the entire bony structure of the legs. Too much jumping will bow the legs. A great deal of running from childhood up tends to render the legs abnormally long in proportion to the trunk.

In a general way we may say that moderate exercise increases the circulation of the blood and therefore the growth and repair of the bones. Excessive exercise, because it may use up the food material in the production of energy, retards growth in the young and weakens the bones of older persons. If there is a lack of organic salts in the foods; in plainer words, if the diet lacks its correct proportion of vegetables of the green kind, the bones in both old and young will lack necessary bone building material and there may be resorption of organic salts from osseous tissue, causing a softening of the epiphises and enlargements of joints as well as pain from the high acidity of the system. Moderate exercise, combined with rational diet and other hygienic measures, is the method of keeping physically young.

Just here it might be well to say a few words about the importance of correct feeding in children for the prevention of infirmities resulting from bone afflictions. If a child is breast fed, the mother, herself, must be fed correctly; this means a diet that includes a balanced ratio of food elements, not from the pseudo-scientific caloric standpoint, merely, but from the standpoint of food combinations that comprise all the sixteen elements necessary to the normal organism. To get all the elements necessary to normal blood supply, which in turn will assure good bone and muscle and nerve structure, one must have a plentiful supply of raw vegetables and fruit along with the meat, fat, starch and sweet of the ordinary popular diet. Everyone should make it a point to get a liberal amount of raw vegetable material into his system daily, and then it will not matter so much what else his diet consists of provided, of course, it does not include things that are positively detrimental. Therefore, coming back to our starting point, if the infant is fed on normal milk from a healthy mother, he will develop normal bones, muscles, nerves and sound teeth. If the infant is bottle fed, he should receive vegetable juices and fruit juices from his fourth month onward. This should be prepared by chopping up vegetables rich in all the organic salts and squeezing out the juices raw, or boiling them and running them through a fine sieve and mixing, say, a teaspoonful to a bottle of milk the first day and then increasing the proportion slightly daily from the fourth month on, until, by the ninth month, the proportion is about half milk and half vegetable, at one daily feeding. Orange juice also should be fed once per day from the fourth month on.

The importance of including such ingredients in a child's feeding is apparent when it can be demonstrated that most bony abnormalities in children are the result of richitis, tuberculosis, syphilitic taint of inheritance, or injuries, all but the last of which can be traced to conditions of malnutrition. Malnutrition means not so much a lack of sufficient food as it does a lack of balanced diet. Since diet plays so important a role in preventing abnormalities it should, logically, come in as an important preventive element in orthopedics and in any discussion of the bones and muscles of the body.

In children, changes from cartilage to bone are incomplete. The bones still contain a large amount of gelatinous matter so that their shape is easily changed by exercise or pressure. Jumping from high positions may displace or distort children's bones and cause abnormal ossification. With the aged, because the bones are so brittle, jumping is dangerous. But if an aged person has kept up moderate exercise from youth and his diet has been properly balanced, moderate jumping will not hurt him.

Next to the study of the bones themselves their articulations should be considered so as to find the possibilities, limits and varieties of motion. The limits of motion in every joint are regulated by the shape of the bones and the ligaments and muscles attached to them. Voluntary movements are limited by the extensibility of antagonistic muscles. Involuntary movements are limited first by ligaments or check bands which are fastened, at least partly, outside the axis of motion. To force a movement beyond the danger limit of the ligamentous bands is to cause rupture of the ligaments, displacement of the interarticular cartilages, or fracture of the bones.

Moderate exercise will retain the mobility of the joints. Lack of exercise will produce immobility. Excessive exercise will lessen mobility by causing absorption of the synovial fluid to go on more rapidly than its secretion. This last condition is often manifested by crackling or grating sounds termed *crepitis*.

GYMNASTIC MYOLOGY.

From a gymnastic standpoint the study of the muscles forms the most interesting part of anatomy. Strictly speaking, myology is a description of the muscles; in a gymnastic sense, it is a study of their functions and a guide to progression from gentle to strong movements.

The muscular system forms a little more than 42 percent of the body weight, and the muscles constitute the largest single organ in the entire organism. In proportion to his size, in comparison to animals, man is the most muscular of the vertebrates, if he is normal. By normal, we mean free from all except the normal and necessary cushions of fat. All the way down the centuries man has had to struggle for his existence and brawn played an important part in his success. Despite the lack of exercise most people are guilty of, the body still shows the results of ancestral muscular prowess. To keep the body in perfect condition exercise is absolutely necessary, unless one's daily occupation is such as to include all the muscles in required activities.

Movements are voluntary and involuntary. Voluntary movements are controlled by the will. Even reflex and automatic movements, which are the same as unconscious neuro-muscular controlled movements, are under control of the will. Involuntary movements are those under control of the sympathetic nervous system, such as the heart beat, respiration, peristalsis, and so on. The will may, and often does, affect these involuntary movements. Respiration and sometimes the heart's action may be affected by the will, but these go on just the same whether or not the will is influencing them.

Where there is good contractility and extensibility in a muscle we find perfect elasticity. The more elasticity a muscle has the better its condition to serve the brain. The best and finest trained muscle has most elasticity but to preserve this it must be exercised regularly.

In a movement of the body all the muscles which act together pulling in one direction to produce the movements are called synergists. The muscles opposing these are called their antagonists. For perfect grace and steadiness in any action the synergists and antagonists must be exactly balanced and under complete control of the will.

We speak of synergists and antagonists only in relation to some definite movement. This means that synergists may be either the flexor or the extensor muscles of a joint. The idea is that we must determine the motion, and the muscles which combine to produce this are the synergists, while their opposing muscular strands are the antagonists of the movement in question. For instance, if we think of arm flexion, the synergists of flexion are the flexors of the arm, and the extensors of the arm are the antagonists of the motion. If we think of arm extension it is the extensors of the arm that are the synergists, and the flexors of the arm are the antagonists, of the movement.

Therefore, synergy and antagonism do not mean much except that they are collective terms which, when clearly understood, save the use of words among trained gymnasts.

We may speak, for instance, of the synergists and the antagonists of gravity. While in erect standing posture, gravity is constantly pulling downward, giving the body a tendency to flex and collapse. The flexor muscles of the body which work with gravity may be called its synergists, and the extensors or erectors which have to work against the flexors to maintain erect posture are its antagonists. Therefore, in good gymnastics we aim to strengthen the antagonists of gravity and at the same time produce extension of its synergists. Both the so-called new system of gymnastics of the French physician referred to above, and the system which advocates the holding of the head as high as possible to develop unconscious neuro-muscular control of the erectors of the body are methods of developing the antagonists of gravity.

Experiment has proven that those muscles contract best which extend most before contracting. Muscular tissue has intrinsic elasticity which gives it a power of recoil like an elastic band. Add all of this natural elasticity to the power of voluntary contraction and the result is emphasized. Therefore, the rule is that the greatest contraction is possible after the origin and insertion of the muscles have been forced furthest apart. This explains the logic of leaning back and carrying the arms as far back as possible before throwing. It also explains why the foot should be carried as far back as possible before high kicking or kicking a football. In arm extension sideways, the closer the elbows are brought to the body the greater may be the force of the extension. This rule holds good in reference to any movement of speed or extension.

From a therapeutic standpoint the so-called slow-leg movement of the Ling system is one of the most useful and least understood of gymnastic procedures. To illustrate this movement, stand with one heel resting on a chair. With the knee of the supported leg kept straight and the hands on the hips, bend forward as far as the pain back of the knee will permit. (Illustration 1.) The pain one feels is the result of extreme muscular extension. As the muscles extend in this way the blood vessels,

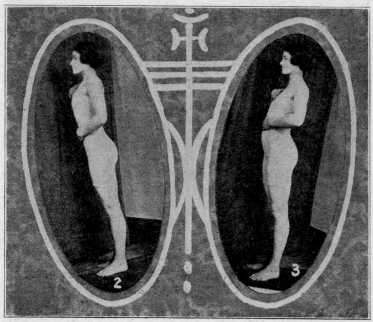

as well as the other tissues, are extended also and a peculiar condition results. As the tissues are extended, the diameters of the blood vessels remain normal so that, while their lengths are greater and their diameters no less, their capacity increases, and thus a volume of blood greater than normal is drawn to them. We thus get a vis-a-fronte, or suction force, which draws the blood from the heart and relieves it in case of strain. After a hard muscular exertion of short duration, when the heart beat is rapid from blood resistance, such a procedure as this would restore it to normal quickly.

Another application of the slow-leg movement is to sit with the legs extended on the bed and, keeping the knees straight, bend the trunk forward as far as possible to draw all the blood one can into the legs. In this way it is possible to draw sufficient blood from the thorax and head to promote sleep in case of insomnia from cerebral congestion. It is also of value in the flushed head and face condition accompanying high blood pressure and threatened apoplexy.

A few words to explain the modus operandi of the slow-leg movement might be advisable. The highest points in the back of the leg are at the buttock, the middle of the thigh and the swelling of the calf of the leg. As the body bends forward, the skin and superficial fasciae are made tense and the greater the extension the straighter becomes the line of the skin so that, as this aligning is with the highest points along the back of the thigh and leg, the hollows or depressions at the knee and just below the buttock are obliterated or filled out with blood. This occurs because as the skin is elevated a suction force causes a retention of the blood present and a distention of the deeper tissues sucks in more blood. There is a negative pressure on the larger vessels that forces them to at least retain their normal sizes and thus, their length increased and their lumens not decreased, blood must come to fill the new space.

The name "slow-leg movement" is, unfortunately, a misnomer. What the Swedish gymnasts really meant by this term was a movement that will produce vascular expansion. In the class of vascular expansion movements are included types that simply cause an easier flow of blood by straightening the path of the vessels. Lying in bed with the arms straight out from the shoulders will straighten the axillary arteries and their branches and reduce the natural friction resistance sufficiently to relieve a very weak heart.

Ling defined the type of movement under discussion as, "A movement in which the passive extension produced is stronger than the active contraction required to perform the movement." Most vascular expansion movements are performed by fixing the leg or legs in such a position that a mass of muscles will be placed on a powerful stretch as the trunk is bent, or allowed to bend, forward. The fact that most movements of this type are performed to affect chiefly the leg muscles has caused them to be erroneously called "slow-leg movements" by the translators of the Ling system. It is this name which has confused American critics of the Ling system.

Professor Hough, for example, has written a "refutation" of the Ling system which has served as ammunition for a number of other misinformed critics, but which shall redound to his discredit and weaken the arguments of his imitators for some time to come among those who really understand scientific gymnastics. Hough's chief bone of contention is this slow-leg movement question. He proceeded to test the efficacy of the slow-leg movement by interpreting its meaning according to its name and, of course, because his premises were wrong, his conclusions must be. He made his subjects run and perform various exertions and tests of endurance and noted how long a time elapsed before the heart beat became normal of its own accord. After establishing a standard average, he then had his subjects repeat their exertions and had them perform such movements as slow flexion of the legs, slow placing of the feet forward and sideways alternately, and other slow-leg movements of ordinary gymnastic type. He discovered no difference in the time of the heart's re-adjustment between allowing it to become normal of its own accord and by using these *slow movements of the legs.* All this simply shows that he did not understand what the Swedish gymnasts had in mind when they described slow-leg movements and he tried to disprove the Ling system before attempting to understand it. His work has misled many who do not care to look further into the Ling system than Hough's critical essay. Such things do not hurt the Ling system intrinsically, but they tend to mislead many and delay the popularity and support, in this country, which this system deserves.

Respiratory movements are employed to reduce a too rapid heart beat after an exercise of endurance. It is well to consider respiratory and slow-leg movements together. If the heart is beating rapidly after an exercise of endurance so that the need of oxygen has been greatly increased because of the great accumulation of carbon dioxide, the quickest way to relieve the heart's distress is through respiratory exercises. If the heart's rate has been increased by a short, but violent exertion we employ a slow-leg movement to normalize the heart. After a combination of endurance and exertion we may need both types of procedures to restore normal heart rate.

The general elasticity of the body is improved and preserved by such activities as running, jumping and vaulting, because these activities require elasticity for correct execution. Vaulting and stunts on the box, horse or buck, tend to establish close co-ordination between the eye and the muscles. The eye grasps the situation at a glance, and the muscles, when under perfect control,

act almost automatically to perform the required movements. This type of co-ordination has been termed muscular timing. With reference to games, sports, occupation or gymnastics, as well as any other form of activity,
there is a general rule that means as much as one can
read into it: within proper bounds, any form of activity
which requires elasticity for its execution will develop
elasticity in the performer; an exercise requiring skill
will develop skill; an exercise requiring strength will
develop strength; an exercise requiring grace will develop
grace; an exercise requiring agility will develop agility.
One might enumerate any number of muscular qualities
desirable for physical perfection and the same rule would
hold. In other words, whatever quality a muscular exertion requires, will react accordingly in the performer.
This rule is absolute.

In a progressive sense voluntary muscular contraction is divided into excentric, concentric and static.
Excentric contraction is where the muscle is in contraction, but giving up the force. Concentric contraction is
where the muscle is in contraction and overcoming the
resistance. Static contraction is where the muscle is in
contraction but holding the position. For example, if one
is unable to pull up to arm bent position on a horizontal
bar, but is helped up to it and then tries to control the
descent (that is, tries to keep the arms from straightening, but is forced to yield by the body's weight), we have
excentric contraction. An example of concentric contraction is where he is able to pull up to bent arms position.
In the same type of exercise, an example of static contraction is illustrated where one is strong enough to
hold the body weight at any position of arm flexion.
These three forms of contraction are given in order of
difficulty and should usually follow this order in difficult
gymnastic feats. From the relation of these three forms
of contraction we get the law that: "In gymnastics no
position should be used as a commencement position for

any movement until it has been mastered as the final position of some previously practiced movement." This is tantamount to saying that until a movement has become automatic it must not be used as the beginning position of a more difficult one of the same class. This also illustrates how it is possible to progress indefinitely in acquiring unlimited unconscious neuro-muscular control of the body.

For the muscles to be at their best they must be used every day, all of them. Healthy working of the muscles needs a healthy state of the body generally. This means that all the hygienic influences must be allowed to play their part. It would require a volume of itself to cover the details of this statement and the writer has done this in another book soon to appear, entitled, "Health in Ideal and Practice." However, it will not be amiss here to mention what these hygienic influences are and to say a few words about each one. These hygienic influences comprise fresh air, sunshine, temperature, water, food and drink, activity or exercise, rest and sleep, clothing, suggestion, the sexual life and the passional life. To name these influences is almost tantamount to stating their laws and significance. It is only by observing the underlying laws of these influences that health can be maintained at its best. The farther away one strays from observing the laws of these influences the farther he will be from perfect health. The nearer and more completely he observes them the nearer he will remain to perfect health. Thoroughly observing these rules means better physical development.

A muscle should never be subjected to continuous pressure from such articles of wear as garters, belts, corsets or even elastic stockings. All such articles interfere with the free flow of blood and lymph and they not only rob the muscles of needed nourishment, but may interfere with contraction. Given a free blood and lymph supply, muscular tissue is kept in best condition by activity. When a muscle is exercised regularly and given sufficient periodical rest, if subnormal, it will grow in size; if normal in size, it will develop finer grain. As the quality of muscular fibre improves, motor irritability will increase and there will grow a closer affiliation between muscle and brain. If exercise is overdone and insufficient rest secured, the muscle will waste away or atrophy.

Normal function of the muscles depends primarily upon oxygen. During contraction muscular tissue draws oxygen from the lymph just as a burning match draws oxygen from the air. The hemoglobin of the blood gives up its supply of oxygen to the lymph fluid, and the various cells of the body, being bathed in this fluid as fish in water, draw on this oxygen supply as they need it. Of course the cells must be nourished in order to function and this nourishment is procured from the blood. Given their proper nourishment, muscles function according to their oxygen supply. If oxygen is not supplied rapidly enough, fatigue sets in. Fatigue is the result of low oxygen supply and an accumulation of carbon dioxide and other by-products of muscular contraction. When one is active too long, or exerts himself too much with insufficient rest, the by-products of muscular contraction may accumulate too fast and he will get all the bad results of muscular exercise and none of the good ones.

The muscles of the human body never reach the stage of absolute fatigue. Absolute fatigue may be illustrated by experiment. If a muscle of a living animal is isolated and an electric current is run through it, it will produce contraction. When the muscle fails to contract under this stimulus a stronger current will again produce contraction, and so on, until a point is reached where the strongest current cannot cause the muscle to contract. Such a muscle is completely worn out. When a muscle of the normal living body is approaching the danger point of fatigue, pain sets in and the muscle must rest. The strongest will cannot cause a painfully tired muscle to contract. Fatigue is a danger signal which indicates the first stage of exhaustion and must be heeded. But the well trained, well nourished muscle, which receives plenty of oxygen, knows no fatigue. The sluggish, lazy, fat individual, who allows his muscular fibres to degenerate into fat, knows fatigue upon the least exertion. In the fat individual the actual size of the muscles may be less than in a slender person, for, although the fat makes his muscles look larger, so much fat has replaced red fibre that appearances are deceiving. Fat interferes with free muscular action and as a result exchange of tissue is slower in the fat than the slender person. It is true that some slender persons have lower vitality than fat ones, but where their health is normal, all other things equal, the slender person is better off than the fat. A simple truth, which may sound as a disparaging statement, is that while absolute fatigue resulting from overwork may never exist in a human being, a state of semi-fatigue due to insufficient physical training is very common.

Overwork and violent athletics may affect the heart. The heart muscles may wear out faster than they can be repaired. In such a case, as the fibres decrease, the walls grow thinner and the heart cavities dilate. The valves do not change as the heart's size increases, but the orifices increase in corresponding degree to the walls so that, in time, the valves prove insufficient to close their orifices and at diastole some of the blood flows back. This is called *regurgitation* and is recognized by the so-called *murmur*. Besides this back flow at diastole, the thinned, flabby walls cannot contract with enough power to overcome the natural elastic resistance of the arteries and we find low blood pressure. When a heart is thus incompetent, owing to thinned walls, or valvular leaks, or both, the pulse is hastened, because nature tries to make up in speed what it lacks in efficiency. So with a dilated, or often so-called athletic heart, the pulse may be high and the pressure low.

The heart muscle is subject to training like all muscles, though this work is complex and requires knowledge of more than mere exercise. To overcome incompetency, one should resort to such procedures as kneading of the muscles, circumduction of the extremities and special respiratory exercises. These will be explained in detail in Chapter V. When the heart muscle has had a chance to recuperate, one should apply easy resistive movements of the extremities. As progress is made with the treatment we find that the pulse rate gradually reduces and the blood pressure increases until a state is reached where both become constantly normal.

Muscular growth depends upon work alternated by rest (and rest sometimes means a change of work), or by massage. Nothing, not even sleep, will restore an exhausted muscle as quickly and completely as massage. Five minutes of thorough kneading given to an exhausted muscle will enable one to repeat what has exhausted it. Experiments have been tried repeatedly to test the truth of this statement, and always, it has been borne out in fact. The test is to repeat lifting a given weight until the muscles are thoroughly exhausted; then to rest five minutes and try to repeat. Never has a subject been able to repeat his first performance after the rest. But, where lifting is followed by five minutes' massage of the exhausted muscles, he can repeat, and, in some cases, subjects have surpassed their records. In Chapter IV is given a summary of the latest results of experiments on this subject.

Co-ordination may be classified as voluntary and involuntary. The voluntary type is under control of the will and the involuntary includes the awkward and unnecessary movements that often accompany any effort. Good gymnastics tend to improve the voluntary and overcome the involuntary. Voluntary co-ordination exists when one has such control that he can easily localize effort to any given region of the body with the exclusion of other parts. When one lacks the power of isolation, he has involuntary co-ordination.

Voluntary co-ordination has been called active repose; that is, when a movement is to be isolated to any given region, the rest of the body is kept from moving, by active control. It requires mental effort to keep a part still which would otherwise fall into some kind of motion as the active parts move.

As an example of active repose, take arm flinging upward. The body should be kept in good fundamental standing position with the chest well forward and head erect, while the arms are being flung forward upward and the rest of the body, from the head to the feet, should be perfectly still. In this case we have active repose of all but the arms. The least swaying of the body or head is an example of involuntary co-ordination, or inco-ordination.

Grace, perfect control, or exactness of form in gymnastics depend upon one's ability to retain muscles or parts in statical activity; that is, to maintain a correct starting position while the active parts perform the movement.

Next to health, the object of gymnastics is to suppress all useless and awkward movements and develop good control. Useless movements are a waste of energy. By developing good co-ordination and isolation one becomes more and more able to concentrate on the parts used and, in time, the least voluntary stimulus will suffice to give the greatest result. Therefore, the aim of educational gymnastics is to cultivate complete control of the powers already present, rather than to produce more muscular force.

ANIMAL DYNAMICS.

Heat in the body is kept up by metabolism. Energy is furnished by food, air and oxidation processes. This energy is partly converted into mechanical work and partly transformed into heat.

One indispensable condition of movement in the body is heat. The problem as to how the muscles are related to heat is not very well understood. But it is well known that there is a close connection between the amount of heat expended and the amount of work performed. Everyone has heard the phrase "warming up to a thing." No athlete can perform at his best if he feels chilled. Outdoor records are equalled or broken only in warm weather. Warm weather is favorable to any bodily exertion. Heat creates in a muscle an aptitude for coming more quickly into action.

Heat always accompanies oxidation. In the living tissues oxidation is going on even while they are at rest, so that heat is ever present. The more active the organ the hotter it becomes. In the body as a whole heat is chiefly produced by transforming energy into mechanical work. The part of the body that is most active usually has the highest temperature; this is true of muscle, digestive organs or brain tissue. But the general bodily temperature is constant at about 98.2 F. If sub or supranormal for any length of time it is an indication of disease. Therefore, during great muscular activity the heat produced has to be gotten rid of and the normal temperature is preserved principally through the process of evaporation of perspiration. Other processes which aid in bodily heat regulation are conduction, convection and radiation.

Conduction takes place whenever heat is transferred directly from one mass to another with which it is in contact. A good example of this is heating a flat-iron on a stove. The heat from the stove is directly communicated to the iron, and then from one particle of the iron to another. Some objects are poorer conductors of heat than others. Air is a very poor conductor; therefore certain fabrics which are porous and contain much air in their meshes when worn next to the skin retain heat better than others.

Convection takes place when a warm body is placed in a fluid, such as water. Heat is conducted from the warm body to the surrounding layer of fluid, but this warmed layer moves off and makes way for a cooler layer which is in turn warmed, until the warmth of the body is used up or has warmed the fluid. Still air does not cool the body, readily, but moving air, or wind, causes a rapid fall in temperature.

Radiation of heat is what takes place from the sun to the earth. Any warm body may radiate heat to surrounding cooler bodies. Although this process is slight from the human body, it at least deserves mention.

Evaporation of perspiration is the most familiar process of cooling the body. What takes place is not clear to all. Place ether on the finger and blow a steady current of dry air upon it and you will have a feeling of cold on the skin as the liquid is evaporated. It has been shown that while evaporating a fluid borrows heat of the surrounding surface. Therefore what cools one is the evaporation and not the secretion of sweat.

During exercise or vigorous work, or when one is surrounded by hot atmosphere, perspiration takes place much more rapidly than during rest. If one is in a hot room, perspiration is the only means by which the body can equalize and preserve its temperature. If the pores are closed by dirt, or if anything, such as a rubber garment, for instance, checks evaporation, bodily heat soon rises, and in some cases this becomes dangerous. Many people reported to have died from the intense heat of summer, really died of an unclean skin. When the skin is clogged, and evaporation is checked, the lungs are strongly taxed, because the elimination of moisture through them is greatly increased and breathing becomes laborious. The power of endurance is greatly lowered, if the skin is unclean.

To summarize we might say that the skin should be kept clean; exercise should be practiced in a cool atmosphere; little and loose clothing should be worn during exercise. A bath should follow the exercise and thicker clothing put on.

EXERCISE AND RESPIRATION.

To the body, the most essential element is oxygen. During activity the amount of oxygen burnt up is so much greater than at rest that, next to pure air, good respiration is most important. Good respiration, according to Ling, is the basis of gymnastics. Unless you can breathe well your physical work is bound to be reduced for lack of endurance. The physical powers will increase with improved respiratory power.

Exercise induces respiration. Even standing position compared with lying position shows a difference in favor of the former. Increased respiration induces more rapid lung circulation, and the exchange of gases is increased. Every great muscular effort is involuntarily preceded by an inhalation. This is to supply an abundance of oxygen and it is also an automatic way of fixing the bones of the thorax so that the muscles attached to them may have a firmer anchorage for contraction.

In "Parks' Practical Hygiene," Dr. Edward Smith's experiments are interesting. According to Posse: "He found that if the quantity of air inhaled in the lying position was taken as a unit, that inhaled at sitting position was 1.18; in standing position, 1.33; walking one mile an hour, 1.90; walking four miles an hour, 5.00; and running six miles an hour, 7.00, etc. Or, in other words, if a man at rest inhales 480 cubic inches of air per minute, while walking four miles an hour he inhales

2,400 cubic inches, and while running six miles an hour, 3,360 cubic inches. The carbon dioxide exhaled is increased in proportion."

During ordinary inhalation the inspiratory muscles, especially the diaphragm, contract, the chest capacity increases and the air is sucked into the lungs. In ordinary exhalation the same muscles relax, allow a recoil of the air cells, and the air is forced out. Under ordinary circumstances respiration is an automatic mechanical action. When the oxygen supply is low, carbon dioxide in the blood stimulates the respiratory center in the medulla to action.

Vital capacity is determined by the amount of air one can forcibly draw into the lungs after emptying them. During forced inhalation the ordinary inspiratory muscles and a few others contract forcibly to elevate the ribs and completely contract the diaphragm. In forced exhalation while the inspiratory muscles relax, the expiratory muscles contract forcibly, depressing the rib and decreasing the chest capacity.

There is but one correct type of respiration for both men and women; that which includes the entire chest. We have the advocates of the diaphragmatic or abdominal type of respiration. Their claim usually is that this type, through the motion of the diaphragm, acts upon the viscera, giving them internal massage and, by producing an oscillation of the intestines, aids digestion and promotes excretion. There is truth in this and their claim rests on fair foundation. But they forget, in their eagerness to defend this type, that the costal type has most points in its favor. The apices of the lungs are not there merely for ornament. The first function of respiration is to supply oxygen and purify the blood, not massage the viscera. There is really no need of bulging out the abdomen at inspiration to exercise the diaphragm. The diaphragm automatically contracts as the first act of respiration, so that if an effort is made to fill the apices of the lungs by lifting the ribs, the bases of the lungs must fill first, unless interfered with by tight garments. Air, like all gases and fluids, follows the line of least resistance. The straightest and easiest path for air to follow into the lungs is downward to the lower lobes. To pass upward to the upper lobes and apices it has to make a sharp turn at the point where the trachea branches upward. Furthermore, cold air cannot rise above warm air. The incoming air is cooler than that already in the lungs, and, therefore, a special effort is required to expand the upper lungs while little or no effort will fill the lower lungs.

It is a mistake to emphasize the abdominal type of respiration as the best for all people to cultivate. All the internal organs of the body are suspended from the spine and lower ribs at the back of the abdominal cavity. This arrangement is correct and as it should be for four-footed animals because, with the body held horizontal, these organs hang straight down and against the anterior wall of the abdomen. They cannot sag any lower than the anterior wall but are free to move forward and backward. When one considers the fact that the roof of the pelvis is higher than the abdominal cavity in four-footed creatures the arrangement of these internal organs also seems logical. But, on assuming the upright position, as the higher apes and man have done, with an internal arrangement that is only adapted to four-footed creatures, instead of the anterior wall of the abdomen becoming the protective limit to the various organs, they simply tend to flop and sag downward and unless every effort is made to hold them up by steady contraction of the abdominal muscles they will gradually drop down and their supporting ligaments become stretched. This condition of general ptosis, or sagging of the internal organs, is increasing rapidly with

increasing laziness and riding in such shaky convey-
ances as many automobiles.

It should be obvious, without going into lengthy
details, that the thing to do is to concentrate every
effort to lift the internal organs, both through development of the entire waist muscles, the natural corset,
and by never making special effort to bulge out the abdomen in breathing. Bulging out the abdomen with
inhalation is so unnecessary and illogical that it can
never be condemned in strong enough terms. In the
first place, for the reasons given above, every effort to
bulge out the abdomen by pushing down on the diaphragm only works with the downward drag of gravity
to establish ptoses. In a later chapter, under the topic
of general ptoses, we explain the symptoms and complications due to this condition. Moreover the effort
to bulge out the abdomen is wasted so far as one's vital
capacity is concerned.

One's vital capacity is determined by the amount of
air which can be inhaled in the deepest possible inhalation. This is dependent upon the efficiency of the entire
thoracic mechanism. A complete inhalation means that
the ribs must be at their freest to rise and spread apart
and the diaphragm must contract to its normal horizontal
level. It is absurd to try to force the abdomen outward
at inhalation because, in order to do so, the diaphragm
has to be bulged downward below its normal contracting
level. Besides, when the thorax is completely filled, the
abdomen will bulge out only as much as the chest is
depressed by the effort. In other words, diaphragmatic
or abdominal breathing implies chest depression. This
is illustrated by figures 2 and 3. Number 2 shows how
the chest may be lifted at inhalation and this will assure
normal diaphragmatic action and cause no depression
of the abdominal organs. In order to bulge out the
abdomen, as in 3, the hands indicate just what happens
to the ribs; and this means that to the extent that the

air is forced down into the abdomen, just to that extent are the stomach and intestines forced downward.

The best way to acquire normal respiration is to center all efforts toward developing the type which one lacks and then, the combination of the two will give the most beneficial results, because it will employ the entire thorax and promote oxidation to its utmost possibility. Respiration is absolutely essential to metabolism. By supplying oxygen it hastens assimilation of food and the elimination of waste matter. Absence of oxygen even for a few minutes will cause death. Vitality is largely dependent upon the ability to exchange carbon dioxide for oxygen. As the ability depends upon the amount of surface over which the blood can be spread in the lungs, and as this amount of surface is determined by the expansiveness of infundibuli or air cells, the importance of full, free respiration becomes apparent. The difference between the chest capacity at inhalation and exhalation determines the expansion of the air cells. The greater this difference is, the better the respiration. Therefore, the more supple the chest the stronger the inspiratory muscles; and the more elastic the expiratory muscles the better. The great importance of proper respiration was recognized by Ling when he laid down the following law: "Any exercise that compresses the chest or interferes with free respiration must be discarded." In the choice of movements in the Ling system this law is always kept in mind.

An exercise that causes a pupil to hold his breath is contra-indicated. Even if the exercise is correct from the standpoint of anatomy, physiology, and psychology, if the pupil cannot do it without holding his breath, it should be postponed until he has developed to a point where he can do it perfectly. This rule seems extreme, but all general rules are extreme in relation to special cases.

The posture of the body during the performance

of any movement largely determines its effect. No matter what exercise one practices, if he does not preserve a correct posture the exercise will in time prove more injurious than beneficial. The posture of the chest is especially important. To keep the chest in proper posture the head must be kept erect with the chin drawn in, and the shoulders well back. Any movement which requires, or in which is maintained, a good posture of the chest will have a good effect. Since the posture of the chest means so much for general effect, every movement must be outlined with relation to its effect upon chest development. As Ling has said: "Every correctly executed movement is in a measure a movement for chest development."

The postures of the head and chest are interdependent. There are muscles attached to the head, neck and upper ribs that establish a very close relation between these parts. If one's occupation causes him to stoop over, or causes the chin to protrude, the consequent relaxation of the sterno-cleido-mastoid allows the sternum to descend and depress the upper ribs. At forward flexion of the neck the fixation of the scaleni muscles is removed and the upper ribs are no longer kept elevated. Thus the chest, over the apices of the lungs, is diminished in capacity and the air cells of this region are compressed. If this condition continues for a long time, that is, if it is repeated with sufficient frequency, the clavicular region of the chest will gradually flatten, its muscles will shorten and, finally, no amount of voluntary effort will suffice to expand it.

As the sternum and upper ribs descend, all the lower ribs and the rest of the respiratory apparatus is allowed to settle. At length, the appearance of the chest at inhalation becomes very much as it should at exhalation. This general settling down affects all the internal organs, so that not only are the lungs handicapped from lack of space, but the heart and large blood vessels are impeded in their functions. The depressed condition of the ribs and sternum also means a lowering of the upper attachment of the abdominal muscles. These muscles, because their extremities are brought nearer together, are easily bulged out by the intestines. Being thus deprived of their support, the abdominal viscera sag, and all this superinduced pressure predisposes to ptoses and hernia. In women, the bearing down of the viscera often produces falling of the womb.

With a depressed thorax, the respiratory function becomes deficient and oxygen is not supplied rapidly enough to meet bodily needs. The system, thus deprived of oxygen, can at best function at very low ebb. The law that action is the first condition of life is very manifest in the human body, for if the activity of any portion of it permanently decreases it will grow less and less capable of performing its function. Thus, when the chest contracts, not only do its muscles shorten and make it still more rigid, but the tissues and air cells gradually undergo a change of structure from want of expansion and recoil and they finally atrophy and become subject to disease.

To preserve healthy lungs we must make them work, and by doing this we improve general health as well. To accomplish this purpose we resort to exercises that will extend the expiratory muscles and thus supple the chest; next, that will strengthen the inspiratory muscles and expand the chest in every diameter; and lastly, procedures that will cause greater activity of the lungs. Arch flexions, heaving, shoulder blade and respiratory movements will supple, expand and correct the posture of the chest. Running, or any exercise in moderation that will increase the need for respiration, will benefit the lungs by activity.

EXERCISE AND CIRCULATION.

The forces that keep the blood flowing through the body are the contraction of the heart, the elasticity of the walls of the arteries, the force of capillarity and the contraction of the voluntary muscles upon the veins. The veins contain valves which compel the blood to flow only in the direction of the heart. Normally there is no backward flow. Centrifugal force and gravity may forcibly affect the flow of blood. Swinging on the rings or holding onto a merry-go-round at great speed, with the feet describing the largest circle, will cause a rush of blood to them that is sometimes sufficient to cause anaemic dizziness or faint. Resting the foot above the level of the head will produce drainage of its blood through force of gravity.

The effect of exercise on circulation is two-fold. As a muscle contracts it presses on the capillaries and squeezes out some of the blood, while it acts as a stopper to the blood in the veins behind it. Since blood in the veins can flow only in one direction, the effect of muscular contraction is to dam it up temporarily. Especially if the muscle is held contracted for some time, the heart is consequently forced to pump harder, but often without success. The law to be learned is that short, frequent contractions will hasten circulation in the muscle, while a muscle kept contracted a long time will offer resistance to the heart. As to the effect of prolonged contraction, we must consider how great a bulk of muscle is under contraction and how long the contraction is continued. Tug-of-war, because it employs all the muscles in hard and long continued contraction, can never prove beneficial to circulation and health. The best that can be said of this type of sport is that some people may be so strong as not to be seriously injured by it. But the majority had better avoid it.

Another force that produces an increased amount of blood to the region of a contracting muscle is vaso-dilation. The muscle cells, as they expand, take up more than an ordinary quantity of blood. Thus does a contracting muscle present an interesting set of phenomena. Each muscle cell seems bent upon performing its own individual function. In response to nerve stimulus each cell swells up and gives out sarcolactic acid, carbon dioxide and other by-products. It takes nourishment from the blood and oxygen from the lymph. The cell may be said to contract upon stimulus without knowing why it does it, and this contraction is the result of its chemical work, that is, the work which produces carbon dioxide, and sarcolactic acid. The combined swelling or shortening of all its cells is what causes a muscle to contract.

The pulse is increased by muscular contraction, partly by the resistance it has to overcome, and partly by the need of arterial blood. The pulse rate is increased by an abnormal amount of carbon dioxide in the blood, just as it grows more rapid at the presence of any poison in the system. Nearly every toxic condition causes an increased heart beat. The increase in heart beat seems to be nature's method of self-defense against poisons. Heart stimulants are poisons, always. Normally carbon dioxide stimulates the heart beat, because more oxygen is necessary. This increased heart beat hastens circulation and respiration, more oxygen is absorbed and assimilated, and there is a more rapid exchange of tissues. Therefore, to make a part grow, exercise it properly. Any active part, whether muscle, organ or brain, needs an increased amount of blood rich in oxygen.

Sometimes we find present a high pulse rate with low pressure. This usually indicates an incompetency of the valves to close properly. That is, as a result of heavy athletics or hard work, the heart has been enlarged rapidly, but the valves did not enlarge proportionately and at the systole they fail to completely close up the passage and part of the blood flows back. In case of regurgitation the heart may compensate by pumping faster than normal; that is, it makes up by speed what it lacks in efficiency. So, where the sphygmomanometer test shows high pulse rate with normal average pressure even though a murmur exists, there is little to fear if the subject will follow proper gymnastic procedures. The heart may be gradually built up as any muscle. But, if the valvular lesion is due to infectious or contagious disease sequelae, gymnastic procedures are limited to the passive in usefulness. Where there is high pressure and normal or slow pulse, we have hardened arteries. Where there is low pressure and high pulse we have a lack of compensation in the heart and the condition is serious. It means that the subject is approaching a stage of heart failure. The proper line of procedure for this condition is explained in Chapter V.

In gymnastics it is possible to equalize circulation by general and specific procedures. In a well balanced gymnastic program the exercises for general effect precede and pave the way for those of localization of special effect. Those who need gymnastics the most are young people and sedentary workers of any age. The time of young people, who are or should be at school, and of sedentary workers, is taken up with brain work; therefore lessons are begun with the leg movements which may be simple but require attention. These will draw blood to the legs, relieve the congestion in the head, and change the mental activity from the intellectual to the motor centers.

Movements of extension are most important. Many of the blood vessels, besides pointing upward and compelling the blood to rise against gravity, are bent at acute angles. The blood, like all liquids, flows best in a straight line, because the straighter the channel the less the resistance caused by friction. In our daily routine we naturally and ordinarily flex our joints much more than we extend them. A flexed joint means bent arteries and veins. Extending them makes blood flow easier. Therefore movements of extension should occupy a prominent position in a gymnastic program. A bed patient with a weak heart may often gain relief by lying on the back, the arms straight out at the sides, to straighten the axillary arteries.

Vascular expansion movements may be overdone. They should only be employed when their need is indicated. The normal heart must have compensatory resistance. Great peripheral resistance may strain it; therefore heavy and long continued strains are bad. Vascular expansion movements practiced when not needed may reduce the heart's natural resistance to the point of danger. The heart's condition, properly interpreted, indicates the kind of movements it needs.

Respiration and circulation are closely related. Thoracic aspiration is an aid to circulation. It occurs at deep inhalation. The capillaries and infundibuli in the lungs are separated by common walls. Through these thin walls the exchange of gases takes place by osmosis. It is readily seen that if the infundibuli are expanded by deep inhalation the distention of their walls means an equal distention of the capillary walls, and therefore an increased capacity for blood in their capillaries. This, therefore, causes a suction force on the blood to the lungs and, if exhalation is not too rapid, the re-adjustment is such as to aid the flow from the right ventricle and it will not retard the flow to the left aurical. A rapid exhalation is liable to cause lung congestion and interfere with pulmonary circulation. Hence, to aid the heart, inhalation should be a little more rapid than exhalation. The frequency of respiration is reflexly regulated according to the need. Respiratory exercises may be active or passive. Types of the passive kind are given in Chapter IV.

Their effects are as the general rule governing all passive movements. Passive movements aid circulation

and as a rule drain a part. Active movements cause
an afflux and flush a part. To flush a part, therefore,
give active movements; to drain it, give it passive movements and active movements to some distal part.

EXERCISE AND METABOLISM.

Exercise rightly regulated causes a rapid and healthy
exchange of tissue. It promotes growth by increasing
the process of assimilation and causes a more rapid excretion of old tissue. An active muscle is always more
richly supplied with blood than one at rest. Up to a
certain point the more active a part the more alive and
normal it is. Where activity becomes too great, destruction of tissue exceeds its reconstruction and loss of
weight results. The constructive process is known as
anabolism; the destructive, as katabolism.

Exercise improves the condition of the blood because
more oxygen is being used during activity and, provided
respiration is normal, more oxygen is being supplied.
Indeed, oxygenation follows the law of supply and
demand. The tissues in activity relieve the blood of its
latent supply of oxygen and other nutritive principles
and the various cells give up their poisonous compounds
more rapidly. The lungs, skin and kidneys rid the system of these poisons more rapidly and the increased need
of oxygen reacts by creating a more rapid respiration.
The blood, richer in oxygen and other constructive principles and flowing more rapidly through the body,
stimulates all the glands, organs and tissues to greater
activity so that every function is stimulated and the
entire organism is refreshed.

This phenomenon is as it should be. Unless there
is a rapid process of metabolism created by activity,
deep respiratory exercises are useless. The exchange
of tissues must be first hastened and then special respiratory exercises will prove useful and logical. To merely
breathe deeply several times without having first created

the need for oxygen by activity amounts to nothing more than an oxygen spree. Indeed, the Sun Worshippers, or Mazdaznan Society members, who used to go out every morning, face the sun and inhale deeply several times until they felt the inflow of "divine principle," were deceived in that the dizziness which they mistook for "divine principle" was nothing but an over supply of unnecessary oxygen that caused a rush of blood to the head. Had they run around the block a few times, or taken a plunge into the lake or performed a few snappy gymnastic movements before inhaling "divine principle" they would have been more benefitted, whatever their own interpretation of their feelings.

Exercise, by increasing metabolism, not only creates a need for more oxygen, but also creates a need for more food. The tissues change rapidly and they need to be renewed. The blood is hastily relieved of its nourishing principles, and this fact is manifested by an increased appetite. This means, better digestion and excretion; more food enjoyed and assimilated. Exercise, therefore, will tend to render one normal; if too fat, the weight is reduced; if too thin, more flesh is taken on.

When one is inactive for a long time the system grows sluggish. The muscle fibres are flabby or undergo fatty degeneration, many of the fibres changing completely to fat. The liver will get torpid from slow circulation and enlarged from overwork. The kidneys are overburdened because they are forced to take on the duties of the skin and lungs, as well as their own. The intestines are usually sluggish, peristalsis is slow, excretion slow, and constipation common. In this condition the lower bowels may be the source of auto-intoxication, for the bowels being incapable of ridding themselves of fecal matter with proper dispatch, gases and toxic principles are rapidly formed and some absorbed into the blood stream. With this general state of inactivity the entire system gets clogged up and nature finds relief through cleansing diseases such as boils, carbuncles, pneumonia, or typhoid fever. A general state of sluggishness usually shows itself by frequent headaches, blurred vision, the blues, lack of snap and energy and then comes a breakdown.

Well regulated exercise, combined with good food, bathing, appropriate dress and the best possible environment, will prevent many of our common ills and save many a doctor's bill. Exercise tends to bring about a perfect equilibrium of functions, which is not merely an absence of disease, but radiant health.

One means of aiding digestion is to hasten general metabolism. But locally, it may be aided by hastening portal circulation. This can be done by exercises that react directly upon the liver and portal veins. Trunk rotation and sideways flexions as well as abdominal and respiratory exercises accomplish this purpose. Trunk sideways flexions are especially beneficial, because, as one bends to the right, the liver is compressed, forcing the blood out of it, and at the same time the portal and intestinal veins are extended and their path straightened, making flow through them more rapid. Bending to the left causes an expansion of the liver, producing a suction force, and, at the same time, a slight compressing of the intestinal veins; thus is a force-pump action produced, hastening circulation through the intestines and liver and stimulating the entire digestive and excretory functions. Trunk rotation and abdominal exercises are supplementary to sideways flexion. They tone up the natural waist region, raise the viscera, and serve as a natural support. Respiratory exercises not only oxygenate the blood, but form a suction force on the inferior vena cava, which drains the liver.

The same exercises are useful and specific in preventing obesity or reducing weight. Fat begins to deposit first at either side of the lumbar spine. When a person begins to grow fat his waist line is the first part to show it.   Sideways bending tones up the quadratus lumborum muscles and prevents fat.   If one is already over stout, general exercise, with a reduction of farinaceous foods, and an increase of eliminative foods such as fruits and vegetables, with the specific application of lateral trunk movements, abdominal and respiratory exercises will reduce him to normal.   Practicing this class of movements is also useful to prevent optoses. The stomach and intestines should be held up by the abdominal muscles.   These, when in proper tonic condition, form nature's corset, keep the viscera up where they belong, and give the natural waist line.   The normal physique shows that the depth of the chest is greater than the abdominal depth.   Any other relation is not normal.   Where the abdominal muscles are not tonic, the viscera are allowed to sag, and, sooner or later, the intestines and the stomach descend and various forms of digestive disturbances result.   A readjustment of conditions by toning up the abdominal muscles will relieve most forms of indigestion.

Corsets are bad for several reasons.   They pinch the waist and reduce the natural corset, or abdominal muscles, to flabby, fatty degenerate layers.   They compress the lower thorax, weakening the respiratory function by interfering with natural expansion of the lower lung area.   They squeeze the liver, sometimes to the point of causing a false lobe that extends several inches lower than it should.   Below the narrowest portion of the corset the intestines are pressed downward, instead of being sustained or forced upward, causing pelvic disturbances of all sorts.   The modern corset is made to measure and does not compress the waist as much as the old styles used to, but there is not a corset on the market which does not limit the freedom of the waist muscles.

It is generally known, but worthy of repetition, that exercise should never immediately follow a meal.

It may precede a meal, but should never be taken sooner than two hours after, for best results. The digestive organs need a rich supply of blood while functioning as vigorously as they do after a meal, and to create a demand elsewhere will give rise to disagreeable or serious complications. Exercise not only interferes with digestion, if taken too soon, but a full stomach itself interferes with freedom of activity. Many animals sleep after a full meal, and this is a safer and more physiological practice than the oft recommended walk.

EXERCISE AND NEURITION.

The relation of brain and muscle is of the highest importance, and our study cannot be complete until this phase of the subject is considered. A well-muscled physique under poor control is not as important as a moderately muscled physique under perfect control. At our stage of civilization brain means more than brawn. Quality not quantity counts in most things. Brawn should be under absolute control of brain to be at a premium.

The ideal of physical education is a harmoniously developed physique to serve as a tool under perfect control of the will. But the brain itself is in a measure dependent upon muscle for perfect balance and health. There is a normal relation that must exist for harmony. To negate the physique as wholly unimportant and to endeavor to make "divine mind" transcend all, regardless of the needs of the purely physical, is unsound. To endeavor to merely develop a massive muscular system, as many "enlarge-your-arm-one-inch-in-one-month" fakers advertise to do, and thus exercise to "keep up and get more" muscle, rather than train the muscle to serve the mind, is wasteful.

What is most needed in our day is good health, and physical efficiency for endurance, stick-to-it-iveness and concentration. How best to develop these qualities is the question of importance.

Muscular power and endurance are created by normal activity. Efficiency is developed as this power is brought under control. Strong muscles, to be of service, must "respond readily to volition for power, speed, agility, gentleness or repose."

The first object of physical education is to develop control of the forces already present. To acquire great strength is of secondary importance. The average individual has more than sufficient power latent within him if he only knew how to make it serve him. There is a limit, not only to absolute force, but to the need of the force possible to everyone, but there is no limit to the possibilities of developing control of powers present or to be acquired, and good control is always of advantage.

To remain healthy, nerve tissue must be used, not abused. Activity means health to any tissue or organ. Our present life tends to develop sensory more than motor irritability. Inactive motor nerves undergo degenerative processes and while this occurs, the sensory nerves grow more irritable. One-sided occupations, such as typewriting, are among the first to show the effects of unbalanced innervation of the body. Nervous prostration is a total unbalance of innervation. The common term "nerves," meaningless in itself, signifies various degrees of unbalance between the motor and sensory nerves and the brain. Balanced activity normalizes and renders more efficient the motor nerves and makes the sensory less irritable. A little daily practice of educational gymnastics is the best preventive measure to any form of nervousness.

Unless a movement compels concentration for its execution it is not educational. It may be beneficial to health, by promoting more rapid circulation and metabolism, but it is not educational in the sense that it brings the brain and muscle into closer relation. Every movement of educational value has a definite beginning and ending, with one or more intermediate positions, and each distinct part must be executed perfectly for best results. When a movement has been mastered, repetition of it has little educational value. One should then proceed to a more complex one.

The nervous energy required to produce a new movement is at first great, but in time it becomes almost nil. A child learning to walk has great difficulty. At first, all his faculties are concentrated upon balancing alone. The least pause in his alertness of attention on what he is doing will cause him to lose his balance and fall. But constant effort soon enables him to get around without requiring his entire attention. As this progress is outwardly manifest there is a specific change going on within. The first mental control of balancing and walking was directed from the brain. But as each controlling impulse travelled down to the legs it left an impression in the motor cells of the spinal cord. As progress set in, more distinct impressions were made on the cord, and less mental control was required until finally, willing to walk was sufficient and the motor centers of the cord controlled the required motion. After walking has become automatic, it is no longer developing. One can then travel for miles and his mind may be occupied with anything and everything but walking. No man would think of developing his mind by resorting to the easiest primary grade books, yet we hear physical educators affirm that the best exercise is walking, because it requires least thought.

Americans oppose Swedish gymnastics, affirming that they are too dry. This is simply another way of saying that thinking is disagreeable. It is the kind of mental functioning that accounts for the fact that in this country, we read nine books of fiction to one of a scientific nature. It is said that the Japanese read nine of scientific nature to one of fiction. After a thorough investigation of all systems of gymnastics, the Japanese have adopted the Swedish system. The real "yellow peril" that a few jingoes love to dilate upon, is our laziness in mental effort.

The automatic drill, set to music, so in favor with the average American educator, is not educational. When a drill has become automatic and set to a given piece of music, the individual fits himself to the set movements and rhythm, and instead of the gymnastics answering his needs he is altering himself to fit the drill. While I served in the militia, some years ago, the company was taught a rifle drill that was very easily mastered, and set to the then popular tune of "Mamie." After practicing the drill for a few weeks it became so automatic that, since that time whenever I hear a strain from "Mamie," I involuntarily start to perform the drill. Such drill work is no more educational than any of the popular dances.

In good gymnastics we practice an elementary movement until it becomes automatic, then the next and next of the same class. A well rounded program for each lesson, with each movement adjusted to the needs of the individual, will require his concentration; it will exercise his entire physique and refresh him. An automatic drill will tire the body without relieving the mind. In controlled gymnastics the mental worker gains rest by the change of activity in the brain.

Gymnastics requiring concentration react on the brain by increasing its growth. While the motor centers are active more blood is drawn to them, exchange of tissue takes place more rapidly, nerve cells are more rapidly developed from need, and there results a closer affiliation between muscle, nerve and brain. The best possible brain is dependent upon a good muscular foundation. Brain tissue, according to the laws of evolution, followed muscular growth. Muscle came first, and nervous tissue afterward as a result of need. In man the brain has reached a higher development than what is simply sufficient to serve muscle, but both are still interdependent. Those whose time is entirely taken up with mental pursuits develop a puny physique which nature soon snuffs off. One does not fit into our physical world unless his physique is at least *adequate* to *his* brain. The muscles depend upon the brain for control, but degeneration of the muscles at least means destruction to their controlling brain areas.

Progression in gymnastics from the standpoint of control is made by first using those that require the least amount of mental effort and gradually changing to forms that require greater concentration. Symmetrical movements, that is, movements in which both sides of the body do the same thing, come first. It is easier to get control of the arms or legs if both sides have the same work to do. Because volition from one side of the brain sends a little impulse to the same side of the body, no energy is wasted when both sides work equally.

Unilateral movements are next in order. Where one side works while the other is resting, concentration or localization of effort is developed. The part of the body that is active requires mental control and at the same time the rest of the body is kept perfectly still. Therefore, while one small portion of the body works, there is retention of position in the rest of the body.

When control has reached that stage of efficiency that enables one to perform a unilateral movement perfectly, the next step is to introduce bilateral exercises. In this type both arms or legs are exercised simultaneously, but for different movements. In this case each lobe of the brain is active for a different movement. This type of movement is useful to develop equal power in each half of the brain.

A symmetrical exercise may be illustrated by extending both arms sideways simultaneously. A unilateral movement is illustrated by extending one arm sideways; then, while it is kept at bend position, the other is extended. Extending one arm upward and, at the same time, the other one sideways, is an example of bilateral work.

As proficiency is acquired in the more difficult types of exercises, by following the same law for the legs as the arms, and by combining both leg and arm movements, one at length attains a standard of control in which the muscles and the brain are so in tune that to will an action is almost identical with doing it. One then possesses what is called muscular sense, which means that in whatever position he is placed, whatever condition surrounds him, from a social gathering to a train wreck, he preserves his presence of mind. This muscular control gives one a full realization of consciousness of his power, which might be termed consciousness of self as contrasted to self-consciousness. Such a degree of self-control gives one power to more easily govern his passions and appetites and paves the way to the highest degree of physical and moral courage.

It is worth while following closely a system of progressive gymnastics that will gradually develop one's powers and in the end give him complete mastery of himself. The constant practice of mere tricks and stunts through play or spectacular gymnastics, tends to develop self-consciousness at first, and self-conceit later on, when the stunt is mastered.

There is morality in physical education which must not be overlooked. It is determined by one's motive. If one practices gymnastics simply to reduce his weight, or to increase his appetite that he may enjoy his food more, or plays games for the sake of victory, he will never realize the pleasure and long enduring benefit of the person who exercises to make his physical body a responsive tool to his mind in order that he may become more efficient to serve the world in his best capacity.

There is another side to the study of exercise and neurition. The constant effort to perform movements that require mental control will develop a close affiliation between the brain and the muscles. (And the closer the brain and muscles are related to each other, the more readily will either affect the other.) The underlying law in Delsarte's system was based on the hypothesis that posture produces feeling. It is also true that feeling produces posture. The skulking attitude of the murderer who is conscious of suspicion and the hang-dog look of the guilty or the timid are examples of feeling producing posture. The actor, to really impersonate and act out one of these conditions, must assume the fitting attitude in order to feel the passion or state of mind and make his acting natural. Therefore we find that posture tends to produce a corresponding feeling, and feeling is manifested by posture. When one tries to conceal his feeling by assuming a posture different from that which his feeling would produce, his false posture is exaggerated.

There is an inter-relation between the sensory and motor nerves. Lack of use of the motor nerves, that is, lack of sufficient activity, causes their degeneration, and at the same time the sensory nerves increase in irritability. When the sensory nerves are hyper-sensitive as a result of the under-use of the motor nerves we find a condition of nervousness. Neurasthenics, of various degree, are usually those who lead a sedentary life which requires great mental and little physical activity. Where perfect harmony exists between the sensory and the motor nerves we find all the functions normal. The sympathetic nervous system is dependent in a large measure upon the harmony between the sensory and motor nerves.

PERIODICITY.

To be of lasting value exercise should be repeated regularly. To endeavor to put all exercise possible into a few hours or days each year, as many do on their summer vacation, and then laze around the balance of the year, doing only what is absolutely required by one's daily work, is worse than useless. It is useless because it has no developing effect. And it is worse than useless because it will render the muscles very sore and may serve as the exciting cause for more serious developments. Exercise may be considered in the same light as suggestive therapy. That is, the oft repeated practice of any set or series of movements will tend to mold the parts exercised according to the nature of the movements, and the posture held while practicing them. Lessons should follow each other frequently enough for the effects of one to last until another is taken. The regularly repeated exercises will create a nutritive change in the muscles, producing new cells and refining the fibres.

Unless exercise is kept up through life, even though one's early years were very active, the muscles and motor nerves will undergo a form of fatty degeneration. The muscles may for a time retain their rounded shape, but microscopic examination shows fat distributed among the muscle fibres or replacing them completely. The motor nerves, from lack of use, become less and less responsive to stimuli and as a result we find a condition of awkwardness, poor endurance and loss of strength, and frequently auto-intoxication.

A repetition not only of the lessons but of the movements themselves is advisable. One should repeat a movement until it is mastered and then go on to the next of the same class. But some movements never cease to be beneficial. For instance, arm flinging upward, or sideways, is always beneficial as antagonistic to the tendency of gravity and daily toil to droop the shoulders. Gravity is constantly pulling down on the shoulders, and most occupations force one to use the pectoral muscles in a stooped position. The effect is to compress the chest and round and droop the shoulders. These arm flingings keep the chest muscles extended and supple the thorax.

For effect in development each movement should be repeated at least three or four times to each side.

This will allow each side to contract and relax alternately and it will also tend to equalize strength and skill. Since the first stimulus sent out from the brain has the best effect on development it is well to begin each movement to the weaker side. In class work, we first do them to the left, because in this way we reach the majority's weaker side first.

For best results exercise, according to one's needs, should be practiced every day, preferably the first thing in the morning, for it has the effect of toning one up and, as it were, set him for the day. One should exercise at least twice a week. Less frequently will only make the muscles sore and the effect of each lesson is nearly lost before the next one is taken. The length of time for each lesson should be regulated by the individual's need. An exercise of 15 minutes each morning is better than two one-hour lessons per week.

INDIVIDUALITY.

The mechanics, physiology and psychology of exercise all have their influence on the individual. As no two persons are exactly alike, exercise must be modified to suit each one. The underlying rules apply to everyone alike, but the methods of applying these rules vary according to each case. The laws which govern physiological functions are necessarily the same in all, yet in their application they must be modified by individual differences. What follows as an absolute effect in the majority may be absent in the minority and vice-versa. What benefits one may injure another. For instance, to supple the chest, elevate the ribs, and increase the respiratory power, arch flexions are best for the majority, because the majority of people have a tendency to droop forward in the upper dorsal spine, depressing the front of the ribs and sternum and fixing the thorax. Bending backward at the upper spine and arching the chest will tend to correct this condition and improve the respiratory capacity. But, in exceptional cases, where the dorsal spine bends forward instead of backward and the ribs are fixed, the practice of arch flexions will render a bad matter worse. The chapter on corrective gymnastics goes extensively into the application of general laws to individual cases.

Suffice it to say here that in making out a program of exercises we should measure the individual by himself. Particular attention must be paid to one's strong and weak points and special procedures should be introduced to strengthen the weak parts, along with the general program to promote harmony of all organs, brain and muscles.

PHILOSOPHY OF EXERCISE.

Exercises should be chosen to fill the needs of the body. In relation to the muscles themselves the aim should be to develop a condition of perfect elasticity. Where one's muscles are soft and flabby, making him loose jointed, to correct this defect the gymnastic work must contain many exercises requiring muscle tensing, as antagonistic movements. If one's muscles are over tense, giving him a condition designated as "muscle bound," he needs exercise of extension and of a limbering nature. When the muscles are properly developed in good tonic condition, the body and limbs show a well rounded surface with gentle swelling where it naturally should be. There should never exist a state in which any part of the body looks like a relief map or wash board. Such a condition shows an unbalanced development. If perfect elasticity exists in the muscles, one can perform with equal facility difficult feats requiring great strength, or balancing feats, or feats of agility and extension requiring great control and extensibility. It is when perfect elasticity exists that the body serves as an efficient servant to the will.

Gymnastic progression is to be considered from

several standpoints. The basis of progression is two-fold. First, from the standpoint of nervous irritability progression is made from the simplest movements, that is, those that require least concentration and control, to the most complex. Secondly, from the standpoint of muscular irritability progression is made from easy to strong movements. The first and most important law of progression is from the standpoint of control. The limit of progression possible from the muscular standpoint is soon attained in any individual. No one can ever get far beyond a certain limit of force, but few ever attain a limit of skill. Therefore progression from the standpoint of irritability of nerves is limitless, but from that of muscle it is soon limited.

Progression is of three kinds: First, from exercise to exercise of the same lesson. For the best results exercises should follow each other in a regular order. The day's order, given in the next chapter, explains why a certain definite order is important. Secondly, progression is made from lesson to lesson by introducing new movements of each type appearing in the day's order, as soon as the preceding have been mastered. One should not go from one exercise to another merely for the sake of variety, but rather for the sake of control. Progression is made from a third standpoint, by introducing games of gymnastic play with young children, gradually changing to specific, concentrated educational gymnastics until full growth is nearly attained when it becomes safe to allow competitive sports and games. Of course, games and play are valuable at all ages, but the emphasis is to be placed upon educational gymnastics, for preventive and corrective purposes at the proper period. Therefore it may be said that progression is from general to special to general. This is true from the third standpoint. It is true of the day's order, in which the first and last groups are general in effect, while the exercises of the middle one are selected for specific effects. Lessons are quite general at first, but soon become very specific, if the laws of progression are closely followed, and then, when good control has been attained, for every type of movement they become general in that more playful work is introduced.

More specifically, in reference to the same class of movements there are many methods of progression in gymnastics. The simplest, crudest and most useless type of progression is illustrated by dead weight lifting where a little is added each day to the dumb or bar-bell, and in time one gets an enormous bulk of muscle which is of little use except to perform one's daily stunts. This method is sometimes called the Milo system, after the Greek, Milo, who, it is said, began carrying a calf across the arena at Olympia every day, and as the calf gained in weight Milo's strength and dexterity increased accordingly until at one of the Olympiads, Milo carried a full-grown ox across the arena. This type of progression is the muscular type which goes from easy to strong.

Progression is made, (1) by duration, that is, increasing the number of times for each movement; (2) by series, that is, by combining two or more simple movements into a series; such as, arm extension forward, upward, sideways and backward; (3) by statical action, that is, by placing the body in some attitude which is to be retained while some active movement is performed; (4) by change of rhythm, that is, when a movement done to count has been mastered, it is practiced by changing the rate of speed for all, or various parts of the motion; (5) by changing the length of the lever, as for instance, in sideways bending where the movement is first done with the arms at the sides, then on the hips, then arms at shoulder height, then extended upward; (6) by shortening the base in the direction of action, as in the same movement just instanced, i. e., sideways bending, first with the feet apart, then together, then heels and toes together, etc.; (7) by increasing the weight, that is, by using dumbbells of increasing weight; (8) by changing the velocity, increasing it in those done most easily at slow or moderate speed, and decreasing it in those done most easily by speed; (9) by going from excentric to concentric to static. For instance, if lying leg elevation is difficult, we begin by flexing the knee, extending the leg upward and then lowering it slowly; that is excentric contraction; later when sufficient strength is acquired, the leg is elevated with the knee straight; this is concentric contraction. When the movement becomes easy in concentric contraction, the legs are kept off the floor and abducted and adducted, or put through a swimming motion. The muscles which keep the legs from the floor while the movement is in practice are in static contraction. (10) In different types of movement, progression is made by changing the moment of weight. In balance movements, for instance, we consider the relation the final position of a movement bears to the line of gravity, as well as its complexity. If we compare heel elevation with toe standing as its final position, to standing on one foot with one knee flexed upward, or hip flexed with leg extended forward, the effect on the line of gravity is obvious, for such a change in the mass of weight will carry the line of gravity forward. This places extra work on the back muscles to keep the trunk erect, besides severely taxing the abdominal muscles. It is a good example of the highest type of progression which is made by causing movements to require more and more co-ordination.

Progression in individual cases is limited or conditioned by the age, intelligence, and sex of the subject. Objectively, progression is limited by the time one has to devote to exercise, the space, conveniences, apparatus and the dress of the individual.

CHAPTER II.

HOME GYMNASTICS.

The following list of exercises is arranged according to the principles of the Swedish System of Gymnastics. The guide in arranging them is Baron Nil Posse's "Handbook of School Gymnastics," and the course in Medical and Hygienic Gymnastics at the Posse Normal School of Gymnastics, Boston, Mass.

The lessons in this series which are planned to meet the needs of the average are typical of the progressive sequence in which Swedish gymnastics are arranged. For best results one lesson should be practiced every day, with every movement performed at least three times to either side. When one lesson has become easy, and every movement mastered, begin with the next, and so on until all are mastered. Then begin with the list of more advanced lessons that follow the second series.

The system is more than a century old. It was founded by P. H. Ling in 1809. It has been experimented with and improved upon by his successors until it has evolved into the best single system now extant. It is not a complete system, though Ling had such an ideal in mind when he founded it. What it lacks is of a competitive and recreative nature. But, as a system to fill the needs of the body, to develop elasticity, control, good posture, grace, vital capacity and all-round health, it has no equal. All the leading nations of the world have adopted it for their schools.

Ling and his followers aimed to arrange a complete system of gymnastics that would comply with the laws of anatomy, physiology and psychology. They succeeded better than they realized. While the reasons given for some of the procedures adopted are not in accord with modern physiology and psychology, the principles are sound.

"The aim of educational gymnastics," writes Posse, "is to develop the body into a harmonious whole under perfect control of the will. It is not to produce a great bulk of muscle, but to cause that already present to respond readily to volition; to improve the functional activity of the body; and to counteract and correct tendencies to abnormal development, especially those resulting from the 'artificial life of civilization.'"

The exercises have been arranged into ten divisions, and each division progressively according to their difficulty and complexity, based upon the laws of mental control and all the physical laws of leverage, gravity and equilibrium. They are arranged and chosen according to their effects upon the body, judging from their action upon the part used and their reaction upon the organism. No exercise is retained in the system which is at all doubtful or injurious in its effects.

Regularity and good order give us the best results in anything. Experience has proven that this is true of gymnastics. In every good gymnastic lesson, the exercises follow each other in the same order. The Swedish system is famous for its "day's order." Progression in each day's order is two-fold: (a) in three groups from general to special to general and (b) from exercise to exercise as follows:

REGULAR DAY'S ORDER.
Introduction.

General {
  Arch-flexions.
  Heaving movements.
  Balance movements.
}

Special {
  Shoulder-blade movements.
  Abnormal exercises.
  Lateral trunk movements.
}

General {
  Slow leg movements.
  Leaping, vaulting, etc.
  Respirating exercises.
}

DAY'S ORDER IN ABSENCE OF APPARATUS.

1. Introductions.
2. Trunk rotations.
3. Arch-flexions.
4. Substitute heaving movements.
5. Balance movements.
6. Shoulder-blade movements.
7. Abdominal exercises.
8. Trunk sideways flexions.
9. Jumping.
10. Slow leg movements.
11. Respiratory exercises.

Such is the order followed in these lessons:

(1) Introductory exercises span the bridge from mental or intellectual to physical activity. They are simple exercises but, when done properly, cause the flow of blood from the intellectual to the motor centers of the brain. They are also given to prepare general control for harder exercises in the same lesson.

(2) Arch flexions cultivate possibility of respiration by stretching the expiratory muscles. They supple the chest and correct drooping head.

(3) Heaving movements increase the ability of respiration by strengthening the inspiratory muscles. Typical heaving movements are done on apparatus, but substitute heaving movements may be done in free-standing work. Besides their effects on the inspiratory muscles these movements develop the muscles of the arm, shoulder and back.

(4) Balance movements cultivate general equilibrium and control and help to attain good posture by their effects on the extensor muscles of the body. We are by nature prone to give up to the force of gravity and allow ourselves to stoop and droop as aged people. Balance movements counteract this.

(5) Shoulder-blade movements produce isolation and co-ordination of the shoulder region. They correct stoop and round shoulders. There are two classes: those for expansion of the chest and those for localization of effect on the back shoulder muscles. The first class precedes and the second class follows marching or running.

(6) Abdominal exercises strengthen the muscles supporting the viscera, improve digestion and promote excretion.

(7) Lateral trunk movements develop the waist muscles, further the effects of abdominal exercises, quicken portal circulation and promote digestion.

(8) Slow-leg movements are movements of passive vascular expansion which diminish blood pressure. They

may be applied in any part of the lesson where this effect is needed.

(9) Leaping and vaulting develop elasticity, control, speed, courage, co-ordination.

(10) Respiratory exercises are movements of deep inhalation and exhalation in which the arms accompany the respiratory act. The position and direction in which the arms are employed largely determine their effect.

There is a law, which is axiomatic, that the body at rest tends to assume the posture it held during activity. This is important to remember. Therefore, a good posture should be maintained during all exercises. The posture itself is of as much importance as the exercises practiced. The position recommended with these lessons is as follows: the heels together; feet at right angles; knees straight; the chest well forward over the toes; shoulders drawn back, but not stiff; the head erect, chin drawn in; arms straight at the sides, hands drawn slightly backward along the thighs. Maintain this position free of stiffness throughout the lesson. Whenever any movement of the legs or arms is practiced, preserve the same relative position of the trunk, isolating the action to the parts used.

These little details make for control. Control and harmony should be your first aim next to health. Then work for power, skill and that which is ornamental. No amount of muscular development will give physical culture until such harmony exists between the mind and muscles that the latter respond readily to all shades of volition for speed, power, dexterity, skill or gentleness.

The following lessons lay the foundation for health and control. They are corrective, progressive and educational in their nature. They will tax the entire muscular system without straining or exhausting. For best results concentrate your attention upon each movement as you practice it. See how much you can get out of it.

The more you watch the details the more perfectly you perform the movement and the more benefit you derive.

We shall offer three series of gymnastic lessons. The first will be for little children; the second series for girls and women. The third series is designed for men or women who desire strenuous daily gymnastics. Of course these are simply average lessons and are at best but limited in their scope. When one considers that it is possible to make up over two hundred different progressive lessons from the Ling system it is clear that these few lessons are but average and limited selections. Gymnastic teachers who wish to utilize these lessons in their work will find the commands in the first lesson descriptions, or in the appendix at the back of the book.

Growing children need no apparatus other than their own bodies. The rapid increase in body weight serves as the very best means of increased resistance. It is a mistake to introduce dumbbells or other weight apparatus too early in the physical training of children. A child's growth is often hindered by following the advice of his elders and taking up weight lifting or strenuous athletic competition too early.

With children, even more than with adults, exercises requiring control are most valuable. As long as one tries to perform movements of control and preserves good bodily posture all the time he is exercising, there is no danger of strain and yet there is every chance of gain in development and strength. Every average person is supplied with all the muscles he needs for general purposes of life provided he gets these muscles under complete control of the will. The weak person is deficient in strength not so much from lack of muscle as from lack of brain and will-control over the muscles present. Any doubt in one's mind as to the truth of this statement will be dispelled if one ever has to struggle with a weak person who suddenly goes insane. The insane person's proverbial strength is explained by the fact that there is complete co-operation between the will and the muscles. If it is possible to establish the closest possible relation between the brain and muscles, an apparently weak person will develop a muscular power that will prove almost as startling as that displayed by the mentally unbalanced. Of course such strength is very seldom needful or desirable, but the example gives an idea of the unrealized powers in all of us.

Another example of the great power of muscles is where there is what is called spontaneous fracture of bone. It sometimes happens that a person who is asleep may produce a sudden pressure on a large nerve trunk and the resulting stimulus which is suddenly sent to the muscles causes a fracture of some bone. For example, while turning over on a couch with exposed strong springs, the sciatic nerve may be pressed upon and the resulting stimulus will fracture one or two of the small bones of the feet. This happens because the sudden contraction of the muscles can be strong enough to rip the tendons loose or break the bone to which they are attached. Therefore it is not so essential to develop a great bulk of muscle as to acquire control of that which is present.

While leading children, who are such perfect little imitators, it is imperative that we keep a good posture. The rule that the body at rest always tends to assume the posture it held in activity can never be repeated too often. Next to proper respiration it is the most important rule in gymnastics.

For little children lessons should not be longer than eight or ten minutes. Tact and ingenuity are necessary and example is of more importance than all the talk imaginable. The disciplinarian of the old school type, that is, the one who commands discipline by stern bearing or frightfulness, such as can still be seen in too many schools, is absolutely out of place with children. A child's attention should be controlled by the element of play. Incorporate picture words or phrases or simple game principles in your appeal.

The useful and simple phrase, "Simon says," is one of the best friends and allies of the teacher. All children can be started early in the little play of "Simon says, thumbs up," and "Simon says, thumbs down." It is a very easy step from this to the gymnastic lesson in which all the desired movements are preceded by "Simon says."

Lesson I.

1. "Simon says, turn your head to the left. Simon says, turn it to the right," and so on, repeating several times to each side.

2. "Simon says, bend your head to the left (Illustration 4), straighten it; bend it to the right, straighten it," and so on, several times.

3. "Simon says, head backward, bend. Simon says, draw in the chin, puff out the chest, and lift it again." Repeat.

These three simple movements are among the most useful for keeping a perfect neck and throat development all through life. If practiced daily, say about ten times each to each side, they will keep the muscles of the neck in tonic state and prevent the disagreeable double chin which so many are worried by. In the backward bending of the head the chin is drawn in during the upward part of the movement so as to assure all the chest expansion and suppling of. the ribs possible. This is one of the procedures that will develop perfect respiration.

4. "Simon says, place your hands on the hips, keep the elbows back, the head as high as possible and rise on the toes quickly. Stay on the toes and make yourself as tall as possible. Now, lower the heels slowly."

This fourth movement is also one which deserves to be practiced frequently because it tends to improve bodily carriage. In its practice, as was said in the preceding chapter, the more speed is put into the elevation the better. In descending from the toe standing, the heels should be lowered very slowly.

5. "Simon says, place the hands on the hips. Now, bend the head backward as far as possible and try to see the floor backward without bending at the waist. Draw in the chin and come up very slowly and puff out the chest." (Illustration 5.) After repeating this backward flexion a few times, "Simon says, with the hands on the hips, bend forward from the hips, keeping the head up. Slowly, come up to position." The forward bend follows the backward bend because there is likely to be a congestion of blood in the small of the back following the first movement and this forward bend, by extending the blood vessels of the small of the back, will relieve the congestion.

6. "Simon says, stretch your arms upward and rise on the toes and reach as high as possible, and try to reach even higher. Now, lower the arms and the heels slowly." (Illustration 6.) To cultivate general body carriage and develop all the erector muscles of the trunk, this exercise is of value to both old and young alike.

7. As a last movement to the first lesson a respiratory exercise is appropriate. "Simon says, lift your arms sideways and breathe in deeply at the same time, (Illustration 7), lift the chest and draw in the chin as you do it; now, as you breathe out, lower the arms slowly."

LESSON II.

"Standing up straight and tall, the head high and the chin in, the chest out and the arms back, let us play 'Simon says.'"

1. "Simon says, bend the head to the left,—lift it up again,—bend it to the right,—lift it up again," and so on. Only the head should be bent; the shoulders should be kept from moving.

2. "Simon says, lift the arms out to the sides and

breathe in as you lift them; lower them slowly as you breathe out."

3. "Simon says, place the hands on the hips; now twist the body to the left, (Illustration 8),—turn it forward again; turn it to the right,—turn it forward again," and so on.

4. "Simon says, bend the arms up and curl the fingers onto the shoulders; from here, imagine that you are in a narrow room and you wish to push the walls apart and extend the arms sideways very hard,—bend them again and extend them." Repeat several times. Forcible extension sideways has a broadening effect on the shoulders. This is of course excellent for growing children.

5. "Simon says, hands on the hips, raise the heels,—keeping on the toes, bend the knees apart, (Illustration 9), stretch the knees slowly and, very slowly, lower the heels."

6. "Simon says, bend the arms across the chest, fingers just touching in front of the chest. Now fling them sideways and back and bend them again,—repeat with count,—one,—two," and so on. This movement is good to expand the chest and correct the posture of the shoulders. It is most effective if the trunk is bent forward slightly from the hips.

7. "Simon says, hands on the hips,—lift the left knee forward, hold while you balance on the right foot, (Illustration 10),—lower the left foot and raise the right knee and hold," and so on.

8. "Simon says, hands on the hips, feet apart, bend as far as possible to the left, (Illustration 11),—raise the body and bend to the right," and so on.

9. "Simon says, lift the arms straight upward and reach as high as possible,—now rise on the toes, and while reaching up hard, walk slowly forward,—now walk backward,—keep your balance—slowly lower the heels." This is an extremely valuable exercise for both young

and old. It will develop all the muscles that co-operate in keeping good posture in standing or walking.

LESSON III.

The two preceding lessons should illustrate amply how to proceed with little children. The work can be as uninteresting as any scientific work usually is, but if such a simple play principle as "Simon says" is introduced it makes all the difference in the world to children. In this simple way their attention is held for ten or twelve minutes easily, and that is long enough for the purpose in mind. To save time and space I shall simply give the commands for the lessons, from now on, as if they were for young or old.

1. "Rising on the toes quickly and coming down very slowly, heels lift!—Heels—sink." Repeat several times.

2. "Head backward—bend. Upward—stretch."

3. "Arms bent, fingers curled onto the shoulders, extend arms sideways as you inhale deeply. As you flex the arms again, exhale slowly. Repeat with count—one, —two," and so on.

4. "Hips firm. Left foot forward—place." The foot is carried forward, toes out, about two foot lengths. "In this position, trunk to the left—turn, (Illustration 12), forward—turn," and so on. Then, "Change feet, one, two. Trunk to the right—turn, forward—turn," and so on, and, when it has been repeated enough times, "Position!" is commanded and this means to come back to fundamental standing with the hands at the sides.

5. (a) "Hips firm, trunk backward—bend,—upward —stretch. The same, one, two," and so on.

(b) "Keeping the hands on the hips, trunk forward —bend, (Illustration 13), upward—stretch," and so on.

6. "Arms upward bend; trunk to the left—turn. Keeping it turned, arms upward—stretch, (Illustration 14),—arms, bend. The same with count,—one,—two," and so on. Repeat with the trunk turned to the right.

7. "Hips firm, heels—lift! Holding this position, reaching up as high as possible with the head, with count, rotate the head to the left and to the right,—one, (Illustration 15),—two," and so on.

8. "Alternate arm flinging upward, beginning with the left, putting all the force in the upward part of the movement, with count,—one,—two," and so on, several times. The trunk should be slightly forward and the head kept from swaying with the motions.

9. "Lie on the back, the arms stretched beyond the head; at one, lift the left leg, (Illustration 16); at two, lower it; at three, raise the right leg and at four lower it. Now, with the count,—one,—two,—three,—four," and so on.

10. "Hips firm,—feet close, heels and toes together. Trunk to the left—bend,—upward—stretch; to the right —bend,—upward—stretch," and so on.

11. "Raise the arms forward upward as you inhale, and lower them sideways backward as you exhale. Now, slowly, with count, one,—two,—" and so on.

LESSON IV.

Every one of the following movements can be made more interesting by employing the "Simon says" command.

1. "Hips firm. Feet close. Left foot forward place, keep the toes pointing straight forward. With count, change feet,—one,—two," and so on.

2. "With count, arm extension forward, upward and sideways. At one, the arms are bent, at two, they are stretched forward, and three, they are bent and at four, they are stretched upward, and so on. Begin, one,—two, —three,—four,—five,—six." Repeat.

3. "Hips firm, heels lift, knees bend, half way down, knees stretch and slowly, heels sink. Repeat with count, —one,—two,—three,—four."

4. "Hips firm, left foot sideways forward—place.

Trunk to the left—turn. Keeping it turned, trunk backward—bend,—upward—stretch," and so on. Then, "Change feet—one, two. Trunk to the right—turn. Trunk backward—bend,—upward stretch," and so on. (Illustration 17.)

5. "Arms bent, trunk to the left,—turn. Keeping it turned, arm extension sideways, with count,—one,—two," and so on. Then, "trunk to the right—turn," and arm extension with count.

6. "Hips firm. Heels—lift!—knees bend,—all the way down, (Illustration 18),—knees stretch,—heels sink. Repeat in four counts," and so on.

7. "Arms bend. Alternate arm extension upward, beginning with the left,—one,—two," and so on.

8. "Lie on the back, the arms stretched beyond the head. Lift the left leg. As you lower it, lift the right, and so on, with count,—one,—two."

9. "Raise the arms out from the shoulders at the sides. Turn the palms forward upward,—turn them down again. Repeat with count,—one!—two," and so on. This is more than a mere hand turning. As the palms are turned forward upward the muscles of the shoulders and back should contract and this movement is rendered into a corrective of the shoulders.

10. "Hips firm, left foot forward—place. Trunk to the left—bend, (Illustration 19), upward stretch. Again, with count,—one,—two," and so on. Then, "Change feet, —one, two. Trunk to the right—bend," and so on.

11. "Arms sideways lift. Palms upward turn. (Illustration 20.) Lift the arms to vertical as you breathe in deeply, and lower them to the level of the shoulders as you breathe out, with count, slowly,—one, —two," and so on.

LESSON V.

1. "Arm extension forward and upward, in four counts—one,—two!—three,—four!" etc. At one the arms are bent upward, at two they are extended forward for-

cibly, at three they are bent and at four they are extended upward forcibly.

2. "Hips firm. Left foot, long step backward—place. Change feet—one,—two," and so on. (Illustration 21.)

3. "Hips firm; heels lift; knees bend, all the way—kneel. Sit back on the heels and spring up to—position!"

4. "Hips firm. Left foot forward—place. Keeping the weight between both feet, trunk backward bend; slowly, upward—stretch." Repeat a few times with the left foot forward and then change the feet and perform with the right foot forward.

5. "Hips firm. Keeping the body perfectly still, with the head high, the left leg backward—lift. Point the toes and keep the knee straight. (Illustration 22.) Leg sink; and, right leg—lift," and so on.

6. "Arms upward bend. Arm extension sideways, palms turned up—one,—two!" and so on.

7. "Lie face down. Place the hands on the hips. Lift the head as high as you can." Repeat a few times.

8. "Stoop fall position, one—(Illustration 23.) two." (Illustration 24.) At one the knees are bent and the hands placed on the floor, the fingers pointing inward; at two the feet are kicked back, the body kept in a straight line. "Foot placing forward and backward—one,—two," and so on.

9. "Hips firm. Left foot sideways—forward—place. Trunk to the left—turn. (Illustration 25.) Forward—turn." Repeat a few times and then, with the feet reversed, the trunk is turned to the right.

10. "Hips firm. Left foot sideways—place. Trunk to the left—turn. Keeping it turned, trunk to the left—bend; upward—stretch." Repeat a few times and then, with the trunk turned to the right, bend to the right.

11. "In five counts, upward jump,—one,—two,—three!—four,—five." At one the heels are lifted, at two the knees are bent, at three the arms are swung upward and brought to the sides again before the landing from

the jump, at four the knees are straightened and, at five, the heels are lowered slowly.

12. "Raise the arms forward-upward as you breathe in and lower them sideways-backward as you breathe out. One,—two," and so on.

The above lessons are typical of the manner of procedure with little children. This method is most useful for teachers who wish to give progressive gymnastics to classes. Should more advanced work be desired one can utilize the list of fourteen lessons which will follow the next program. These lessons begin with the simplest of gymnastics and progress in safe gradations. With the simple addition of the "Simon says" commands, a teacher will find sufficient work for an entire season for the average class. Much of the time can be taken up with games and other play activities and thus supplement the gymnastics.

Mothers and guardians often ask for a well balanced program that might serve for daily practice when once memorized, without the need of following a long progressive list. While this is not the best method of assuring a perfectly developed body, yet, if there are no deformities present, the following program will prove adequate for the average child. Let each movement be practiced ten or more times to each side, and, along with correct eating and the observation of other hygienic laws, the child's health will be kept at its best.

1. "Arms bent, fingers onto the shoulders, extend them, with all the force possible, forward, upward, sideways and downward, with count,—one!—two,—three! four,—five!—six,—seven!—eight," and so on. The exclamation points indicate when the extension takes place. At the even numbers the arms are bent with the elbows close to the body.

2. "Stand with back to the wall, about two feet away. Arms upward—stretch. Bend backward slowly until the fingers touch the wall. Keeping the chest well

up, raise the heels a few times, with count,—one,—two,"
and so on.

3. "Arms upward stretch. Trunk forward—bend,
try to reach the floor,—upward stretch,—to the right
turn, forward—bend, upward stretch,—to the left turn,
forward—bend, upward stretch," and so on.

4. "Hands on the hips. Heels lift! Remaining on
the toes, deep knee bending with count,—one,—two,"
and so on, then, "Slowly—heels sink."

5. "Arms forward bend. With count, forcibly, arms
flinging sideways,—one!—two,—one!—two," and so on.

6. "Heels lift! Knees bend—kneel. Fingers locked
behind the head. Trunk to the left—turn, (Illustration
26),—forward turn, to the right—turn,—forward turn,"
and so on.

8. "Hands on the hips. Feet close. Trunk to the
left—bend, (Illustration 27),—upward—stretch, to the
right—bend,—upward—stretch," and so on.

9. Practice various hops, jumps, dancing steps, or
running games. Rope jumping will also do at this time.

10. "Arms sideways lift. Palms forward upward
turn. Lift the arms to vertical as you inhale, and lower
them to shoulder level as you exhale, with count,—one,—
two," and so on.

Lesson I.

1. Keeping the body in good posture,
without moving the shoulders, turn the head
forcibly from side to side. (Illus. 28.)

2. Observing the same rule as in the
Introduc- above, flex the neck to the left and then to
tion the right. (Illus. 29.)

3. Hands on hips, fingers, in front,
thumbs behind, (1) rise on the toes quickly,
(2) lower the heels slowly. In practicing
the exercise, keep the weight forward over

the balls of the feet so that as you rise on the toes you feel a tendency to fall forward. Counteract this by contracting the muscles of the back. (Illus. 30.)

4. Raise the arms sideways slowly to shoulder height and at the same time breathe in deeply. Lower them slowly as you breathe out. (Illus. 31.)

5. Hands on the hips, feet apart, turn the body to the left and then to the right as far as possible without bending the knees or moving the feet. (Illus. 32.)

6. (a) Hands on the hips, drop the head back and arch the chest. In practicing this movement localize the bending to the upper spine. (Endeavor to see the floor backward without bending at the waist.) (Illus. 33.) One should have always come up slowly from arch flexion. If the body is raised too suddenly, dizziness results because the blood rushes to the head. (Vide: Centrifugal force, Chap. I.)

(b) Hands on the hips, bend forward from the hips, keeping the head up, shoulders back. (Endeavor to touch the chest to the floor and keep the eyes on the ceiling.) (Illus. 34.)

7. Arm extension upward and forward in four counts, keeping the body steady, moving just the arms. (1) Bend the arms upward, elbows close to sides, fingers curled onto shoulder (Illus. 35), (2) stretch them upward, (3) bend them, (4) stretch them forward, etc.

8. Hands on hips, (1) rise on the toes, (2) bend the knees half-way, (3) stretch the knees, (4) lower the heels. (Illus. 36.)

9. Alternate arm flinging upward, beginning with the left. Keeping the elbows straight, chest well out, head erect, (1) fling the left arm up, carrying it vertically forward-upward with force, (2) as you lower the left fling up the right, etc. Keep the body steady. Isolate the motion to the arms. (Illus. 37.)

10. Hands on hips, feet apart, bend as far as possible to the left and right. (Illus. 38.)

11. Raise the arms forward-upward, inhaling deeply as they go up. As you lower them, sideways-backward, exhale slowly. (Illus. 39.)

LESSON II.

1. Bend the head backward. As you stretch it up, draw in the chin so as to produce a lifting of the ribs. (Illus. 40.)

2. Rise on the toes quickly. Lower the

Introduc- 3. Arms bent upward, (1) carry them
tion heels slowly.

sideways slowly as you inhale deeply, (2) as you flex them exhale.

4. Prepare to jump, (1) rise on the toes, (2) bend the knees half-way, (3) stretch the knees, (4) lower the heels.

5. Hands on hips. Left foot forward, toes turned out. The feet far enough apart to measure two foot lengths between the heels; weight between both feet. Twist the trunk to the left a few times. Repeat with the right foot forward, twisting body to the right. (Illus. 41.)

6. Repeat Exercise 6 of Lesson I.

7. Arm extension sideways and backward in four counts. (1) Bend arms upward, (2) stretch them sideways forcibly, (3) bend them, (4) stretch them downward-backward forcibly, etc. [Illus. 31 for (2).] (Illus. 42.)

8. Hands on hips. Keeping the body steady, knees straight, raise the left leg backward as high as possible without inclining the body forward. As the leg is elevated point the toes downward. Repeat with the right. (Illus. 43.)

9. Arms extended upward rise on the toes and reach upward.   (Illus. 44.)

10. Run in place.   (Illus. 45.)   The arms are bent, forearm close to the chest; keep up on the toes.

11. Arms sideways, shoulder high.   Turn the palms upward forcibly a few times.   To execute this movement correctly and get full benefit, make the rotation upward take place in the shoulder.   You should feel a tension in the back muscles.

12. Lie on the back, arms extended back of the head.   Flex the left knee up, extend it, and lower the leg slowly.   Repeat with the right.

13. Hands on hips, bend the trunk as far as possible to both sides, without bending the knees.   (As Illus. 38, with heels together.)

14. Upward jump in five counts.   (1) Rise on the toes, (2) bend the knees, (3) fling the arms upward, spring from the floor and bring the arms back to the sides before landing.   Land with the knees half-bent as in position (2) of prepare to jump, (4) stretch the knees, (5) lower the heels.   Aim to get a good landing first.   This will give control.   (Illus. 46 shows the beginning of the jump and the position at landing.)   (Illus. 47 shows the body in the air.)

15. Arms bent forward, elbows shoulder high, wrists straight, fingers straight.   Fingers about four or five inches apart in front of chest.   (Illus. 48.)   This gives good starting position without compressing the chest.   (1) Carry the forearms sideways slowly as you inhale deeply.   (Illus. 31.)   Bring them back forward as you exhale slowly.

LESSON III.

Introduc-tion   1. Hands on the hips; feet apart.   Rise on the toes quickly.   Lower the heels slowly.

2. Alternate   arm   extension   upward.

Bend the arms upward, (1) extend the left upward, (2) as you flex the left, extend the right upward. Put force in the extension. (Illus. 49.)

3. Arms bent forward as Ex. 14, Lesson II. (1) Carry them sideways as you inhale, (2) flex them as you exhale.

4. (a) Hands on hips; feet apart. Turn the trunk to the left, keeping the body turned, drop the head backward and arch the chest. (Illus. 50.) As you come up let the head come last, chin drawn in, so as to raise the ribs. Repeat with the trunk turned to the right.

(b) Hands on hips, feet apart. Bend forward from the hips.

5. Hands on hips, left foot forward, toes straight forward, weight between both feet, rise on the toes a few times, holding the position a few moments each time. Do not allow the feet to rotate sideways. This is a balance movement for control. (Illus. 51.)

6. Arms bent forward; fling them sideways forcibly to expand the chest.

7. Run in place.

8. Hands on hips, bend the body half-forward from the hips, keeping the head well up, shoulders back. While holding this posture, twist the head to the left and right. (Illus. 52.)

9. Lying on the back, arms extended back of the head, raise the left leg upward, knee straight. Repeat with the right. (Illus. 53.)

10. Hands on hips, feet close, i. e., heels and toes together. Bend as far as possible to the left and right. (Illus. 54.)

11. Hands on hips, rise on the toes. Keeping the heels off the floor, spring the feet apart and together a number of times.

12. Raise the arms sideways-upward and at the

same time breathe in deeply. Lower them sideways-
backward and at the same time breathe out.

1. Hands on hips, (1) place the left foot
diagonally forward, that is, carrying it two
foot lengths in its own direction, (2) bring
it back to position, (3) carry the right foot

Introduc-
tion

2. Arms bent upward. (1) Carry them
out, (4) back to position.
sideways slowly, palms turned up, and
breathe in as they go out. (2) Flex them
as you breathe out.

3. Prepare to jump, in four counts. (As
in Lesson II.)

4. (a) Hands on hips, turn body to the left; keeping
it turned, bend backward. Repeat with body turned
to the right. (As Illus. 50, with heels together.)

(b) Hands on hips. Bend forward from the hips.

5. Turn the trunk to the left. Arms bent upward.
Stretch them sideways forcibly a few times. Repeat
with the trunk turned to the right.

6. Hands on the hips. Rise on toes; as you lower
the heels, raise the toes; as you lower the toes, raise
the heels, etc., alternately. Preserve a good posture of
the trunk throughout.

7. Arms bent upward, extend them sideways forcibly, the palms turned up.

8. Run in place.

9. Arms shoulder-high at the sides, feet apart, bend
the trunk half-forward, keeping the arms in their relative position, head well up. Holding this position, twist
the head to left and right. (Illus. 55.)

10. Rise on the toes, bend the knees all the way
down, place the hands on the floor, fingers turned inward,

about four or five inches apart. (Illus. 56.) Carry the left foot back and then the right, thus supporting the weight on the hands and toes. From the head to the heels the body should be in a straight line. (Illus. 57.)

11. Hands on hips, the left foot forward, toes turned out. Bend the trunk to the left. With the right foot forward, bend to the right. (Illus. 58.)

12. Forward jump in five counts. (1) Rise on the toes, (2) bend the knees and carry the arms back preparatory to the spring (Illus. 59), (3) spring forward as you swing the arms forward and, just before landing, bring the arms to the sides, landing on the toes, the knees half-bent, (4) stretch the knees, (5) lower the heels.

13. Raise the arms sideways to shoulder height; at the same time rise on the toes and inhale deeply. (Illus. 60.) As you lower the arms and heels, slowly exhale.

Lesson V.

Introduction

1. Arms bent upward, stretch them sideways alternately, palms turned up.
2. Prepare to jump in four counts. turned up, raise them upward as you rise
3. Arms shoulder high at sides, palms on the toes and breathe in. (Illus. 61.) Lower them to shoulder height and at the same time lower the heels and breathe out.

4. Hands on hips, left foot forward, toes pointing straight forward. Twist the trunk to the left. (Illus. 62.) Repeat to the right with the right foot forward.

5. (a) Carry the left foot two foot lengths in its own direction, arms shoulder high at sides; turn the body to the left and bend backward, allowing the arms to sag slightly as the trunk is arched. (Illus. 63.) Bend backward a few times; then repeat the movement

with the right foot forward, trunk turned to the right.

(b) Arms extended upward, feet apart, bend forward from the hips. The head should be kept in line with the body, the arms in line with the ears. (Illus. 62.)

6. Arms bent upward, turn the body to the left. Keeping body turned, stretch the arms upward forcibly. Repeat with the body turned to the right.

7. Hands on hips, rise on the toes and hold position. While holding position turn the head to the left and right. (Illus. 63.)

8. Keeping the head erect, chest well forward, elbows straight, fling both arms upward forcibly. They should travel forward-upward.

9. Run in place.

10. Arms shoulder high at sides. Bend the trunk half-forward from the hips. While holding this position turn the palms of the hands forward-upward forcibly. (As Illus. 72 with the heels together.)

11. Rise on the toes, bend the knees and place the hands on the floor, fingers turned inward. Spring the feet back so that the weight rests on the hands and toes. From head to heels the body should be in a straight line. Repeat a number of times, springing the feet forward and backward. As the feet are sprung forward, let the knees come outside the elbows.

12. Hands on hips, left foot forward, toes pointing forward, bend body to the left as far as possible. With the right foot forward, repeat to the right. (Illus. 64.)

13. Ninety degrees turning upward jump, in five counts. (1) Rise on the toes, (2) bend the knees, (3) fling the arms upward as you spring upward and turn so as to land facing to the left, knees half-bent and hands at the sides, (4) straighten the knees, (5) lower the heels. Repeat with turn to the right.

14. Raise the arms forward-upward; at the same time rise on the toes and breathe in deeply. Lower

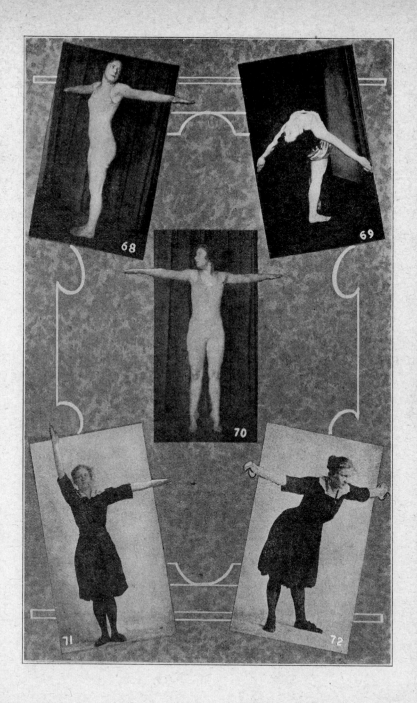

the arms sideways-backward; at the same time lower the heels and breathe out.   (Illus. 67.)

LESSON VI.

1. Raise the arms sideways-upward; at the same time rise on the toes and breathe in.   Lower them sideways-backward; at the same time lower the heels and breathe out.

Introduction
2. Arms bent forward.   Arm swimming in three counts—(1) carry them forward, hands slightly everted, (2) fling them sideways forcibly, (3) flex them.   1 and 2 should be run together when the movement is mastered.

3. Prepare to jump, in four counts.

4. Arms shoulder high at sides, feet close.   Twist body as far as possible to left and right.   (Illus. 68.)

5. (a) Carry the left foot forward, and keep the toes straight forward throughout the movement.   Arms shoulder high at sides.   Bend backward a few times. Repeat with the right foot forward.   (Illus. 69.)

(b) Repeat (b), Exercise 5, Lesson V.

6. Arms bent upward, turn body to the left.   Keeping the body turned, extend the arms upward and forward in four counts.   (1) Stretch them upward, (2) bend them, (3) stretch them forward, (4) bend them.   Repeat with the body turned to the right.

7. Arms shoulder high at the sides, rise on the toes; while holding this position turn the head to the left and right.   (Illus. 70.)

8. In two counts, the left arm upward and the right arm sideways, stretch.   (Illus. 71.)   (1) Bend the arms upward, (2) stretch the left arm upward and at the same time stretch the right sideways.   In the upstretched arm the palm is turned inward; in the other it

is downward. Change arms with count. (1) Arms flexed, (2) the right up and the left sideways, etc.

9. Run in place.

10. Arms sideways, shoulder high, feet apart. Bend half-forward from the hips. Holding this position, turn the palms upward forcibly a few times. (Illus. 72.)

11. Repeat Exercise 11 of Lesson V.

12. Hands on hips, feet apart, turn body to the left. Keeping it turned, bend to the left. Repeat to the right with the body turned to the right. (Illus. 73.)

13. Sideways jump in five counts. (1) Rise on the toes, (2) bend the knees and carry the arms to the left (opposite to the side you jump). (3) Swing the arms forcibly toward the right as you spring to the right, and, before landing, bring the arms back to the sides, landing knees half-bent, (4) stretch the knees, (5) lower the heels. Repeat to the left.

14. Arms bent forward, carry them sideways slowly; at the same time place the left foot forward (inclining the body forward by raising the right heel), as you inhale deeply. (Illus. 74.) As you flex the arms, draw the foot back and, at the same time, exhale. Repeat, carrying the right foot forward.

LESSON VII.

1. Raise the arms forward-upward. At the same time rise on the toes and breathe in deeply. Lower them sideways-backward; at the same time lower the heels

Introduction   2. Hands on hips, feet close. Foot placing and breathe out.

ing forward with heel elevation, in eight counts. (1) Place the left foot forward, (2) rise on the toes (Illus. 75), (3) lower the heels, (4) bring the foot back, (5) right foot forward, etc.

3. Arms bent upward, stretch them sideways forcibly, palms turned up.

4. Arms shoulder high at sides, twist the body as far as possible to the left and right. (See Illus. 68.)

5. (a) Feet apart, arms shoulder high at sides, bend backward.

(b) Feet apart, arms extended upward, bend forward from the hips; from the hips to the fingers should be a straight line.

6. Fingers locked behind the head, keeping the elbows well back, head erect, chest out, rise on the toes a few times. Remain upon the toes a few moments each time. (Illus. 76.)

7. Arms bent forward, bend the body half-forward from the hips. While holding this position, fling the arms sideways forcibly.

8. Run in place, or up and down room.

9. Arms bent upward, feet apart, bend body half-forward from the hips. Holding this position, stretch the arms sideways and backward in four counts. (1) Stretch them sideways, (2) bend them, (3) stretch them downward-backward, keeping the shoulders back, (4) bend them, etc.

10. Assume stoop fall position described in Exercise 8, Lesson IV, body in one line from head to heels. Holding this position, turn the head to the left and right. (Illus. 77.)

11. Hands on hips, left foot forward. Turn the trunk to the left. Keep it turned while you bend sideways to the left. Repeat with the right foot forward, trunk turned to the right. (Illus. 78.)

12. Arms bent upward, turn the body to the left. Keep it turned. In four counts stretch the arms sideways and upward.

13. Hands on hips, left foot forward, rise on the

toes. Change feet by jumping upward, drawing the left foot back and the right forward, etc.

14. Arms bent upward, feet close, turn the trunk to the left. Keeping it turned, extend the arms sideways, palms turned up, and at the same time breathe in. (Illus. 79.) As you flex them, breathe out. Repeat with the body turned to the right.

LESSON VIII.

1. Arms bent forward, feet close, turn the trunk to the left. Keeping the body turned, carry the arms sideways slowly and at the same time breathe in deeply. As you flex the arms, breathe out. Repeat with the body turned to the right.

2. Hands on hip. Place the left foot crosswise forward, the left heel in line with *Introduc-* the toes of the right foot, toes of both feet *tion* turned outward. (Illus. 80.) The body should be square forward regardless of position of the feet. Holding this position, rise on toes a few times. (Illus. 81.) Repeat with the right foot crosswise forward.

3. Arms shoulder high at sides, turn the palms forward-upward forcibly a few times.

4. Arms shoulder high at sides, feet at right angles; carry the left foot diagonally forward, i. e., in its own direction. Holding this position, twist the body to the left. (Illus. 82.) Repeat to the right, right foot forward.

5. (a) Right foot forward, right hand on the hip, left arm extended upward. Bend the upper body backward. (Illus. 83.) Repeat with the right arm extended upward, left hand on hip and left foot forward.

(b) Arms extended upward, bend forward from the hips.

6. Arms bent upward, turn the body to the left; holding this position, extend arms sideways and then backward in four counts. Repeat, body turned to right.

7. Fingers locked behind head, feet apart. Rise on the toes and hold a few moments each time.

8. Arms straight forward, shoulder high, palms turned in. Lean the weight forward, chest prominent, head erect. Fling the arms sideways forcibly, turning the palms downward as they go out. (Illus. 84.)

9. Running or rope skipping.

10. Arms bent forward, bend the trunk half-forward from the hips. Holding this position, fling the arms forward and sideways in a swimming motion.

11. Lie on the back, fingers locked behind the head, elbows kept on the floor. Grasp some weight. Flex the knees up, straighten them and, keeping them straight, lower the legs slowly. (Illus. 85.)

12. Hands on hips, place the left foot diagonally forward as in Exercise 4 above. Turn trunk to the left. Keeping it turned, bend to the left as far as possible. (Illus. 86.) Repeat to the right, right foot forward, trunk turned to the right.

13. Arms flung sideways, upward jump, in five counts. (1) Rise on the toes, (2) bend the knees, (3) fling the arms sideways-upward as you spring up from the floor, bringing them back to the sides before landing on toes, knees half-bent, (4) straighten the knees, (5) lower the heels. (Illus. 87 shows the body after leaving the floor.)

14. Arms bent forward, as Exercise 1, feet apart, turn the trunk to the left. While keeping it turned, carry the arms sideways as you inhale. Flex them as you exhale. Repeat the movement with the trunk turned to the right.

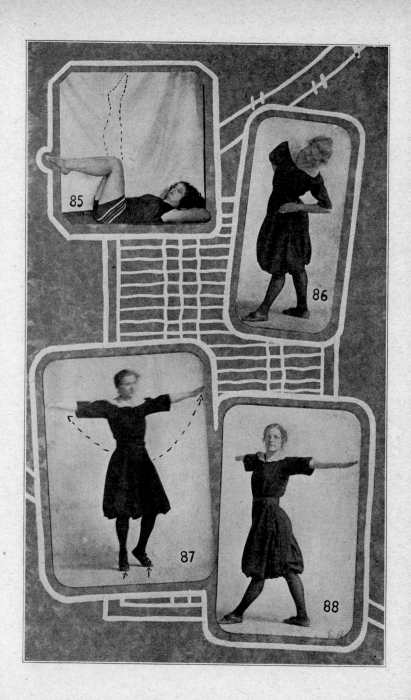

LESSON IX.

1. Arms bent forward, carry them sideways slowly as you inhale deeply. Flex them as you exhale.

Introduction

2. Arms bent upward. Stretch the left arm upward, palm turned in, and at the same time stretch the right arm sideways, palm turned down. In two counts change arms. At (1) bend the arms, at (2) right arm up and left sideways, etc. (Illus. 71, Lesson VI.)

3. Prepare to jump, in four counts.

4. Arms sideways, shoulder high; left foot forward, toes turned out. Twist the trunk to the left. (Illus. 88.) Repeat to the right with the right foot forward.

5. (a) Left arm extended upward, right hand on the hip. Turn the body to the left. Keeping it turned, bend backward a few times. (Illus. 89.) Repeat, with the right arm up, left hand on the hip, the body turned to the right.

(b) Arms extended upward, bend forward from the hips.

6. Arms bent upward, turn the body to the left; stretch the arms forward and upward in four counts. Repeat, body turned to right.

7. Fingers locked behind the head, left foot forward, toes pointing forward. Rise on the toes and hold a few minutes. Keep the weight between both feet, do not rock forward and backward, but rise straight up. Repeat with the right foot forward. (Illus. 90.)

8. Arms shoulder high at sides. Fling them forward and sideways by starting with arms at sides, palms down. (1) Curl the fingers downward and flex the arm so that as the hand gets close to the body, the elbows close, the palm is turned upward, (Illus. 91),

and stretch the arms forcibly forward. (2) Reverse the movement, flexing slowly to the shoulders and extending forcibly sideways. Make the movement each way a continuous one.

9. Running or rope skipping.

10. Arms bent upward. Bend the body half-forward from the hips. Holding this position, practice the Arm Exercise 2 of this lesson.

11. Repeat Exercise 9 of Lesson VIII, except that the position of the arms is changed. In this lesson, lock the fingers behind the head, keeping the elbows from leaving the floor as you practice the leg lifting.

12. Hands on hips. Twist the trunk to the left. Keeping it turned, bend as far as possible to the left. Repeat to the right, trunk turned to the right.

13. Jump upward in five counts, flinging arms and legs sideways. (1) Rise on toes, (2) bend the knees, (3) spring upward, and, as you leave the floor, fling arms sideways-upward, elbows straight, and legs sideways, knees straight, and bring the arms to the sides and heels together just before landing on toes, knees half-bent, (4) straighten the knees, (5) lower the heels. (Illus. 92 shows the body after leaving the floor.)

14. Feet close, turn body to the left. Raise arms forward-upward; at same time inhale deeply. Lower them sideways-backward; at same time exhale slowly.

LESSON X.

1. Arms bent upward. Carry them sideways slowly, palms turned up, and at the same time inhale deeply. As you flex them, exhale slowly.

Introduction

2. Hands on hips, rise on toes. Holding this position, twist the head to the left and then to the right.

3. Hands on hips. Lunge diagonally forward, carrying the left foot in its own

direction far enough to measure three foot lengths from heel to heel. In this position the body should be in a straight line from the head to the rear heel. Keep the rear heel on the floor. These details are important for control. Repeat to the right. (Illus. 93.)

4. Arms shoulder high at sides. Left foot forward, toes of both feet pointing forward. Twist the trunk to the left. Repeat to the right, right foot forward. (See Illus. 116.)

5. (a) Arms bent upward, bend the trunk backward. While holding it bent, extend the arms sideways a few times.

(b) Arms extended upward, flex the body forward from the hips.

6. Arms bent upward, elbows close to the body; turn the trunk to the left. Holding it turned, extend the arms forward and sideways, in four counts. Repeat with body turned to the right.

7. Hands on hips. (1) Rise on the toes, (2) bend the knees down to sitting. Spread the knees as they go down, keep head erect, chest out. (3) Straighten the knees, (4) lower the heels. (Illus. 94.)

8. Arms bent upward, bend the body half-forward, extend the arms forward (Illus. 95), and, while holding this position, fling the arms sideways forcibly. Keep the body steady; move only the arms.

9. Running or rope skipping.

10. Arms bent upward; feet apart. Bend the body half-forward. Holding this position, practice the arm movement described in Exercise 2, Lesson IX.

11. Rise on the toes, bend the knees, place the hands on the floor, fingers turned in, about four or five inches apart, elbows inside knees. With a spring carry the feet back far enough so that the body is straight from the heels to the head, weight borne by the hands and toes.

Spring the feet forward, again, knees outside the elbows, etc. (See Illus. 58.)

12. Hands on hips; feet close, i. e., heels and toes together. Turn the trunk to the left. Keeping it turned, bend to the left as far as possible. Repeat to the right, trunk turned to the right.

13. Half-step forward jump in four counts. (1) Step forward with left foot, (2) spring forward, flinging the arms forward at the same time and bringing them back to the sides to land on the toes, knees half-bent, head erect, (3) straighten the knees, (4) lower the heels. Repeat, stepping forward with the right foot. The step and jump run together.

14. Feet close. Turn the trunk to the left. Keeping it turned, raise the arms sideways-upward, inhaling deeply as they go up. Lower them sideways-backward, exhaling as they come down. Repeat with trunk turned to the right.

LESSON XI.

1. Arms sideways, shoulder high, palms turned up. Raise them upward and at the same time inhale deeply. As you lower them to shoulder height, exhale slowly.

2. Practice Exercise 1, Lesson I.

Introduction

3. Hands on hips. Lunge straight forward, carrying the left foot far enough to measure about three foot lengths from heel to heel. Body inclined forward in one line from heel to head; rear foot squarely on the floor. Repeat with the right foot. (Illus. 97.)

4. Arms shoulder high at sides. Left foot forward, toes of both feet pointing forward. Twist the body to the left as far as possible. Keep it turned while you flex and extend the arms sideways a few times. Repeat to the right, right foot forward. (Illus. 98.)

5. (a) Arms bent upward, feet apart, bend the

trunk backward, and, while holding this position, extend the arms sideways a few times. (As Illus. 94, except that the feet are apart.)

(b) Arms extended upward, bend forward-downward from the hips.   (Illus. 99.)

6. Feet apart, turn the trunk to the left. In eight counts, stretch the arms, forward, upward, sideways and backward. (1) Arms bent, elbows close to the sides, (2) stretch them forward forcibly, (3) bend them, (4) upward forcibly, (5) bend, (6) sideways forcibly, (7) bend, (8) downward-backward forcibly, etc. Repeat with the body turned to the right.

7. Arms extended upward, feet apart. Rise on the toes a few times, remaining up a few moments and reaching upward. (Illus. 100.)

8. Arms shoulder high at sides, bend half-forward from the hips. While holding this position of the trunk, practice Exercise 8 of Lesson IX.

9. Running or rope skipping.

10. Arms bent upward, elbows close to sides. Bend half-forward from the hips. Holding this position, extend the arms sideways alternately, palms turned upward. (1) Extend the left sideways, (2) as you bend the left extend the right out, etc., putting force in the extension.

11. Hands on hips, rise on toes, bend knees and kneel. Keeping the body straight up, without sitting back onto the heels, incline the body back from the knees as far as possible. (Illus. 101.)

12. Hands on hips. Place the left foot upon a chair, knees straight. Bend the body back as far as possible. Repeat with the right foot up. (Illus. 102.)

13. Hands on hips. Rise on toes. Without allowing the heels to descend, and without bending the knees, leap forward by merely springing from the ankle.

14. Arms shoulder high at sides. Raise the shoulders up and back as you inhale, allow them to descend

as you inhale. In this movement the hands do not describe a larger circle than the shoulders. This exercise is valuable to normalize the heart rate after a run.

LESSON XII.

1. Raise the arms forward-upward and at the same time breathe in deeply. Lower them sideways-backward while breathing out.

Introduction

2. Without moving the body, fling the arms straight forward-upward alternately.

3. Hands on the hips, feet close, i. e., toes pointing straight forward. Lunge forward with the left foot, then with the right.

4. Kneel. Arms shoulder high at sides. Twist to the left and then to the right. Do not sit back on the heels, but keep straight at the hips. (Illus. 103.)

5. (a) Arms extended upward, place the left foot forward. Bend the trunk backward. (Illus. 104.) Repeat with the right foot forward.

(b) Arms extended upward, bend forward downward from the hips.

6. Arms bent upward, left foot forward, turn the body to the left, hold this position while extending the arms sideways a few times. Repeat with the right foot forward.

7. Arms extended upward, feet close, rise on the toes and reach upward. Repeat a few times.

8. Arms sideways, shoulder high, bend them half-forward, so that the elbows are at right angles. Keeping the elbows shoulder high, fling the forearm upward a few times. Put the force in the upward fling. (Illus. 105.)

9. Running, hopping or rope-skipping.

10. Arms extended upward, feet apart. Bend the body half-forward, hold this position and bend and stretch the arms upward forcibly a few times.

11. Lying on the back, fingers locked behind the head, raise the legs upward alternately, first the left, then the right.

12. The left arm extended upward, right hand on the hip. Bend to the right a few times, then changing the arms, bend to the left. (Illus. 106.)

13. Hands on the hips, raise the left leg back slightly, rise on the toes of the right foot (keeping head erect, shoulders well back), and leap forward by springing from the ankle joint merely, keeping the right knee straight. Repeat with other foot. (Illus. 107.)

14. Arms flexed forward, feet apart, turn the trunk to the left. Holding this position, carry the arms sideways slowly as you inhale deeply. As you flex the arms, exhale. Repeat a few times, then turn to the right and repeat.

Lesson XIII.

1. Raise the arms sideways to shoulder height; at the same time flex the knees halfway and inhale deeply. As you lower the arms and stretch the knees, exhale slowly.

2. Arms shoulder high at sides, (1) gradually curl up the hand and arm so that *Introduction* as the hand is close to the body (the elbows close), the palm is turned upward, and stretch them forcibly forward, palms up. (2) Reverse the movement, flexing slowly to the shoulders and extending forcibly sideways. (See Illus. 91.)

3. Prepare to jump, i. e., (1) rise on the toes, (2) bend the knees half-way, (3) stretch the knees, (4) lower the heels slowly.

4. Fingers locked behind the head, feet apart. Keeping the elbows well back, twist to the left and right. (Illus. 108.)

5. (a) Feet close, arms extended upward, carry the left foot forward. Keep the toes of both feet straight forward as you bend the trunk backward. Repeat with the right foot forward.

(b) Arms extended upward, turn the trunk to the left and bend forward. The same to the right. (Illus. 109.)

6. Arms bent upward, left foot in front of right, toes pointing forward, turn body to left. While holding this position extend the arms upward forcibly. Repeat with right foot forward, trunk turned to the right.

7. Left foot in front of right as in above exercise. Arms extended upward, rise on the toes a few times, staying up a few moments each time. Repeat with right foot forward. Do not allow the feet to turn sideways. (Illus. 110.)

8. Arms bent upward, feet apart, bend body half-forward. Keeping head up, stretch the arms upward a few times.

9. Running, hopping or rope-skipping.

10. Arms extended upward, bend trunk forward half-way. Keeping the head up, moving arms in line with ears, lower them to shoulder height and raise them slowly a few times. (Illus. 111.)

11. Hands on hips, kneel on the left knee far enough back so that both knees are at right angles. Keeping body in straight line from head to knee, incline backward as far as possible from the knee. Repeat with the weight on the right knee. (Illus. 112.)

12. Left arm up, right hand on hip, bend body to right as far as possible a few times. Repeat to left with arms reversed. (As Illus. 106, but feet together.)

13. In five counts upward jump with 180 degrees turn. (1) Rise on the toes, (2) bend the knees, (3) fling

the arms upward and spring up, turning around a half-circle, and bringing the arms back at the sides before landing, with the knees half-bent, trunk erect, (4) stretch the knees, (5) lower the heels. Repeat with turn to the right.

14. Feet apart, turn to the left. Keeping the body turned, raise the arms sideways to shoulder height as you inhale deeply. As you lower the arms, exhale. Repeat, the body turned to the right.

LESSON XIV.

1. Arms shoulder high at sides, palms turned upward. Raise the arms and at the same time bend the knees and inhale deeply. As you lower the arms to shoulder height, stretch the knees and exhale.

Introduction

2. Hands on hips. In series place the feet forward alternately and rise on the toes. (1) Place left foot forward, (2) rise on the toes, (3) lower the heels, (4) bring the foot back. Repeat with the right foot, etc. Keep the weight between both feet.

3. The left arm extended upward, the right arm at the side, palm turned up. Moving the arms together, lower the left to shoulder height as you raise the right upward. (See Illus. 118.)

4. Lock the fingers behind the head, elbows well back, head erect. Rise on the toes and bend the knees all the way down and kneel. Twist the body to the left and right. (Illus. 113.)

5. (a) Feet apart, arms extended upward, turn the trunk to the left and bend backward. (Illus. 114.) Repeat with the trunk turned to the right.

(b) Arms extended upward, feet apart, turn to the

left and bend forward a few times. Repeat to the right.
(Illus. 115.)

6. Arms bent upward, elbows close to sides. Toes
pointing straight forward, place the left foot forward.
Turn the trunk to the left. Holding this position, stretch
the arms sideways forcibly a few times. Repeat with
the right foot forward, trunk turned to the right. (Illus.
116.) (See Illus. 98 for arms bent.)

7. Hands on hips. Place the left foot forward. (1)
Rise on the toes, (2) bend the knees outward, weight between both feet, trunk and head erect, (3) stretch the
knees, (4) lower the heels. Repeat with the right foot
forward. (Illus. 117.)

8. Feet apart, arms bent upward. Bend half-
forward from the hips. Stretch the arms forward.
Holding this position, fling the arms sideways forcibly.
(Compare with Illus. 95.)

9. Running, hopping or rope-skipping.

10. Arms bent upward, bend half-forward from the
hips. Stretch the left arm up and the right sideways,
palm turned up. Practice the arm exercise described in
Exercise 3, above, while holding this position. (Illus.
118.)

11. Hands on the hips. Place the left foot on a chair.
Bend sideways a few times. Repeat with the right foot
up. (Illus. 119.)

12. Left foot forward, toes of both feet pointing forward. Right arm extended upward, left hand on hip.
Bend as far as possible to the left. (Illus. 120.) Repeat
to right, left arm up, hand on hip, right foot forward.

13. Hands on hips, feet apart. Rise on toes. Spring
up. Strike the heels together and spread them out again
before landing. Keep it up rapidly.

14. Arms bent upward, elbows close to sides, feet
apart. Turn the trunk to the left. Holding this position,
stretch the arms sideways slowly, palms turned up and

121 122 123 124 125 126

Violet Heming

inhale deeply as they go out. As you flex the arms exhale slowly. Repeat with the trunk turned to the right.

There are many women who would like to practice exercises daily but who do not feel that they have time to follow out such a list as that given in the last fourteen lessons. There is frequent demand for a single typical program that would serve day after day. The following program is illustrated with poses by Violet Heming, of stage and movie fame. For the average woman who has no organic afflictions, these exercises will prove sufficient to keep the body graceful, firm and agile. These exercises will also maintain a slender and strong waist.

1. With the feet apart, the arms out from the shoulders, twist the trunk rapidly from side to side. (Illus. 121.) Repeat several times to each side.

2. Feet apart, arms out from the shoulders, bend backward as far as possible. (Illus. 122.)

3. Arms extended upward, twist to the left, bend and touch the fingers to the floor without bending the knees, straighten the body upward, twist to the right and bend again, and so on alternately.

4. Arms out from the shoulders, palms turned upward, elevate the arms to vertical as you raise the left leg sideways. (Illus. 123.) Lower the arms to shoulder level as you lower the left leg and raise them again as you raise the right leg sideways, and so on alternately several times.

5. The arms bent in front of the chest, fling them sideways forcibly as you lunge forward with the left foot, (Illus. 124.) As you bring the foot back, bend the arms again; then fling them sideways again as you lunge with the right foot, and so on alternately several times.

6. Place the hands on the floor, the knees bent in squat; kick the feet back and bring them to the beginning position again ten or more times.

7. Arms extended upward, bend to the left and then

to the right as far as possible, ten or more times.

8. A graceful exercise is to rise on the toes, the arms back, (Illus. 125). As you bend the knee all the way down, swing the arms downward and forward, (Illus. 126), and without stopping the motion fling the arms sideways and backward as you rise to the beginning position up on the toes. This should be repeated several times without stopping.

9. Raise the arms forward upward and rise on the toes as you inhale deeply; lower the arms sideways backward and lower the heels as you exhale slowly.

The following six programs are more advanced and they do not follow the laws of progression as closely as the preceding lessons. They are designed to meet the needs of advanced pupils who want more difficult work. Where it is feasible, apparatus may be introduced. If the pupil has access to a gymnasium, where he may use the apparatus indicated, better results will be obtained. These lessons will also be found useful to teachers who wish to give their classes advanced Swedish gymnastic lessons.

LESSON XV.

1. Head flexion backward. Also sideways.

2. Heel elevation.

Introduction

3. Arms bent upward. Lunge forward as you extend the arms upward, first with the left, then the right foot. At the lunge, the body, from the rear heel to the fingers, should be in a straight line. (Illus. 127.)

4. Prepare to jump, (1) rise on the toes, (2) bend the knees, (3) stretch the knees, (4) lower the heels.

5. Elevate the arms sideways upward

as you rise on the toes and inhale. Lower
the arms and heels slowly as you exhale.

I. (a) Standing with your back toward the wall,
about two feet from it, extend the arms upward and bend
the body backward until the hands rest against the wall.
While in this position, without holding the breath,
elevate the heels a few times. (Illus. 128.)

(b) Arms extended upward, feet apart, bend forward as far as possible without losing the relative position of the arms and head. (See Illus. 62.)

II. Practice "chinning" on a bar or trapeze. Preserve a good posture of the body while doing this. (Illus.
129.) Do not kick or swing the legs in the movement.

III. (a) Hands on the hips. Raise the left leg forward, knee straight, toes pointed. (Illus. 130.) Without
in the least altering the body, carry the leg outward as
far as possible (Illus. 131) and then backward; then, with
slight knee flexion, carry it forward again. Repeat with
the right leg.

(b) Hands on the hips, carry the left foot crosswise
forward, that is, the heel of the left foot about one foot
length's distance in front and in line with the right foot,
the toes of the left foot pointing diagonally to the left.
Keeping the trunk squarely forward, (1) rise on the toes,
(2) bend the knees (Illus. 132), (3) stretch the knees,
(4) lower the heels. Repeat a few times, then practice
it with the right foot crosswise forward.

IV. (a) Arms forward, palms turned in, fling them
sideways forcibly, gradually turning the palms downward
as they move sideways. The reason for turning the
palms downward in all arm flingings sideways is so as to
get the greatest possible expansion of the chest without
pain. The pain referred to is felt between the shoulder-
blades when the arms are flung sideways so that the
palms face forward as they get in line with the shoulders.

(b) Arms bent half-forward, elbows shoulder high.
Fling the forearms upward, by rotating the upper arm,

elbows kept steadily at shoulder height. (See Illus. 105, Movement 8, Lesson XII.)

V. Marching and running, or the equivalent.

VI. Arms bent upward, bend the body half-forward from the hips. While holding this position, slowly extend the arms upwards a few times. The body, from the hips to the head, should be in one line, and the hands should move in a line parallel with the ears, so that, when the arms are extended, there should be a straight line, or an arch backward, from the hips to the fingers.

VII. Rise on the toes, bend the knees, place the hands on the floor, fingers pointing inward, elbows inside the knees (Illus. 58) ; now kick the feet backward, keeping the body in a line from the head to the heels (Illus. 59). While holding this position, elevate the left and right leg alternately, keeping the knee straight and pointing the toes of the elevated leg. (Illus. 133.)

VIII. Arms extended upward, place the left foot forward. Rotate the trunk as far as possible to the left. (Illus. 134.) With the right foot forward, rotate to the right. Do not allow the arms to lose their relative position to the head as the trunk is rotated. There is a tendency to carry the right arm forward and the left arm backward, as the body is rotated to the left, and vice-versa.

IX. Rise on the toes, bend the knees, place the hands on the floor. Kick the feet backward; then turn the body to the right so that the weight is supported on the left hand and the outside of the left foot. The right hand is on the hip. While holding this position elevate the right a few times, keeping the knee straight and toes pointed. (Illus. 135.)

Turn face downward, weight on the hands and toes; then, to the left, so that the weight is on the right hand and right foot. Left hand on hip. Repeat the leg elevation. Then turn forward, spring the feet forward and come up to position.

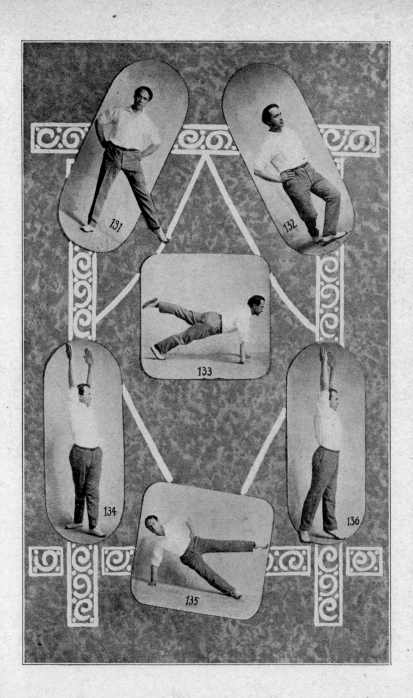

X. Arms extended upward, rise on the toes and reach upward. While holding this position walk slowly forward and backward. (Illus. 136.)

XI. (a) Practice vaults on the horse or buck.

(b) Twice upward jump. (1) Rise on the toes, (2) bend the knees, (3) as you swing the arms upward spring up, bringing the arms to the sides before landing, knees half-bent, (4) repeat the jump, (5) stretch the knees, (6) lower the heels.

XII. Arms bent forward, elbows shoulder high, hands in front of the chest, fingers and wrists straight. (1) Carry the arms sideways as you step forward with the left foot and at the same time breathe in. Carry the chest well forward, head erect. (2) As you flex the arms and exhale, carry the right foot forward, etc. After repeating this for three or four steps, practice with stepping forward with the right foot as you inhale, and the left foot as you exhale.

LESSON XVI.

1. Fingers locked behind the head, raise the heels a few times. (Illus. 46.)

2. Arms bent forward, fling them sideways a few times as you lunge forward, first with the left, then the right foot. (Illus. 137.)

Introduction
3. Prepare to jump. (See Exercise 4, Lesson II.)

4. Arms bent upward, extend them sideways forcibly, palms turned up.

5. Raise the arms forward-upward as you inhale. Lower them sideways-backward as you exhale.

I. (a) Back toward the wall, about two feet away from it, arms extended upward. Bend backward and rest the hands against the wall. While holding this posi-

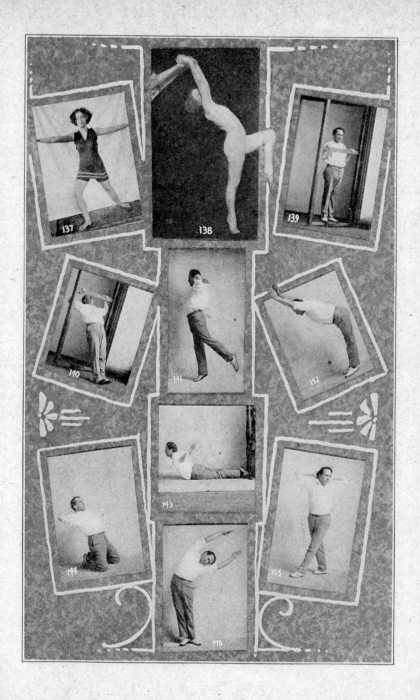

tion, flex the knees upward alternately, beginning with the left. The uplifted knee should flex at right angle, toes pointing down. (Illus. 138.)

(b) Arms extended upward, bend forward as far as possible without bending the knees or rounding the back.

II. (a) Traveling rings.

(b) Horizontal bar. Fall hanging, arm flexion. Have the bar about shoulder high, grasp it with the palms facing away from the body (Illus. 139), then spring the feet forward so that the weight rests on the heels (Illus. 140). While in this position, flex the arms. Do not allow the hips to sag, but keep the body in line from the heels to the head.

III. Lock the fingers behind the head; rise on the toes. While balancing on the toes, and without disturbing the posture of the body, raise the left and then the right leg backward alternately, keeping the knee straight and pointing the toes of the elevated foot. (Illus. 141.)

IV. Arms extended upward, bend forward from the hips; lower the arms forward to shoulder height. (See Illus. 95.) Fling them upward a few times. (Illus. 142.) Finish with the arms up before you straighten the trunk.

V. Marching and running or, with the hands on the hips, rise on the toes, bend the knees to sitting on the heels. In this position hop about.

VI. Lying face down with a weight on the feet, arms bent; arch the body upward, and, while holding this position, extend the arms sideways forcibly, the palms turned up. (Illus. 143.)

VII. Fingers locked behind the head. Rise on the toes, bend the knees all the way down, kneel. In this position, without sitting back on the heels—that is, keeping a straight line from the knees to the head—incline the body backward from the knees. (Illus. 144.)

VIII. Fingers locked behind the head, feet pointing straight forward, carry the left foot forward about two foot lengths. Keeping the elbows well back, and the weight between both feet, turn the trunk as far as possible to the left. (Illus. 145.) With the right foot in front, turn to the right.

IX. Arms extended upward, bend to the right and then to the left, as far as possible, without bending the knees. (Illus. 146.)

X. Rope climbing, or hanging on the horizontal bar; bend the knees up to right angle. While holding them up, straighten them forward alternately. (Illus. 147.)

XI. Jump to opposite sides, in six counts. In jumping first to the right, then to the left, proceed as follows: (1) Rise on the toes, (2) bend the knees and at the same time carry the arms to the left, (3) with a swing of the arms downward and to the right, spring to the right, (4) Immediately upon landing, with the arms straight, to the right, swing them downward and to the left as you spring to the left, and just before landing, bring them to the sides to land with the knees half bent as in all landings. (5) Straighten the knees, and (6) lower the heels. Repeat, taking the first jump to the left, etc.

XII. Raise the arms sideways upward and at the same time raise the heels and inhale deeply. As you lower the arms and the heels slowly, exhale.

LESSON XVII.

1. Heel lifting.

Introduction

2. Hands on the hips, elevate the legs sideways alternately, beginning with the left. Do not allow the body to incline to the side opposite the elevated leg. The trunk is kept erect by making a slight effort to elevate the opposite shoulder. (See Illus. 131.)

3. Arms bent forward. Fling them

sideways as you lunge forward. (See Illus. 137.)

4. Raise the arms sideways to shoulder height and, when they are almost up there, turn the palm forward-upward forcibly, and at the same time inhale deeply. Turn the palms downward and lower the arms slowly as you exhale.

I. (a) Back toward the wall, standing two feet or more from it. Arms extended upward, bend backward and rest the hands against the wall. Travel downward by moving the hands alternately until you reach your limit; then travel upward and rise slowly. (Illus. 148.)

(b) Arms extended upward, left foot forward, bend forward as far as possible without bending the knees. (Illus. 149.) Repeat with the right foot forward.

II. Horizontal bar work. Anything the pupil enjoys, provided it does not compress the chest. A valuable exercise is to fix the bar at shoulder height, grasp it as in Exercise 2, Lesson XVI, spring the feet forward to fall hanging as Illus. 139. Then, in one movement with a hard pull of the arms spring the feet back as far as possible to arch-hanging position. (Illus. 150.)

III. Arms shoulder high at the sides, palms turned up; raise them to vertical and at the same time elevate the left leg sideways, and raise the heel of the right foot. (Illus. 151.) Balance in this position a few seconds, then lower the arms to shoulder height, lower the left leg and right heel. Repeat the movement raising the right leg and left heel, etc.

IV. Hands on the hips, lunge sideways-forward to the left. The body should be in a straight line from the heel to the head. (See Illus. 93.) Holding this position, raise the arms forward. Fling them sideways forcibly a few times, the palms turning downward as the arms travel back.

V. Marching or running, or the equivalent.

VI. Lying face down with a weight on the feet, arms bent, arch the body up and hold this position while you extend the arms upward a few times. (Illus. 152.)

VII. Lying on the back, fingers locked behind the head, elbows kept resting on the floor, without bending the knees, raise the legs to vertical a few times, keeping the toes pointed. (Illus. 153.)

VIII. Heels and toes together, place the left foot pointing straight forward, weight between both feet, turn as far as possible to the left. This movement requires good balancing power. There is a tendency to shift the toes from side to side to keep from falling; guard against this. (Illus. 154.) With the right foot forward, practice to the right.

IX. Arms bent upward, feet apart, bend the trunk to the left and when the trunk is bent nearly as far as possible, extend the arms upward. Flex the arms as the trunk is straightened. Repeat to the right, etc. Illustration 146 shows the trunk bent sideways, but the heels are together. In this movement the feet are apart, and as the arms are extended the position of the body corresponds to the illustration.

X. Practice the dip on parallel bars, or between two chairs. (Illus. 155.)

XI. Various running high jumps; plain, with turns, and with arm flinging, landing as in the standing jumps.

XII. Arms bent forward, carry them sideways slowly as you take a half step sideways-forward, first to the left, then to the right alternately, and inhale deeply. As you step, raise the heels of the rear foot and exaggerate the chest expansion. Illustration 156 shows the body at inhalation. Illustration 46 shows the starting position.

LESSON XVIII.

1. Raise the arms sideways and rise on

153 154 155 156 157 158

the toes as you inhale. Lower the arms and heels slowly as you exhale.

2. Hands on hips, without bending the knee or disturbing the position of the body, raise the left leg backward. Lower it, and raise the right leg. (Illus. 41.)

3. Various bilateral arm extensions. (1) Arms bent upward, (2) extend the left arm upward and at the same time the right sideways; the palm is inward in the upward arm and downward in the sideways one.

Introduction (Illus. 71.) Change arms a few times, with count; at (1) bend them, at (2) extend the right upward and left sideways, etc.

Arms bent, extend the left upward and the right forward. Palms inward in both. Change in the same way as the above exercise. (Illus. 157.)

Arms bent, extend the left sideways, palm turned down and the right forward, palm inward. Change with count. (Illus. 158.)

4. Prepare to jump, in four counts.

I. Repeat Exercise 1 of Lesson XVII (a) and (b).

II. Flying rings: various swings and cut-offs.

III. Hands on the hips, raise the right leg backward and at the same time slightly flex the left knee and bend the body forward until it is horizontal or slightly arched from the head to the pointed toes of the left foot. (Illus. 159.) Hold a few seconds, then repeat on the right foot. This is called horizontal half standing position.

IV. Keeping the elbows and wrists straight, and without allowing the head to duck forward, fling the arms forward-upward forcibly as you lunge forward with the left foot. (Illus. 160.) Repeat with the right foot, and so on, alternately.

V. Marching and running or the equivalent.

VI. Lying face down with a weight on the feet. Lock the fingers behind the head; keeping the elbows well back and the head up, arch the body up from the floor. (Illus. 161.)

VII. Take position explained and illustrated in Exercise 10, Lesson IV. This is called stoop fall position. Spring the feet forward and through the hands. To accomplish this lift up onto the fingers as the feet move forward.

VIII. Arms sideways at shoulder height, feet apart. Twist the trunk rapidly from side to side. (Illus. 162.) Keep the arms straight from the shoulders throughout the movement. There is a tendency for the left arm to come forward as you turn to the right, and for the right arm as you turn to the left. Guard against this. This exercise is a splendid developer of "nature's corset."

IX. Take side fall position, explained and illustrated in Exercise 9, Lesson XV. As the weight is borne on the left hand and side of the left foot, extend the right arm upward; then, while holding this position, elevate the right arm and right leg. (Illus. 163.) Repeat the exercise from the right.

X. Work on the ladder. In absence of a ladder, hang on a horizontal bar and elevate both legs forward, knees straight, toes pointed. Hold them in this position a few seconds, and repeat. (See Illus. 177.)

XI. Ninety degrees upward jump, "Start." Practice the upward jump with the usual start: (1) rising on the toes, (2) bending the knees, and (3) springing up with a fling of the arms upward and a quarter turn to the left, thus landing facing left from where you started; (4) spring up again with a quarter turn, and so on a number of times. Then, practice jumping a series with turns to the right.

XII. Arms shoulder high at the sides, palms turned up. Elevate the arms as you rise on the toes and breathe

in deeply. Lower the arms to shoulder height, as you
lower the heels and breathe out.

LESSON XIX.

Introduction

1. Raise the arms forward-upward and
at the same time breathe in deeply. Lower
them sideways-backward slowly as you
breathe out.

2. Hands on the hips, raise the left leg
sideways; then, the right, alternately.
(Illus. 131.) Exercise 2, Lesson XVII.

3. Arms swimming as described in Exercise 2, Lesson VI.

4. Horizontal half standing position,
Exercise 3, Lesson XVII. (Illus. 159.)

I. (a) Arms bent forward, arch the trunk backward
and, while holding it arched, extend the arms sideways
forcibly a few times. (Illus. 164.)

(b) Arms extended upward, bend forward to the
floor without bending the knees. If possible touch the
palms to the floor.

II. Horizontal bar, or flying ring work.

III. Arms bent forward, take horizontal half standing position on the left foot. While holding the position practice arm swimming. Repeat on the right foot.

IV. Hands on the hips, lunge sideways-forward to
the left, that is, carrying the foot in its own direction
three foot lengths. (Exercise 3, Lesson X, Illus. 93.)
Turn the trunk to the left and raise the arms forward.
While holding this position, fling the arms sideways
forcibly. (Illus. 165.) Repeat in lunge position to the
right.

V. Marching and running, or the equivalent. Low
down dance is good if one is able. The arms are extended forward, the legs bent to squat. Kick the right

foot forward, and change feet in one spring. Keep it up rapidly. (Illus. 166.)

VI. Arms bent upward, take horizontal half standing position. Extend the arms sideways, palms turned up. While holding this position, elevate the arms a few times. (Illus. 167.)

VII. Take stoop fall position. (Illus. 59.) Raise the left leg, keeping the knee straight and the toes pointed, as you flex the arms. (Illus. 168.) Lower the leg as you extend the arm, and repeat, raising the right leg, etc.

VIII. Feet close, that is, heels and toes together; arms out shoulder high at the sides. Twist the body rapidly from side to side without shifting the feet, and observing the same rule about the arms as in Exercise 8, Lesson XVIII.

IX. (a) Hands on the hips, flex the trunk to the left, raising the right leg at the same time. (Illus. 169.) The same to the right.

(b) Prepare for cart wheel: Arms out at the sides, bend to the left until the left hand rests on the floor, the right leg elevated, and the right arm reaching over the head ready to bear the weight in complete turn. (Illus. 170.) Repeat to the right.

X. Horizontal lever. Rest the elbows against the front of the hip bones and gradually assume a horizontal position, head up, toes pointing. (Illus. 171.)

XI. (a) Various vaults on the horse.

(b) Sideways forward jump: Keeping the trunk forward, (1) step out with the left foot in the direction it is pointing and, (2) with a swing of the arms, leap in the same direction, landing in the usual way with the knees half bent and the hands at the sides, (3) straighten the knees and, (4) lower the heels. Repeat, stepping out with the right foot.

XII. Raise the arms forward-upward and at the same time turn the trunk to the left and rise on toes

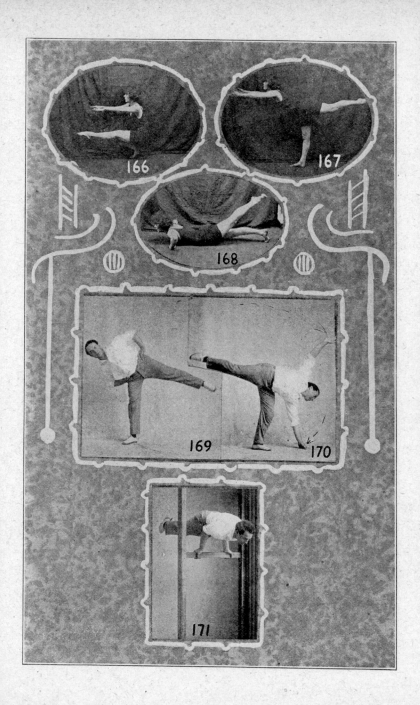

166

167

168

169 170

171

as you breathe in deeply. As you lower the arms slowly, turn the trunk forward, lower the heels and breathe out. The same with turn to the right.

LESSON XX.

1. Head rotation and backward flexion (Exercise 1, Lesson I), also (Exercise 1, Lesson II).

2. Arms extended upward, feet apart; (1) rise on the toes, (2) bend the knees (Illus. 172), (3) stretch the knees, (4) lower the heels.

Introduc-tion

3. Arms bent upward, lunge sideways-forward to the left and at the same time extend the left arm upward and the right arm downward. (Illus. 173.) The body should be in a straight line from the rear heel (which is kept on the floor), to the upraised arm. Repeat to the right with the right arm up and left down, and so on.

4. Raise the arms forward-upward and at the same time rise on the toes as you breathe in. Lower them sideways-backward as you lower the heels and breathe out.

I. (a) Fingers locked behind the head, feet apart, turn to the left. Keeping the body turned, bend backward a few times. Keep the elbows well back as you arch the upper spine backward. (Illus. 174.) Repeat with the trunk turned to the right.

(b) Arms extended upward, turn to the left and bend to the floor a few times. Repeat with the trunk turned to the right.

Instead of the above arch flexion, which is difficult enough, if one is able, he might practice the following:

(a') Arms extended upward, feet apart, bend back-

ward to the floor. With a slight spring of the fingers come up to position as slowly as possible. Repeat a few times. (Illus. 175.)

(b') Arms extended upward, bend forward to the floor, without bending the knees, touching the palms if possible. (Illus. 176.)

II. Hang on the horizontal bar and flex the legs forward at the hips. Knees straight, toes pointed. (Illus. 177.) While holding this position spread the legs apart, and bring them together again. Then, still holding the legs forward, flex the arms. Keeping the arms flexed, spread the legs apart and bring them together again. (Illus. 178.) Repeat as many times as possible.

III. (a) Fingers locked behind the head, rise on the toes, and, while holding this position, flex the knees alternately up to right angles. (Illus. 179.)

(b) Arms extended upward, take horizontal half standing position on the left foot. (Illus. 167.) Hold for a few seconds; then, as you erect the trunk, carry the arms straight forward and, without touching the floor with the right foot, elevate the right leg straight forward. (Illus. 180.) Preserving this posture of the arms, right leg and body, bend the left knee all the way down. (Illus. 181.) Extend the left leg and, from position picture in Illustration 180, go back to horizontal half standing position, and so on, in a continuous movement. Repeat on the right foot.

IV. Fling the arms forward-upward forcibly and at the same time take a lunge forward with the left foot far enough to rise on the toes of the right foot with the rear knee straight, the forward knee at right angle and the trunk erect. (Illus. 182.) In one count, change feet forward as you lower the arms and fling them upward again.

V. Running or, "low down dance," described in Exercise 5, Lesson XIX.

VI. Lying face down, with a weight on the feet,

the arms extended upward, arch the body upward and, while holding it arched, lower the arms to shoulder height and raise them again a few times. Illustration 137 shows the movement of the arms.

VII. (a) Stand about three feet away, facing a support, or any place where you can hook one foot. With the right hand on the hip, the left arm extended upward, raise the left leg forward and hook the foot. Holding this position, bend the body backward to horizontal a few times. (Illus. 183.) Repeat with the right foot up, arms reversed.

(b) Practice the hand balance, and, if possible, walk on the hands. To practice the hand balance, place the hands about two feet from the wall and swing the feet up, one leg getting a good swing before the foot of the other leaves the floor. The feet stopping against the wall will prevent you from falling over. While the feet are resting against the wall, stiffen the wrists and fingers so as to get the feet away from their support and balance a few seconds. (Illus. 184.) If one is able, this time in the lesson is proper for walking on the hands. (Illus. 185.)

VIII. Arms extended upward; preserving this posture of the arms, and without shifting the position of the feet or bending the knees, twist the trunk rapidly from side to side.

IX. Cart wheel. Following up (b) of Exercise 9, of the preceding lesson, with plenty of speed as you bend sideways, turn completely over, shifting the weight from the left foot to the left hand, then to the right hand and right foot, and up again. For perfect form the arms and legs should be kept straight. Practice first to the left, then to the right. (Illus. 186.)

X. Horizontal lever on the hand. To balance on the left hand, rest the left elbow against the crest of the hip bone; grasp the bar with both hands and gradually bring the body to horizontal; then extend the right

arm in line with the body. Practice the same on the right hand. (Illus. 187.)

XI. Kip up. Lying on the back, the arms bent, palms turned forward, curl the legs over the head and rest the hands on the floor beside the head. (Illus. 188.) With a sudden kick upward, arch the body, very much as Illustration 175, and push hard and suddenly against the floor to spring up. In the upward spring, with the final push of the hands, bend the knees and bring the feet under the buttocks.

XII. Practice various vaults on the horse, with and without turns. In absence of a vaulting horse, practice the hitch kick. In the hitch kick with the left foot, get the lift by swinging up the right leg as you spring from the left, and, while the body is in the air, kick as high as possible by bringing up the left foot and at the same time pulling down the right. (Illus. 189.) From the kick you land on the right foot.

To kick with the right foot begin by swinging up the left leg, and so on.

XIII. Raise the arms sideways to shoulder height, turning the palms forward-upward (rising on the toes just as the arms are almost turned), and inhale deeply at the same time. Gradually turn the palms downward as you lower the arms and heels, and exhale.

Advanced Gymnastics.

What is the end aimed at in the Ling system? is a question sometimes asked. What are the most difficult stunts possible to perform without particular strain? It has already been explained how, if each lesson is made up by using one movement from each of the nine divisions, one can be given a new lesson every day for a few hundred days. In other words, instead of having to resort daily to the same short routine of memorized, uninteresting movements of the "Daily Dozen" type, or other systemettes and tabloid systems, which may no more meet the needs of the person practicing them than a baby jumper fits an adult, one may have a series of progressive lessons so arranged as to meet exactly and interestingly the needs of the health seeker.

The aim of good gymnastics, as already said, is to develop the entire body into a harmonious whole under perfect control of the will. It is not to develop a great bulk of muscle of the dime museum freak type, but to make that already present finer in texture and tone to serve, rather than handicap, the brain. Most people have enough muscle without needing to develop more bulk and everyone can gain by trying to improve control and elasticity of motion. A good development means a smoothly rounded and firm, but not ridged, surface at every region of the body. Such muscle is soft and pliable when at rest, but very hard when in contraction. Such muscle will respond readily to volition for strength, speed, skill, gentleness or repose.

To acquire a perfect muscular development is often the work of a life time, and it is worth all the trouble. If one can perform with ease movements which surpass in complexity the ordinary actions of everyday life it will mean that all ordinary actions are performed with the greatest ease and grace. This will of course mean the highest type of physical efficiency.

One form of efficiency test for physical development is the skill and control of the individual in question. Rarely do we find anyone who can perform with perfect grace and ease the extremely advanced types of free standing exercises. The illustrations accompanying this discussion show stunts that will serve as goals for the most ambitious. Indeed, a few of these stunts are beyond the scope of even physical training. They rather belong in the category of special tests of flexibility which is only possible after one has practiced from earliest infancy to acquire and preserve extremely flexible joints.

La Sylphe, the well known dancer and contortionist,

can perform with perfect ease what hardly one person in a million ever approaches. She has perfect control and consciousness of her physical self, which is something quite different from self-consciousness. She can hold for several seconds without quavering the most difficult gymnastic positions. Not all of the extreme tests she can perform are of great gymnastic value. But of those that are, we select a few and describe them in nearly the regular day's order.

1. With the feet pointing straight forward, the left foot about two foot lengths in front of the right, the arms straight upward, she can turn to the left at least a quarter of a turn farther than most people can. (Illus. 190.) Of course, with the feet reversed, she can twist the same way to the right.

2. As a simple balance movement, with the fingers locked behind the head, one leg elevated backward, she balanced on the toes of one foot for four seconds without the least quaver. (Illus. 191.)

3. The backward bending is always difficult. Beginners are advised to practice going down holding onto a support. La Sylphe shows a simple bend which is beyond the possibility of most people. (Illus. 192.)

4. The plain backward bend, touching the hands to the floor, is very easy for her. (Illus. 193.)

5. A difficult method of backward bending is to stand with the feet apart, the arms extended upward; then twist the body to one side and bend. (Illus. 194.)

6. Bending forward and touching the toes without bending the knees is more than most people can do. This is too easy for La Sylphe to take seriously. (Illus. 195.)

7. To make a stunt of forward bending, twist the body to one side and then touch the floor. (Illus. 196.)

8. It is common to develop the power of lifting the arms and one leg sideways without tilting the body to the side of the supporting leg. But to perform this stunt

Posed by La Sylphe

and balance for a few seconds on the toes of one foot is a rare achievement. (Illus. 197.)

9. All young dancers love to acquire ability to perform the arabesque. A dancer posing for a picture will always suggest the arabesque. This corresponds to the horizontal half standing position of gymnastics. Rarely ever can we find one who can perform the arabesque correctly on the toes of one foot. La Sylphe held this position for over three seconds without a quaver. (Illus. 198.)

10. To perform the reverse of the arabesque is a test of strength of the abdominal muscles and almost a defiance of the law of gravitation. La Sylphe performed it with perfect ease. (Illus. 199.)

11. To stand with the feet apart, the arms out from the shoulders and, keeping the arms in line with the shoulders, that is, not allowing the distant arm to come forward at the limit of motion, a quarter turn to either side, is possible to most people. La Sylphe can make more than a half turn to either side. (Illus. 200.)

12. It is a test for most people to even kick as high as the head. La Sylphe can kick straight up without apparent effort. She stood and raised her knee almost to the level of her shoulder and then straightened the leg up and held it there a few seconds. (Illus. 201.)

13. Many people can, with practice, acquire the ability to squat and kick the feet forward alternately, but few can hold the body in balance on one foot. La Sylphe held this balance as easily as most people feel when seated. (Illus. 202.)

14. A few limber dancers can make the foot touch the back of the head in a kicking motion. Fewer can pull the foot up till it touches the head. La Sylphe can lift her foot backward straight up over her head. This, like all other stunts, she can do equally well to each side. (Illus. 203.)

15. It is quite common for flexible girls to rest one

knee on the sole of the other foot and force the upper foot to the back of the head, while resting the weight on the elbows. This is no longer a stunt to La Sylphe. (Illus. 204.)

16. Many can do the split. But few can do the split, then turn the trunk around and bend backward, touching the hands to the floor. (Illus. 205.)

CHAPTER III.

GAMES, SPORTS, ATHLETICS AND DANCES; THEIR ACTIVE
PRINCIPLES AND CORRECTIVE APPLICATIONS.

All methodical gymnastics, no matter of what system, are likely to become tedious to one who practices them. This is especially true if one repeats the same routine movements from day to day, as in practicing the common type of tabloid system with never, or but seldom, a change. It is less true where one changes exercises with definite progression from day to day, but even in the practice of such a system the work will prove tedious unless a certain amount of play is introduced.

Games and sports are not absolutely necessary to perfect physical development, but they are the most popular and most generally indulged in of all forms of financially unproductive activities. If one has the right spirit he will keep up the practice of a few carefully selected exercises through life and get keen enjoyment without needing the encouragement of games and sports. The splendid health preserved by a hygienic life furnishes the zeal required to keep up the interest. It might be added that, for the sake of self-control and discipline, it is far better to practice without the addition of the phonograph. One whose will power is not better than the phonograph must be in a pitiful mental state.

Most games and sports are one-sided and if any one is indulged in frequently for a long time uneven development is likely to result. Every game or sport taxes some set of muscles or region of the body more than the other portions and in time will prove more detrimental than beneficial. Still, this very fact may be taken advantage of in outlining a personal program.

Besides the pleasure to be derived from games or sports, all have some special use from a development standpoint. After a brief analysis of their general characteristics we shall group them according to their active principles and then indicate in what cases they should be applied. By active principle we mean the fundamental elements of a game or sport in relation to its chief effect upon the participant; that is, the reaction according to the most constant and compulsory activity required.

For best results hygienic gymnastics should come first, in order to develop a good physical foundation. Where necessary, in conjunction with hygienic gymnastics, corrective gymnastics should be employed. Games and sports of the strenuous type should never be employed to any great extent except as a topping off, or fruition to the other work. In their employment, games and sports should be selected according to the individual's needs to render him strong and skillful where he is weak and awkward. This is, of course, speaking from a therapeutic standpoint as well as that of physical perfection.

One need not feel an aversion to the idea of selecting games with a view to their therapeutic effect, because, the selection once made, all idea of therapy may and should be forgotten in getting the pleasure out of the game. The time to think seriously is when one is deciding which game he shall practice. Then, once in the game, he should abandon himself to the spirit and joy of it.

It would be needless to our purpose to enumerate in detail the characteristics of games as a whole. We have to group them and analyze the general characteristics or take single typical ones for more specific details. Games vary from the intense labor of wrestling, tug-of-war and college football to the intellectual type, such as chess, and the sentimental type, such as postoffice. The first and the last types mentioned are likely to strain the heart, but in a different way.

In general it is best for boys and girls less than eighteen to keep from violent efforts such as weight-lifting, shot-putting, boat-racing and all games or sports requiring a high degree of special skill or long continued exertion. Because of our abnormal modes of living in civilization, and because daily training is not continued as it should be, it is best for those past their thirtieth year to practice no games or sports requiring great speed or strain. The majority "settle down" to some vocation or profession soon after their twentieth year. Because of "dignity" or because of loss of incentive for activity (they perhaps won the girls they were after through their athletic efforts), at thirty they are fat and lazy or thin and nervously weak.

If girls were active as boys are from childhood up there would never need to be special rules laid down about what is and what is not safe for them to practice. Because of the foolish practice, since the decline of the Roman empire, of mothers wearing corsets and later hobbles and tight shoes, jumping and skipping rope are examples of what girls should not practice after puberty. Corsets, said the late Dr. J. W. Seaver, of Yale, have reduced women's backbones to backaches. No matter how well fitted they may be, and it is only recently that an attempt has been made to scientifically fit them to the wearer, corsets always interfere with the free activity of the waist muscles and thus render flabby the region of the body which it is most important to keep firm and tonic. In the past corsets have tended to impose a pressure from above onto the pelvic organs and caused all kinds of weaknesses and ailments. Some of these weaknesses have become hereditary to such a degree that female complaints have come to be taken as a matter of course. Specialists in women's diseases have waxed rich through specializing on conditions most of which might be prevented by simply beginning with young girls and developing their waist muscles and forbidding the use of corsets. Indian women who have never worn corsets do not know such sufferings as white women. The defenders of the corsets now claim that they so adjust this apparel as to support the abdominal organs. This, of course, is possible and probable but even this is not as sanitary and logical as to develop the muscles which should naturally hold up these organs. For every prop nature collects its toll in weakening the parts that are relieved of their normal function.

The corset does not err in being ugly, but in being unphysiological. It is a weak argument to denounce the corset because it spoils the wearer's natural waist line. As a matter of fact there are many waist lines that might be improved by being spoiled. Any change might be better than the natural in the fat. It is the fat who are most likely to wear the tight corset, because they try to appear slender by wearing a garment that only succeeds in giving them the appearance of a meal bag with a string around its middle. What ought to be done is to develop the natural corset through such procedure as outlined under the treatment of obesity in the last chapter.

If the devil, if there is one, had formed a league with the god of vanity and the shoe manufacturers to abuse human feet he could hardly have done worse than has actually been accomplished. With most people trying to wear shoes several sizes too small for them, and the shoemakers trying to fit the feet to their peculiar fancies rather than trying to fill the needs of the wearers, we find that chiropodists are becoming more and more popular. Tight shoes have reduced the human foot to such a state that one or more toes have had to be amputated in many cases and this fact has led to the statement that the small toe is no longer necessary. Neither is the large, nor any toe. If this state of affairs continues our feet will lose one toe after another until we become cloven-hoofed, even before death, or solid-hoofed as the horse.

Such statements may sound ridiculous but the facts warrant their utterance. With the wrong shape in most shoes and the endeavor in everyone to make the foot look smaller than it is, the toes are literally fields of corns, and bunion joints are becoming more common. Instead of allowing the feet free play, such tight shoes interfere with the function of the muscles; and arches are often affected and the foot's natural spring is lost. Shoes with special arch supports do not remedy this condition. Only the natural free play of the feet can ever normalize their musculature. Wrong shoes have been made and worn for so long that it now amounts to a special adventure in business to produce sensible shoes. Indeed, it is a mark of distinction for a shoe firm to attempt the normal. But it should require no argument to persuade anyone that the flexible, low-heeled, straight inside line and broad-toed shoe is the best for all uses, whether play or ordinary activities.

It is bad for a person past thirty to practice exercises requiring speed or strain, or for girls past puberty to remain active, for the same reason that it is bad for a person with rheumatism of the legs to practice jumping or high kicking, or for one with broken back to sit up. In other words, because all are as lazy by nature as they dare be and get by, no one does anything that will not pay in money. Through some perverse mental twists most people seem to think that it is policy to be as inactive and lazy as they can afford to be. Even to the average human being it should be plain that if pleasure is the end and aim of life, one can get more of it while in health than in disease. Real, vigorous, robust, joyful health is not merely a state of mind. It is an achievement that has to be paid for by the individual enjoying it. Of course, we have to except inherited weaknesses, but, for the normal, the mere observance of the laws underlying the hygienic influences enumerated in the first chapter will assure agility, grace and health through life.

Keeping in condition for games and sports is considered by many as something close to the mysterious. Many have an idea that to excel one must place himself in the care of some professional who will give him a formula and, presto, some record will be shattered. This is a false view which is made most of by those who gain most from it. Without natural ability, or ability acquired after a long continued practice of special training, no one can be made into a world beater in any line by the best professional coach that ever lived. The fact is that what counts for most in any phase of life is the oft-repeated mite rather than the short and strenuous effort. A little study of a few minutes each day kept up through life will keep the mind fresh and accomplish more than the most concentrated course in the best university in the world. From the health and physical efficiency standpoint the few minutes of well selected exercises practiced every day will accomplish what no concentrated course under the best instructor in the world can begin to accomplish. This is true in relation to keeping oneself fit for any game or sport.

As a concrete example, take the baseball players who do nothing but eat, drink and loaf about through the winter. It is always hard to get them into playing condition in the spring. Such baseball players have the shortest careers in the major leagues. On the other hand, those who do a little practicing in handball, indoor baseball, basketball, or any other form of physical training daily, or work about the home or farm daily, get into the best playing shape early in the spring. If a little exercise, including running, throwing and shadow batting with an elastic exerciser, were practiced daily during the winter the spring training would be unnecessary for physical conditioning, although the practice games in the spring should never be neglected.

People in general do not like set work or regular programs. They enjoy games, because in games there is always the element of chance and possibility of the unexpected. The trouble is that most people have a favorite game or sport and practice it to the exclusion of other activities. When one is near perfection in his physical training he soon reaches a standard where his favorite game is the one he happens to be playing. Base-ball, tennis, golf, football, hockey, polo, handball, any and all, are keenly enjoyed where one plays for the fun of it. This is the spirit of play that is worth cultivating. Victory is not as important as participation in a game. Good health and amusement should be our first consideration.

COMBATIVE ACTIVITIES.

For most people to enjoy play activities there must always be the element of opposition or combativeness. First in interest and importance we might consider a group of combative activities including fencing with foil, broad-sword or rapier, single-stick drills, broom-stick play, boxing, hand-wrestling, jiu-jitsu, tug-of-war and so on. In all of these the object is to conquer the oppo-nent by physical force and skill. Victory is won by masterful employment of muscular resistance, aggress-iveness, yielding or trickery.

FENCING.

From the traditional, picturesque and physical edu-cation standpoint no sport surpasses fencing. It would be interesting to enter into the history and evolution of the fencing art but this is not necessary to our purpose. The fine points of fencing are intricate and require years to be mastered but, when one really means to acquire skill in the art, these years will not be tedious. However, one need not possess the skill of the great Bertrand, one

Georgie Sewell 206 Irene Delroy

207

of the most famous fencers of all times, in order to derive benefit and pleasure from the sport.

A moderate and correct use of the sport develops keen sense of touch or what is termed muscular sense, cunning, agility, grace, quickness, good generalship and elasticity of muscles. Because the mind must never wander if one would fence successfully this sport produces a close relation between the brain and the muscles. Indeed, the attention is kept so alert that fencing causes great nervous waste compared to the muscular exertion required in its performance. As one progresses in the art of fencing he improves in co-ordination, strategy, patience and self-reliance, and the combative feature always proves exhilarating. It is one sport in which brain counts for more than brawn and, as practiced nowadays with the rubber-tipped foil, a woman can compete with a man without being favored in any way.

The "on guard" position, with one arm up in the air—not merely for ornament but to be extended along the side of the body at the lunge and lifted again to assist in regaining position—is one in which all the muscles are alert and, at times, the test of skill is so closely countered by evenly matched opponents that perspiration breaks out even without many lunges. The finest work is done with the fingers and slightly with the wrist, the arm alone being extended in the riposte and the entire body in the lunge. (Illus. 206 and 207.)

The lunge to the right taxes the extensor muscles of the right leg and the adductors of the left. Carried to excess it will overdevelop these particular sets of muscles. The constant repetition of the lunge to the same side, with the head held high, may cause a slight upper dorsal spinal curvature. To prevent or counteract this and to render fencing a complete developer one should practice with the left as well as the right side; at least one should practice the lunge to the weaker side every day. After practicing fencing for a while one acquires a

208

degree of grace and consciousness of one's powers that is evident in every movement or position.   (Illus. 208.)

In broad-sword fencing there is more muscular exertion and less nervous waste than in foil fencing.   There is more of the entire arm and shoulder swing and the unused arm is held folded behind the back to keep out of harm's way.   Of course there is less of the muscular sense developed, less brain and more brawn needed.   In modern days the use of the single-stick or even a broom-stick has been found almost as good and certainly simpler from the equipment standpoint than the sword.   The attacks and parries are simpler in broad-sword or single-stick than they are in foil fencing and to one who has mastered the fundamentals it is easy to arrange sequential attack and defense movements that make up interesting drills for classes (Illus. 209), or for partners to perform and for spectators to watch.   Indeed, most of the sword play on the stage is of the type of such simple drills and many who deport themselves creditably in such performances before the average audience know no more about French fencing than the average bricklayer knows about French pastry.

BOXING.

Boxing has been well named the manly art of self-defense. If properly practiced it will develop self-reliance and self-discipline. It will teach one his limitations as well as his physical powers. It requires no more equipment than the natural physique and the padded fist for apparatus and in the employment of these good brain action and judgment are of more consequence than brute force. Our anaemic reformers who would suppress all boxing because some have abused the sport should themselves learn to use their fists. If they did this they would soon learn that a good sound thrashing properly administered to the lowbrows who have injured boxing by their foul tactics would go farther toward final reform than all suppressive or prohibitive laws ever devised. The fact that

209

210

Jack Dempsey

people from all walks of life pay up to the million to witness a championship test of boxing ought to decide the kind of legislation we require.

Boxing, to be carried on successfully, must be supported by careful living and close observation of all the factors that influence health. To be in the best condition to uphold the championship standard one must exercise every day. (Illus. 210.) The normal physique with endurance and the correct use of nature's weapons will furnish no end of healthful enjoyment. It will also develop powers that may prove of great service in emergencies.

Carried to excess, or in the hands of the natural bully, boxing will increase arrogance and self-conceit. Carried to excess from the muscular standpoint, when practiced to the exclusion of other exercises, it will produce round shoulders because it over-develops the muscles in front of the chest and neglects the back shoulder muscles. To keep the shoulders square and assure a supple chest for free respiration, a boxer should practice rowing or exercises with a chest weight or elastic exerciser while facing the machine.

Those who classify boxing as a brutalizing and degenerating sport might stop to compare it to various forms of business. In boxing you must not strike an opponent when he is down, yet how many times has the law supported the mortgagor in dispossessing the poor widow or the financially embarrassed owner of a home? If you strike an opponent below the belt you forfeit a match in the ring. Let the various salesmen and business people acknowledge a wee small percentage of the times when a customer was taken advantage of and boxing will prove the most respectable business of all. Even in warfare boxing is used as one of the chief factors in conditioning the fighting men, yet in the actual battles every time a leader can deceive and take advantage of his enemy and murder men by the thousand he is ennobled by it. Everything about boxing except the gambling element is open and above board. Boxing is not to blame for the gambling that goes with it. I have known boys to place bets with their offering money on the number of times the preacher would use the word God in his sermon.

BAG PUNCHING.

Although one may disapprove of boxing surely he cannot but approve of bag punching. Bag punching is one of the very best developers of endurance and fistic skill that we have and yet no bruising is possible from it. The best way to use the punching bag as a conditioner and educator is to have a platform with its floor and ceiling on four posts, well braced at the corners. This will prevent shaking of the house and also prove a noise deadener. The ceiling should be high enough to allow a rope of seven or eight inches when the swelling of the pear-shaped bag is on level with the throat. With this arrangement it is possible to punch forward or sideways with arm swings, or even to spin around and also stand with the back to the bag and use the elbows and the fists from the sides to exercise all the muscles of the shoulders. Rapid bag punching kept up for a few minutes will tax the heart and the wind as much as a run of the same length of time, but with less actual strain than the run might produce. Bag punching will develop the hitting muscles and a close co-ordination of the eye and the fist as well as establishing a form of rhythmic action of the arms that no other activity can equal.

HAND WRESTLING.

Hand wrestling is perhaps the best, safest and most easily practiced of combative exercises. It requires no special preparation. It is done by opponents clasping hands, standing with the outside of the forward feet touching, their rear feet well back and the knees slightly bent so as to maintain a firm base. (Illus. 211.) By pulling, pushing and twisting, with the clasped hand only, and not with the head or shoulder or free hand, against the opponent's body, each endeavors to cause the opponent to move either or both feet, according to what they agreed to determine the fall. Each time one causes his opponent to move a foot he wins a point. This exercise should be practiced with the left hand as much as with the right (Illus. 212) and it will produce an even development of wrist, arm and shoulder and all the muscles of equilibrium. Hand wrestling on a thickly padded floor would prove excellent for locomotor ataxia patients or any individual whose equilibrium is poor.

WRESTLING.

Wrestling, especially catch-as-catch-can style, is the most popular form in our country and is fast surpassing other styles in other countries. It is a form of combative exercise which requires strength, endurance, skill, good generalship and clever defense as well as courageous offense. The catch-as-catch-can style includes the finest points of all other styles, namely, collar and elbow in which each holds his opponent at the left elbow with his right hand and at the collar with his left hand; the Swiss style in which they hold at the knee and the waist; the Græco-Roman style in which all holds are above the waist and tripping or leg holds are barred; the Japanese style, which can hardly be called wrestling but consists merely of pushing an opponent off a high stand and in which mass and weight count for more than skill.

A weakling should never wrestle except with his peers. Once he has developed skill and strength it is safe to try himself against stronger opponents. Continued for years at the exclusion of other and more relaxing exercises wrestling would develop a great bulk of muscle possessed of little elasticity. Wrestling develops the flexors more than the extensors, especially of the arms. The average wrestler is slow, massive, muscle-

211

212

bound and awkward. A little mixture of activities will help to develop the ideal wrestler who is agile, tricky and graceful. (Illus. 213.) Great benefit may be derived by the correct use of wrestling, if one keeps in good physical condition. Like every strenuous sport, if carried to excess and only practiced spasmodically, it is likely to produce an athletic heart which tends to shorten one's life.

TUG-OF-WAR.

Little need be said about tug-of-war. Like heavy weight lifting, this form of sport is always a strain instead of good training. Those on professional tug-of-war teams who are able to stand the strain for years prove their own muscular efficiency rather than the efficacy of the sport. Even the strongest are in danger of straining themselves by it. Tug-of-war is not to be recommended as a general practice. It is true that a tug-of-war match taxes the entire musculature at once but it does it in so strenuous a way as to overtax the lungs and the heart and develop a tight, muscle-bound condition and slow, laboring gait.

JIU-JITSU.

Jiu-jitsu can hardly be classified as a form of wrestling. It is more in the nature of self-defense. It might be classified as something which American wrestlers call "dirty work." Every effective hold or trick in jiu-jitsu places an opponent at one's mercy, that is, it forces him to yield or suffer a broken bone. Jiu-jitsu is a combative sport a knowledge of which enables even a weakling to master one much superior in strength. It is a system of holds which are secured by yielding just enough to take advantage of an opponent's strength and by locking or twisting the arm, neck or leg, or by pressing upon a superficial nerve center, causing him to cringe or collapse to the ground or into a worse and more punishing hold. It is difficult to get a good instructor in jiu-jitsu and therefore it is not well known in our country. It is not

Johnny Meyers

213

214

to be recommended as a system of physical culture but merely as a method of self-defense. The few Americans who have combined antagonistic gymnastics with a few jiu-jutsu tricks and called it "a thorough Japanese system of physical culture" knew what they were about. They acted upon Peter Barnum's famous statement about the American public.

RUNNING AND BALL GAMES.

Basketball, baseball, football, college football, playground football, lacrosse, handball and tennis may be considered as fairly representative of running and ball games. Speaking generally these games develop elasticity, strength of leg, greater peristalsis, better endurance, stronger heart action, higher blood pressure, more rapid respiration and a hastened exchange of the body's tissues. From a psychological standpoint these games are especially effective in developing presence of mind, judgment and coolness in relation to the unexpected. They develop a power of concentration by requiring non-expectant attention and they produce a high type of co-ordination.

BASKETBALL.

Basketball is the best and most strenuous of indoor games. It requires such quick thinking and concentrated attention that it is nervously exhausting. It is made up of quick starts and stops with periods requiring extreme muscular exertion. (Illus. 214.) It is filled with opportunities for bang-up grandstand activity that is often too evident in athletes who are conceited and arrogant. The game is so strenuous that it severely taxes the heart. One of the worst features of basketball is that it is played indoors where the air is usually vitiated at a time when fresh pure air is very necessary.

Basketball is a game for the strong and well trained. It may be played by weaklings but they do not bring out its characteristic features. For the well trained and vigorous it condenses a great deal of muscular exertion of the entire body in a short space of time.

Played to the exclusion of other sports or in the entire absence of gymnastics basketball might produce erroneous posture from the over use of the chest muscles especially on the side of the throwing or passing arm. Over development of the legs in comparison to the upper body may be one of the results of basketball. Pelvic congestion in women may be produced by this game. It may prove dangerous to those who have organic heart afflictions. The nervous strain or mental unrest often evident in players who are to participate in championship games is more a matter of individual weakness than a result of the game itself.

BASEBALL.

Baseball is the most popular of our American games. It possesses all the best features of basketball and is an excellent all round game for pure sport. It is filled with possibilities and unexpected situations which keep both players and spectators on the alert. The best feature of baseball is that it is played out-of-doors. As a game it is exhilarating, requires and develops quick thinking and action, judgment, co-operation or team work and concentration. It particularly develops the running and throwing muscles, deep respiration and the general bodily rotators according to which side one throws or swings his bat. If one throws from one side and bats from the other he will obtain a more even development than the entirely one-sided player. The conceit and arrogance evident in some baseball players, as in the case of basketball, are not due to the game itself so much as to the mental weaknesses of the players.

Moderately used baseball will promote good carriage, co-ordination between eye and muscle, elasticity, good lung action, increased metabolism, good digestion, improved appetite, increased peristalsis and better endurance. If the left hand is used as well as the right and if the upper body is trained to balance the lower body development one should be able to continue high standard playing years longer than the average player lasts. For winter training one should use the elastic or spring exerciser, standing with the back to it, and go through throwing motions many times each day. He should then face the machine and go through rowing movements and other exercises to keep the shoulder region balanced. It would be well also for the one-sided player to practice extra throwing motions and practice batting with the weaker side.

The pitcher is usually short lived in comparison to other players because his task is so pronouncedly one-sided and nothing much is done either to balance his work or to preserve his powers. He should practice throwing with his weak arm and also use exercises to keep the shoulders from rounding or drooping. When a pitcher is unusually valuable to a team it would be entirely possible to preserve his powers for a longer time and use him more frequently than is now found common. During a hard game the pitcher's arm and shoulder should receive thorough kneading of the muscles between every inning. This kind of kneading will rest and entirely restore a tired arm and may improve it on cool days. While instructor in one of our playgrounds, at the annual tournament between the eleven playgrounds, when each team to win must play at least four games in one day, instead of having two or three pitchers to draw from, I used the same boy, who was unusually efficient, and he won the championship by pitching through all the games. Between every inning his arm and shoulder were thoroughly kneaded and he showed no signs of weakening during any of the games although his opponents tried their best to worry him. At a very important interscholastic meet at the University of Chicago in 1905, with several teams tied for first place and

two hundred and five schools represented, my broad
jumper was kept out of two trials and the muscles of his
legs and hips were carefully kneaded. In his first and
last jump, which was the final for all the others, he won
second place, which was sufficient to give Lewis Institute
one point more than all the other schools and win the
banner. This kind of treatment of the muscles would prevent many athletes from going stale and strains might
never result if they were warmed up to the heat of the
test they are to undergo. Of course, all of this is only true
in relation to scientific kneading. The usual rub which
consists merely of rubbing on alcohol in any direction
irrespective of the direction of blood flow, or slapping the
skin to toughen it, would be valueless in such cases.

Considered from a therapeutic standpoint baseball
is useful in many ways and especially in cases requiring
a change in mental activity from the intellectual to the
motor centers, as indicated in neurasthenia, in paranoia
and slight paresis. In prisons to keep convicts healthy
and efficient in their work baseball has been found useful.

FOOTBALL.

Football, Gaelic or association, is a game which
requires a high degree of bodily control, especially active
repose, for there is so frequently a desire to use the
arms and hands, an action which the rules prohibit. The
head and shoulders may be used to bounce the ball, but
the feet and legs do most of the actual work. Great
endurance is required because of the size of the field and
amount of running. Control of the feet and legs is highly
developed by this game, but the upper body is badly
neglected. The typical player shows the unbalanced
effects; the shoulders are sloping and undersized, the
arms scrawny, but the body below the waist shows a
high type of development. There are many players who
show good general development but they have inherited
or developed their physiques. Football requires over use

of the legs in relation to the upper body and strongly taxes the heart and lungs. Because it is played in the open air, if not overdone, it will improve the heart power. Counteracted by selected upper body work it is an ideal sport.

COLLEGE FOOTBALL.

College football has grown more popular than baseball because the teams playing under one color usually belong to the institution they represent. The football season is short and the exhibition witnessed by the spectators may be the culmination of months of preparation and training. College football is an all round developer and strenuous taxer of the entire mechanism, nervous and muscular. It combines catch-as-catch-can wrestling, running, basketball, features of association football, greater team-work than baseball, generalship and self-discipline, bang-up activities and opportunities for individual grandstand stunts.

College football is splendid for those trained for it or for those who play with their peers. When weaklings play against opponents who are much their superior in strength, as is often the case with preparatory and grammar school teams, there is always danger of strain or injury. Anaemic reformers who would suppress college football because of the few injuries recorded against the game every year should consider all the facts. Raw, untrained, growing boys should not take part in the game but there is no good reason why well trained, hardened athletes should be kept from it. College football is known to be so strenuous that the prospective players are put through a system of training that prepares them for all exigencies of the game. The game requires great power of endurance, speed, strength and tenacity for shoving and grappling, and the entire physique must be hardened to prevent injuries from hard jolts and falls.

Therapeutically, when college football is played true to form, that is, vigorously, courageously, thoughtfully

and aggressively, little can be said except that it is a
test of one's mettle and physical education rather than
a benefit. If no injuries result from the game the player
is benefitted because of his careful training for it and he
is exhilarated by the sport itself. The modern open style
of play has rendered college football almost free from
danger, yet the game is the best modern substitute for
the ancient gladiatorial combat. Whoever can stand a
few strenuous games of modern college football gives
evidence of possessing superb health and vigor, but if
he values his health as he should he will not continue
this game any longer than he has to under the
circumstances.

PLAYGROUND FOOTBALL.

Playground football is a game which is not well
known, but it proved such a useful sport and general
favorite at McKinley Park playground a few years ago
that a few words should be said about it. The game
requires at least fifteen players to each side and even
a larger number have frequently been used. The game
brings together some of the features of basketball, football and college football. Everyone who has played the
games knows the temptation to kick the ball in a basketball game, to pick it up or bat it with the hands in football,
or to pass it back and forth in any direction in college
football. The rules of playground football permit all
these features. But there is no tackling or mass play
permitted in this game.

The game is started as in basketball, and the ball,
once under way, may be kicked, passed with the hands or
caught from an opponent's kick for a fair catch and disposed of, without interference, by the catcher. The players are arranged at the discretion of the captain and distributed to guard and pass much as in basketball. The
playing field is about two hundred feet long and one
hundred wide and the goals consist of posts set ten
feet apart and twenty-four feet high. There is a cross

bar at the top and one six feet lower. Throwing the ball, that is about the size and dimensions of an association football, through the rectangle or "window" scores two points. If the ball is kicked through the window it counts five points. When the ball is out of bounds after a try at goal it goes to the opponents or goal defenders. When the ball is out of bounds at the side lines the playing is governed as in basketball. There have been several fouls classified and after their committal, instead of free tries at goal, three class (a) fouls, or one class (b) foul count for one point for the opponents. As there are few reasons for stopping play during the game it is very fast and strenuous sport.

There are more possibilities for team work than in basketball and very intricate plays have been developed. Although it offers a chance to use the arms as in basketball, the foot work is so much greater than the upper body work that it proves an unbalanced activity from a developing sense. Combined with upper body work, however, it proves an ideal game because it combines many interesting features of other games, and eliminates the dangerous features of tackling and mass formation plays of college football.

LACROSSE.

Lacrosse, which might well be called the real American game because it originated among the Indians, will never be as popular as baseball or football, because it lacks the elements of chance of the former and the necessary headwork of the latter. Team work in lacrosse is not as essential as skillful maneuvering of the crosse. A few players on a team adept at catching, carrying or passing the ball are often seen playing all around their opponents and they are sufficient to determine whatever team work may be possible. The muscular side of lacrosse corresponds in a degree to basketball. There is much more leg work than arm work. Of course the arms are used in carrying and manipulating the crosse but this is a light piece of apparatus which in no great degree taxes the muscles of the arms, as the running and dodging about do those of the legs. Therefore, as in all running games, the chief developing effect of lacrosse is on the legs. A high degree of muscular sense is required for effective use of the crosse in catching, scooping, retaining or passing the ball at various rates of speed and for various distances.

The crosse compels one-sided activity because it is so made as to be usable from only one side. Unless made expressly for left-handed individuals the crosse is so bent and the mesh so woven that it must be carried right hand back of the left, that is, the right hand gripping near the end of the stick and the left hand free to slide up and down. Passes are always made with the lift from left to right at the upper part of the swing. This necessitates using the right side muscles at the waist region more than those of the left side. If lacrosse were practiced to the exclusion of other activities it would produce unbalanced development.

Like all running and ball games lacrosse will develop strength of leg, elasticity of body generally, muscular sense, good eye and muscle co-operation and a high type of co-ordination. It will develop power of endurance, increase peristalsis and excretion, and improve appetite. If used to excess it can develop the unfavorable conditions that result from any strenuous activity.

TENNIS.

Tennis is one of the best of the popular games. Enough of the game may be mastered to enable one to derive most of the benefits without necessarily becoming expert. (Illus. 215.) But one may play for many years, from childhood to maturity, and always feel that he may yet become absolute master of all the fine points of the game.

It is a game requiring cool and quick judgment as well as great endurance and agility. It will develop a keen sense of honor and fair play because the lines are not always visible to one's opponent and thus one has to announce whether the play is fair or foul.

Tennis is a game in which a woman who is proficient may equal or surpass most men. The competition between an expert woman and a man may be real and tax the ingenuity and strength of the man to the utmost. The great liveliness of the tennis ball and the lively tension of the racket strings require a deftness of muscular control that approaches the type of muscular sense developed by expert fencing. Tennis is by no means a lady's game, as some wags have said, because to be proficient at it means a high degree of physical efficiency. (Illus. 216.)

Tennis has so many good points to recommend it that it needs little defense. But there is one bad feature to the game. The racket can only be held by one hand. If each hand were employed alternately there would be nothing more required to render it a complete developer except the addition of such a sport as breast stroke swimming or exercising with an elastic exerciser while facing the machine. For development's sake one might play one set right and one left handed, or practice shadow strokes left handed. The constant swings downward and forward in striking tend to pull the shoulder into drooping position, but the type of work mentioned above will prove adequate to counteract this.

The constant starts and stops required in tennis, together with the deft use of the racket, will develop coordination between the eyes and muscles. The game will develop elasticity, strength of leg, endurance and muscular sense. An expert player can tell without looking at the racket at what angle he is carrying it or striking the ball.

215

216

217

HANDBALL.

Handball is a game that is played both in or out of doors. It requires great co-ordination between the hand and the eye. Few games equal this one in showing the limitations as well as the possibilities of the human hand. The ball is often hit deftly with either hand, but we usually find a player who has a favorite hand. The chief stroke in hitting the ball is one corresponding to the uppercut in boxing, that is, a swing of the arm from the side of the body, forward and upward, employing the anterior muscles of the shoulder and chest.

The posture of the body in handball is that of a slight stooping with the chin protruding, thus depressing the chest. The muscles chiefly used are those that tend to draw the shoulder forward. The forced attitude of the head in watching the ball tends to droop it. The lower body and the legs are employed in the twists, bends, starts and stops required in the game.

As a game handball has many fine points to recommend and few to condemn it. The faulty developments that may result from this game are to be counteracted according to corrective gymnastic principles. A slight variation from real handball may be played by using a tennis ball against any smooth wall.

HOCKEY.

Field hockey, ice hockey, hurling and ice polo are types of group games in which the object is to send a puck or ball into the opponents' goal and prevent them from reaching your goal. In all of these games, while the rules governing them are different, the muscular activity is very similar, although there are points in favor of ice polo and ice hockey. In field hockey and hurling, one is allowed to strike the ball only from the right hand side, whether or not you are right handed. The stick is held so as to hit, stop or pass from the player's right to left. In ice hockey you are free to strike, stop or pass from either side, but you are not allowed to raise the stick above the hips. In ice polo might governs at times. It is not an organized game but it has always been popular among boys. In New England we were as free in our maneuvers as the Indians ever were in their lacrosse games. With a broad, free swing at the ball, allowed to raise the stick as high as we chose, also allowed to pass the ball forward as well as sideways or backward, actively skating about, every player for himself, we obtained plenty of exercise if we did not develop much skill.

ICE HOCKEY.

Ice hockey required such a degree of self-restraint in handling the stick and the rules were so binding that it had a wholesome civilizing effect upon us boys, but the rule requiring that the stick be kept below the two-foot level compelled us to maintain a stooped posture. The team work enforced upon us in order to play winning hockey was a first rate lesson in co-operation. We soon learned that by combining efforts we could accomplish far more than by playing everyone for himself. The fact that ice polo and ice hockey are played on skates renders these sports valuable and worthy of encouragement even though one may never master all the finer points of ice hockey.

FIELD HOCKEY.

Field hockey was developed as a woman's game and there are so many unnecessary rules governing and restraining the players and encompassing them within limited portions of the field that men will never take this game away from them. The rule requiring that the stick be used only from the right and kept below the two-foot level may render the game safer but it also renders it tamer. The head is drooping in much of the active part of the play and the stick always moving from right to left with the shoulders drooped forward cannot attract praise for the game. If only a player were allowed to take a full swing as in ice polo or in the drive in golf when no opponent is close by, it would render the game more attractive. The feet should be employed more in stopping and dribbling the ball, and when a player has the ball and starts dribbling she should keep the ball moving with her feet much of the time and use her stick to lift the sticks of her opponents from it. There are so many little tricks possible, but not practiced, that are not prohibited by the top heavy governing rules that our interest can not be keen for the game. (Illus. 217.)

HURLING.

Hurling is a game as active and nearly as wild as ice polo, except that the ball must always be struck from the right hand side, as in field hockey, but in hurling a player may raise his stick as high as he pleases for a hard swing. "Shinny on your own side" is frequently heard from the participants in a hurling game and if the offending opponent remains on the wrong side after being warned he is likely to receive a stroke below the knees. Aside from the little thrills furnished by hot-headed players, hurling is a strenuous game which requires a vast amount of leg work and one-sided upper body work. To play the game effectively one takes frequent chances of getting hurt unless he is nimble footed and observes the rules, such as they are. This game is the antithesis of field hockey, but is not played very much in this country.

The effects of the above four games are to overtax the legs in comparison to the arms. All tend to produce drooping head and the last two mentioned develop a one-sided arm and shoulder condition. The fact that they are all played out of doors in the cool or cold seasons of the year speaks much in their favor.

GOLF.

The difference between ice-polo, or "shinny," and golf is as great as the difference between the unwashed savage finger and knives and forks in eating. Golf has

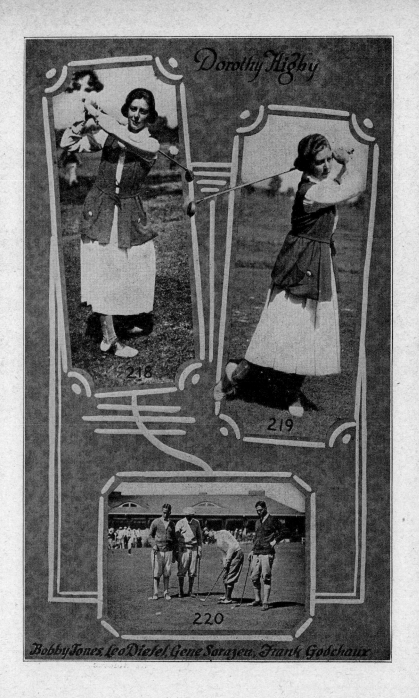

Dorothy Higby

218

219

220

Bobby Jones, Leo Diegel, Gene Sarazen, Frank Godchaux

been called the gentleman's game and one is surprised at the great number who have become devotees to the game, although the Binet tests still place them in the infant class. There is more literature on golf than on almost any other single game or sport.

A cold analysis of the game should be interesting. Golf is one-sided, decidedly so, no matter how many "authorities" say differently. The stroke is always from one side, unless one is ambidextrous, or tries to be so for health's sake. In right-handed people the swing is full and free, from over the right shoulder down and toward the left, up to and around the left shoulder, including a twist of the body toward the left. (Illus. 218 and 219.) Needless to say that the opposite is true of left-handed people. Granted that the player hit the ball, now comes a walk. There is valuable exercise in this walk if one carries his own sticks, but "gentlemen" employ a caddy. The player's eyes might be benefitted by watching his own ball and seeking it when lost, but, again, the "gentleman" confers this favor upon his caddy. The result of compelling the caddies to gain all the real exercise of this outdoor game while the "player" tries to attain the nineteenth hole as quickly as possible has been that most of our best players and champion golfers are from the former caddy class. The present champion, Gene Sarazen, is an ex-caddy. (Illus. 220.)

The tanned skin and the gay attire do not form the best feature of golf. The game takes one out into the open air and sunshine and no matter how poorly one plays he is sure to derive benefit. One thing is certain, a player is seldom overtaxed, except in a nervous and mental way during an important tournament. To play well requires good co-ordination between the eyes and the arm muscles. This point should be emphasized more by golf enthusiasts. Gauging distance accurately in the approach and then crystallizing this estimated distance into the perfect stroke means a knowledge of sticks,

angles, force and power of cool calculation which are
only possible after years of patient application. To be
a top-notcher in golf is proof that one possesses very
great skill, because there is no game in which so many
can play well. Perhaps there is less of the element of
chance in golf than in many other games, but unless one
is in the finest physical condition during a tournament
there is always the chance of losing one's courage and
with it all chances to win a championship.

For a change of eye activity from the close vision
work of teachers, newspaper editors or profuse readers
golf offers a splendid opportunity. It is strange that
oculists do not recommend it more. To keep one's gaze
fixed on a spot or the general area where the ball landed
and then walking toward it after a drive means that
the eyes are gradually adjusted from distant to close
accommodation and the vision or concentration of the
player is improved by it.

Golf never injured any one unless he allowed himself
to serve as a bunker. Without meaning to desecrate the
holy of holies of the golf devotee, measuring golf purely
from its activity standpoint, it can be compared to a
walk in the country with occasionally a little arm work.
Indeed, aside from its effect on vision and co-ordination,
the purely muscular development from golf can be
equalled by a walk with a walking stick and occasionally
knocking the head off a daisy. If this summary seems
too plebeian to our "gentlemen" golfers, we might refer
them to the history and origin of the game.

To render golf a complete developer it should be
played to both sides. This is entirely possible and prac-
ticable. Procure right and left-handed sticks and play
alternate holes or course left and then right. It does
not take long for one to acquire enough skill to really
enjoy a competitive test between his right and left hands.
As a supplementary sport breast stroke swimming is
ideal. If swimming is unavailable, a little work each

day at an elastic or spring exerciser, facing the machine throughout the exercise, will complete ambidextrous golf as a perfect developer.

CROQUET.

Croquet has never developed a single athletic heart; it has never been accused by reformers of promoting gambling; and it is perhaps the only game that has never been threatened by blue-law mongers with suppressive statutes. It develops a certain amount of coordination between the eyes and the arm muscles. It requires skill to aim straight and pass the wickets or strike an opponent's ball. The stooping required tends to limber and develop the back muscles, but it must never be classified as a reducer. Its gymnastic effect is bad because it requires so much stooping and drooping of head. Croquet has been recommended as a reducer because it produces forward bending, and it has been taken for granted that this uses the abdominal muscles. This idea is incorrect. While standing up, as the body is bent forward, the work of the movement is forced onto the back muscles as soon as the head gets beyond the line of gravity. This bending is really a back exercise and will be explained in Chapter IX.

BOWLING.

Bowling is one of the most popular of indoor sports. Though one-sided, the exercise is very beneficial, but the environment in the bowling alleys is usually bad. The close vitiated air, thick with smoke, in which it is played, and the late hours it usually induces one to keep, are points against it. But these conditions are not caused by bowling; they are simply evils that accompany it and are dependent upon the individual bowlers.

The muscular effects of bowling are one-sided. The favorite arm is always used in rolling the ball and the other is neglected. Long continued bowling produces an over developed right arm and a much weaker left

Vivian Oakland

221

222

arm in right-handed people and vice-versa. The work of the legs is also somewhat specialized. In right-handed bowlers the ball is supported in the right hand in front of the body and the left hand serves to steady it. (Illus. 221.) At the movement to roll the ball the right arm swings backward with the ball and at the same time the left arm and the left leg move forward and the trunk bends slightly to the right as the body surges forward. The feet are far enough apart for the left knee to be bent at right angle and the foot flat on the floor, the knee is bent down till only the right toes press on the floor to anchor the body from sliding over the line. (Illus. 222.) Thus, in the principal movement of bowling the muscles in the legs that are taxed most are the back muscles of the left and the anterior muscles of the right. Since bowling is so pronouncedly one-sided the best way to counteract this is to bowl as much left as right handed.

Bowling in itself has great advantages especially if one uses the left as well as the right side. It is filled with excitement and offers a splendid opportunity for individual satisfaction as well as amusement. It is a vigorous exercise, but not of a straining nature, and women have become quite proficient in it. It will produce a fine arm and shoulder development, though the flexors are affected more than the extensors. The main therapeutic tendency of bowling is to deepen the chest.

SWIMMING.

Swimming is one of the best of all round exercises and a useful art to learn if one wishes a complete education. Breast-stroke swimming has the evenest developing effect because all the work is done symmetrically, both sides doing the same thing at the same time. The body is kept in an ideal posture for chest development and correct shoulder and head carriage. The side stroke performed alternately, or as long on one side as on the other, is also a well balanced developer. The crawl stroke, the best for speed swimming and employed by the present sensational champion, John Weismuller, (Illus. 223), requires a high degree of bodily control. It is a very complex movement with the arms, head and legs performing varying types of motions although all in rhythmic repetition. After practicing this style for a while it becomes as automatic as any other but never as easy on the performer.

Properly practiced swimming will give one a smooth, muscular, well rounded form. (Illus. 224.) It will develop elasticity in the muscles and correct faulty posture. Breast-stroke swimming could not be improved upon as a single sport for bringing about shoulder and head correction and chest expansion. Indeed, it can be safely recommended as an antidote to almost any other unbalanced activity.

Swimming establishes in one a high degree of self-reliance and courage, that is enhanced by diving, which properly belongs with swimming. Swimming teaches one way of overcoming nature, or, at least, to successfully combat it as long as endurance lasts. If swimming is over indulged in, it is likely to develop massive shoulders. There is always danger when one attempts long distance swimming in cold water because one may get cramps or the heart may give out. Moderation and frequent repetition are better than infrequent long doses.

ROWING.

Rowing in catboats or in the pleasure boats in parks and at summer resorts has a slightly different effect from rowing in a racing boat or shell with a sliding seat. The chief effect of rowing is on the back and the shoulder muscles with a slight taxing of the abdominal muscles. With the sliding seat the legs are also brought into play and the abdominal muscles are much more powerfully taxed than in the ordinary boat. Moderate practice will greatly benefit health, because with it go fresh air and sunshine. Besides affecting the muscles mentioned above, rowing also benefits the respiratory apparatus because the activity of the sport produces deep respiration and no position in any part of it need compress the chest.

To summarize, rowing develops and corrects the shoulder region, strengthens the abdominal muscles, increases respiration and promotes digestion and metabolism. Speed rowing develops combativeness and perseverance. Because of the limit to the speed possible to a rower and the length of time required to cover a distance which seems very short from over the water, rowing develops patience, peace of mind and a certain sense of rhythm and automatism.

Back water rowing part of the time will emphasize the work of the abdominal muscles as well as the extensors of the arms. If the chin is kept in and the head carried high, great benefit and no malformation can result. One who is master of back watering can turn a boat around very easily. Instead of rowing with only one oar and letting the other drag, pull with one and at the same time back water with the other and the boat will spin around. This is so simple that even a child can do it. (Illus. 225.)

CANOEING.

Canoeing is far more interesting than rowing because it is less monotonous and usually more risky. A certain amount of risk requires a more alert state of mind, develops concentration, and prevents one from losing interest.

Canoeing is usually done with a single paddle. The stroke itself requires special attention in order to keep the canoe going straight. The canoe is usually so light that one can go over shallow water, on inland streams and lakes, and it is very easy to carry the canoe over a portage from one stream or lake to another. In primitive surroundings, among the timber in unsettled coun-

J. Weismuller
Swimming Champion

223

224

Sarrah
Haussen

225

226

227

228

Rose Johnson

229

tries, a canoe and camping trip offers tempting attraction.

Most people know canoeing only from the standpoint of factory made products on pleasure lakes. (Illus. 226.) The gymnastic side of canoeing may be considered apart from its most attractive features. The real Indian style of stroke in canoeing requires a position of body and employment of the arms that, in time, tend to deepen the chest. The arms and shoulders, and nearly all the upper body muscles are benefitted, but the legs get no exercise. The lungs are benefitted by the forced expansion of the upper chest and the increased respiration due to the exertion. The psychological effects of canoeing are improved courage from the risky nature of the sport, a certain sense of secure repose resulting from the feeling of safety in spite of the chances taken, and power of distant observation developed by watching the shore for guidance or for game.

If canoeing were over indulged in and all the paddling done from one side, it might produce one-sided muscular development, perhaps scoliosis, and a weakening of the legs from lack of use. It is said that along the Amazon river, where savages live most of their lives in canoes and trees, their arms are as large as their legs because they constantly use their arms in paddling and climbing and only sit on their crossed legs.

ARCHERY.

Archery is a wonderful outdoor sport. It is a survival of the ancient practice of the use of the bow and arrow in hunting and warfare, and deserves much more popularity than it has at present. As a sport it may be gentle or powerful in its effects, according to the strength of the bow one chooses and the frequency and length of time he practices shooting.

Archery is graceful and picturesque in every detail. (Illus. 227.) The standing position, the uniform angle at which the feet are held, the erect trunk, high carriage of the head and the backward inclination of it as the archer draws, then the slight tipping forward as he looses his arrow, all these points can only react in promoting good chest expansion and deep respiration as well as graceful carriage generally. Stringing the bow, nocking the arrow, covering the point of aim, which develops such close relation between eye and muscle, drawing, holding, aiming and loosing, all done with the arm and shoulder muscles while the rest of the body is erect and in active repose; all these details are important and effective in developing self-control and gracefulness.

Archery would prove a complete gymnasium in itself if it were only practiced to both sides. The chief action, which is drawing the bow, employs especially the back shoulder muscles, the extensors of the left and the flexors of the right arm. This action tends to broaden the shoulders and develop a full chest. It should be utilized to prevent narrow and shallow chest in the consumptive type of child. All one needs is to hold the bow in his right hand and draw with the left to affect the other side and thus balance and complete his development. There is walking enough incidental to this sport to properly develop the legs without making special effort that way.

SKATING.

Skating on ice, an almost unknown and ancient practice in cities, has gymnastic and therapeutic values that are worth considering. Skating consists of a series of balance movements in which the weight is borne by one leg after the other has given the stroke. The free leg is used, with the arms, to preserve equilibrium and then moves forward to carry the weight of the body in the next stroke. In fancy skating the stroke consists of short curves with the body inclined inward in relation to the curve, with the free leg and the arms employed to preserve equilibrium. The pivot in all curves is the center of gravity influenced by the laws of centrifugal force, leverage and penetrating energy.

The effects of skating are plentiful and good. The chilly and crisp winter air compels one to action in order to keep warm. This activity reflects upon the body by promoting metabolism and increased respiration. Nearly all the good effects of running and running games, added to the best effects of balance movements, will result from skating. Skating tends to establish perfect equilibrium and correct posture. It develops elasticity of muscles, grace of motion, and strengthens the muscles of the calf, thigh and waist region. The erectors of the spine are also exhaustively employed in long continued straight away speed skating. (Illus. 228.)

Skating is very exhilarating. There is much satisfaction felt in the ability acquired and interest in the limitless possibilities ahead. But, in one's eagerness to achieve, skating may be carried to excess, and the same bad results as from excessive running may be noted: heart dilatation, lung congestion and, in women, pelvic congestion.

ROLLER SKATING.

Roller skating is similar to ice skating and therefore needs little special consideration. As it is usually practiced indoors or at least on dusty pavements it is less hygienic than ice skating. (Illus. 229.) The stroke in roller skating is in a straight line, the body carried well forward. There is little of the curved stroke effect noted in ice skating and roller skating offers less opportunity for fancy play. The effects of roller skating are similar to those of ice skating.

SKIING.

Skiing, or Swedish snow-shoeing, has been steadily growing in popularity in this country. Ordinarily the skis are used for swift travel over the snow. Progress is made by sliding over the snow, alternately pushing one foot at a time and carrying it forward with a lifting

230

Hanger   Omtvedt   Berger

231

232

and sudden dropping of the heel for propulsion. The feet move straight forward in a parallel line. Sometimes, to aid progress and preserve equilibrium, especially on crusted snow and on inclines, one or two poles are used.

Skis are used by many of the woodsmen of our northwest to cross lakes speedily and for rapid travel over well beaten trails with supplies from settlement stores. The hunters sometimes use skis for swift travel. With the Laplanders and other northern Europeans it is said that skis are a necessity. So dependent are they upon these that to lose or break a ski often means loss of life. In our country skiing survives chiefly as a winter sport. The effects of skiing are much the same as skating and running though in a much less degree. They develop strength of leg and equilibrium and give one a sense of man's superiority over nature.

For developing pure daring few sports surpass the form of skiing used in exhibition work. A special shoot with a smooth hump at the bottom is used by the competitors and it is a thrilling sight to see them slide down and leave the bottom of the shoot to sail through the air. (Illus. 230.) They slide down this shoot, acquiring great speed with the descent, and just as they reach the hump they nearly squat and spring up to add as much as possible to the elevation of the body through the air; then the penetrating energy gained from the descent carries them up to 150 feet or more from the take off. In order to establish a record a skier must remain on his feet in the landing and slide over the snow. This form of skiing requires and develops courage, great strength of leg, and good physical control; it is a proof of great personal bravery. The leaders in the skiing world at present, Haugen and Omtvedt, are clear-eyed, sturdy Scandinavians. Their work has placed our country in the lead in this sport. (Illus. 231 and 232.)

SNOW-SHOEING.

Canadian or Indian snow-shoeing can hardly be called a sport; yet it is frequently used for exercise and, since it requires a special method of walking a few words in explanation would not be amiss. Many people in our northern states practice snow-shoeing for exercise. In the north woods of this country and in Canada everyone uses snow-shoes at some time or other for hunting, packing supplies over the snow, or simply for long distance walking in the winter. With snow two or three feet deep through the winter there is no other method of travel except Esquimo fashion or on skis.

To walk on snow-shoes requires less power of equilibrium than with skis. Although rapid progress is not as easy as with skis, heavy burdens may be carried more easily on snow-shoes. The steps are taken by carrying the moving foot outward to avoid striking the ankle of the other leg, and far enough forward to keep from placing one shoe over the edge of the other. If the edge of the forward shoe rests on the edge of the rear one when the next step is attempted the walker is sure to trip forward into the snow. A few minutes of practice is all that is required to clarify these remarks.

The effects of snow-shoeing are much the same as those of ordinary walking, strengthening the muscles of the legs and developing endurance and perseverance. Progress on snow-shoes can never be rapid, although, over a well hardened trail, one is capable of a slow jog. But a great deal of snow-shoeing would tend to slow one's running speed. The fact that snow-shoeing can only be practiced out of doors in crisp weather makes it a desirable sport. It gets one into the bracing air and offers enough activity to keep him warm, without overtaxing his strength.

WALKING.

Walking, it is affirmed by those who have never adequately analyzed the needs of the body, is the best of all exercises. Measured by the great number whose health has been improved by taking up regular walking it can be said, in a loose sense, that walking is the best of exercises, merely because most people take so little of what may be called exercise. It is a universal human trait to do as little as one dare and get by, for all are lazy by nature and few persons attempt more than their daily occupation requires. It follows that whenever one is moved through persuasion,—seldom self-persuasion,— to take up exercise for health's sake, in nearly every instance he will select walking. This is because walking is so simple, so elemental and so convenient.

Because any exercise is better than none, in one who has remained inactive for a long time walking in the open air will make such a change that he will become an ardent advocate of this "best of exercises." The sudden change from indoor inactivity and slow internal decay to outdoor activity and renewed rapid cellular exchange in the muscles could also be attained through scores of other forms of activity, and some much better than walking, if they only were practiced long enough. Any activity will promote metabolism or the exchange of cells within the tissues and this will rejuvenate the individual to a degree that will react by making him want to tell others how good he feels and why they should adopt his method.

There are many reasons why walking is not the best of exercises. The most important reason is that walking requires so little mental control. All other factors equal, as was explained in the first chapter, that form of exercise is most valuable which requires most thought, because, aside from the health factor, it creates a closer affiliation between the brain and the muscles. Walking is so automatic and simple that one can walk hundreds of miles without having to give it a single thought. The only way to render walking educational as well as healthful is to vary the speed and frequently

233

234

practice toe walking. Another reason why walking is not the best of exercises is that it employs the lower body so much more than the upper. There is no way of walking to render it a balanced developer. It is a conservative statement to say that the legs receive hundreds of times more activity than the arms. Every move one makes, except while lying down, requires use of the leg muscles. While the arms may be said to move almost as frequently as the legs, very seldom must they bear the entire body weight. The arms and general upper body therefore need special consideration along with walking.

If one wishes to make walking the main part of physical training, besides changing the rate of speed while on the road, one should add such activities as bag punching and rowing, or chest weight exercises while facing the machine. A combination of this kind would keep one in excellent condition for as long as it is continued regularly.

For best results in walking one should wear low heeled, broad toed shoes, easy fitting garments and if he carries luggage and camping material they should be evenly distributed over both shoulders and not hung from only one. It is obvious that if one habitually carries a burden upon the same shoulder it will develop an unbalanced condition that, in the young, might produce lateral curvature of the spine.

On long journeys many have the habit of carrying a stick across the shoulders and flexing the arms over it. (Illus. 233.) This is done with the idea that it will keep the shoulders straighter and render walking easier. This does seem to make walking easier but, because it employs the muscles in front of the shoulders to hold up the stick, it tends to round, rather than straighten the shoulders.

BICYCLING.

For a wonderful airing with mild exercise nothing will ever surpass the bicycle. So far as people's health is concerned it is too bad that the automobile came when it did. The bicycle was just being perfected at the time the automobile made its appearance and because of the natural impulse of all human beings to rush to the new, and their inherent laziness to avoid exertion, the automobile eclipsed the bicycle. However, at the present writing interest in the bicycle has been revived to such an extent that the manufacturers are running night shifts and increasing their old plants, and repair shops are being established and old ones renovated.

The frequent sight of boys and girls riding bicycles is causing many old men and women to feel young again. (Illus. 234.)   It is recalling vividly the days of the bicycle's great popularity. Whether it is the constantly increasing rates of transportation and the increasing cost of automobiles and gasoline, or whether it is simply the opposite swing of the pendulum, is not clear, but it is a fact that so far as the bicycle is concerned the good old days are with us again.

Unlike the hatred fostered by the auto between the autoist and the pedestrian, the bicycle creates a free masonry among all—riders, pedestrians and men and women about town. The bicycle is a natural bond of friendship and promotes good fellowship. The old League of American Wheelmen will no doubt be revived with a co-ed department. Many of the oldtimers have been seen in their back yards shyly testing out the old rusty bicycles, polishing and oiling them up and trying to ride them again. There is no doubt that many of them will at length condescend to purchase modern makes, but it is doubtful if the bond of fellowship between rider and steed will ever be as strong as it used to be.

There is something about a bicycle that cannot be explained. It must be experienced to be realized. Just the other day I saw a little boy pushing his bicycle along. He had a punctured tire and was carrying the injured member in one hand as he pushed his precious steed with the other. I wanted to talk to him.

Has anyone over thirty escaped this most memorable of experiences, the punctured tire? Does it not recall the days when, if one remained near home, he might ride over tin cans, tacks, nails and glass and escape a mishap, but if he ventured a long distance from home he would get a puncture from even a lump of dirt?

We sat down, the boy and I, and examined the tube and discussed the puncture. As I handled the bicycle,— though never given to sentiment,—I felt queer as I recalled the day when, riding through Westboro, Mass., just as our party was turning down into the wonderful new state road, smooth as a floor, I heard the familiar whistling hiss of the punctured tire. We all had to stop for about twenty minutes while the tire was mended, for we always carried the repair kit, but none of us could explain how the puncture was made.

Everybody loves a bicycle and the least mishap to this iron steed brings forth words of sympathy from all passers-by, from the policeman to the street urchin. "Dat's too bad," said the policeman, "but you've got de fixin's and it all comes under de headin' o' sport. Where'ye from?"

"Marlboro."

"Well, nine miles ain't so fur." Then, true to form, as he picked up the bicycle to feel it over, he said, "Ah, me by, she's sure a daisy." A little boy then approached and timidly passed his hands over the smooth handle bars. As we made smiling remarks to him, the lad got over his timidity and pushed the button to ring the bell a few times. Two young ladies teasingly asked how it would be to walk home. And so it went in the good old days.

Now, if we are re-entering a similar period, may God speed the day. The roads are much better than the ones we knew, but there are a great many automobiles on them. Nevertheless, there are many good roads that are not infested by this modern nuisance where one can live again the golden days of the '80s and '90s. We do not see the high wheeler any more, but the modern "safety" is returning in ever increasing numbers.

It seems sacrilegious to compare the romantic bicycle with the motorcycle. When the motorcycle is made oil-proof, noise-proof, smell-proof and vibration-proof, it may then challenge a comparison. But as long as it lacks the human propelling element it cannot hold the place of the old fashioned bicycle in the hearts of true devotees.

What sense is there in traveling a hundred miles an hour with no special place to go and no special reason for such speed? On the bicycle, at least, the speed seldom becomes dangerous and one is always conscious of what he is doing. Then there is the exercise of the legs that is afforded by bicycle riding. This sport is like walking, only more so. Combined with rowing and bag punching, it is ideal.

HORSEBACK RIDING.

If the bicycle can grow into one's affections as much as it has in the past, how much more genuine regard one might acquire for a horse. There are many tales of the attachment between rider and horse that seem stranger than fiction.

"In some respects," wrote the Autocrat, "saddle leather is better than sole leather." As a brief analysis of the sport will prove, it was not mere prejudice that brought forth this statement.

Frequently you hear the statement that getting exercise on horseback is tantamount to developing your physique in an easy chair. However, because the rider is seated is no proof that his muscles are idle. As long as the horse remains motionless the rider may rest comfortably, but as soon as he moves the active role begins. The horse's motion causes the rider to be constantly on the alert to maintain equilibrium.

The most important single point in good gymnastics is to maintain correct posture. Correct posture is dependent upon the erector muscles of the trunk. To develop a correct posture one must frequently exercise the erectors of the spine. The gentle swaying of the rider's body forward and back with the motion of horse causes a constant activity of the abdominal and back muscles. The back muscles, especially, are taxed, because of the constant tendency of the trunk to fall forward. In addition to the work of these groups of muscles the adductors of the thighs are used a great deal.

So marked is the need of strong adductors that, from the habit of clinging to their horses day after day, year after year, we sometimes see western ranch men, or cowboys, so bowlegged that they say a greased pig could run between their knees without soiling their trousers. We deduce from this that, to prevent knock-knees, horseback riding would form a pleasant remedy.

The impulses received by the rider from the movements of the animal tend to constantly disturb the line of gravity in the body so that all the muscles of the trunk are employed. Horseback riding may not develop such athletic forms as result from selected gymnastics but it does give splendid training of the waist region. The muscles of the waist, comprising the rectus, the obliques and the transverse abdominals, as well as the lateral spinal muscles, constitute nature's corset. When these muscles are in tonic state they preserve a beautiful natural waist line and support the organs of the abdomen, so that no amount of jarring can prove unhealthy.

By reacting so forcibly upon the waist region of the body horseback riding promotes appetite, normal digestion and increased peristalsis, thus preventing constipation. These facts alone are sufficient to establish the advisability of riding frequently. Good appetite and digestion and normal bowels are among the best signs of health and prove powerful factors in making life enjoyable.

The advantage of exercising out of doors where the light and fresh air can reach the skin and the increased respiration induced by the activity itself, all are conducive to pure blood, clear skin and good complexion.

236

James Thorpe

The great exhilaration created by horseback riding certainly tends to keep up one's spirit and prevent the blues. The feeling of mastery, of one's superiority over nature, in the consciousness that one's will governs not only his own body, but that of a very powerful animal, is very satisfying. Alertness of body and mind are induced by a brisk horseback ride; the varying speeds of travel and the varying nature of the road prevent one's mind from dwelling upon morbid thoughts and idle dreams. (Illus. 235.)

Horseback riding has, of all sports, the most interesting and perhaps most ancient traditions. Even farther back than the days when "man's mind runneth not to the contrary," it was the sport of king and peasant. Riding was then a sort of duty rather than a hygienic and pleasurable practice. With so many labor and exertion-saving devices, it has now become a new duty to keep active, and no form of activity can surpass horseback riding for those who can afford it.

It is too bad that our reformers have completely stopped horse-racing, instead of regulating it. It is an exciting, pleasurable and healthful sport. By taking away horse-racing the gambling element that has hovered around the race tracks has not been cured. If one wants to gamble, he will do so, in spite of all the laws, and over any sort of competition or chance medium. In many respects it would be far better to bring back horse-racing under strict regulation than to keep it, as it is at present, a sport only for the rich and a gambling sport for all gamblers through the news reports.

ATHLETICS.

Years ago, before the amateur associations were formed, there were many abuses of athletics. Although these bodies have not always been above reproach, it would be unjust to assume that they have not greatly improved all athletic activities. However, the heads of the Amateur Athletic Union might have   stretched

a point a few years ago in the case of Jim Thorpe, the
greatest athlete who ever lived. The A. A. U. had a rule
that if, at any time in life, a person had accepted money
for any physical activity, he was forever after in the
professional class, and not only could he not compete
against others who were amateurs, but, if the others
knew that such an athlete had been guilty of violating
this rule they were themselves to be classified as pro-
fessionals and prohibited from competing on the amateur
list except after being re-instated by the union. Jim
Thorpe (Illus. 236) won the world's championship in the
pentathlon and the decathlon at the Olympic games at
Stockholm in 1912. There was no competitor who came
close to his averages. After performing so creditably
and getting possession of the prizes, it was found out
that, as a boy, this Indian had accepted a few dollars for
playing Sunday baseball in some out of the way town of
the south. For the sake of glory and diplomacy, James
E. Sullivan, little czar of the Amateur Athletic Union,
dispossessed Thorpe of his laurels and accorded them to
the athletes who stood second in the decathlon and pentathlon. Had the Scandinavians who had come such poor
seconds possessed a single drop of sporting blood they
would have refused to take such laurels from Thorpe. It
is only in this country that amateur rules are so extreme
and sweeping. It is because of such rules that many play
summer baseball for money under an assumed name so
that they can afford to go to college with the money thus
earned and perform as amateurs on their college teams.
Would it not be better to allow a person to be professional
in one sport and amateur in another? This is permitted
in golf and it has not injured the sport.

Nearly every school and college provides in some
way for games and athletic sports. The students who
take part are usually healthy, not so much because of
their activities but rather because they have to be in
order to withstand the training or straining. At present
the purpose of athletics seems not so much to promote

the health of the students as to win athletic meets and the average student is neglected for the sake of a few select performers who receive the attention of the coach. It is always splendid to develop a winning team but, in the long run, would it not be more to the purpose to try to average up the weaklings than to improve the superior physiques merely for victory?

Besides causing a neglect of the majority of students in the endeavor to bring out winning combinations the methods of procedure in many institutions tend to so strain as to undermine the athletes. This is not due so much to athletics and competition as to the wrong application of them. When an institution comes out victorious at a meet we should think of the cost of the victory as something beside financial expense. How many athletes' hearts may have been injured unless special advice is given and followed? How many of the members of a team are developing a one-sided condition that may lay the foundation for future ailments? Nature is not always to blame for the fact that veteran athletes frequently die of heart failure at an age when one would expect them to be near their best physical condition. There are laws governing the body that should be observed and, until they are, we can expect shallow thinkers to explain injuries and fatalities by saying, as we frequently hear, that "Such mishaps are only nature's toll for the good derived from activities."

One naturally asks, what might be offered as a remedy for all these defects? It is easy to find faults, but how remedy them? Although it has been said by many that it would prove impractical, it is a fact, nevertheless, that all athletic tests should be done equally to both sides. It is to be hoped that women, now that they are entering every domain that men once claimed as their own, will profit by their brothers' mistakes and establish the logical way to practice athletic competitions. There is no serious argument against any form of athletics if only the body is kept balanced, by the stunt itself done to both sides, or by supplementing selected gymnastics or play activities to balance the general activities. The quickest way to re-establish equilibrium in a one-sided individual would be to neglect the strong side for a while and perform entirely with the weak side until both are equalled. When both sides are about even, to maintain such balance, one should perform as much left as right. Whatever sport or exercise one takes up he should follow a scheme by which he can produce symmetrical development.

Unless one is an all round athlete it is absolutely certain that he will develop some portion of the body at the expense of some other part. Even the all round athlete will neglect his weaker side more or less. It is true that there is hardly one form of athletics in which all the muscles are not brought into play, but if we compare the difference in the amount of strain and control of the muscles directly taxed with the slight exertion and want of control of the other muscles the unevenness in the distribution of effort is soon apparent.

As an example, let us consider shot putting. Assuming that the athlete is right handed, he holds the shot with his right hand and balances on his right foot. The weight being on the right, the waist muscles and the left spinal muscles have to contract to keep the trunk erect. The first hop is on the right foot. From the hop he lands on both feet and, to achieve the twist for the put, the internal rotators of the left thigh and the external rotators of the right thigh become active in co-ordination with the right pectoral, the deltoid and the extensors of the right arm. Trailing further the succession of muscular action, all the muscles of the trunk involved in twisting to the left and the sudden extension of the right leg at the same time as the arm is extended are included in performing this feat. The left arm and leg and all the antagonists of the muscles really exerted are only called into action to help balance the body in the put.

Many athletes specialize on the shot put, but some also include the discus (Illus. 237), the javelin (Illus. 238), and the hammer. These four events only dovetail together into a pronounced one-sided combination. The shot put, the discus throw and the javelin require more pronounced twisting of the body to the left than the hammer throw, but the last event includes a larger group of muscles in somewhat the same twisting. In the shot and javelin events the extensors of the throwing arm are brought forcibly into play at the final movement of the feat, while in the discus throw it is the flexors of the throwing arm that are especially taxed. In the hammer throw the flexors of the right arm and the extensors of the left, as well as the muscles of the entire back, are used. The main point in each event is to get a rapid twist of the body to the left. The discus and javelin are classical and beautiful. The javelin has been taken up by women (Illus. 239) and it has proven interesting and free from strain.

Close examination of an athlete who has done nothing but put the shot for a few years will disclose evidences of deformity. His right arm is much stronger and a little larger than his left. There is often a slight difference between the legs. The most pronounced fault is in the spine where a curvature with its convexity to the right is often evident.

If you compare the spine to a balance, the erectors corresponding to the weights, you can readily see that if the muscles of each side are equally strong equilibrium exists and the spine is erect. But if the muscles of one side are too strong the equilibrium is lost and the spine bends with the concavity to the stronger side, just as the balance would tip to the side of the greater weight. If one develops the muscles of one side and entirely neglects those of the other the trained muscles will improve at the same ratio as the neglected ones lose. That is why we are likely to find lateral spinal curvature in the shot putter who specializes.

237

238

Hoffman U. of Mich.

239

240

Following the same principle, examine the shoulder girdle. The bones are loosely fixed and depend upon the muscles of the chest and upper back for their position. When all these muscles are balanced the shoulders and chest are carried in the ideal position. Because of the activities of everyday life, or from most of our athletic events, it is common to find the chest muscles shortened, the back ones extended, and the shoulders drawn forward and downward. Unless the work of the above four events is counteracted by antagonistic activity deformities will occur. The shot putter, discus and javelin throwers will probably have round and sometimes drooping shoulders. The hammer thrower is less likely to show such deformities because his feat tends to develop the back shoulder muscles, but he can make it a complete developer if he will throw left as much as right handed.

In jumping and hurdling there is also a favorite side. Every athlete has a favorite "take-off" leg. Actual measurement has shown that the girths of the take-off leg exceed those of the weaker member. We know, through the findings of osteopathy, that there are often twists of the hip and lower spine produced from one-sided exertions. These will lead to lumbago, sciatica and, in women, to pelvic ailments. Women especially should be careful to equalize their jumping efforts. (Illus. 240.) To make the work even and thus maintain equilibrium, whether high or broad jumping, one should take off first from one foot and then from the other. One can do this and lose nothing in ability, but rather acquire reserve power. Even hurdling might be made perfectly symmetrical if one hurdled from the left and right foot alternately.

Of all the track events the most pronouncedly one-sided is the pole vault, yet it offers the best opportunity for all round and balanced development. The all round development which is now gained from this event is far from symmetrical. Nearly the same faults observed in shot putting are obvious in the athlete who does nothing but pole vault for a while. In the pole vault the athlete runs with the pole resting on the left hand, the right hand assisting to balance it. (Illus. 241.) Thus, in the run the right spinal muscles are taxed more than the left. After the body leaves the ground in the take off, the muscles of the abdomen and then those of the right side of the spine again do the chief work in lifting the legs and the body over the bar. During this action the arms may move up along the pole but the real lift is achieved by the left arm pushing and the right hand pulling against the pole. All of this emphasizes the over use of the right as compared to the left spinal muscles. If the pole vaulter practiced from the left as much as from the right his event would prove a wonderful developer.

Barring the heavy hammer throwing event, if all recorded organic troubles which are charged against athletics were truly reported the majority could be traced to running in its various forms. This is not due to the fact that running is in itself injurious but to the methods taught runners. The coaches understand very well how to get speed and strength into their runners but few seem to understand how to conserve these powers. Expert horsemen might teach a lesson in this. A good jockey was never known to take his horse right from the stable into the race. The usual way is to run it up and down the track so as to warm up the muscles and thus prepare them and the heart gradually. A warm muscle is in the first stage of contraction and an exercised muscle is a warm muscle. After the race the expert jockey allows his horse to gradually lessen the speed until it becomes hardly more than a walk. The idea is to gradually work the horse up to the speed of the race and then gradually work it down again. Experience has proven conclusively that this scheme will produce the best results on the heart and muscular system.

There is no difference between the muscular system of a horse and that of a man. If the jockey were to do as most coaches do, he would allow his horse to lie idle until the moment of the race and immediately after the race he would allow it to drop down in a heap to recover. Everyone who has considered the physiology of the body should know that any exertion is dangerous unless the muscles are prepared for it and that no one should suddenly cease a strain without gradually moderating his exertion. It is best for all runners to warm up to the race and after it to go on running, gradually lessening their speed until the lungs and heart action are normalized again. Of course, all runners, as well as hurdlers and jumpers, should practice upper body activities to maintain a balanced development.

It is often affirmed with truth that our athletes surpass those of ancient Greece. In the actual records the ancients have been surpassed. But, while records and victory are the first consideration with us, with the Greeks these were secondary to physical perfection and beauty. A young lady remarked a short time ago: "I shall never forget the first track meet I went to. I expected to see Apollos and Adonises, but when I beheld the ugly, unsymmetrical, round-shouldered athletes who constitute our record holders my consternation can hardly be imagined." Her remark was not at all exaggerated. Athletics as conducted today tend to produce just such specimens as she described. What we need is a revision of rules to induce athletes to develop harmonious bodies. Indeed, prizes might be offered for symmetry and beauty of development as much as for skill in performance.

All athletes must be encouraged to avail themselves of the benefits of the gymnasium until all parts of the body are properly developed. When track work is taken up, enough properly selected gymnasium work should be followed to counteract the evil effects of the athletic events. Before an athlete is allowed to take part in competitive work he should be required to fulfill a high standard of symmetrical development as well as the usual

organic test. No argument should be necessary to make one appreciate the great satisfaction to be derived from physical perfection. The reward for such development lies in the thing itself. It is not easy to make the majority see it from such a light and therefore other inducements are necessary.

If the gymnasium training has been done as it should be, the track work should not be allowed to undo all. That the same ideal be upheld on the track field the following method might be tried out. In the shot put the athlete might be given three trials with the right and three with the left. The average between the longest put with the right and the longest with the left could then be taken and this would stand as his trial put for qualifying. When the finals come, all who have qualified could carry on in the same way until the winners are determined. Whatever form or style the athlete uses for his put he should be compelled to do exactly the opposite from his weaker side. In the discus, the javelin and the hammer throws the same principle should obtain. In the high and broad jumps the athletes might be allowed three trials from each foot and the average computed from the best of each and that might stand for either the trials or finals. Thus, the pole vault, perhaps the most picturesque of the field events, could be made into a complete gymnasium if only both sides were used equally. In all athletic events the same scheme could be carried out. Even in the hurdles it should be required that they be cleared from each foot alternately. As for the running events, enough was said above except that upper body development should be emphasized.

The ideas here expressed have been suggested to those in authority, who answered that these suggestions were impractical. But they are no more impractical than the one-sided work that is now in vogue. If athletes were trained from the start to perform in this manner, they would like it as well, and competition could be as keen and far more interesting to spectators as well as beneficial to participants. The health and future welfare of all athletes should be considered most seriously—not simply victories and records.

GYMNASTIC GAMES.

The above sports and games constitute a list of the typical popular forms of recreation. But unless one is in good health he can hardly participate in any of them and frequently good health is injured by taking part in some of them. Without resorting to corrective or hygienic gymnastics many seek to establish a high state of health within themselves by some form of play that will qualify them for the most strenuous of games or sports. Although it is difficult by play to supplement or counteract the evils of play, a number of games have been invented for this purpose. These gymnastic games lack the spontaneity of most of the popular games but, when their value is emphasized and their practice is guided by the needs of the individual, much good can be obtained.

There are hundreds of gymnastic games explained in detail in books devoted to that subject. For our purpose we shall select a few of the best for correcting given defects.

The medicine ball is the best and most useful of recreative exercising apparati. It may be used out of games, simply by being tossed about in various ways. The developing or corrective effect of its use depends upon the throw. It may be thrown as any object with one or both hands, pushed as a shot or heavy weight, thrown backward over head, thrown between the legs, thrown underhand or sideways with both hands. The force used is according to the individual's strength and the weight of the ball. No well equipped gymnasium should be without medicine balls of various weights.

The medicine ball might be used from the weak side by athletes who specialize in shot putting or any other one-sided field event. Where one has used the chest muscles more than the back shoulder muscles he might counteract the deformity or muscular unbalance by swinging the medicine ball backward and tossing it over his head as far as possible several times each day.

In circle ball, circle touch ball, dodge ball, straddle ball (Illus. 242), straddle pin ball and all such games, where the object of the game is to strike a player or object, or dodge the ball, the throws can be made by employing a motion of the arm or arms that will be corrective in its effect. By throwing for corrective effects there can be just as much pleasure in the games and much more benefit to the player. The game may be given new interest by varying the styles of throw.

Captain ball is one of those games that may accommodate almost any number of players, but the most popular number is ten players to each side. The field should be at least sixty feet long and divided into halves by a center line. At the center of each half is a circle for the captain, and at the four corners are slightly smaller circles for the captain's partners. For each player in a circle there is an opponent who is allowed to run about and capture the ball and pass it to his team-mates across the line, but they must not cross the center line nor step into the circles. The play is started by two of the players jumping for the ball at the center of the field. Each tries to bat or pass the ball to one of his team-mates in the circles across the line. The object is to get the ball to the captain, but it must reach the captain from one of the side circles to count a point. Another way to count a point is to make a circuit of the circles. The circle players must not step out of their circles. The ball must not be kicked, nor can a player take a step after catching it. As a practice game for basketball passing and catching this game is valuable. (Illus. 243.) It has most of the qualities of basketball but in a milder degree.

Volley ball is a splendid game because of the fine control of the hands it develops and the fact that it com-

pels an upright standing posture. It has some of the
elements of tennis in that it requires a batting stroke
sufficient to carry the ball over the net but, the ball
being light and the court limited, the stroke must be
so regulated as not to carry the ball out of bounds. Volley
ball should be popular for all who have scrawny shoulders
and prominent collar bone, because the forward upward
stroke that is used so much tends to correct such defects.
The holding of the head high to watch and control the
ball also tends to improve the carriage of the head and
chest and expand the ribs.

Hill Dill is a pure running game that every child has
played at some time in life. It has various names in
different parts of the world. In Massachusetts, where
I played it as a boy, it was known as Monny Moss. It
is a simple running game that develops the muscles of
the legs and improves endurance. It has no more developing value than common "tag."

Hang tag is one of the most valuable games for the
playground and gymnasium, or as a picnic game. A
player saves himself from being tagged by hanging by
the hands. If the players do not move about enough to
give the It man a chance to tag them he has the power
to call out: "All change!" and every player must leave
the spot where he is hanging and find a new one. At
any time a player changes his place if he decides to hang
from a support already occupied, the first one there has
to move because the last to come always has best claim
to the support. This adds to the game's liveliness. The
effects of this game are to strengthen the arms and
shoulders, raise the rib, benefit the respiratory apparatus and furnish the legs sufficient work to give an all
round development.

Indian club wrestling (Illus. 244) is a splendid game
to promote nimbleness. Where one is pulled and pushed
around and jerked rapidly about by players to either
side, at the same time doing his best to keep from
knocking down the Indian clubs, and endeavoring all the

while to force the other players to do so, there is a variety of activity that more or less taxes all the muscles and has as a predominant characteristic the effect of developing nimbleness and balancing power.

Chicken fight is a game in which each player holds up one foot with one hand and with the free hand tries to make his opponent lose his balance and touch the upraised foot to the ground. (Illus. 245.) It is a good developer of nimbleness and, if practiced to each side, will prove a balanced developer.

Bull-in-the-ring is a well known and popular boy's game which tends to develop powerful shoulders and arms and a tenacious grip.

Stick wrestling can hardly be called a game, as it has no special organization features. It might be classified with hand wrestling. (Illus. 246.) The game consists in opponents taking an even hold on a stick and by pulling, pushing and twisting in various ways, to make the opponent let go. It is a very effective way to strengthen the wrist and forearm and develop grit.

Tournament is a beautiful game from the traditional standpoint and for exhibition purposes. A large sized and strong boy serves as war charger and he carries a light weight boy on his shoulders. The rider carries a long stick, or pole, well padded at one end. This serves as his spear. The object of the game is for each rider to dismount his opponent. The horses and riders either pair off or make it a free for all and an elimination contest. Besides furnishing no end of amusement for rider and onlooker, this sport has several developing effects. The boys playing the part of horses are taxed about the shoulders, arms and legs, and practically the entire musculature is exercised. The riders need strong adductors of the thighs to remain seated. These are the muscles that are taxed in horseback riding. The riders also need strong abdominal muscles for pushing forward while clinging to their chargers. Their arm and shoulder muscles are also brought into strong activity. Unless

244

245

246

counteracted by rowing, breast-stroke swimming or special work on the exercisers, the effect of this game on the rider will be to produce round and drooping shoulders.

One of the best games to counteract the bad effects of nearly all round shoulder developers is arch-ball. The players in this game stand in two or more rows of even length, one player behind the other. A line serves to mark where the first player should stand. The ball, either a medicine or basket ball, is dropped backward over the head while the trunk is bent backward, causing a slight arch-flexion; the next player catches it as it comes down and passes it on to the next, and so on to the last who runs forward to the front of the line and starts the ball down again. At each round, as the last player is running forward with the ball, all take a step backward so as to leave sufficient space for the runner to take his place and at the same time keep the line its right length. This is repeated until the player who stood at the head of the line in the beginning has come back to his first position. The line finishing first, wins. There is as much pleasure from this game as from any of the same type and the backward bending renders it above all others in value.

The above survey of the characteristic games and sports is brief, but it brings out the chief effects of the most popular of them. Some writers are so imbued with the spirit of play that they advocate the use of games to the entire exclusion of formal gymnastics. "Play is natural," they say, "and only when one plays is he responding to nature's call for activity." So far this is true, but, in our modern civilized life nearly all occupations, which are by no means natural, and nearly all games call for a greater use of the flexors than the extensors of the body, and nearly all cause a stooping posture of the trunk and drooping of the head. Because of this one-sidedness in our daily work corrective gymnastics are necessary.

Indeed, because our daily life is in many respects artificial, it is but natural that artificial means like corrective exercise should be found necessary.

ROPE BALANCING.

Before closing this chapter, dancing should be considered briefly. There is a form of balancing activity that has been rendered a cross between the dance and tight rope balancing and it is such a valuable contribution that it deserves special mention. Bird Millmann has acquired such skill on the wire or rope that she can balance on her toes and perform a series of genuine ballet steps to music. (Illus. 247.) The slack wire, slack or tight rope, do not seem as popular now as they used to be in the past. There was a time when all boys tried themselves out at it and with nothing but great benefit. At first, by using a balancing pole and keeping the rope only a few inches from the ground, a sense of equilibrium far in excess of anything natural can be developed. As this sense of equilibrium improves the rope or wire is fastened higher and higher from the ground until the height seems to make no difference. Miss Millmann has mastered this balancing stunt so that she can run back and forth and balance on her toes and perform dancing steps that make it seem as if she were held up by wires. As evidence of how much the mind has to do with the entire balance test, she has told me that she is no better at walking a track rail than any ordinary person. She does not feel that she has to concentrate in this simple stunt and therefore her balance is like that of the average. On the wire, however, while conscious of the fact that a misstep may mean serious injury, her mind is alert and all her powers are concentrated on her dangerous feat. Although very few can ever hope to equal or surpass such extreme skill, for a short cut to perfect equilibrium walking a rail or a rope at a low height would prove helpful. The effects of balance movements have been so thoroughly covered in chapters one and two that no more need be said here.

DANCING.

Conventional dancing is the most general, most popular and the least valuable from a gymnastic standpoint. The physical effects of all dancing are on the legs and feet, very much as in walking or running, except that the stuffy and often smoke-laden atmosphere of the dance hall and the tight, stiff, obstructing garments limit the possibilities of physical benefit. The automatism of the rhythm certainly does not develop one's mental control of the body. The shifting styles of dancing which have been popular for the last few years, beginning with the tango, the maxixe, the one step and the hesitation, on to the dances of cabaret and underworld origin, have none of them been gracefully developing. There seems at the present writing to be a movement back to the beautiful waltzes and adaptations from the folk and classical styles. These may never come into general popularity, but they are to be encouraged. This is not said from the moral uplift standpoint, but because of the gymnastic and developing value of these activities. The law of gymnastics that the body at rest tends to assume the posture it held in activity is true for dancing as much as for other activities. Go to any dance hall and observe the protruding chins, the forward throw of the heads, the sunken collar bones, the body slump, the gawky outward angle of the elbows and the knees and the dragging of the feet.

Dancing in some form or other has been so universally practiced and for so long a time that it would require more than an ordinary lifetime of incessant labor to prepare an exhaustive history of it. With all races and nations in all parts of the earth dancing has formed a part of their religious rituals and social diversions. Most of the nations of Europe have developed their own folk dances. Among the tribes and peoples who never danced from sheer joy and amusement, secret dances

247

Bird Millman

were part of their ceremonies accessible only to initiates. Even among the Puritans, who condemned all dancing as carnal, there developed the Shakers, who invoked the holy spirit by frenzied rhythmic movements of the body.

The intolerant spirit of the Puritans that manifested itself in England by enacting laws against "play acting, dancing and other carnal sports" still survives among some of our censors. One of the most ridiculous exhibitions of prudery in history occurred when Margaret of Valois after marrying James V, of Scotland, danced the salta and died a few days later of consumption. The Puritans of Edinburgh declared that her death was a celestial punishment for having gyrated in that naughty French dance. Such a view of the dance is based upon the fact that, in mediaeval days, when all joys were suppressed, whatever records of the ancient and classical dances we now possess were written by the monks or priests, because no one else could write, in those dark days when the church ruled supreme. Besides these biased records we have only such statuary and such vases with their pictures of the dance as were not destroyed by these holy men.

It is all very well to be just good, but it is better to be good for something. For those who do not aim to suppress dancing in general, but look upon it as a mere frivolous amusement, it might be interesting to know that dancing as an art is of historical importance. The character of a people may be safely judged by its amusements. This perhaps explains why so much of our stage dancing borders on the daring and defiant: the blue law gentry are so busy trying to suppress all. When filth is not suggested by censors' charges and brothel ideals, dancing is only a manifestation of pure joy, consisting of bodily movements performed to music, song, clapping or pounding and subject to definite rhythmic rules. In the hour of mirth all people's minds should be unrestrained; the environment, the music and the individual's ability determine how mirth shall be expressed. The

248.

national ideal determines largely what the nature of the predominating dances shall be. Among the Greeks dancing was so beautiful that the sculptors perpetuated in marble some of the characteristic steps and poses (Illus. 248), and these statues have inspired many of our most wholesome and entertaining dancers. In Turkey, Italy and Spain the dance in general was of a voluptuous nature. In France we find the correct, dainty, graceful, ceremonious type of ball room dances and minuets.

NATIONAL FOLK DANCE.

What shall we say of the dance in our country? We have seen changes from the skirt to the shirt dance, the last perhaps an exact reaction to the suppressive work of the Puritans, and we have seen all kinds of fads and spasmodic developments. There is not much that is aesthetic about any of these. The chief attraction about any new dance is its novelty. The most popular type of stage dancing is the eccentric and tricky kind.

One of the most popular exponents of the modern stage dance is Marilyn Miller. (Illus. 249.) When she started as a dancer on the stage she performed very gracefully as an interpretive and toe dancer. Now, however, most of her work is of the eccentric type. She herself prefers the classical style of dancing but her managers and public demand the eccentric forms. In some of the foot divertisements for which she is so popular, she might have her arms tied to her sides and still gain applause. As a nation we are still far from being artists.

The only approach to a folk dance in our entire country is to be found among the southern highlanders. They are a group of folks who "ain't carin' a which nor whither" about the troubles of the outside world. They have lived apart for about three centuries and it is only recently that we have really learned anything about them. Most people have thought of them merely as moonshiners. As a matter of fact they possess other interesting and attractive traits that are worth considering, but for the

249

Marilyn Miller

present purpose we are only concerned with their peculiar form of dancing, or "play," as they call it, for they
are so intensely religious that the word dance must not
be used.

Because of their religious beliefs, which are as stern
as those of the early Puritans, there is no such thing
as dancing allowed among them. In some of the lower
highlands, "twistifications" are not altogether under the
ban, but, "way back of beyond," in the region of western
North Carolina, where there have been few outsiders,
all "twistifications" are condemned by the church. The
natives call their show "play" and will resent any other
name. When mountaineers are resentful, they are very
resentful.

The play usually takes place "when the crops are
laid by," that is, after the last cultivating of the corn
in the hot part of the summer, when there is a slack
time in the farm work. Then an outsider may, if they
are not too suspicious of him, witness a sight worth
going miles to see. The tall lanky fellows, in their "store
bought clo'es," with their women in calico fineries, meet
and greet one another with "How yo' all?" "Tol'able."
"Yo' all must come an' see us." The men deport themselves as gracefully as the best Chesterfieldian exponent
could. They gather from a picturesque string of loca-
tions, from "Silver Creek Knob way," from "beyan
Epley place," from "yen side of Lone mountain." They
gather at dusk so as to end their play early, for there
are no street lights in the mountain trails.

The play is a mixture of the quadrille and English
country dances, with traces of old Irish jigs. Probably
it was originally danced in sets of four, but since there
is not room for more than one set in their little cabins,
and because as many as possible wish to take part at
the same time, they play in circles of eight couples.
(Illus. 250.)

The steps are all sorts of jigs and a kind of hitchy
two-step. The men do all the capering and show off

Mountaineer's Play
Reproduction by Ridge Women's Club
CHICAGO.

250

while the women are "put around" where it pleases the men. Partners never come nearer to each other than holding hands, usually at arms' length. To begin, the men salute their own partners and then swing the lady on the left and then swing their "own woman." The first man then shuffles toward the center of the circle, turns to the second couple, to his right, swings the lady of the second couple and then goes back and swings his "own woman" again. He shuffles again to the center of the circle, turns to the third couple, swings the lady of the third couple and then goes and swings his "own woman" again. As the first man goes to the lady of the fourth couple the second man capers to the lady of the third couple and both swing the ladies simultaneously and then caper back to swing their "own women" again. So, each man falls in with the lady two couples ahead of him and back to his "own woman," until at length all are swinging together like dervishes. As a sort of chorus, after each figure, all men swing the ladies on their left and then their own partners again and then promenade around in a circle; then the first man begins the next figure. This goes on for a long time in seemingly unending variety. It may not be dancing but it gives the mountaineers thrills, the onlookers pleasure and, simply as a matter of ethnological policy, at least, the "play" should be preserved true to form.

The music for this "play" is unique. The old fiddler and banjo player who performed for them simply played by ear scraps of old tunes resembling old Scotch reels and some Irish and English country tunes which they had learned from their fathers. The time of the music might be described as six-eight or two-four. Miss Merrimen, the pianist, who was with Mrs. Gour at a "play," wishing to accompany the violin on the piano, had the violin tuned to concert pitch, but when the fiddler tried to play he was absolutely lost and said the fiddle was not right this way. The violin had to be tuned down again. The fiddler's pride was hurt, as an artist's should be, because they were trying to improve his music, and he said, "A woman's allers findin' somet'in' to do that a man cain't find no sense in nohow."

These mountaineers have been here as long as any group that makes up our nation, and what they have is something that has never been influenced by the outside world. But there is a true American folk dance which the whites have not tried to understand and which, therefore, they have never appreciated at its true worth—the American Indian dance.

Before the white man came, the Indian was free from the restraints and refinements of civilized life. He was solitary and independent, obeying his natural impulses and inclinations and the dictates of natural judgment. Surrounded by vast lakes, boundless forests, majestic rivers and trackless plains, he travelled about on hunting trips or merely to satisfy the wanderlust. His wild paradise developed in him a proud stoicism that was at times striking and sublime. If early writers misinterpreted his stoicism for stubbornness, and misrepresented his deeds, it was because of bigotry and self-interest. The Indians had no chance for redress in the early days and if they suffered in silence they suffered acutely. Because of the long continued abuses perpetrated against them the Indians tried to retreat to forest fastnesses and keep away from the whites. But it has come to pass that they are rising above their misfortunes and becoming factors in our civilization. Many have decided to play the game of life in the white man's way and they have acquired wealth and prominence.

On the reservations are left only remnants and wrecks of powerful tribes. From the Iroquois and the Mohawk tribes—which were the strongest of the six nations whose activities in the colonial wars determined America for the English instead of the French—there has come forth a young Indian princess who has buried the hatchet forever. She was fired with an ambition to show the artistic side of Indian life and approached her task with perfect assurance, simplicity and spontaneity.

She possesses a natural sense of rhythm and music realization that most dancers require years to master before they show an artistic grace that equals the highest art. The gorgeous display of colors such as surrounded the Indians in their native life presents a stage setting that should appeal to everyone. Her work has been greatly approved by, and she has received tokens of appreciation from, the best judges of the terpsichorean art in the leading cities of Europe. Her physique is so beautiful and well proportioned that she presents an attractive picture from any angle and in any garb. (Illus. 251.) Her ability is such that she can dance appropriately to any music she hears. But, on our American stage, her "Indian Act" is not favored and she has been reduced to jazz and buck and wing dances.

Among the Indians the girls were not supposed to dance. Their part consisted of slight rhythmic lifts of the shoulders with slight knee bendings and head tossings in time to the song and dance the men were performing. (Illus. 252.) It was the braves who did the dancing and strutting about. Therefore, White Deer has been exhibiting the dances of the male Indians. Her father, a famous dancer among the Mohawk chiefs, taught her many of the interpretive dances which might have died with him. One of these dances, peculiar only to the chiefs, was the staff dance, or the dance with the flag. Few people know that the Indians had a flag. It consisted of a long stick with eagle feathers attached. (Illus. 253.) In this dance the chief enacted many of his brave exploits and the most important facts in the history of his life were brought out.

The dance among the Indians has a deep significance and is at times quite awe inspiring. Almost every emotion and phase of life are interpreted by dance and appropriate song. Because early observers did not understand the significance of the Indian dances and possessed

Princess White Deer

no artistic sense they condemned and misinterpreted it as wild and meaningless raving. According to White Deer, most of the Indian dances are built each around a unique step which might be termed the keynote of the sketch. Through the entire dance the same step is continued and the head, arms, body and facial expressions, along with appropriate paraphernalia, help to convey the dancer's meaning. There are the corn dance, the thanksgivings dance, the wedding dance, the staff dance, the braves' dance (Illus. 254), and many others which do not permit of description here. White Deer has made a selection of the most typical and picturesque movements of the various dances and assembled them into a few attractive composites of her own which she can perform with the vim and wild abandon of the worthiest brave. The wonderful muscular development she possesses speaks volumes for her type of work. There is so much action in most of these dances that it assures a more nearly harmonious development than any other style except possibly certain acrobatic features of the eccentric dance.

White Deer has come out of the wilds to offer the best of the artistic side of Indian life and hopes that in this way the ancient hatred, prejudices and misunderstandings will be cleared away between the paleface and the red man. She believes we should exchange ideas instead of bullets. But, instead of the reception and appreciation she expected and deserves she finds herself constrained to perform attractions of the lowest standard. Is the American public too blind to appreciate and grant the consideration her efforts and material merit?

It may seem strange to the reader to find so much said about a few styles of dance in a book that purports to limit itself to the health side of activities. It is important that we try to get together all the elements that will give us a national folk dance or dances. At present the eccentric style bids fair to prove the foundation of our future folk dance, if any is ever to appear. In any case there are elements of the last two dances that should be included.

Folk dances, like favorite old folk songs, will always remain popular among those who appreciate the real in the traditional. All nations but ours have had some folk dances. We cannot enter into a lengthy description or analysis of all of these but we might say a few words about some of the most typical. From the vigorous Hungarian and Russian Cossack dances to the colonial minuets, there have been all kinds and grades of activity, of course, mainly of the legs. At any rate, many of these dances have had great influence in preserving the best phases of the life of various nations. Among the most picturesque of these have been the Swedish and the Polish folk dances. Besides the old songs and tunes that have been preserved with these dances, the colorful costumes that belong to various clans, or cantons, or families give us pleasure. Illustration 255 shows Martha Hedman dressed in one of the Swedish folk dance costumes.

The Polish folk dance is an excellent example to consider. Poland is famous for its musicians and for its music with its national note of melancholy. For centuries Poland has been regarded as the buffer state between Germany and Russia. The country has been used as a sort of football by these two more powerful neighbors, and many years ago she was deprived of her independence. Her present status is but a continuation of the trials that this nation has endured for centuries. As a result of the long continued uncertainties and oft-repeated shifts in the nation's life, the people have developed in their suffering a certain mixture of hope and doubt. The women especially have reflected the nation's life, because they, more than the men, have stood the brunt of the sufferings and disappointments. Balzac has described the Polish woman, as an "Angel through love; demon through fantasy; child through faith; sage through experience; man through brain; woman through heart; giant through hope; mother through sorrow; poet through dreams." Because they feel less responsibility, the men of Poland do not reflect the national composite nature.

In the universal and complete trouble of Poland the peasants and royalty were brought into close relation. The beautiful national dances of the country, which seem like attempts to drown sorrow and disappointment by living over the old glorious days, were performed by all alike, peasants and nobles frequently taking part in the same dances. In the early days these dances were performed to vocal music and later to instrumental accompaniment.

The polonaise is characteristic of the ancestral splendor of the country. In the early days it formed a sort of court dance when all, from the highest officials to the lowest and meanest of the court personnel, marched solemnly before the king and queen. The proud spirit of an independent western people was always manifested in this dance. The costumes worn added greatly to the beauty with their slight touch of the oriental. At first, the marching part of the polonaise was done with weapons, which were laid aside for the dance proper. The ancient custom in which the couple of the highest rank was followed by the others in order of their rank is still observed. The beautiful polonaise of Chopin, in its various forms, reflects the spirit of the old aristocracy.

The mazurka, which is a typically Polish dance, is full of life and expression and reflects the popular mind more than any other. (Illus. 256.) The name, which means turning around, or perplexity, indicates the wild, romping nature of the dance. It is danced in sets of four, six or eight couples. It is full of motion and expresses rustic qualities with warlike and sad passages. Some of the more popular conceptions express love, sorrows and regrets of exile. The various mazurkas were once named after great personages, such as generals and statesmen. The mazurka used to be danced to old Christmas tunes, but the modern developments have been very

Martha Hedman
Folk Dance
Costume
Credit Gentle N.Y.

255

256

Marie Houyng

much improved by the musical accompaniments provided by Polish composers. Chopin has composed mazurkas that added a melancholy beauty to the dance.

It will be a long time before our nation develops a folk dance that will reflect as accurately its national experiences as the mazurka has done for Poland. But we are a young nation and have not yet found ourselves in an artistic sense. When we do, it will be through efforts and developments from within our borders and not by purchasing the art treasures of Europe.

At present more and more of the European artists are settling within our borders and setting up their studios to teach or exhibit their work. The first and most important lesson they are teaching us is that there is no short cut or royal road to artistic achievement. Unless one is born a genius he must grind for years getting the foundation for a true artistic career. We have had a few extreme productions of our own brewing. La Sylphe, for instance, with a thorough European foundation mixed with our American eccentric style of dance, (Illus. 257), has proven a popular stage favorite for years, but she has exerted little influence toward a national school of dancing. Perhaps the reason is due to the fact that so much of her best exhibition work is of the contortionist type which is beyond the ability of everyone.

To become an expert interpretive dancer requires more than a mere wish and a fat purse. One who lacks good health is handicapped in dancing as in any other pursuit. Too much dancing, even of the classical interpretive type, will not furnish a well-proportioned physique. The very best exponents of the best modern schools of dancing do not often show a balanced development. Many are wonderful performers but their legs are so out of proportion with their upper body that they often seem deformed. Pavlowa, however, one of the greatest dancers of all times and by far the best living dancer, possesses a well proportioned body of the grace-

La Sylphe

257

ful, slender type. (Illus. 258.) Pavlowa spent all her life, from the age of five, preparing for her career and her work consisted of a musical training as well as the daily grind of technique work. Not until she was past twenty was she permitted to exhibit in public. In this country there is such eagerness to rush a child to the stage that mothers will prefer to place their children in charge of teachers who have influence with stage managers rather than go to teachers who will compel them to drill daily in all the details of dancing fundamentals at the bar, (Illus. 259 and 260), or before a mirror, (Illus. 261). There is no other way to build up the correct dancing foundation except to practice daily, even by the hour, for many years, and thus render the body a genuine interpretive instrument to depict musical compositions so that any onlooker can understand them.

One of the chief troubles is that most people of this country believe that any graceful pose or attitude and series of bodily movements in time to any sort of music is dancing. There are many ambitious boys and girls who believe they are qualified for the stage after a course of twelve lessons under the instructions of impostors who capitalize such gullibility. Of course, when the dress parade idea predominates in their mothers' minds, there are many simple little dances of the Mother Goose interpretive type that can be mastered by the children and exhibited at tea parties and birthday parties and at exhibitions that end courses of lessons. With the beautiful children growing up all about us, it requires little effort to display attractive sights. (Illus. 262.) But, if ever we are to have a school of dancing that will truly represent America, it will have to be a final composite form with elements of all the nationalities and traits that make up our nation. What this will finally be no one would dare predict.

For our future American national dance there must be a solid foundation laid in the coming generation. In all properly conducted education we proceed from the

Anna Pavlowa

258

general to the special to the general again. The kinder-garten is the place where little children begin to control the use of their hands and to discern colors and master various fundamentals that form a foundation for the grade studies. At the beginning of the year the work should be of a general nature. Then the special work that each or the majority need most is given. Toward the end of the year we find the general and more amusing work. The same rule applies in gymnastics, both in each lesson and in a season's work. The body is set for the specific work by movements that fix the posture and correct the carriage of the entire body.

In dancing about the same rule applies. The children are first given free standing work until they have mastered enough sense of rhythm, balance and general muscular control to have a real concept of what is expected of them in a dancing sense. When the children have mastered these fundamentals they are ready for the work at the bar which enables the pupils to isolate the muscular effort to special movements that finally establish precision and perfect control. They consist of rond-de-jambes, toe balances, arabesques and other limbering and control exercises. These are repeated over and over and such work at the bar is continued all through a dancer's career. Indeed, this kind of daily work is as essential to a dancer as finger exercises are to the pianist. As time goes on, of course, these bar exercises become more intricate, but they are never aban-doned without detriment to the dancer's grace and skill.

EURHYTHMICS.

One of the most important elements for building the future American dancing school is the study of the Eurhythmics of Jacques Dalcroze. This form of training bids fair to revolutionize training for the dancing art and for a musical education. His work also borders on the dramatic and is essential to the best work in this field also.

In our first chapter it was explained why music has little value in gymnastics. From an educational viewpoint, for bringing about a close affiliation between the brain and the muscles, music has no value in gymnastics. If one thinks of an exhibition in club swinging, wand drills or set and memorized calisthenics, where the object is primarily to please the audience, music is fitting. But it must never be forgotten that in order to perform well to music a pupil must have his movements memorized and he must fit his actions to the tempo of the music, thus requiring no mental concentration on his work. If his movements were not memorized but are to be done to music, his mind is divided at best between the music and the movements. Therefore, for bringing about the closest relation between the mind and the muscles, to acquire a physique that is a perfect tool to the brain, the best type of gymnastics is the kind done to command, and not to music or in imitation of the instructor.

When it comes to training a child for music or dancing, however, the problem takes a new aspect. In establishing a real sense of rhythm and tone values the greatest difficulty for the average child is to master the lengths and values of notes and rests. This is far more difficult than reading the musical scale. Most graduates of our musical conservatories are clever technicians but seldom complete musicians. Most dancers, interpretive, acrobatic or otherwise, possess great ability for performing leg divertisements but rarely do they display evidence of a real grasp of the full value of the musical composition to which they perform. In the dancer the rhythm may be felt but it is not expressed appropriately because the proper co-operation between brain and muscle was not established correctly or early enough. Even music masters, with a complete knowledge of music and supplied with all the musicians' technical equipment, cannot do themselves and their musicians justice at times, because they lack the finer muscular sense development required to convey their meaning while leading.

The most perfect interpreter of good music is the human body, but it must have been trained carefully and for a long time in sensing notes and tone values. The grand opera of the future shall be very different from the present standard, not in composition but in interpretation. This shall be brought about when every student of music—vocal or instrumental—dancing or dramatic interpretation has been trained in eurhythmics. As one of the most important steps to perfect rhythmic realization, Dalcroze urges physical education so as to render the body a perfect physical instrument. Physical perfection and control are to interpretive dancing what harmony is to music.

The ultimate aim of eurhythmics is to develop pupils to the point where they will not only go through appropriate movements in correct time, but really feel the motive behind the musical composition. In the interpretive arts technicians are common but reasoners rare. As we have students and translators of Greek language but few interpreters of Greek thought, so do we have many who can perform cleverly upon a musical instrument, or sing or dance cleverly, but few who can grasp the spirit of the composer and render a correct interpretation. To get so in harmony with the feeling of the composer at the time he composed as to feel the naturalness of doing just what he did and nothing else is a quality which eurhythmics aims to develop and render common. The great composers were complete musicians, not merely technicians, and in certain moods they were irresistibly driven to give expression to their feelings through what we inherit as musical classics. Until our artists of interpretation and expression, bodily, vocal or instrumental, master all that eurhythmics is aiming at, every performance will leave one who understands, with the feeling of "room for improvement."

For best results eurhythmic training should begin early in life. The age of five is not too young. Children are made to march to music with changing rhythm.

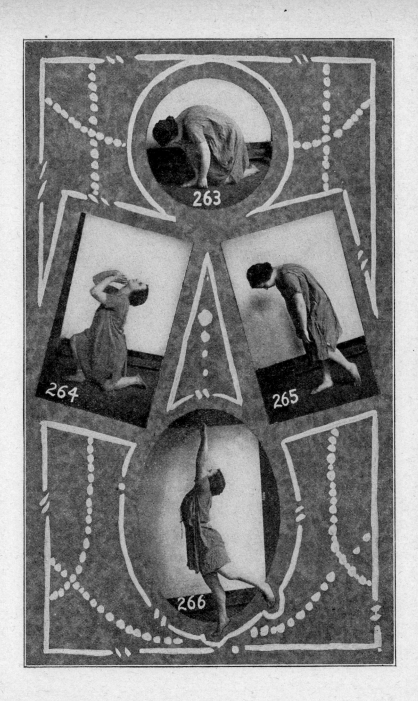

Various measures, notes and rests, at varied tempos are introduced and the pupils gradually trained to mark time to them. In marching the feet are moved to the note value and the head is nodded; the arms and later the body are moved to the various tempos. The pupils are thus taught to "realize" rhythm. As skill is acquired the pupils are given more complex work. For instance one arm may beat two, while the other beats three. While the arms are thus engaged in "realizing" different rhythms, the head may be nodding at some other rhythm and the body swaying at still another. Thus is efficiency in "realizing" the most complex rhythms acquired.

One point that is emphasized above all others in eurhythmic training is that motion must always continue in interpreting music. Attitudes are rests between motions and should not be mistaken nor used for the purpose of expression. Extremes of movements are not aimed at. What Dalcroze keeps iterating and reiterating is that a musical tone is expressed by shading movements. Shading movements to interpret music might be taken as the keynote of eurhythmics. The force or spirit or intensity of the music is expressed by motions or movements which begin from a starting point that is determined by the quality of the composition to be expressed. This is called the point of departure. For instance, the crescendo and diminuendo may be expressed in eurhythmics by making the point of departure lying down and coming up in a series of changes to sitting or kneeling; or beginning at kneeling and rising to erect and reaching posture and then to kneeling again (Illus. 263, 264, 265 and 266); or from standing with the arms out from the shoulders and elevating and bringing them down again in as many distinct steps as there are notes; or by walking and running or leaping and back to walking and standing, and so on. In each case the point of departure is to be determined by the music and its significance to the one who is interpreting it.

Briefly stated, the aim is to render the body a perfect

instrument for the brain and this is acquired by conscious effort and drilling at first, until to hear a tone or tune is to immediately interpret it in an automatic reactive manner. When a pupil has become proficient in eurhythmics he naturally favors classical music above the ragtime type of popular music. Of course, after one has mastered the power of expressing all types of rhythms and to correctly value tones and musical phrases, the next and most natural step in advance is to take up interpretive dancing or acting or singing. The physique, the feet, legs, arms, body work, the facial muscles of expression, and the appropriate dress, all play their part in good interpretive work.

The physiological effects of dancing in all forms resemble those of running. Of course, they all promote metabolism, increase respiration, develop endurance and, when they include upper body work or are combined with it, they are always beneficial. Anatomically speaking, much dancing will over develop the lower body and the legs and produce poor shoulders and arms. Dancing is usually amusing and exhilarating.

Therapeutically dancing is to be classified as leg work. The arms and body are employed but hardly to compare in amount with the foot and leg work. Interpretive dancing and eurhythmics develop a sense of rhythm, grace, self-command and harmony between the brain and the body. When dancing in all its best forms follows a perfect body development it puts a finishing touch and rounds out the individual's consummate skill. With a perfect physique, ability in artistic dancing means a completed physical being. Add to such a combination a well balanced and cultivated brain and you have a mature and complete personality. But such exists only in theory. Nearly all artistic dancers so far have possessed what has been politely called temperament, which simply means a narrow intellect with uncontrolled conceit.

Most people are not so much concerned about developing themselves into complete personalities as they are to learn some quick method for offsetting or concealing their weak points. The thing about physical training that interests girls most is how they can prevent or correct double chin, fill the hollows of their necks, reduce their waists or their hips with the least exertion possible. The next concern is how the greatest amusement may be obtained from exercise.

Boys, when questioned on physical training, think first of learning self-defense and next of acquiring enough skill and power to excel in some favorite sport. But the same rule holds for both boys and girls. To excel in any sport or game one must have a strong physique naturally and to keep up one's prowess there must be a constant practice of such work as will normalize and maintain the normal.

Summarizing this chapter briefly:

To develop strength of arm and wrist one should practice such play activities as hand wrestling and stick wrestling or bull-in-the-ring.

To improve equilibrium one should use hand wrestling, Indian club wrestling, chicken fight, skating or skiing.

To improve muscular sense nothing surpasses foil fencing, tennis, handball, volley ball, eurhythmics and interpretive dancing and golf.

For one who is awkward, clumsy and muscle-bound: fencing, handball, basketball, tennis, golf, skating, dancing and any activities that require nimbleness and accuracy without much strength are recommended.

For lumbago and stiff back: croquet is beneficial.

For the soft, cowardly boy: boxing, bag punching, wrestling, and any of the sports that require courage are important.

For the flat chested person: canoeing, boxing and bag punching will prove helpful.

To develop courage and self-reliance practice boxing, bag punching, wrestling, jiu-jitsu, single stick, broad sword fencing, skiing, skating and swimming.

To develop hardiness the anaemic or consumptive type should use snow-shoeing, skiing, skating, bag punching, rowing, canoeing and camping.

To develop self-control and a sense of fair play: all games are excellent but especially golf, tennis and boxing.

To develop grit and stick-to-it-iveness or perseverance are bull-in-the-ring, high diving, ski jumping, college football, boxing, wrestling, stick wrestling, tug-of-war, swimming and rowing.

To develop endurance: running and all running games, lively dances, bag punching, swimming and skating are helpful.

To develop concentration: use baseball, lacrosse, tennis and fencing.

For neurasthenics we advise: baseball, tennis, handball, volley ball, medicine ball, hang-tag and horseback riding.

To correct round or drooping shoulders practice: breast-stroke swimming, arch ball, throwing the medicine ball overhead, rowing and hang-tag.

To promote combativeness and fair play combined, most athletic feats, football, playground football, boxing and all competitive activities are excellent.

For general development use: swimming, canoeing and camping, horseback riding, eurhythmics and all activities, or a few selected ones balanced by special work.

The rule to follow is to determine in what respect one is weak and then practice the games, sports or play activities that require activity of the type of the weakness one would correct. The general rule governing the effects of gymnastics applies with special force in the play field.

CHAPTER IV.

MEDICAL GYMNASTICS

"Medical gymnastics," says Baron Posse, "means systematic exercise of the muscles and other tissues for therapeutic purposes. While no distinct line can be drawn between hygienic and medical gymnastics, it will however be found that a majority of the medico-gymnastic procedures differ from ordinary gymnastics, even though these are used as auxiliaries in special cases." Perhaps as clear a line of demarcation as can be drawn might be indicated in the statement that any movement, passive or active, prescribed or practiced for corrective or curative purposes would come in the category of medical gymnastics; while any movement, or procedure, practiced simply to promote or maintain health in the individual would be classified as hygienic. Therefore, the purpose for which a movement is employed determines whether it is medical or hygienic.

Medical gymnastics includes, besides auxiliary gymnastic procedures, all massage procedures. These are friction, kneading, circumduction, pressure, percussion and vibration; all of which may be regarded as passive exercise of the muscles. Massage makes it possible for the average healthy person to keep in good state of health without exertion, if he has recourse to treatment periodically as many do. Since the muscles must be used to be healthy, and since many people are lazy or indifferent in this respect, the masseur has a fruitful field before him. But the financial is the least important feature of massage.

Massage is extremely useful on many cases, especially where there is soreness or inflammation, as in sprained ankle, lumbago, or over-exhausted muscles. It is true that massage is in many respects but a general procedure, as compared to the specific procedures of osteopathy. But it is also true that massage becomes a useful adjunct to much osteopathic treatment, under the term, manipulation. It is usually employed in relaxing muscles previous to lesion setting.

"Through the Middle Ages, massage was followed by the monks in the monasteries, and by priests, who had the reputation of healing diseases by the laying on of hands. Ling became interested in this method of healing as a result of having rheumatism in his shoulder. He began fencing and his ailment grew better. He continued to fence and in a short time the rheumatism had disappeared. Although he was not a physician, Ling had a knowledge of anatomy and physiology, and he at once started his investigations which were to be of such benefit to mankind." Although he claims to have based most of his work upon the physiology of a century ago, nevertheless, with the new discoveries and rapid development of this science, his system, though in most particulars unaltered, is still in accord with the physiology of today.

Before considering the details of each division of massage, it might be well to consider briefly some of the latest findings in this science.

Graham, in "Recent Developments in Massage," tells of Mosso and Maggiora of Turin, who carried on several experiments and report, among other findings, their observation of the fatigue curves of the right and left middle fingers. The test understands the maximum voluntary flexion every two seconds, with a weight of three kilos. Records were taken at 8 and 11 a. m. and 2 and 5 p. m. without massage. On the following day, under the same conditions, as the day previous, except that a friction and kneading of three minutes preceded the lifting, the average results proved that the muscles could do twice the work after massage.

Maggiora also proved that an extension of the period of massage did not improve the results. Five minutes seems the maximum period of massage for best results. Friction and percussion gave almost the same results; but kneading gave better results than these two, while alternating all three gave the best results of all.

It has been the writer's experience that massage is the most useful procedure in connection with athletes; or as a preparatory measure to heavy work of any kind. The rub-down of the average trainer accomplishes very little. But a scientific application of massage will bring excellent results: results that are impossible otherwise.

If a part is cold, extreme care should be taken before making a strenuous effort with it. Massage—that is, circumduction—should be used to draw the blood to it, and then exercise should warm it up to the proper state. The best procedures, if time permits, are kneading and circumduction.

During contraction of a muscle the cells swell, and at relaxation they contract again. During this process, a rapid exchange of tissue takes place, thus promoting metabolism. Properly regulated action will increase the number of muscle cells, and the general system is benefitted. But, in violent work, there is such a rapid breakdown of tissue that the waste material accumulates more rapidly than it can be gotten rid of; therefore soreness sets in. In such a case, and there are few conditions more common, there is not a more efficient procedure than proper massage.

Where a part is depleted, from fasting, malnutrition, over exertion, or during convalescence, massage is one of the best procedures. But in such cases, for best results, massage requires manual dexterity. And this can only be acquired by practice. Massage will promote nutrition, and hasten restoration in depleted parts. Even in cases where the patient has taken no food, a proper application of massage will temporarily restore normal strength.

Massage affects the blood flow primarily. Its effects upon the nerves are not so marked. Maggiora found that if the brachial artery is shut off so as to produce a local anaemia, the finger can contract eleven times; after a massage of three minutes, with the current still shut off, the finger could contract nine times. While in the normal state the finger contracted 265 times, thus proving the need of free blood supply.

It has been long recognized that massage improves muscle tone, postpones the onset of fatigue, or hastens recovery from it, and relieves pain. To prepare an athlete for a contest, a general massage treatment is unequalled in its effect. A student of the Posse Gymnasium, during a gymnastic exhibition, found that his arms felt so weak that he could not perform his feats. We took him to another room where we thoroughly kneaded his arms for about five minutes, with the result that the athlete excelled his previous performances.

After a hard contest, or feat of some kind, or after a heavy day's work a few minutes kneading of the affected muscles will enable the subject to repeat or continue his performance.

Massage is a form of passive exercise, as already said, but it is better than the active kind in that it feeds the muscular tissue, and at the same time produces less fatigue or waste of nervous flow or tearing down of tissue. It increases the number of red and white corpuscles, removes peripheral resistance, hastens the blood flow and thus stimulates the circulation, nutrition and excretion. It is not as specific as osteopathy in these last three respects, but it is a very valuable adjunct.

PASSIVE PROCEDURES.

Friction: Very little need be said about friction. Friction simply means a rubbing or stroking of a part with one or both hands, together or alternately, in the

direction of the venous blood flow, or along the path
of a nerve. Graham says that "the manner in which
a carpenter uses his plane represents this to-and-fro
movement very well." The pressure should not be so
great as to chafe the skin. Where friction has to be
prolonged as in severe sprain, or "house-maid's knee,"
cocoa-butter or vaseline should be used.

The effect of friction is very soothing. The skin
temperature is raised; effusions and exudations are
pushed along in the capillaries; the brain and cord are
mildly stimulated; ordinarily the cutaneous nerves are
soothed, but in pathologic conditions, as neurasthenia,
these nerves are irritated.

Friction may be used as a finishing up of kneading,
or as a primary procedure to lead up to kneading, which
is deeper in its effect. This applies particularly in such
cases as sprains and various inflammations.

Kneading: Proper kneading is done so that the
pressure is given in the direction of the venous current.
Begin nearest the heart in whatever member or region
of the body you are kneading and press the tissues heart-
ward. Give two or three squeezes and then move the
hand about half its width, away from the heart, giving
a new series of rotary squeezings and then moving the
hand again. Thus one works away from the heart, but
at each manipulation squeezes toward it. The hand
should not glide over the skin, but rather move the skin
and surface tissues over the deeper ones. As much tissues as the hand will hold or as the tissues will permit,
should be grasped. On large surfaces, as the back and
chest, the flesh cannot be picked up, but the flat of the
hand is used to press the flesh on the bones in a rotary
motion. On the arms and legs, the hands may be used
simultaneously or alternately, each grasping all the tissue
possible between the heel of the hand and the cushions
of the fingers. The thumb acts as a fifth finger, rather
than in opposition to them. Wherever possible the flesh
is stretched from the bone and moved in as large a

circle as possible without gliding on the skin, the squeezing coming as it moves heart-ward.

The chief effect of kneading is not on the arteries and large veins where the flow is rapid, but on the capillaries where the flow is very slow. By beginning nearest the heart, the capillaries are emptied in one region and as the hand is moved away and presses from below a double force works to empty the tissue. There is a suction force above and a pressure from below. Traveling down a limb in this way, the hand overlapping the portion already kneaded each time it is moved, will bring about quicker and more complete results than the old method of beginning at the extremities and moving toward the heart.

In giving a *general treatment* to get the best results in the quickest time, treat as follows: Left arm, left leg, right arm, right leg, chest, abdomen, back, and last, the neck and head. In each part give whatever procedures are necessary.

In *treating the arms,* begin at the shoulder, and travel to the fingers, the pressure being upward while the hands move downward. The same rule holds for the legs. Whatever part or region is to be drained of its old blood and supplied with new, the pressure should always be applied first nearest its outlet.

The part kneaded determines the portion of the hand used. On large surfaces the entire hand is used flat, pressing against the bones. Sometimes both hands are employed separately, moving simultaneously, or alternately. Or, to exert more pressure, one hand may be used to press the other. As the hands are used in this way, wherever possible, the tissues should be picked up and given the circular squeeze. For example, in kneading the chest, with the flat of the hand or the cushions of the fingers, as the swollen portion of the pectoral muscle is gone over, it should be picked up and treated as the muscles of the arms or legs.

Without going into minute detail the general rule

is to fit the hand to the part treated. On large surfaces, the entire hand; on smaller, the cushions of the fingers and heel of the hand; on smaller still, the ball of the thumb against one or more fingers; on the face, about the eyes, and regions where no flesh can be picked up the pressure is applied gently with the tips of the fingers. Therefore, if one knows the general direction of the venous flow and fits the hand to the part treated, being careful not to glide on the skin, he has the essentials of good kneading.

In *kneading the abdomen,* for constipation, the general rule of kneading holds good; that is, to start near the outlet. The principle is very much the same as in emptying a thin rubber tube filled with putty. The best way is not to begin at the distal end from the outlet and attempt to move the entire column at once, but, begin a short distance from the outlet and squeeze out a small portion of the mass. Then, move back and squeeze a little more, and so on, until the entire mass has been moved, section by section. One begins at the sigmoid flexure and, with a circular motion, presses the bolus toward the rectum. Press two or three times in one spot then move away. The pressure is kept up in the direction of the rectum but the hands gradually travel back from the sigmoid flexure up the descending, transverse and ascending colons. Much special kneading is necessary at the region of the caecum as well as at the sigmoid flexure. Impaction is very common in these parts as a result of chronic constipation. Many a patient has been operated on for appendicitis when his only trouble was a caecum inflamed from impaction.

Kneading of the small intestines is neither as important nor difficult as that of the large intestine. It is given to stimulate peristalsis rather than to mechanically empty this region. There are two methods of applying it. One is to press transversely with the hand in a back and forth motion; that is, with the operator standing at the patient's right side, the heel of the hand would press the small intestines from the right side toward the left, and then, as the hand is pulled back, the fingers then dig deeply to the left of the small intestines and then draw them toward the right. The second method is to describe a circle with the edge of the hand along the margin of the small intestinal area, pressing toward the umbilicus with whatever part of the hand is touching. As this kneading is applied one describes as large a circle as possible with the hand, so that the heel of the hand, then the outside edge of the thumb, the finger tips and the ulna side of the hand successively press the intestines in a concentric circle.

Circumduction is commonly called rolling of a joint. Posse's definition is quite explicit: "Some part of the body describes, with a longitudinal axis, the surface of an imaginary cone, the base of which is at the free end of the part moved, and the apex at the joint in which the movement takes place. Circumduction can be active or passive."

In giving passive circumduction one hand steadies the moving joint while the other grasps near the next. The speed is less for a large than for a small limb. The circle should be as large as the joint permits or as its effects demand. The duration is limited by the sensation of resistance. When applied, as in stiff joints, to promote freedom of action, it is slow. When applied to reduce the blood supply in a part it is comparatively slow. The act of slowly describing a large circle with a limb alternately stretches and contracts the blood vessels and then hastens the circulation away from it. But rapid circumduction, through centrifugal force, holds or draws blood to a part.

Circumduction, it may be said, produces about the same results as kneading, only it affects the deeper and larger vessels to a stronger degree. It promotes absorption of nourishment from the blood, renders more pliable the tendons, ligaments and fasciae, removes articular adhesions, makes the cartilages thinner and when prolonged, it induces relaxation of attention and acts as a hypnotic.

It may thus be used as a soporific; as a regulator of circulation; as a substitute for, or as preparatory to, kneading.

Active circumduction, that is, where the pupil or patient executes a circumductory movement unassisted, has different effects than passive. It retards the venous circulation in the moving part, because of the active muscular contraction around the articulations. The flow to the active part increases according to the speed of motion. The cerebral influence to the part increases. The heart's action is accelerated through increased arterial resistance. The prolonged movement will produce hyperemia in the active part. Thus, its effect is the reverse of passive circumduction.

As nothing in medical gymnastics on *nerve pressure* would add to the repertoire of the up-to-date physician, we shall omit a discussion on this subject. All superficial nerves are accessible for either stimulation or inhibition. To inhibit pain, gradually increase your pressure on the nerve center or trunk; hold firmly for perhaps fifteen to thirty seconds; then gradually reduce the pressure. To suddenly apply and remove deep pressure has the effect of stimulation, and increases rather than soothes pain. To stimulate a nerve center or trunk apply intermittent or vibratory pressure.

Percussion, commonly called hacking, is very general in its effect, and deserves little consideration. It is divided into digital, ulna, palmar and fistic. The digital type is given with the tips of the fingers, on the head and sternum. Short percussion has the effect of stimulation on the nerves, produces constriction of the blood vessels, and tends to loosen phlegm and mucus in bronchitis. Therefore, digital percussion of the head would tend to reduce congestion; of the chest, it would promote expulsion of catarrhal accumulations. Prolonged percussion produces vaso-dilation and has a soothing or inhibitory effect on the nerves.

In every type of percussion the wrist is loose, and the hand kept quite limp, so that the effect may be penetrating without bruising. In applying the digital type, the wrist is loose and the tips of the fingers are struck smartly against the part treated. In the ulna type, the wrist is loose, the fingers are spread apart and slightly flexed, and the outside edge of the little finger strikes the part treated. As the little finger strikes, the others simultaneously close up on it to increase the penetrating impact, with a dry, bony sound. Ulna percussion is particularly useful when applied in thoracic troubles, and along paralyzed or weak nerve paths. Palmar percussion is a form of slapping with the wrist held loose. Its only use in osteopathy is in conjunction with ulna percussion of the chest. It is applied at the lateral costal region to promote coughing and expectoration. Fistic percussion is given by striking the palmar side of the closed fist, with the wrist held loose, over the sacral area. It is applied to a patient who is in knee-chest position, when treating retroversion uteri. As the right hand percusses, the left hand is employed at the abdomen to give a traction to the patient's viscera away from the pelvis.

Vibration: In medical gymnastics vibration is usually applied manually, but physicians who use vibration, with very few exceptions, use the electric vibrator. The advantages of the medical gymnastic method lie in the fact that the hand can be better adapted to a given surface than the applicator of a vibrator.

In favor of the mechanical vibrator, it can be said that the vibration, though not so fine, is more even, and it can be prolonged indefinitely. The operator, when giving manual vibration, becomes easily exhausted and, when he has treated a few cases, his vibration becomes irregular and less effective. This cannot be charged against mechanical vibration.

The effects of vibration are to promote metabolism, increase mobility in a part, break up adhesions, change neurition and increase venous circulation. It stimulates paralyzed parts, acts as a counter-irritant and promotes resorption or repair. Short vibration tends to stimulate both the nerves and local blood circulation by producing vaso-constriction. Prolonged vibration has the opposite effect.

ACTIVE MOVEMENTS.

As already stated, all movements which are performed by the operator, without any effort on the part of the patient, are passive. But if the patient performs, or mentally tries to perform, a movement, it is active. A patient, as for instance, a paralytic, may strive harder than a healthy person to perform a given movement without getting any response in his muscles, but the fact that he wills it makes the movement active. This statement may seem paradoxical, but it is nevertheless true. All active movements begin and end in the brain. That some active movements originate in the spinal cord, is true; such movements are active, but also reflex or automatic movements. The active movement under discussion is the kind which the patient makes a conscious mental effort to perform. So that, as in the case of the paralytic, even though his muscles do not respond to the will, still, the fact that he wills a movement makes it active. This feature is particularly important in the treatment of paralysis. If the operator takes hold of the part, and tells the paralytic to perform a certain movement and, while the patient is mentally striving to perform it, he performs it for him, the result is to gradually re-establish a relation between the brain and the muscle. Whether one re-establishes a new nerve path, or restores a deranged nerve, is not clear, but it has been the writer's experience that when this principle is followed in treating paralytics, greater improvement results than by any other method. Movements which the patient makes a conscious effort to perform but which, owing to his incapacity, have to be performed by the operator, are called assistive.

In the assistive movement we have the conscious mental effort, and the response in the shape of the movement, even though performed by an outside power. Besides the assistive movement, we have the single and the resistive.

Active movements are further divided into excentric and concentric, and, in respect to the single, the static type. These forms of movements, from the contraction standpoint, have been explained in Chapter I.

Under medical gymnastics then, we have the passive and the active movements. The active movements and their subdivisions have been considered, but a word or two may be added in regard to the single and the resistive types. The single is where the patient, or pupil, performs the entire movement without any outside help or resistance. All educational or free standing gymnastics, such as those explained in Chapter II, are examples of this type. The resistive type is the most important in medical gymnastics. In these movements the operator guides, and at the same time resists, the effort of the patient. The amount of force or resistance used is regulated by the strength of the patient. They should always begin and end gently, and they should be smooth and even. In applying a course of treatments where resistive movements are indicated, it generally follows that these movements are at first excentric, then, concentric. In many cases they are concentric from the beginning; mild at first, then, increasing gently in force.

The general effects of active movements are to increase cerebration, promote or re-establish co-ordination, increase voluntary control, and promote motor, and lessen sensory irritability. On the circulation, their effect is to increase blood pressure and heart beat. They improve metabolism by rapidly tearing down old cells and promoting newer and fresher cell life. That is why rational exercises so tend to rejuvenate all who practice them. They tend to harden fibrous tissue, render muscular tissue more efficient and healthy, lessen adipose tissue and promote general excretion. The local effect of an active movement is to increase the blood flow to the part used, promote nutrition, neurition and muscular sense.

In medical gymnastics, active movements are used to increase arterial circulation, increase nutritive activity, promote cerebro-motor activity and develop efficiency. In a local sense they are used to increase absorption and nutrition, cultivate motor innervation, increase muscular strength, and restore absent movements.

In giving resistive movements Posse says: "that the resistance should always be applied at right angles to its lever (so that the lever of the weight does not change during the movement), as this gives a steadier movement, one more comfortable to the patient. The only change in the resistance should be one of pressure (weight), which is made to increase as the lever of the power grows (toward the middle of the movement). The resistance throughout should be so moderated as to give a movement of uniform velocity—slow rather than quick —and motions done in pushes and starts, or with so much resistance as to cause vibration should be discouraged, as neither is in accordance with the laws of normal muscular contraction and produce undesirable effects on muscle fibre and motor nerve, they usually being types of overwork. Moderate the resistance carefully according to the patient's strength, and remember that medical gymnastics are not combative exercises (wrestling) but that even a slight resistance is enough to increase the muscular activity with consequent effects over that of ordinary everyday life, or of single movements. The purpose is to get some exaggeration in the effect of the active disorders; on the other hand, the resistance is often driven to the patient's utmost power (his nervous capacity inside the limits of normal fatigue), since it is then a question of getting the utmost pressure for displacement of bone, cartilage, etc."

There are many typical movements which might be described in detail, but it is not necessary to our purpose to do so. Before going into the application of general principles a word or two on the general divisions might be said. In resistive movements we have those of flexion and extension, elevation and depression, adduction and abduction, and rotation. Those of flexion and extension explain themselves. They should be given, in regular progression in force and complexity, according to the strength and need of the patient or pupil. For circulatory purposes in depleted conditions these movements should be applied first to the smaller joints, and later to the larger, until the trunk flexions and extensions can be practiced. In restoring movement or control of a part incapacitated by such ailments as paralysis, dislocation or fracture, begin the movements at the larger joints and progress to the smaller. The movements of elevation and depression are such as lifting of the arms or legs, or coming up to sitting from lying position, and these can be applied according to the needs. Those of adduction and abduction explain themselves, if the meaning of the word is understood, and as more will be said about these under corrective gymnastics, this will suffice here. The movements of rotation are such as turning of the arm to palm up or down, or turning the head or trunk from side to side against resistance.

All of these movements will be brought into application in the chapter on Corrective Gymnastics, and it is well to say, that they are divided into such classes chiefly for convenience in study. In actual bed-side or office practice these names and classifications are forgotten, and movements are given according to each case. The thing to do is to consider carefully what muscles are weak and what strong, for what effect resistive movements are given (that is, whether for control, strength or circulatory effects), and then apply them accordingly.

RESPIRATORY EXERCISES.

There is one class of movements which should be considered by itself before taking up the application of medical gymnastics. Respiratory exercises are particularly important, because, as Ling explained, all gymnastic movements are, in a sense, respiratory exercises.

If a movement tends in any way to impede or prevent free respiration it should be rejected or delayed until one has reached that stage of development which enables him to perform it without interfering with free respiration. No matter what exercise or work one is performing, he should seldom allow himself to assume an attitude which in any way compresses the chest and causes him to hold the breath.

Respiratory exercises are deep respiration accompanied by some movement of the arms, head, or arms and legs together, which will emphasize the expansion and increase the suppleness of the thorax. These are divided into the assistive type, in which the operator does the expanding of the chest while the patient inhales; the single, as in educational or home gymnastics; and the resistive type, in which the pupil or operator offers some resistance to the movement performed to increase the chest expansion.

The effects of respiratory exercises are many. Most important is that they produce thoracic aspiration. Thoracic aspiration, in plain words, means a suction force created in the thorax by the great expansion of the capillaries in the lungs. As the chest expands and the lungs become filled with air, the minute blood vessels are caused to expand also and their capacity is increased so that a greater amount than ordinary is drawn to them, and thus this suction force decreases the work of the heart. The general pressure in the veins is diminished, the contraction of the right ventricle is lessened and the blood passes onward as water in a force pump. At exhalation the reverse is true. Therefore, "by making inhalation comparatively rapid, its effects may be heightened; and by making the exhalation slow, its effect of retardation can be reduced to a minimum, so that the total effect of the respiratory movement will be diminution of blood pressure and acceleration of the venous circulation," and, at the same time, there will be a quickening of the lymphatic circulation. Oxygenation of the blood and general elimination are increased.

Respiratory exercises should be applied for general effects on venous circulation. They should be used at the beginning, middle and end of a daily program, and in a treatment, they are often advisable after every other movement. These exercises are sometimes used especially to affect the portal circulation, the heart beat and to expand the air cells. Their effect on the portal circulation will bear explanation. Through assistive chest expansion the suction in the vena cava becomes five or six times as great as it is during ordinary respiration. This suction empties especially the hepatic veins, which are the nearest vessels flowing to the heart and thus the flow through the liver is hastened.

In administering or practicing respiratory exercises it is well to remember that these movements should follow the rhythm of the individual's respiration. Exhalation should always be slow, but inhalation is somewhat quickened. There should be a short pause after the exhalation, as occurs naturally. Overlooking this pause or prolonging the duration of the respiratory exercises will make the patient dizzy, owing to the rush of blood to the head.

The most important respiratory exercises will be explained as they apply to given cases in the next chapter.

CHAPTER V.

APPLICATION OF MEDICAL GYMNASTICS IN OSTEOPATHY.

It would be a waste of time and an imposition upon the reader's patience to attempt to present the details of applied medical gymnastics in every form of disease where it is indicated. This has been done by a number of writers to whom the novice is referred. And for the healer of any school who has a knowledge of diseases and their treatment, it is useless to enter into the details of technique in each disease. Therefore, we shall consider the application of medical gymnastics in a general sense, and as they apply to classes of diseases. But in a few cases, where special explanation is advisable, it will be briefly given.

DISORDERS OF CIRCULATION.

Among diseases of the circulation, myocarditis and endocarditis can be benefitted by passive procedures such as kneading, circumduction, and respiratory movements which will hasten the return current. The treatment for endocarditis may be a little stronger than in myocarditis. While the heart is being relieved by the procedures that help it perform its work, easy resistive movements of the extremities may be applied, and thus, the entire system, heart included, is gradually brought to normal.

Valvular heart troubles may be treated somewhat as myocarditis and endocarditis. A typical program following the osteopathic adjustment which will always help is as follows:

(1) Passive shoulder circumduction and respiration.

(2) Circumduction of the ankle joint.

(3) Kneading of the arms and legs.

(4) As (1).

(5) Circumduction of the hip joints.

(6) Circumduction of the shoulder joints.

(7) As (1).

(8) Abdominal kneading.

(9) Resistive foot and wrist flexion and extension.

(10) Heart vibration.

(11) As (1).

(12) Seventh cervical percussion.

Such a program might be repeated at each treatment. Progress consists of increase in force of the resistive movements of the smaller joints, gradually leading up to resistive movements of the larger joints. In treating heart cases it is well to warn the patient against raising the arms above shoulder height. All procedures or exercises which call for arm elevation while the patient is sitting or standing should be avoided for a long time as least.

In *fatty infiltration* of the *heart*, progressive educational gymnastic work is useful. Sometimes the course of treatment might begin by such a program as in valvular heart trouble, and gradually lead up to single exercises as explained in Chapter II.

In *arteriosclerosis*, friction, kneading, light resistive movements of extension, such foods and procedures as promote elimination through the skin and kidney are helpful.

In *varicose* veins, elevate the part and give special kneading, then keep an elastic bandage on between treatments. At night, cold pack is beneficial. The mattress should be elevated from the hips to the feet so that the feet are kept eighteen inches higher than the hips.

While discussing circulatory conditions it might be well to sum up a few of the general principles that are worth remembering. Movements of any part of the body will usually increase the circulation toward and within it. We can decrease the amount of blood in a part by giving passive movement here and an active movement at a distal part. Muscular contraction alternately extends and shortens the blood vessels, forming a suction, and it thus hastens the circulation, especially in the veins. As a rule, active movements increase both the circulation and heart action, while passive movements increase the circulation and at the same time reduce the action of the heart.

By increasing the blood supply to any part, whether muscular, glandular, nervous or bony, we get increased nutrition. By hastening the venous circulation waste matter is hurried away to the excretory organs. All active movements are stimulants to muscular, bony and other tissues and increase their growth and quality.

Movements stimulate absorption and hasten endosmosis, diffusion and filtration. The osteopath can promote all of them through the vasomotor system. But absorption cannot be induced beyond a certain point. The law of supply and demand settles this question. While the osteopathic procedures may bring about a supply to the tissues, they cannot correspondingly increase the demand. But the increase of waste caused by muscular action, and the expenditure of the blood elements thus promoted, must be replaced by material from the digestive organs. Hence, the connection between the muscular action and absorption is direct. Therefore, exercise increases appetite, aids digestion, by stimulating the secretions necessary to the process of digestion, and it also increases defecation and general excretion.

It is true that the condition and functioning of the nerves have much to do with the condition of the body. But it is also true that if they lack sufficient exercise, the nerves soon begin to degenerate and grow irritable and abnormally sensitive.

DISORDERS OF RESPIRATION.

Before entering into a discussion of specific ailments, let us consider a few typical respiratory exercises.

(1) Wing sitting shoulder circumduction with respiration. (Illus. 267.) The operator stands back of the patient who is sitting on a stool and, grasping the latter's axilla, he lifts the shoulders up and back, while the patient inhales deeply; then, as he releases his hold, and the shoulders are allowed to resume normal, the patient exhales slowly. In this exercise the patient should be thoroughly relaxed. This movement is good for a tired patient, or for one who has a weak heart. Or it is commonly used wherever any of the effects of passive respiration are needed. The effect of this movement may be increased by the operator leaning back and forcing his hip against the patient's shoulders, thus creating a strong expansion of the chest.

(2) Rest sitting shoulder circumduction is the same as wing sitting, except that the patient's hands are locked back of the head and the elbows kept well back. This movement is stronger in its effect than the preceding and, in heart cases, or any depleted condition, it should not be applied except to increase the force of the former.

(3) Reclining two arm elevation. The patient is reclining, or lying with arms loose at the sides. The operator grasps his hands and lifts his arms forward-upward and stretches them up and back at the end of the movement. The patient inhales deeply during this movement. As the patient exhales, the operator carries his arms down along the couch or bed to first position. In this movement the arms of the patient travel about the same path as in Illustration 268, but he is passive, while the operator puts him through it.

This movement, and all like it, tend to supple and expand the chest, stretch the chest muscles and the forced inspiration not only produces thoracic aspiration, thus aiding the circulation, but the vacuum caused in the chest by the forced expansion and the general lifting of the upper intestinal organs also tends to lift the viscera and relieve pressure on the pelvic organs. This movement is valuable in uterine anteversion. The more horizontal the body in this movement, the stronger the effect on the viscera.

(4) Wing standing heel elevation with chest expansion. (Illus. 269.) In this movement the patient stands in good posture, with the hands on the hips. The operator stands behind him and grasps his elbows. Then, he commands the patient to rise on the toes and inhale and, as the patient does so, he forces the elbows together from behind, thus producing great chest expansion. As the patient exhales and lowers his heels the operator releases his pressure. This movement is useful in producing chest expansion, correcting round shoulders, and for general chest development.

(5) Rest standing chest expansion is another movement of the same class as the last. (Illus. 270.) The operator stands on a stool close to and behind the patient. He braces his body back of the patient's shoulders and grasps his arms below the axilla. Then, as the patient inhales, he forces the arms up and back, at the same time pushing forward with his body, thus producing strong chest expansion and, in a stronger degree, all the effects of wing standing shoulder circumduction. This movement might be made still stronger by lifting the patient's arms up overhead and lifting him up almost off the floor as the operator leans back. (Illus. 271.) For general chest development and shoulder correction, this is a powerful exercise. Many variations of this movement can be given. Instead of standing, the patient might sit, while the operator stands behind him, and thus produces the expansion.

(6) Stretch grasp standing chest expansion. (Illus. 272.) The patient grasps a bar or trapeze overhead and, as he inhales, the operator pulls, or pushes, him forward (apply the force first between the lower part

of the scapulae), until he is forced to rise onto the toes. As the operator releases the pressure, the patient exhales. This is a powerful movement, which exaggerates all the effects of those described above. To increase the strength of this movement, the operator might push until the patient's feet leave the floor (Illus. 273), thus giving an extremely powerful respiratory and expansive movement. For general chest and lung development in advanced pupils, or in patients who can stand violent work, this class of movements is indicated.

The above movements are merely types illustrating the various classes in quality and force. They can be varied to suit the patient's need. Progress can be made through repetition, by the force applied by the operator, or by the change in the position of the arms and body in applying them.

Another type of movements, which is given for expulsion of mucus and phlegm rather than for the general effects aimed at in the above, may be illustrated.

(7) Standing arm elevation sideways, with chest percussion. (Illus. 274.) The operator stands in front of the patient and, as the latter raises his arms sideways to shoulder height and inhales, he percusses lightly over the sternal area. As the patient exhales, he may place his hands at the sides of the patient's thorax and vibrate or shake them. This usually loosens the phlegm in lung troubles, such as bronchitis, and gives rise to a cough that soon rids the patient of much waste material. Even in cases where consumption is threatened such a treatment might help. But of course, in advanced cases, where there is danger of hemorrhage, and in any serious lung condition, such a movement is contra-indicated.

This same movement may be increased in its effect by the operator placing his hands just back of the patient's axilla, inside his arms, and, as the patient inhales, he gives a palmar percussion down along the lower ribs and forward to the sternum where he winds up with ulnar percussion up the sternum. Then, as the patient exhales, he applies vibration with his hands at the lateral costal area.

This movement can be made still stronger by the patient raising his arms up, overhead, instead of only to shoulder height. Or, any of the above movements can be made stronger by the aid of an assistant who will do the operator's work while the latter guides and percusses or vibrates.

So much for description of movements. The reader ought to be able to develop others now, or alter them into harder or easier ones according to his needs.

In *rhinitis,* all osteopaths use friction along the facial veins to promote good drainage from the head. Vibration over the frontal area and deep respiratory exercises should also be used.

In such ailments as *laryngitis, pharyngitis* and *tonsilitis,* thorough kneading of the neck muscles, to relax them and free the circulation, along with proper osteopathic adjustment will aid materially in removing the trouble. Vibration applied over the inflamed area is very soothing and helpful. In kneading the neck, stand at the head of the patient, who is lying on the back, place the fingers under and along the back of the neck, then lift his head up and away from the body, so that its weight is borne by the hands. Thus you give a stretching of the neck and at the same time the thumbs are busy kneading the front of the neck and throat. A rolling downward pressure with the fingers may accompany the downward pressure of the thumbs. Or, while kneading in this way, you may at the same time stretch the neck from side to side. Set whatever lesions exist, and then lift the ribs.

In *pleurisy,* kneading and vibration help to relieve the patient by their soothing effect.

In *deformity* resulting *from pleurisy,* that is, where one side of the chest shows a depressed or contracted condition, special respiratory exercises to expand the depressed side and thus create a balanced condition, should be prescribed. There are many possibilities here to the medical gymnast which the "ten finger" osteopath cannot do much with. As a type of possible respiratory movements, suppose the right upper costals to be depressed; let the patient turn to the right, then bend the head backward and slightly to the left and at the same time let him extend the arms sideways, palms turned up, inhaling deeply as the arms are extended. As the arms are flexed let him exhale. (Illus. 275.)

Another exercise of this type would be to place the left hand on the hip, the right hand back of the head, the body turned to the right, and the head bent as in the above movement. While holding this position, with the mind fixed on expanding the depressed area, let him breathe deeply a few times. (Illus. 276.) Several others can be worked out in this way. (See one-sided chest defects, Chapter VI.)

For *bronchitis,* thorough kneading of the chest muscles, with digital percussion over the sternum and general chest vibration, will be found helpful. Respiratory exercises with percussion are indicated here.

In *emphysema,* give percussion over the entire thorax and resistive arm adduction. Resistive arm adduction means to resist while the patient draws the arms forward, keeping the elbows straight, starting from the position with the arms out at the sides. This will tend to contract the chest muscles and thus indirectly force the lungs to normal by constricting the chest.

Tuberculosis of the *lungs* is one of those diseases for which every school of healing claims the best cure, but if you come down to elementals, you will find that all resort to about the same forces in successfully treating it. The prevention of tuberculosis is more important than its cure. The successful cure, in cases that are not too far advanced, consists in placing the patient in an environment where he will get an abundance of fresh air, good food, water, bathing and outdoor life generally. But although these forces prevent or cure such trouble, there should be added a course in educational gymnastics and osteopathy such as would establish proper adjustment and develop the respiratory mechanism. There is nothing so effective in preventing tuberculosis as good power of respiration, which means a supple, well developed chest and shoulders. It seems needless to repeat here that all respiration should be done through the nose. Chest percussion and vibration, and such exercises as trunk rotation and sideways flexion that directly affect the digestive organs, are all beneficial. Therefore, a general course in health culture in all its aspects is indicated in the consumptive constitution. In children who show a tendency to consumption because of a narrow or phthisical thorax, an early start should be made to correct this defect and prevent the disease. Besides sunshine, fresh air, outdoor activity and plenty of vegetables in the food, corrective exercises to broaden the chest should be used. The outline given for consumptives in Chapter IX should be followed.

In advanced cases of consumption, where outdoor life and vigorous activity are too violent, the passive procedures of medical gymnastics with mild resistive exercises, are indicated. It is useless to outline the specific procedures that might be used, for the reader can easily scheme out the proper ones. The aim should be not to work about the lungs too much because of danger of hemorrhage, but to draw the blood away from this inflamed area by circumduction and resistive movements of the legs. Let the lungs regulate themselves after everything possible has been done to remove obstacles. Placing a weak patient on the back so that the ribs are held elevated will cause the apices of the lungs to work normally and, as recovery sets in, progression in procedures is indicated.

DISORDERS OF DIGESTION.

The chief cause of these disorders is improper food, or incompatible food combinations. Many healers seem to take no cognizance of this important fact and though they claim that they watch the patient's dietary still they proceed with their treatment in a way that indicates that they only consider the condition of the digestive organs themselves as important in their treatment. Many physicians suffer from indigestion and constipation, themselves; yet they treat others for these ills, paying almost no attention to the food question.

The simple rules: of thorough mastication; little or no drink at meals; plenty of vegetable foods to balance the dietary and thus furnish the essential salts; simple food combinations; reduction in quantity of starchy foods, and observance of such laws of compatibility of foods as seldom to allow starches and acids or starches and sugars to be eaten at the same meal; of eating one's fill of only one or two compatible dishes, are seldom observed.

Granted that the dietary is attended to properly, there should be no digestive trouble present, unless there are maladjustments that come within the osteopathic province. If all seems right and yet there is a sluggishness in the digestive function, such movements as trunk rotation, sideways flexion, abdominal exercises, respiratory exercises, outdoor activity and games, are very helpful.

In *enteralgia,* or intestinal cramps, let the patient lean forward, the arms hanging loose and relaxed, and knead the abdomen, inhibit sub-sternally, give vibration, and active trunk circumduction. Such respiratory exercises as passive shoulder circumduction are beneficial.

In *constipation,* laxative foods, as figs, prunes, green onions, celery, or raw salads, are indicated. The patient should make an entire meal of such foods. If necessary, several meals of just such foods are helpful. Many live exclusively on raw foods and, if they take them in proper combinations and proportion, only benefits result. But most people like rich combinations of cooked foods and constipation is perhaps the most common ailment known.

Deep abdominal kneading, trunk movements, rotation and sideways flexion, abdominal exercises, jumping, active games, etc., with proper diet are indicated. If this does not bring results, and if osteopathy is slow, a very valuable procedure consists in lying on the back, with the pelvis raised, then inject about a quart or more of warm water and, as it passes in, knead the abdomen deeply for a few minutes so as to mix well and soften the bolus. Such a procedure is more effective and less potent of evil results than salts, or copious enemas.

In *prolapsus* of the *rectum*, place the patient in knee-chest position (Illus. 277) and give strong sacral percussion. Give percussion in incline stoop fall position. (Illus. 278.) If the patient is strong enough give him back, neck and elbow stand (Illus. 279), with various leg exercises. Also give lying on the back, arms extended, grasping some object, and in this position let him practice various leg elevations, such as are explained in Chapter VII. Vibration of the perineum and rectal vibration are helpful. To give rectal vibration insert a rectal applicator and vibrate while the patient is in back, neck and elbow position, or in incline lying position. The cold sitz bath to finish this treatment, or taken at night before retiring, is a valuable adjunct.

In *hemorrhoids,* fasting, gradual evacuation of bowels, internal rectal kneading, perineal vibration and sitz bath will help any treatment or constitute an effective treatment in themselves. What was said about food in constipation applies here.

DISORDERS OF NEURITION.

Neurasthenia can be divided into two types, (1) that of *spinal* origin, (2) that of *cerebral* origin. The first type means an exhausted physique that requires rest and restorative procedures. In this type the treatment should consist largely of rest, soothing massage, with the proper osteopathic procedures, and the treatment should gradually be worked up to active gymnastics.

The cerebral type is found in those whose daily occupation requires a great deal of mental and little physical work. The motor nerves may even have undergone fatty degeneration, while the sensory nerves have increased in irritability. In the cerebral type the treatment from the beginning includes educational gymnastics. Such work as outlined in Chapter II illustrates the line of procedure.

Sciatica is an ailment which osteopathy can successfully treat. All the soothing procedures in the treatment of this ailment have been known to medical gymnasts. The setting of lumbar and hip lesions is what osteopathy has added to this treatment. The setting of the innominate or lumbar lesions does not always relieve the pain at once. To aid this, foot and hip extension, slow leg movements, deep kneading and inhibition are the soothing procedures.

In *neuritis,* in conjunction with osteopathic adjustment, inhibition, kneading and passive extension of the muscles and nerves are always beneficial. A peculiarity of neuritis is that activity will relieve, while rest of the part will increase, the pain. In this respect neuritis may be easily differentiated from rheumatism.

Paralyses of *central origin* can be but little benefitted by medical gymnastics. Those of *superficial,* or *spinal origin,* may be greatly aided. Proceed with your treatment by kneading, circumduction, percussion and vibration, and then give assistive and later resistive movements of the weak parts. If there is any voluntary motion of the fingers or toes possible the cells are not entirely destroyed and a new nerve path may be developed or the old one restored. But it takes time and perseverance. Though the patient cannot move a part in a given direction, through partial or complete atrophy, still the connection between the brain and motor nerves may be improved by properly applied assistive movements. Suppose the flexors of the forearm to be paralyzed, the arm will remain straight, owing to the inability of the flexors to counteract the normal tonic contraction of the extensors. In this case, if the patient is told to flex the arm, and he makes a voluntary effort to do so, the fact that he wills it makes it an active movement, though the arm remains unflexed. Now, with this process going on in the patient's brain, if the operator flexes the arm for him, through his assistance there is produced an active movement. There is the stimulus sent forth from the brain and the response in the arm, and thus, there gradually grows the normal connection between the center and the periphery. This rule holds good with any part of the body which should normally be under control of the will.

Chorea, or *St. Vitus' dance,* is greatly benefitted by educational gymnastics, which establish proper voluntary control of the muscles and thus create a condition under which the individual can inhibit his muscles from the wasting, meaningless jerks. Not much gymnastic work should be given at first, as the patient is easily exhausted. There is so much nervous energy wasted through the uncontrolled movements that little is left for directed effort. It is well at first to give movements of muscular isolation.

Epilepsy is an affliction that few forms of treatment can help. During an epileptic fit little can be done except to loosen the clothing; allow a free supply of fresh air and keep the patient from injuring himself. Forcing the edge of a folded towel or stout piece of rubber or wood between the teeth will keep him from gnawing the tongue or lips, and keeping the head low, and turned to one side to permit the saliva and phlegm to pass out will prevent choking.

Between attacks is the time to bring proper treatment to bear. The first and most important thing is to reduce the amount of food consumed, and to regulate the diet with a view to supplying necessary elements in their proper proportion. Properly applied gymnastics to develop control will be found invaluable in this condition. Competitive sports, and every form of exciting exertion, should be eliminated. The combined application of water, sun and air baths, diet, exercise and osteopathy will give the very best results.

Infantile paralysis can be greatly aided during the reconstruction period. Gentle kneading and percussion, leading gradually to resistive movements, combined with the necessary osteopathic procedures will be found most efficacious. Find out what movements are difficult and gradually develop the muscles so as to restore control of these movements. It may be possible to develop new cell areas and thus restore proper nerve control of atrophied parts by assistive movements described in the treatment of paralysis. In your treatment begin at the central and work toward the peripheral end of a limb or part. For instance, suppose the legs are paralyzed, begin at the hip joints with assistive exercise, then resistive. As soon as it is controlled to any degree, begin with the knee, etc.

Whether we should expect complete restoration of motion after an attack of infantile paralysis depends upon the extent of the paralysis. Light cases will be fully repaired, but extreme cases will never fully recover even after years of treatment, though they may show marked improvement for a time. Whatever the degree of paralysis, whether the prognosis is good or bad, and by whatever method the patient is treated, medical gymnastics is always indicated, for, even if the patient does not improve, such treatment will prevent further degeneration.

Locomotor ataxia is a symptom, not a disease, and it is difficult to cure by any method, but nothing equals the combination of medical gymnastics and osteopathy. Where the case is so advanced as to be beyond recovery, properly applied treatment will at least delay progress of the disease and prolong life. But if there is any substance left to work on, the proper combination of medical gymnastics, by assistive, single and resistive movements will restore normal muscular control. It is well to teach the patient to regain his muscular control by such procedures as walking between a pair of rails for support, later with canes, and, as soon as possible, give educational gymnastics. Frenkel's system of treatment for locomotor ataxia, which has proven so efficient, is based upon the progressive gymnastic idea.

In advanced cases the treatment follows the same general laws as in paralysis. Begin with the larger joints and assist in the simplest movements until a slight degree of control appears; then resist as far as the patient can go and assist further. As soon as the patient has acquired sufficient control to begin work by himself, prescribe exercises that he is to practice every day. (See Chapter IX.) In prescribing home exercises advise the patient to practice movements that require more concentration than ordinary movements of daily life.

A peculiarity about the treatment of locomotor ataxia is that progress is very rapid for three or four weeks and then there is a pause in progress, during which treatment does not seem effective. This pause lasts about two weeks, when progress again becomes comparatively rapid. This should be made plain to the patient so that he will not become discouraged when progress ceases temporarily.

Occupational neuroses, as the name indicates, are not due so much to a misplaced vertebra, or to an abnormal dietary, as to the one-sided muscular exertion necessitated by one's occupation. Such neuroses are the result of long continued over use of a few muscles, and a partial or complete under use and neglect of their antagonists. Lesion setting will accomplish little if antagonistic muscular exercise is not given. To inhibit osteopathically, or to inject morphine may relieve the pain, but the cure lies in creating normal balance between the over used muscles and their antagonists. Such exercises as resistive extension of the fingers and thumb, all together against an elastic band, or, one at a time, against specific resistive movements, will restore harmony. Study to find out just which muscles are affected and, by isolating the action of their antagonists, restore equilibrium.

Hysteria is an unbalanced mental condition which could be materially benefitted by properly regulated educational gymnastics. Where harmony exists between the body and the mind such a condition as hysteria is impossible. One of the quickest ways of restoring harmony, where it does not exist, is to appeal to the mind through the physical.

Cephalgia, or sick-headache, can be relieved by friction downward along the facial and cervical veins, scraping the fingers through the hair from the forehead to the occiput, and slow head circumduction. These procedures will be found helpful and, though palliative in nature, should be included with the osteopathic adjustment.

Fractures should be treated by gentle kneading from the second or third week after the accident happened. Complete restoration of movement as well as knitting of the bone can best be effected in this way. To attempt to restore motion before the bone is completely knitted would be dangerous. But gentle kneading will aid in the osseous reconstruction. The bandages and splints should be removed for the treatment and replaced after as much as possible of the exudation has been removed and good circulation restored. As soon as the bone is set, that is, at about the third or fourth week, gentle passive movement can be safely given; then, assistive, single and resistive, according to the patient's strength and needs.

Knead and percuss the flabby muscles. Be sure of the axes of motion and the joints' limitations before attempting active movements. Make use of a lubricant in treating the skin, and stretch it as much as the patient can stand, so as to break up all adhesions and thus hasten complete restoration of motion.

Kneading is the best procedure to remove venous

congestions and edema, but one should stop at enough. In fact, it is better to do too little than too much, for too much kneading may delay, or even prevent the healing process.

Dislocations should be treated by massage. After the dislocated joint has been reduced, the tenderness can be best removed by kneading and slow circumduction.

Sprains. The sooner a sprain is treated the better. If treatment can be applied immediately after the sprain occurs there will result but little inconvenience from it. It is well, if convenient, to first bare the joint and allow a stream of cold water to run on it. If the patient cannot stand the stream directly over the sprain, have him place the joint in a vessel of water and allow the water to flow into the vessel in a steady stream from several minutes up to half an hour. While the part is under water it is well to grasp it and give gentle squeezing of the swelling toward the venous flow.

After bathing the joint in cold water give plenty of massage to reduce the swelling as much as possible. In your massage use a lubricant to save the skin, because a thorough treatment requires much deep kneading over a small area and it is easy to bore through the skin unless the lubricant is used. In the case of an ankle sprain, start with gentle friction upward, beginning at the spot below the swelling and stroking upward, several inches. Then, beginning at about the middle of the leg, knead deeply, pressure upward, and work down to the seat of the trouble, over which the kneading must be very gentle at first. Gradually increase the force of the kneading over the swelling until it is strong enough to remove the exudation and thus reduce the swelling. After treating the part, bandage it tightly and at night apply a cold pack. Apply the pack tightly. Allow the ankle to rest in the pack for perhaps 24 hours; then treat it again. But there is no reason why such a sprain should not be treated more frequently. It is often possible to restore an ankle fully within a day or two by two or three treatments each day.

From the beginning, give passive movement, and if not too painful, resistive movement to the sprained part. In applying circumduction, do not carry the foot inside the median line, for the structures on the outer side of the ankle have been stretched or ruptured by the sprain and they need no further stretching. Encourage the patient to use the ankle a great deal despite the pain. Let him walk as soon as he is able to stand, even if he requires the use of canes. Encourage all forms of activity of the ankle except the statical. After the second day, even in the most severe type of sprain, the part should be used. The average sprain can be healed in from four to seven days. In the hip or shoulder more time is required. With proper treatment, no joint need remain stiff as the result of a sprain. If a sprained part is left to itself, or is treated by the old method of immobilization, it will grow stiff and remain so for a long time. In many cases joints are stiffened for life as a result of improperly treated sprains.

In a *strain* of the muscles, ligaments, or tendons, kneading for ten or fifteen-minute periods will soon restore the part. A strain is usually accompanied by an osseous lesion which osteopathy can reduce. But kneading should be resorted to for the strained tissues.

Synovitis is best handled by rest and kneading of the part. It usually occurs in a tendon that has been overtaxed and what it needs most is rest from the straining work and a good blood supply such as kneading will create. The application of a cold pack, at night, is also helpful.

Bursitis, or "house-maid's knee," is inflammation of the bursa of the patella, with a fluid deposit about the joint. Deep kneading with percussion and immobilization for a time will be found helpful. At times the application of splints and elastic bandage is indicated for a continued pressure to keep out the fluid. Dashing cold water on the knee after kneading will also aid recovery.

Rheumatism may be benefitted by kneading and vibration, as well as by osteopathy, but for permanent results, for the real cure, the diet has to be attended to. It is the writer's opinion based upon the experience of several years' practical demonstration that proper diet and exercise combined will do more toward eradicating and preventing rheumatism than all other so-called cures. Proper exercise means muscular movement based upon the needs of the individual. Proper diet means the consumption of plenty of green vegetables and fruits. Most people do not eat enough of these foods to supply the essential organic salts which keep the blood normal. Every day some green vegetables, such as lettuce, spinach, celery, onions, or cabbage, should be eaten. The more of these are eaten raw the better. Everyone needs them. No one who gets enough of these foods will suffer from inflammatory or articular rheumatism.

Arthritis deformans may be removed, or much benefitted, by proper diet along with local massage, wet packs, and constitutional osteopathic treatment. In smaller joints give principally passive procedures. In shrunken joints, graduated resistive movements are indicated. To break up adhesions, or lax contractures, mechanical vibration is a valuable adjunct. While the muscles are under forced extension, or the mobility of the joints is being restored, prolonged vibration is indicated.

In gout, constitutional treatment, regulated diet and educational gymnastics are indicated.

VARIOUS PTOSES.

There is a condition which seems to be on the increase in these days of Fords and other shaking means of transportation. This condition is called ptosis (gastroptosis and enteroptosis), or, in plain language, dropping of the stomach, or of the intestines, and sometimes of some of the other organs. The chief signs of such a condition are gas and distress after each meal, often vomiting, retching and heavy feeling at the stomach. Then there is usually constipation and later auto-intoxication or self-poisoning. The teeth are next likely to go bad and all the symptoms which were manifest are classified as results of focal infection. The teeth are never infected from without. It is the blood that first goes bad from lack of balanced food and the teeth, like every other tissue, become victims and not causes. Were there more attention paid to the balancing of foods to assure all the elements, and enough coarse foods to compel normal use of the teeth, there would never be such pus sacs at the roots of the teeth as result because the teeth are not used enough; then wholesale tooth extraction would never take place. From the standpoint of ptoses, however, we are now concerned with the prevention, or reparation, by natural methods, of the original weakness which preceded all the symptoms mentioned. And these symptoms and complications are not the only ones; in fact we might mention all the rectal conditions which orificial surgeons accept as causes, but which in reality are but results.

To prevent ptoses of any sort it is imperative that the muscles of the abdomen and waist be kept in tonic condition, because they are the natural supporters of the abdominal organs and unless they hold up the viscera these will settle down onto the pelvic roof and cause all manner of malpositions and displacements. First in importance in assuring normal support for the abdominal organs is the integrity of the region of the spine from which the nerves to the abdominal muscles and organs originate. If there are any bony lesions here the exercises or dieting practiced to relieve the digestive and postural abnormalities will prove of little avail. If these lesions are corrected, however, and the diet and exercises are practiced faithfully, surgery will never prove necessary, provided a suitable device is utilized to support these fallen organs until nature has regained general normal efficiency in this function.

The exercises which are of most value in this work are given in Chapter VII, in the treatment for inguinal hernia. The same exercises used for toning up the abdominal muscles will suffice. If one wishes for a greater variety, the program for obesity explained in Chapter IX will prove valuable. Before practicing any exercises one should lift up the fallen organs by assuming knee-chest position, illustrated in picture 277. While in this position, exhale completely and then flatten the abdomen. The suction force, resulting from the empty lungs and lifting of the diaphragm which must precede flattening of the abdomen, will lift all the fallen organs to their normal level or nearly to it. The patient then lies on his back and, with the hands, lifts the abdominal contents away from the symphasis pubis. Then the exercises are practiced for ten or fifteen minutes. These exercises should be practiced in the morning and at night before going to bed, but they must always be preceded by the lifting of the organs through knee-chest position and manual lifting.

It seems advisable to say that the position of the abdominal organs should be detected by percussion and, in case of doubt, by X-ray of the abdomen. This is essential to make sure of the habitual level of the stomach and transverse colon. After one knows the level of the stomach it is simple to determine where to begin and how much to raise the fallen organs at each application of the strips of adhesive plaster. There are many methods used for holding up fallen organs but none surpass the *right* use of adhesive plaster, if the patient's skin does not react unfavorably.

To apply adhesive strips for ptosis of the stomach and intestines, precede the application of the plaster by having the patient prepare in the same way as preceding exercises. After the knee-chest with exhalation, the operator should do a little lifting of the organs while the patient lies on the back, the knees bent. When the organs are lifted about two inches higher than they

were, stick two pieces of adhesive plaster of about three
by four inches in size, obliquely, one over each anterior
spine of the right and left ilia. (Illus. 280.) These
pieces will act as buffers to prevent rolling up of the
oblique strips to be applied next. Granted that the
stomach was low down, begin at the left inguinal region
and apply the plaster across and slightly obliquely upward to pass over the buffer piece just above the crest
of the right ilium and then onward up the back to the
left scapula, or just below it. The strip of plaster follows a line obliquely upward, so as to keep it from
wrinkling. This means that there is no arbitrary rule
except the general upward oblique direction, because
different people vary so in size and shape. (Illus. 281.)
The next strip of plaster is applied opposite the last;
that is, beginning at the right inguinal region, it is carried obliquely upward over the buffer piece at the left
ilium and passing just above the crest of the bone, around
the side and up the back, crossing over the other strip
and continuing to a point just below the right scapula.
(Illus. 282.) A strip of plaster, about two and a half to
three inches wide and long enough to nearly reach the
back at each side, is stuck on over the two oblique pieces
at the front. (Illus. 283.) This completes the job so
far as the stomach and intestinal support is concerned.
Should it be found desirable to hold up the lower intestines from bearing down over the roof of the pelvis, along
with this lifting of the abdominal organs, or even as a
procedure by itself, a band of plaster, about two and a
half to three inches in width and nearly long enough
to reach around the body, is placed with its lower edge
just above the line of the symphasis pubis and carried
horizontally and firmly around to the back. (Illus. 284.)
Before applying this strip of plaster there should be
placed a strip of gauze or cotton bandage over the pubic
hair so as to render removal easier when the plaster
has served its purpose. In all these cases, the plaster is
left on from one to two weeks and then removed, after

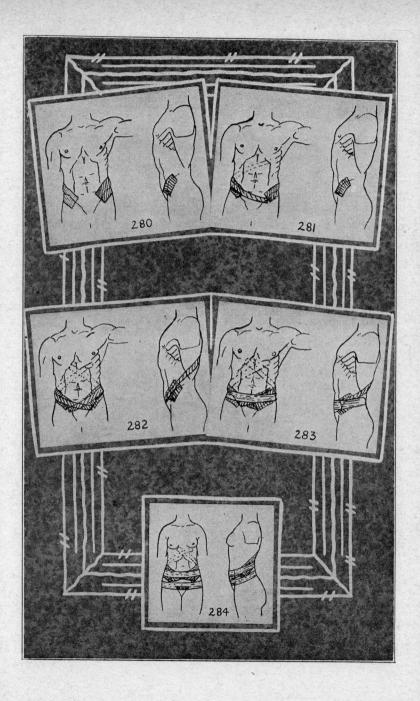

a hot bath, with naphtha or chloroform, which dissolves the adhesive part. Bathing is possible all the while one carries such plaster because it requires special pulling to loosen it. Should the edges roll up during a hot bath they are easily smoothed down again after the bath. In the case of ptoses the tapes are applied an inch or two higher each time they are changed, but, of course, the pelvic band is always applied at the same level.

It is extremely important in all cases in which the plaster strips are used for supporting the stomach and intestines to pay special attention to the patient's diet. Where there has existed a ptosis condition for a long time it has become nature's way to react by producing a great amount of gas daily which causes distress and oppression in the abdomen, not to mention gas pressure pain in the spleen and heart and interference with lower lung respiration. When the plaster strips are first applied, if one tries to accomplish too high a lift at the first application he is likely to increase the kind of distress from which the patient has suffered. Therefore, it is necessary to progress slowly and also see to it that all gas-producing food mixtures are eliminated and only such food eaten as will not distress.

CHAPTER VI.

CORRECTIVE GYMNASTICS.

Principles of Corrective Gymnastics.

Corrective gymnastics means gymnastics practiced to correct anatomical defects or deformities. Hygienic gymnastics are practiced primarily for health. Properly regulated hygienic gymnastics are always corrective in the sense that no movement is practiced which is doubtful or injurious in its effects.

According to sound gymnastic principles, the posture of the body during any exercise is considered of extreme importance in its relation to the results desired. There is a saying, an axiom, in fact, that the body at rest always tends to maintain the position it held during activity. Therefore, during exercise one should assume and preserve as nearly as possible throughout the exercise, the habitual posture of the body he would like to cultivate. By keeping this principle in mind one may transform any useful exercise into a corrective movement.

There are two ways of applying corrective gymnastics: one is by the individual himself, through his own efforts with or without apparatus; the other, by the properly applied movements resisted or exaggerated by the operator. Everyone who has given the matter a thought is conscious of his own defects, and if he will exercise with the idea in mind of developing the opposite condition to that of his defect, he can do a great deal for himself. The major part of one's success depends upon his own determination to succeed. With determination, the best results can be gained by resorting to daily individual effort and periodical aid from the medical gymnast.

In considering the principles of corrective gymnastics let us review briefly the anatomical mechanism involved. Every muscle or group of muscles pulling in one direction has an opposing muscle or group pulling in the opposite direction. When the individual's health is normal and the muscles are in perfect adjustment and proper tonicity, the position of the part they control will be normal. The adjustment of the bones is important, but the bones are really passive factors, and the normal position of a part is maintained by its bony structure if the muscles controlling this structure are in tonic state.

If the muscles lack this tonic state we find some defect in their antagonistic relation. One muscle, or set of muscles, is stronger or weaker than its antagonist and there is an unbalance, or shortening of the stronger and lengthening of the weaker side. Such deformities as result from this unbalance usually prove serious with the individual, although the ultimate result is so remote from the original cause that their relation is overlooked. But the damage is done just the same.

Among the deformities commonly found as a result of this unbalance are round-shoulders, drooping-head, drooping-shoulders, lateral curvature of the spine, swayback, bow-legs, knock-knees, pigeon-toes and others. These deformities cannot always be traced directly to an unbalanced antagonistic muscular relationship. But wherever we find these deformities, an unbalanced antagonistic relation exists between the muscles; that is, the muscles on the concave side of the deformity are shortened and those on the convex side are lengthened. Sometimes, after the bony structure has become set in its deformity, the muscles on the concave side are not only shortened, but they are also flabby, atrophied, or changed to fibrous tissue from lack of use, while those on the convex side, because of their over-use in simply supporting a part, are not only lengthened but hypertrophied as well. A thorough examination of a bad case of round-shoulders or scoliosis will bear out this fact.

As to the causes of these conditions, many might be mentioned, but we shall limit ourselves to general principles rather than specific cases. The osteopath needs little persuasion to be convinced of one of the most common, though, up to within the last few years, least understood, of causes—that is, the contraction of any muscle or group of muscles caused by the inflamed condition of the nerves controlling it. These nerves may be inflamed through various causes, but chiefly through some subluxation or mal-adjustment of the bones. Re-adjusting this part would have removed the inflammation and restored the muscles to normal tonicity. But, after this condition has obtained for a few years, simply re-setting the vertebra will not correct the deformity. Re-adjusting of the bones with re-establishing of the proper antagonistic relation between the muscles controlling the part will bring better results than either method used singly. The muscles must be restored to normal for a part to remain in proper adjustment after treatment.

The result of one-sided work is to create a lack of equilibrium in the anatomy of the individual. This lack of equilibrium results in deformity, and the deformity affects health or the resistive power of the body directly. The most important rule in correcting defects is that we should endeavor to contract the relaxed and relax the contracted. Note which muscles are weak and which strong, and strengthen the weak until they balance their antagonists. If one is in doubt as to how to proceed, he should note what movements he is most awkward in and practice those particularly; for we are weakest in the movements we need most, and the movements that are easiest to us are the ones least needed. By proceeding in this way one will create normal elasticity, restore structural balance, correct defects and promote health.

Applied Corrective Gymnastics.

DROOPING-HEAD.

This condition indicates that the muscles on the back of the neck are extended, allowing the head to hang forward. The side neck muscles (sterno-cleido-mastoids), attached to the sternum, clavicle and mastoid process of the occipital bone, are also relaxed, because as the head drops forward, the extremities of these muscles are brought nearer each other and this allows the sternum and the sternal ends of the ribs to drop. Therefore, flat chest and drooping head usually go together. To establish proper carriage of the head and chest, the muscles at the back of the neck must keep the head well back. The muscles at the sides and front of the neck attached to the chin must contract and keep the chin in. This fixes the upper attachment of the sterno-cleido-mastoid muscles far enough back for it to properly support the sternum.

Drooping-head is often the result of occupation which causes the head to be bent forward most of the time. Mental depression, bashfulness, will frequently cause one to droop the head forward with that familiar hang-dog expression.

To correct drooping-head we must strengthen the muscles of the neck, especially the erectors of the head. We must cultivate in the patient a consciousness of correct carriage of the head. This means more than the mere exercise indicated in such a case. It means developing courage, optimism, and pride in the personal appearance dependent upon posture. There are many books on the subject of success and optimism that would assist.

Among the special exercises indicated are resistive neck extension. This is done in standing (Illus. 285); stoop standing (Illus. 286); and reach grasp stoop standing (Illus. 287). Forward lying neck extension (Illus. 288) is also valuable.

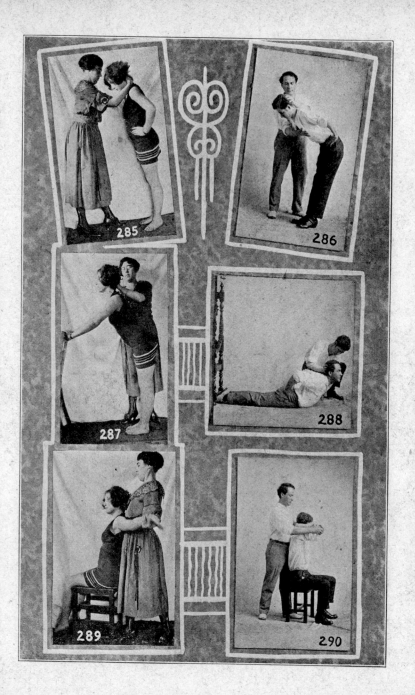

In each of the above the operator offers resistance.
Where the pupil has to depend upon himself, the
following exercises are valuable:

1. Head flexion backward. See Exercise 1, Lesson
II. (Illus. 40.)

2. Hands on the hips, bend the trunk forward from
the hips, keeping the head high. While holding this
position rotate the head to left and right.

3. Stand about a foot from the wall, facing away
from it, lean backward and rest the head against it.
Keep the arms at the side or on the hips. Now allow
the body to sag a little, and spring up to erect by a sudden contraction of the muscles of the back of the neck.

ROUND-SHOULDERS.

Strictly speaking, round-shoulders indicate a condition in which the chest muscles (transverse fibres of the
pectoralis and deltoid) are over-contracted and the posterior shoulder muscles (transverse fibres of the trapezius, supraspinatus, teres minor and posterior fibres of
the deltoid) are relaxed and the shoulders are drawn
forward, but not downward. Round-shoulders seldom
occur alone. It is usually accompanied by drooping-shoulders and drooping-head, and these conditions must
be overcome separately by their specific procedures.

As specific exercises to correct round-shoulders, the
following will be found effective:

I. Without apparatus or external resistance.

1. Arms forward, shoulder high, palms in. Fling
them sideways forcibly, turning the palms downward as
they move back. Isolate the exercise to the shoulders,
by keeping the chest forward, head erect and chin drawn
in during the exercise. See Exercise 4 (a), Lesson XV.

2. Body bent half-forward from the hips, arms forward as Exercise 1; practice the same arm movement.
See Exercise 8, Lesson VIII, Illus. 84.

3. Lying face down with a weight on the feet, bend
the arms forward and practice arm swimming.

4. Arms bent forward, carry them sideways slowly as you inhale deeply. As the arms travel back with this inhalation carry them as if pressing against something to emphasize the bulging forward of the chest.

5. Arms bent forward, fling them sideways forcibly as you lunge forward, first with the left and then the right foot. Exercise 2, Lesson XVI, Illus. 137.

II. Resistive.

1. Patient sitting on a stool, the operator standing behind him. Patient's arm forward from the shoulders. The operator offers resistance as the patient carries them sideways, and when the patient has carried his arms as far back as he can, the operator pulls them back as far as the pain in the stretched muscles will permit. (Illus. 289.) The patient's chin should be kept drawn in during this exercise. The resistance offered by the operator need not be great. This is no wrestling match. Only enough resistance is necessary to exercise the posterior shoulder muscles.

2. Patient sitting on a stool, fingers locked behind the head, elbows forward; head erect and chin in throughout the exercise. The operator stands behind and offers resistance as the patient carries the elbows back and then forces them back to hyperextension of the pectoral muscles. (Illus. 290 and 291.)

3. The patient standing, fingers locked behind the head. Operator stands behind him, on a stool if necessary, and resists as the patient carries the elbows back, then leans back and pulls the patient over his chest. (Illus. 292.)

4. Patient takes long lunge backward so that the forward knee is bent at right angle, the rear knee straight and the weight of the rear leg is supported on the toes. While balancing in this position, arm extended forward, the patient abducts the arms against the operator's resistance. (Illus. 293.)

5. Lying face down with a weight on the feet, the patient arches the body upward, raises the arms forward

and abducts the arms against resistance offered by the operator. (Illus. 294.)

III. With apparatus.

1. While facing a chest weight or elastic exerciser, the patient abducts the arms against the machine's resistance. (Illus. 295.)

2. Patient takes fall hang position and flexes the arms, keeping the elbows well out. Exercise 2 (b), Lesson XVI, Illus. 139 and 140.

3. Rowing, especially if the elbows are kept up as high as possible, is corrective of round-shoulders.

4. Standing in a swing and "pumping up" is also corrective of this defect.

DROOPING-SHOULDERS.

Drooping-shoulders usually accompany round-shoulders, but the muscles involved are different. In drooping-shoulders the lower or oblique fibres of the pectoralis major, the pectoralis minor and, to a certain extent, the coraco-brachialis muscles are at fault. They are shortened, often through over-development from such as parallel-bar work, and their antagonists, the posterior fibres of the deltoid, the lower oblique fibres of the trapezius and to some extent the latissimus dorsi, are weak and over-extended, thus allowing the shoulders to droop forward.

To overcome this condition we must employ such movements as cause forcible contraction of the posterior over-extended muscles and forcible, or passive, extension of the anterior shortened muscles.

I. Without apparatus or external resistance.

1. Alternate arm flinging forward-upward. Exercise 9, Lesson I, Illus. 37.

2. Arms forward from the shoulders, palms turned in. Keeping the chest well forward, head erect, chin in, weight on the balls of the feet, and, without moving any part of the body but the arms, fling the arms upward forcibly. Lower them slowly to shoulder height and repeat the fling a few times. (Illus. 296.)

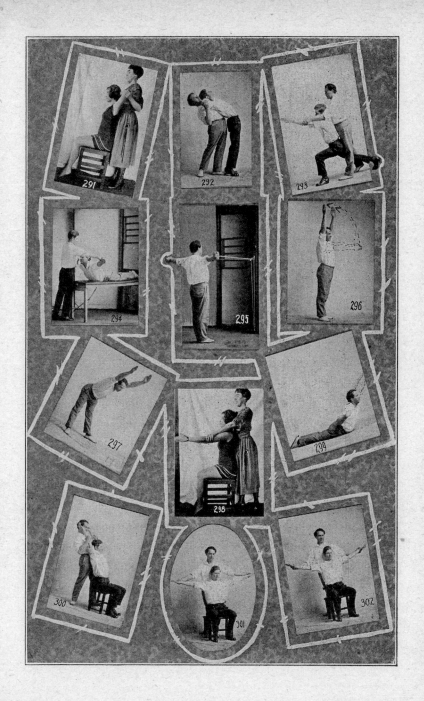

3. Arms shoulder high at sides, turn the palms forward-upward forcibly. This exercise should not be merely a turning of the palm by rotating the forearm, but a rotation from the shoulder. When done properly the muscles behind the shoulders and down the back to the waist are contracted forcibly with the upward turn of the palm.

4. Arms bent upward, bend the trunk half-forward from the hips. While holding this position extend the arms sideways, palms turned up. Illustration 72, with the heels together.

5. Arms shoulder high at sides, bend half-forward from the hips, and while holding this position turn the palms forward-upward forcibly. Follow the directions given for Exercise 3 of this series. Illustration 72 shows the position of the trunk, arms and hands when the palms are turned upward.

6. Arms shoulder high at sides, palms turned up, feet apart, trunk bent half-forward from the hips. (Illus. 72.) Preserving a good posture of the head, and carrying the arms in line with the ears, or back of them if possible, elevate the arms a few times. (Illus. 297.)

7. Lying face down with a weight on the feet, arms bent upward, arch the trunk upward, more from the shoulder and head region than from the waist and, while holding this position, extend the arms upward a few times. (Illus. 298.)

II. Resistive.

1. The patient sitting, or standing, with his arms straight forward. The operator, standing behind him, reaches forward, grasps his arms above the elbows (Illus. 299) and offers resistance as the patient elevates the arms, and when the patient has gone as high as he can the operator forces the arms back to hyper-extension of the chest muscles. (Illus. 300.)

2. Patient sitting, arms out at the sides. The operator stands behind and takes hold of the patient's hands, fingers at the palms, thumbs over the backs of the hands.

(Illus. 301.) As the patient turns the palms forward-upward, the operator offers resistance and when the patient has gone as far as he can the operator shifts his hold, bringing the thumbs in the patient's palms, fingers at the backs of the hands, and twists the patient's arms a little further. (Illus. 302.) In this movement the patient should preserve a good posture of the trunk and head, and perform the arm rotation by employing the muscles of the shoulders and back. See explanation to Exercise 11, Lesson II.

3. The patient stands with the trunk bent half-forward from the hips, arms forward from the shoulders. The operator stands to one side, places one hand lightly over the patient's inter-scapular region, and the other arm is held over and across the patient's arms. (Illus. 303.) As the patient elevates his arms the operator offers slight resistance. When the patient has elevated his arms as high as he can the operator shifts his resisting arm to the under side of the patient's arms and, while bearing down at the inter-scapular area, he forces the arms upward to hyperextension. (Illus. 304.) In this exercise the patient must preserve a good posture of the trunk and head. The position requires control and the operator should not make his resistance so strong as to cause the patient to assume a faulty posture.

4. The patient lunges forward with the left foot, the body is inclined in line with the backward leg. The arms forward as in the above exercise. The operator standing on one side offers resistance as the patient elevates the arms, following the observations on the above exercise. (Illus. 305.) This movement should be repeated with the right foot forward.

5. The patient takes a lunge backward sufficiently far to rest the weight on the toes of the rear foot, the rear knee straight, the knee and hip of the forward leg bent at right angles. The trunk is erect and the head kept high and erect throughout the exercise. The arms are forward from the shoulders. The operator stands

behind and offers resistance as the patient elevates his arms, carrying them back to hyperextension of the chest muscles.   (Illus. 306.)   Repeat the movement a few times with the right foot backward.   The patient must preserve good balance in this movement.

III. With apparatus.

1. While exercising with the chest weights or elastic exerciser, stand facing the machine and elevate the arms forward-upward.

2. Stand facing the exerciser, arms half-bent forward; carry the forearms to half-bent upward position. (Illus. 307.)

3. Arch hanging position; hold for a few minutes. (Illus. 152.)

4. Flinging a medicine ball, or weights, over head is excellent for both drooping-shoulders and kyphosis. Standing with feet apart, weight in the hands, lean forward, swinging the weight between the legs; suddenly erect the trunk with a full swing of the arms and fling the weight backward over the head.

KYPHOSIS.

Kyphosis is a marked abnormal posterior curvature of the dorsal spine.   The condition may be due to tuberculosis where gymnastics are contra-indicated.   It may be due to rachitis where gymnastics will be useless, unless a diet is followed which supplies the necessary bone-forming materials.   It may be due to occupation requiring a stooping forward, or to ignorance of proper standing posture, or to laziness.   The last type is amenable to gymnastics, especially in the young.   In grown up and old people the posture is hard to correct, though not always impossible.

Kyphosis should not be confused with round or drooping shoulders, though it usually accompanies these. It cannot be corrected so well by exercises for these conditions as it can by special exercises that localize the action particularly to the deformed part.

Specifically, kyphosis is not a shoulder defect, but a condition in which the spine is bent backward, between the shoulder-blades, to an abnormal degree. The sternum is usually depressed and the ribs overlap at the front, though, in some cases, the sternum stands forward high and prominent and the ribs are elevated, giving the entire thorax a barrel-shaped, bulky appearance. The muscles, especially in the common type of kyphosis— that is, where the back is round and the chest depressed —are elongated at the back. They are thick and firm and have extensibility without much contractility or recoil. The habitual posture of the body has kept them on a stretch, causing them to bear the entire weight of the upper body in a state of static, excentric and negative contraction. The chest muscles are usually shortened from lack of stretching through antagonistic force. Or they may be flabby and weak from lack of use altogether.

To correct kyphosis the exercises given for drooping-head are helpful. But there are a few special exercises that are more specific in their effects.

I. Exercises without apparatus or external resistance.

1. Flex the head backward as you inhale deeply. As Exercise 1, Lesson II, Illus. 40, with respiration.

2. Hands on the hips, trunk bent half-forward from the hips, keeping the chest as prominent as possible, head high, with chin drawn in, rotate the head from side to side. Exercise 8, Lesson III, Illus. 52.

3. Hands on the hips, arch the upper body backward. Exercise 6, Lesson I, Illus. 33.

4. Arms out at the sides, trunk bent half-forward from the hips; while holding this position, turn the palms forward-upward forcibly and at the same time bend the head backward. (Illus. 308.) In turning the palms upward make the muscles of the shoulders and back work forcibly.

5. Lying face down, arms out at the sides. Elevate the head without arching the trunk upward from the

hips. While keeping the head elevated rotate it from side to side, and at the same time turn the palms forward-upward.

(1) As you rotate the head to the left turn the palms upward, (2) as you rotate it forward, turn the palms down again, (3) as you rotate it to the right turn the palms upward and (4) as you rotate it forward, turn them down again, etc. (Illus. 309.)

II. Exercises with assistance and resistance.

1. The patient's arms are forward from the shoulders, the operator stands behind and resists as the patient raises the arms and flexes the head backward. When the patient has carried the arms as far as possible the operator forces the patient's spine forward by lifting him over his chest as the patient pulls back on his arms. (Illus. 310.)

2. The patient standing with hands on the hips. The operator stands at the patient's left, facing toward him, and places his left hand at the patient's chest and the right hand behind his head. As the patient inhales deeply he flexes his head backward against the operator's resistance. (Illus. 311.) The operator's left hand is used merely to steady the movement and brace the patient, the right hand does most of the work. The patient's endeavor should be to flex the head and upper back forcibly and at the same time inhale to elevate the sternum.

3. In this movement the operator should have an assistant. The patient stands with arms extended upward, the assistant assumes a firm position, one foot in front of the other behind the patient, and places his hands, one over the other, at the crest of the patient's curve. The patient bends backward, and as he does so, the operator, who is standing in an advantageous position, behind or beside the assistant, grasps the patient's arms and presses them back. (Illus. 312.)

4. The patient stands with arms extended upward. As he flexes forward, the operator, standing to his right,

places his left hand at the curvature and presses downward, while his right arm is held across and above the patient's elbows where he forces the arms upward. (Illus. 313.)

5. The patient is sitting on a stool; the operator stands behind and places his knee against the patient's curvature. He then lifts the patient's arms up and back as he presses forward with his knee. It is advisable to place a pad between the knee and the patient's back. (Illus. 314.)

III. Exercises with apparatus.

1. Patient in arch-hanging position, the operator resists as he flexes the head backward. (Illus. 315.)

2. Patient stands with arms extended upward, grasping a bar overhead. The operator stands behind and forces the spine forward by pressing at the curvature. (Illus. 316.)

3. Patient in arch-hanging position, head held high; he elevates the arms alternately, with head rotation. As the left hand is lifted, the head is rotated to the left; as the right is lifted, the head is rotated to the right, etc. (Illus. 317.)

4. Patient hanging, face out, with a pad behind the curvature. The operator forces the body backward to increase the correcting effect. (Illus. 318.) If there is a lordosis condition accompanying the kyphosis, the patient should draw up the knees against resistance, or raise the legs forward to horizontal, while hanging. (Illus. 319.)

SHALLOW CHEST.

Shallow chest means a condition in which the antero-posterior diameter of the chest is abnormally short. The term "flat chest" does not necessarily mean shallow chest. In kyphosis, for instance, the chest is usually flat in appearance because of the depressed rib condition, but the antero-posterior diameter may be normal, or even above normal. In shallow chest, both the sternum and dorsal spine are straight or nearly so. Sometimes, in

this defect, the dorsal spine is anterior instead of posterior, with the sternum straight or sunken.

Shallow chest is a difficult condition to correct by gymnastics alone. Osteopathy must play its part, but even the combination of these two frequently fails. Very little can ever be done for a full grown person whose bones are set. Excellent results are to be expected in children.

The exercises for shallow chest should be designed first to elevate the sternum by loosening and elevating the ribs. Respiratory exercises are especially effective for this purpose. All exercises for chest expansion are good, but with every exercise that tends to expand the chest an effort must be made to produce a posterior curve in the dorsal spine. By flexing the head forward and keeping it flexed during any exercise for chest expansion, the effect will be a rounding out of the back and a lifting of the sternum that will ultimately increase the antero-posterior diameter. The following exercises will deepen the chest:

I. Without apparatus or external resistance.

1. Head flexed forward, making the upper back as round as possible, arms flexed with the hands resting over the chest. Inhale deeply and lift the ribs against the hands. Endeavor to force the hands out as far as possible. (Illus. 320.)

2. Head flexed forward, extend arms forward with all the speed possible. As in Illus. 35, with the head flexed.

3. Head flexed, fling the arms forward-upward with all the force possible. (Illus. 321.)

4. Head flexed forward. Raise the arms forward-upward slowly as you inhale deeply and expand the chest to the utmost. Lower them sideways-backward as you exhale. As Exercise 11, Lesson I, Illus. 39, with the head flexed.

5. Fingers locked behind the head, pull forward on

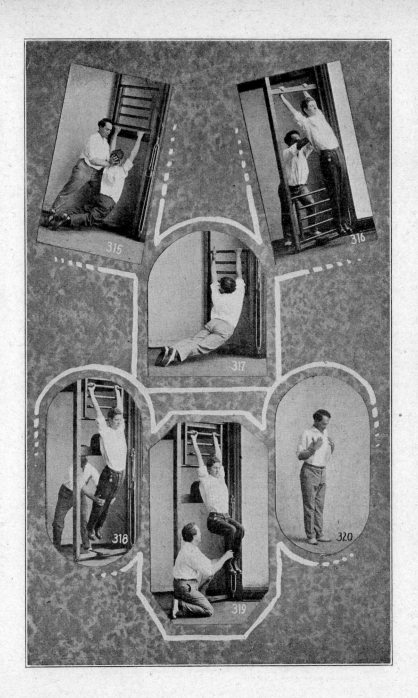

the head as you inhale deeply and endeavor to expand the chest. (Illus. 322.)

II. With assistance and resistance.

1. Patient sitting, head flexed forward, arms extended upward. The operator stands behind, grasps his hands, and offers resistance as the patient pulls down, flexing the arms, elbows well out at the sides, and inhaling deeply to expand the chest. No resistance is offered as the patient extends the arms and exhales. (Illus. 323.)

2. Patient standing, head flexed forward, hands on the hips. The operator stands behind, grasping the patient's elbows. As the patient inhales and rises on the toes, the operator forces his elbows back to increase the chest expansion. (Illus. 324.)

3. Patient standing, head flexed, arms extended upward. The operator stands behind him and pulls his arms back as the patient inhales deeply. (Illus. 325.)

4. Patient lying on his back, head elevated, resting on a pillow, arms extended forward. The operator, standing at the patient's head, resists as the latter carries his arms up and back while inhaling deeply. (Illus. 326.)

III. With apparatus.

1. Lying on the back, feet toward the exerciser, head elevated, resting on a pillow, carry the arms from the sides, straight upward and back of the head as you inhale deeply. As you bring the arms back, exhale. (Illus. 327.)

2. Standing, head flexed forward, holding light dumbbells, fling the arms forward-upward as you lunge forward, first with the left foot, then with the right.

3. Patient hanging, head flexed forward, the operator stands behind and places one hand each side at the angles of the patient's ribs, and presses inward and forward to expand his chest. (Illus. 328.)

4. Standing facing the chest weights, feet apart, head flexed forward as the arms are lifted, carry the arms down between the legs and up over head. (Illus. 329.)

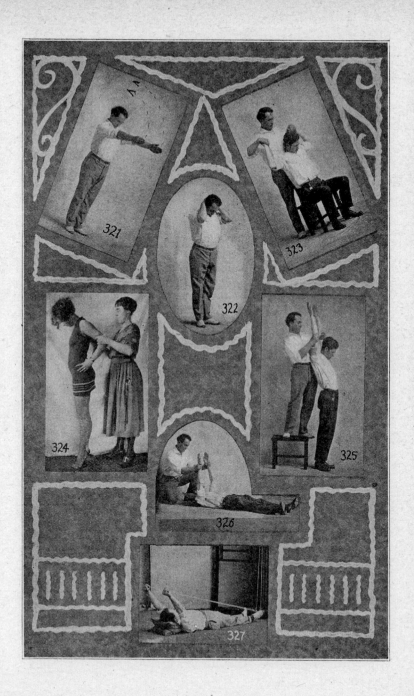

5. Practice throwing a baseball, or any light object, with each hand alternately. Or, the same effect may be obtained with an elastic exerciser. Standing with your back to the exerciser, go through the throwing motion with the right and then the left hand alternately.

NARROW CHEST.

In this condition the lateral diameter of the chest is less than the normal average. The chest is narrow from side to side, and sometimes this condition accompanies shallow chest, but not for long, because persons having such a defect do not live long.

The anatomy of narrow chest is a condition in which the ribs are depressed laterally. From the first rib down they all form an acute angle downward at the sternal and spinal attachments. The lower the rib the more acute the angle.

The corrective work must be such as to raise the ribs laterally. Any exercise in which the arms are speedily extended sideways, or elevated sideways-upward, will tend to correct this defect. The attachments of the muscles to the lateral portions of the ribs and to the arms above, give us a purchase upon them which aids in their lateral elevation. Added to this is the effect of lateral elevation at deep inhalation. By making a special effort to raise the upper ribs anteriorly and laterally, through contracting the scaleni, sterno-cleido-mastoid and internal intercostal muscles, we add to the effect of arm raising.

I. Exercises without apparatus or external resistance.

1. Raise the arms sideways-upward and inhale as they go up. Lower them sideways-backward and exhale as they go down.

2. Extend the arms sideways, putting all the speed possible into the extension.

3. Arms shoulder high at the sides, palms turned upward. Raise the arms up to vertical and at the same

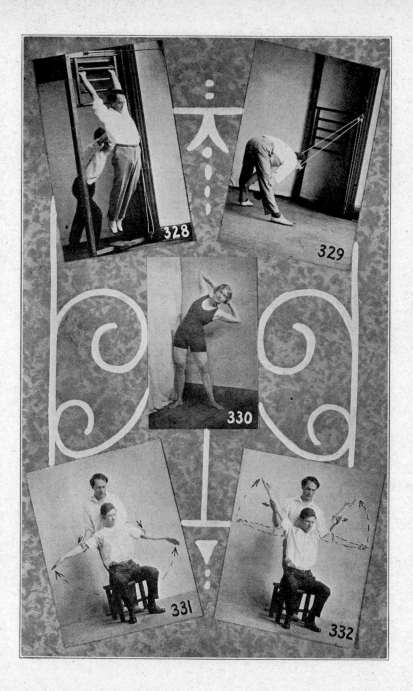

time raise the left leg sideways. As you lower the arms to shoulder height, lower the leg. As you raise the arms again, raise the right leg, and so on, alternating with the legs. See Exercise 3, Lesson XVII, Illus. 153. In this exercise, however, do not rise on the toes, as is shown in the illustration referred to.

4. Fingers locked behind the head, feet apart, bend as far as possible to either side. (Illus. 330.)

5. Rise on the toes, bend the knees all the way down; place the hands on the floor, fingers pointing inward, kick the feet back, and turn to the right, thus resting the weight on the left hand and the outside of the left foot. The right arm is extended upward along the head. While thus balancing the weight, elevate the right arm and right leg a few times. Then, change sides and elevate the left arm and leg. See Illus. 163.

II. With assistance and resistance.

1. The patient seated, arms hanging at his sides; the operator stands behind and, grasping the patient's arms just below the elbows, he offers resistance as the patient elevates his arms sideways to shoulder height; and at the same time, the operator combines with his resistance a slight outward traction on the patient's arms. When the patient's arms are at shoulder height he tries to hold them there, while the operator forces them down to the sides, combining an outward pull on the patient's arms with his downward pressure. (Illus. 331.) Throughout this exercise the patient should preserve a good trunk and head posture.

2. Patient seated, arms extended sideways from the shoulders, palms turned upward. The operator stands behind and takes hold of the patient's wrists. As the patient inhales and elevates his arms the operator offers resistance, and when the arms are vertical the operator pulls up on them. (Illus. 332.) As the patient exhales and lowers his arms the operator resists.

3. The patient seated, arms bent upward. The operator stands behind and grasps his hands. As the

patient inhales and extends his arms upward the operator resists. The elbows must travel sideways as far
as possible from the body. The operator resists as
the patient flexes his arms and exhales. (Illus. 323.)

4. The patient seated, his arms flexed upward; the
operator stands behind him and grasps his forearms
a little above the wrists. The operator offers slight
resistance as the patient extends his arms sideways and
at the same time inhales deeply. As the patient's arms
reach complete extension the operator forces them out
still farther. (Illus. 334.) As the patient flexes the
arms the operator offers slight resistance.

5. The above exercise is increased in force with the
aid of an assistant. The operator and his assistant stand
at either side of the patient, and each grasps one of the
latter's hands. They offer resistance as the latter extends
the arms sideways and at complete extension they pull
out to emphasize the movement. (Illus. 335.) Both
offer slight resistance as the patient flexes his arms.

III. With apparatus.

1. Standing with your left side to the exerciser, left
hand grasping handle, right hand on the hip, elevate
the left arm sideways upward a number of times. (Illus.
336.) With your right side to the exerciser, left hand
on the hip, elevate the right arm.

2. Hanging on a horizontal bar, hands grasping as
far apart as possible, swing the legs from side to side.

3. Arms extended upward with or without dumbbells, feet apart, bend as far as possible to the left
and right.

4. Hanging on a horizontal bar, hands grasping as
far apart as possible, the operator resists at the ankles
as the patient abducts the legs. (Illus. 337.)

5. Practice on the travelling rings.

ANTERIOR DORSAL.

In this condition the spine, instead of rounding back
gently at the shoulder region, curves forward and makes

the back appear very flat. This condition usually accompanies shallow chest, but it may exist with a comparatively full chest. There is a false notion prevalent that with a straight dorsal spine one should be straight and broad of shoulders, but even if this were true, the condition is one that weakens and lowers the resistance of the thoracic organs.

Osteopathy has shown that the normal spine is gently curved posteriorly between the shoulder blades. A spine that is too straight or anterior at the dorsal region predisposes to lung, heart and stomach disturbances.

The exercises given for correcting shallow chest are of service in treating anterior dorsal. There are not many specific exercises for anterior dorsal that do not have a deleterious influence on the chest. It may be said that this is compensated for by the fact that anterior dorsal condition is quite uncommon. Another interesting fact is that nearly all gymnastic movements may be made corrective of anterior dorsal curvature.

In Chapter I we explained why the head should be kept erect and the chest forward during exercise. In the average individual the inclination is to develop a posterior dorsal condition and gymnastics must be so arranged as to counteract this tendency. A condition of anterior dorsal renders it imperative, for the individual so afflicted, to violate the general law of gymnastics. Since the body at rest tends to assume the posture it held during activity, then, to correct anterior dorsal one should endeavor to slightly round the upper back, by, or during, exercise. Walking with a drooping head, working over a bench with the head bent forward, reclining the body backward with the head kept forward as one does while reading in a Morris chair, or playing such a game as croquet, will tend to correct anterior dorsal.

Exercises to correct anterior dorsal.

1. Head flexion forward. With the chin drawn in, flex the head as far forward as possible.

2. Lock the fingers behind the head, keeping the chin drawn in, pull forward on the head, and round the upper back as much as possible.

3. Lying on the back, with the chin drawn in, elevate the head as high as possible. (Illus. 338.)

4. Back-of-neck-and-elbow-stand. Lie on the back, raise the legs and curl them over the head. Place the hands at the small of the back, keeping the elbows as far apart as possible and thus support the body on the back of the neck and elbows. As Illus. 279. By kicking upward forcibly one is able to travel by short jumps while in this position.

5. The patient seated, locks the fingers behind his head. The operator stands behind him and passes his hands beneath the patient's axillae, and, palms facing forward, grasps his wrists. He now makes the patient fall backward and by pulling on the wrists, forces a rounding of the shoulders. (Illus. 339.) While holding the patient in this position he works his body forward and back, and from side to side, thus extending the posterior dorsal muscles from various angles.

6. The patient facing the stall bars, stands about two feet away from them and bends forward until the back of the head rests against the bars, and he reaches up and back and grasps one of the bars with both hands. (Illus. 340.)   He then allows the feet to slide backward and the hips to sag. (Illus. 341.) If strong enough he raises the body to vertical, a few times. (Illus. 342.)

ONE-SIDED CHEST DEFECT.

A common sequel of pleurisy is a sunken rib condition of the upper chest, most frequently on the right side. The depressed ribs are usually fixed and immovable, thus rendering the lungs less capacious than normal.

During a case of pleurisy, the patient tries to lie with the weight resting on the afflicted spot. This lessens the pain during the acute stage of the disease, but it also favors the production of adhesions that ultimately fix the ribs in a state of immobility. Corrective exercises in such a case must cause an expansion of the depressed rib area, and thus gradually remove the adhesions and restore normal lung action.

For the sake of clearness in explanation we shall prescribe for a depressed upper rib condition at the right side. All the exercises explained are with such a hypothetical case in mind. By just reversing the exercises in every respect, we can affect the left upper rib area. These exercises are also very good where the apices of the lungs are threatened or slightly affected by tuberculosis. In this case they should be done alternately to either side.

I. Exercises without apparatus or external resistance.

1. Feet apart, raise the arms forward-upward as you twist the trunk and head to the left and at the same time inhale deeply. As you turn the trunk forward, lower the arms sideways-backward, and exhale.

2. Head turned to left, bend it diagonally backward and to the left as you inhale. (Illus. 343.) As you elevate the head exhale slowly.

3. Left hand on the hip, right hand behind the head, body turned to right, head turned to the left, bend the head and upper body diagonally backward and to the left as you inhale. (Illus. 344.) As you stretch the head and trunk to erect posture, exhale.

4. Hands on the hips, body turned to the right, head turned to the left and bent backward. This is the starting position. (Illus. 345.) The exercise consists in straightening the head upward, while keeping it turned, and at the same time inhale deeply to expand the upper right thorax as much as possible. (Illus. 346.)

5. As number 4, except that the upper trunk, as well as the head, is bent backward in starting position. (Illus. 347.)

II. With assistance and resistance.

1. Patient standing, trunk turned to the right, head

turned to the left. The operator stands on a stool behind him. As the pupil elevates his arms forward-upward and inhales deeply, the operator reaches over and offers resistance and, when the pupil's arms are as high as he can carry them, the operator pulls them back over his chest, exerting the greatest force on the right arm. (Illus. 348.)

2. Patient sitting, arms extended upward, trunk turned to the right, head to the left. Operator stands behind and grasps the patient's hands. As the patient flexes his arms and inhales the operator offers resistance. (Illus. 349.) The patient exhales as he extends his arms to starting position, the operator does not resist this arm extension.

3. As number 2, except that the patient's head is flexed backward at starting position, and brought to erect posture with inhalation.

4. Patient sitting, trunk turned to the right, head turned to the left, right hand behind the head, left hand cn the hip. The operator stands behind with the side of his knee against the patient's scapular region, his right hand grasping the patient's right arm above the elbow, his left hand at the patient's left axilla. As the patient inhales, the operator forces his right arm back to expand the right upper thorax. (Illus. 350.)

5. Patient sitting, fingers locked behind the head, elbows forward; the head is turned to the left and bent backward; the upper trunk is slightly inclined backward and to the left. The patient preserves this position of the trunk and head throughout the exercise. The operator stands behind the patient, grasps his elbows, and offers resistance as the latter carries them backward while inhaling deeply. When the patient has carried his elbows backward as far as possible, the operator carries them back a little farther, pressing a little harder on the right than on the left. As the patient exhales, his elbows are carried forward without resistance. (Illus. 351.)

III. With apparatus.

1. Patient standing, arms extended upward and grasping a horizontal bar, his head is turned and bent to the left. The operator stands behind, places his hands at the patient's interscapular region and pushes forward and toward the right as the patient inhales deeply and rises onto his toes. (Illus. 352.)

2. Patient hanging on an incline bar, right hand higher than the left, the head is turned to the left and bent backward. As he elevates the head, he inhales deeply to expand the right upper thorax.

3. Repeat number 2 with forced chest expansion. (Illus. 353.) The operator stands behind the patient, places his hands at the latter's interscapular region and pushes forward and toward the right at inhalation.

4. The patient takes arch-hanging position, his head turned to the left. Keeping the head turned, he arches it upward and backward as he inhales. (Illus. 354.)

CHICKEN-BREAST.

Chicken-breast is a defect that may have a strong influence on a patient's general health. The chest is narrow and peaked at the front with the sternum very prominent. Even if the patient's health is not affected by the condition, he is usually conscious of it, and his mental attitude may have a depressing effect upon his organism.

In children this condition may be removed by making use of the exercises outlined just above, for one-sided chest defect. But, in treating chicken-breast, these exercises should be used alternately to both sides. In the above list, the exercises apply especially for a right upper rib depression. By just reversing every step of each exercise, the effect is centered on the left upper ribs. Repeat each exercise at least three times to either side.

In addition to the above exercises for chicken-breast, every procedure explained in treating narrow chest will

be found valuable, because chicken-breast needs a lateral expansion force as well as a rib lifting one.

In a bad chicken-breast defect in a child or youth, the plaster cast is of great value. The proper application of the cast is on the same principle as the method of treating spinal curvature, explained in Chapter VIII, except that the jacket is made to exert a pressure at the sternum and angles of the ribs.

In a bad case of one-sided chest defect, the plaster cast may be used on the same principle as for chicken-breast. In this case the pad is applied, and the window cut out only at the area of the depressed ribs.

LORDOSIS.

Lordosis or sway-back is the common condition of deep anterior bend at the waist. People develop such a defect from weak anterior lumbar muscles (psoas-iliacus), and weak abdominal muscles, or from a wrong conception of correct standing posture. Many a child, and often an adult, when told to stand up straight, simply settles the trunk backward from the waist, deepening the anterior lumbar curve and thrusting the shoulders and head forward. Wrong conception of correct standing posture is one of the chief causes of lordosis in those who have never taken exercise or been told what correct standing posture means.

Lordosis is not only a postural defect but it is often the cause of much physical suffering. It means weak, flabby abdominal muscles and tendency to, or presence of, hernia. It predisposes to optoses of different kinds because the abdominal muscles fail to properly support the viscera. In women it means that the abdominal organs bear down on the pelvic organs and often produce a tipping of the uterus that may, in addition to menstrual pains, cause bladder or rectal troubles. Optoses may also cause adhesions between the intestines and the uterus or ovaries.

Lordosis is not difficult to correct because the exercises indicated are easily understood. But they must be practiced regularly and for a long time. Because of this fact the treatment is often considered difficult.

To correct this defect one must practice exercises that will stretch posterior lumbar muscles and strengthen and shorten the anterior lumbar and abdominal muscles. The following are typical:

I. Exercises without apparatus or external resistance.

1. Lying on the back, raise the legs. If this movement is too difficult, begin by bending the knees upward, straightening the legs and lowering them slowly with the knees kept straight. As soon as you are strong enough, keep the knees straight as you raise and lower the legs. (See Illus. 153.)

2. Lying on the back, fingers locked behind the head, elbows resting against the floor. Keeping the knees straight, elevate the feet and, holding them a few inches from the floor, spread the legs out and bring them together a few times.

3. Lying on the back, practice leg swimming. Bend the knees up onto the chest, spread the legs apart as you straighten the knees, and then draw the feet together. Practice this exercise a few times without resting the weight of the legs between movements.

4. Lying on the back, with the feet under some heavy object, hands on the hips, flex the body up to sitting posture.

5. Lying on back with the feet held down as in Exercise 4, arms extended and kept in line with the ears; flex the body up to sitting posture. (Illus. 355.)

II. Exercises with resistance.

1. Patient lying on his back on a table, his hands grasping the sides near the head of it. As he draws one knee up to his chest, the operator offers resistance. (Illus. 356.)

2. Patient on a table, as for Exercise 1. As he flexes both knees up to his chest, the operator offers resistance. (Illus. 357.)

3. Patient lying on a table, hands grasping the head of it. As he elevates both legs with the knees straight, the operator offers resistance. (Illus. 358.)

4. Patient lying on the back, feet strapped down, hands on the hips. As he comes up to sitting, the operator offers resistance. (Illus. 359.)

5. Patient on table as for Exercise 4, except that the fingers are locked behind the head and the elbows kept well back. As he comes up to sitting the operator offers resistance, and then, pushes him forward as far as possible to extend the posterior lumbar muscles. (Illus. 360.) This exercises, strengthens and shortens the anterior and stretches the posterior lumbar muscles.

III. With apparatus.

1. Hanging on a horizontal bar, flex the knees upward to right angle.

2. Hanging on a horizontal bar, flex the knees up as in Exercise 1, and, holding them up, straighten them forward alternately. (Illus. 177.)

3. Hanging on a horizontal bar, raise both legs forward from the hips, keeping the knees straight. (Illus. 177.)

4. Hanging on horizontal bar, legs held horizontally forward from the hips, spread them apart and bring them together a few times. (Illus. 177 and 178.)

5. Most cases of lordosis are compensated for by a posterior dorsal condition often verging on a kyphosis. Assuming that the case under treatment is typical, we can combine an exercise that will correct the lordosis with a force that will affect the kyphosis. The patient, while hanging on a horizontal bar, may practice any of the above four exercises while the operator stands behind and pushes forward at the interscapular region. (Illus. 361.)

POSTERIOR LUMBAR.

This defect does not exist as commonly as lordosis, but where it does exist, it is usually causative or indic-

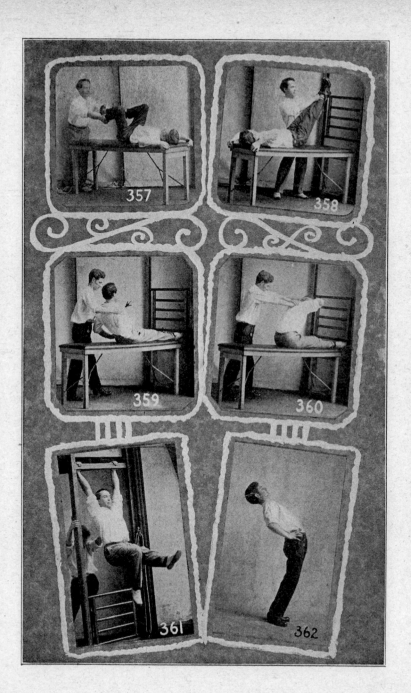

ative of pathological conditions. Chronic constipation, rectal troubles, and pelvic disturbances leading to menstrual complications in women, usually accompany this defect. With posterior lumbar we find, almost without exception, a rigid, straight, or anterior dorsal spine, digestive irregularities and lung or heart weaknesses.

This defect is usually acquired by improper standing and sitting postures, by occupational postures or exertions, and by nervous irritations due to intestinal indigestion resulting from long continued improper feeding which keeps the intestinal nerves constantly irritated, the reflex effect causing tension in the anterior lumbar muscles. These muscles remain in a state of contraction and thus cause a concavity at the posterior abdominal wall where there should be a convexity. Externally we have the convex posterior lumbar instead of the normal concave.

Whatever the cause or causes, the muscles at the front are shortened and those at the back lengthened abnormally and the correction is accomplished by exercises that extend the anterior and shorten the posterior lumbar muscles. Since posterior lumbar is usually accompanied by anterior dorsal, some of the exercises are given to affect both defects at once.

I. Exercises without apparatus or external resistance.

1. Hands on the hips, bend backward at the waist, keeping the head up. (Illus. 362.)

2. Hands on the hips, elevate the left and then the right leg backward, alternately. (As Illus. 43, except that the head may be allowed to droop slightly.)

3. Lying face down with a pillow under the chest, raise the legs as high as possible from the table, either alternately or together. (Illus. 363.)

4. Lying face down with a weight on the feet, hands on the hips, arch the body upward from the waist, the head being allowed to droop a little. (Illus. 364.)

5. Lying on the back, arch the body upward at the

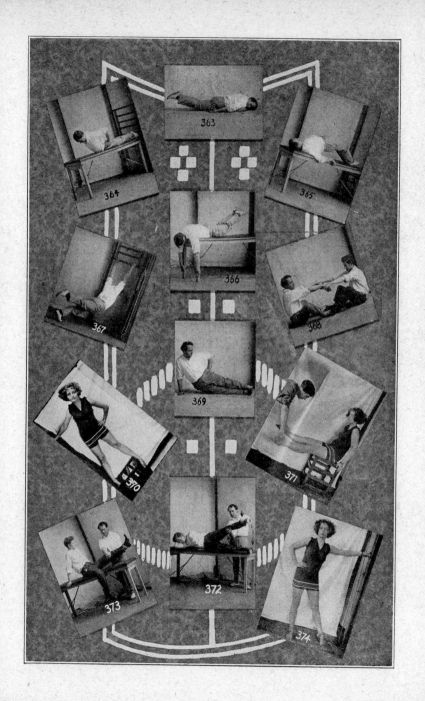

waist, resting the weight on the heels and the shoulders. (Illus. 365.)

6. Patient lying face downward, his head unsupported and projecting beyond the end of the table, a pillow under the chest, arms hanging down and hands grasping the legs of the table. The legs are lifted as high as possible from the table, knees kept straight. (Illus. 366.)

II. Exercises on apparatus or with resistance.

1. Practice 3, 4 and 6, of the above against resistance.

2. Arch-hanging, head drooping, alternate leg elevation. (Illus. 367.)

3. Stick wrestling on the floor. Opponents sit with their feet pressed together, hold a stick and at a given signal each tries to pull the other up from the floor. (Illus. 368.)

4. The so-called "slinker-slouch" walk is corrective of posterior lumbar and anterior dorsal.

KNOCK-KNEES.

This defect is usually found in the slender, lanky, flabby-muscled and loose-jointed individual. The subject usually shows a need of general resistive exercises to give firmness and strength to his muscles. From the muscular standpoint the local defect means extended internal and shortened external leg muscles. Frequently, there is a joint defect that is independent of the musculature. In such a joint defect the internal tuberosities of the tibia and femur may be too long, or the interarticular cartilages may be thickened on the inner side.

The treatment for knock-knees is both active and passive. The active form consists of exercises that tax the inside, or adductor muscles, and extend the outside, or abductor muscles of the legs. In this way the adductors are strengthened and shortened and the abductors are correspondingly extended. This method of procedure gradually brings a force to bear that will constantly draw in at the top and bottom of the legs and cause the knee joint to go out, at the same time altering the adjustment within the joint proper, whether cartilaginous or osseous.

Such a correction cannot be accomplished in a few days or weeks but requires months or years. The treatment is based upon the idea of creating a new cell-adjustment habit by repeating the effort toward correction. As metabolism goes on in the joint it accommodates itself to the corrective force exerted.

The passive treatment, which should always accompany the active, consists in using braces that press outward at the knees and inward at some point above and below it.

There are many types of braces made which are more or less serviceable. Any corrective appliance should be such as may be worn at night during sleep. Padded boards placed on the outside of the legs, with the pads resting against the outside of the thigh and leg, made secure by bands at the top and bottom and with a broad elastic tape strapped securely around the knee, thus pulling it outward, will prove efficient. A simpler method is to place a pillow between the knees and then strap the ankles together. As long as the knees are unflexed this will prove corrective.

I. Exercises without apparatus or external resistance.

1. Walk on the external edges of the feet and at the same time endeavor to keep the knees as far apart as possible.

2. While in standing position, force the heels together, or as nearly together as possible, and at the same time force the knees apart.

3. Take side fall position and allow the body to sag so as to extend the outside muscles of the supporting leg. (Illus. 369.)

4. Foot grasp side fall position, leg adduction. Patient rests the inside of the supporting foot on the edge of a chair or stool and, while bearing his weight on this

foot and the opposite hand, he lifts the other leg a few times. The free hand may rest on the hip, as the illustration shows, or it may rest on a chair to help balance. (Illus. 370.)

II. Exercises with resistance.

1. The patient sitting, his legs extended forward and apart. The operator stands in front of him and, holding at the ankles, resists, as the patient adducts the legs. (Illus. 371.)

2. The patient lying on his right side on the table. The operator stands behind him and holds the patient's left leg with the right hand inside the knee and the left on the outside of the ankle. The leg is lifted up without resistance; then, as the patient pulls it down, the operator offers all the resistance he can at the knee, that is, lifting up here, and, at the same time, he pushes downward at the ankle. (Illus. 372.) In this movement we have resistive exercise of the adductors, and passive extension of the abductors, the forces working as the arrows point.

This exercise is repeated as many times for one leg as for the other. With the patient lying on his left, the operator behind him, the left hand is at the knee, the right at the ankle.

3. A variation of number 2 may be given with more force by having the patient sit astride the table and adduct one leg at a time. For example, to exercise the adductors of the right leg, with the patient sitting, his hands grasping the sides of the table just behind him, the left knee, or inside of left foot, pressing against the edge of the table, the operator stands to his right, grasps the inside of the right knee with his left hand and the outside of the ankle with his right hand and, as the patient adducts the right leg, the operator resists by pulling hard with his left hand, and at the same time he pushes in at the ankle with his right hand. (Illus. 373.) Reverse to exercise the left leg.

In treating a child, too small to straddle a treating

table, one leg should be held or strapped down while the other is exercised as above.

III. Exercises with apparatus.

1. Adduction of the leg against a chest weight or elastic exerciser. (Illus. 374.) Exercise first one leg, then the other.

2. Horse-back riding is excellent to correct or prevent knock-knees. In this sport the adductor muscles are in constant use, so much so that one who rides horseback from childhood may develop bow-legs.

3. The use of braces, home made, or of the patent kind, or, placing a pillow between the knees and strapping the ankles, as already explained, are procedures that may be regarded as passive exercise by means of apparatus.

BOW-LEGS.

The exact opposite condition to that explained in knock-knees obtains in bow-legs. The internal, or adductor muscles, are the stronger and shorter, and the external or abductor muscles are the weaker. Constant use of the adductor muscles, as in horse-back riding, will develop bow-legs. But there is often an osseous condition, such as rachitis, which results in malformation. When bow-legs are the result of rachitis, correction is almost impossible. Braces, which give a constant pressure inward at the point of greatest outward curve along the shaft of the tibia and outward at the knee and ankle, may, in time, produce passive correction. This is especially true in children where the outward bend is not too marked. In very young children, it is possible to produce correction without patent braces by simply placing a pad inside of the ankle and knee joints and a wide strap or bandage at the point of greatest outward bend on the tibia.

Exercise will correct the form of bow-legs acquired by occupation, that is, where the entire leg is bowed from the hip to the ankle, with the greatest outward bend at the knee. These exercises should be such as to force in the knee and force out the ankle and foot by pressure, and by strengthening and shortening the abductors, and extending the adductors of the legs.

I. Exercises without apparatus or external resistance.

1. Walking on the inside edges of the feet, at the same time keeping the feet apart and forcing in the knees.

2. Standing with the feet apart and pressing in the knees, either by pushing in with the hands or by contracting the external muscles of the legs.

3. Support side fall foot eversion. The patient bears the weight of his body on one hand and the outside of the foot, steadying himself by holding a chair with the other hand. While in this position he everts the supporting foot. (Illus. 375.) Repeat on the other side.

4. Support side fall, leg elevation; supporting foot everted. The patient take side fall position as in Exercise 3, everts the foot, and, while holding this position, elevates the upper leg a few times. If control is good enough he should rest the upper hand on the hip, instead of on a chair or other support. (Illus. 376.) Repeat on the other side.

5. Side fall leg elevation with self-resistance. The patient takes side fall position. The supporting foot is everted and kept so. The upper hand is placed against the thigh. As the upper leg is elevated, the patient resists with his hand. (Illus. 377.)

II. Exercises with resistance.

In all of the following exercises the effect is increased by keeping the foot of the working leg everted all the time it is exercised.

1. Patient sitting, legs extended forward with the knees straight. The operator stands in front of him, grasps his ankles and resists as the patient spreads the legs apart.

2. Patient lying on his right side on the table. The operator stands behind him, places his right hand outside

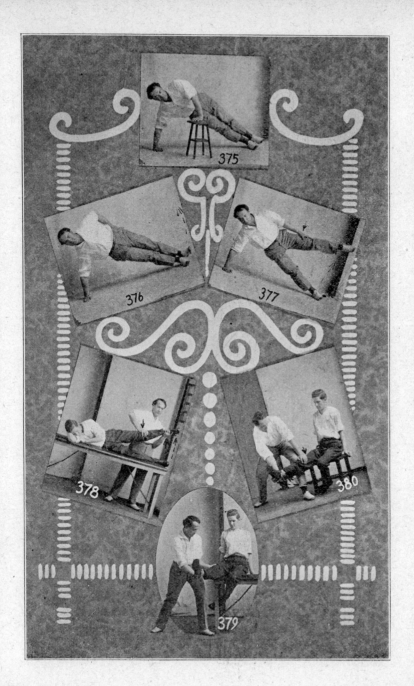

of the patient's left knee and his left hand inside of the patient's ankle. As the patient elevates the left leg, the operator resists by bearing down with his right hand and at the same time gives passive extension to the adductors by lifting up with the left hand. (Illus. 378.) Reverse for the other leg.

3. To make this second exercise stronger the patient sits on the side of a table close to the end. To exercise the right leg, the patient sits on the left side of the table near its end. This brings his right leg nearest the end, where the operator can work to advantage. The patient's left knee is curled under the table to grip it firmly; the hands grip the opposite side of the table, thus allowing the body to settle backward firmly. The right knee is straightened forward. The operator standing near the end of the table, to the right of the patient, places his left hand outside the knee and his right inside of the ankle. As the patient forces the leg outward, the operator resists by pressing inward at the knee and at the same time he gives passive extension of the adductor muscles by pulling outward at the ankle. (Illus. 379.) Reverse in every respect to exercise the left leg.

4. For the same purpose as in Exercises 2 and 3, the force may be increased by using a chair or stool instead of a table. To exercise the patient's right leg, the latter is seated with his left foot hooked inside the leg of the chair. His hands clasp the sides of the chair. The right leg is extended forward with the knee straight. The operator stands at the patient's right, his left knee pressed against the outside of the patient's right knee, his right hand clasping the patient's right ankle. The left hand steadies the patient's knee. The operator's right foot is about two feet behind the left. Both his knees are partly bent to allow freedom of motion. As the patient carries his right leg outward, the operator offers resistance with his left knee, which is allowed to straighten backward slowly to adjust itself to the patient's movement, and at the same time, to extend the

adductor muscles he pulls outward at the ankle. (Illus. 380.) To exercise the left leg, every part of this exercise is just reversed.

III. Exercises with apparatus.

1. To exercise the right leg, the patient stands with his left side to the exerciser, hooks the exerciser to the right foot and raises the right leg sideways. (Illus. 381.) To exercise the left leg the position is reversed, and the exerciser hooked to the left foot.

2. Sitting or lying, with an elastic band attached at the ankles, the patient spreads his legs apart against its resistance.

3. Patent braces that exert outward pressure at the knee and ankle and inward pressure at the tibial curve; and, the use of pillows attached between the ankles, and straps attached to press in at the greatest outward curve of the tibiae, may be regarded as passive exercise of the legs that will correct the defect.

FLAT-FOOT.

Flat-foot, or broken arch, is a very common complaint. The loss of the arch is due to muscular or ligamentous weakness, or to paralysis of the muscles. Such a condition as infantile paralysis will produce flat-foot. In rachitis, owing to the bony softness as well as muscular weakness, we frequently find flat-foot. Flat-foot sometimes occurs from birth. Normally, the arch begins to form soon after birth, but in some cases it never develops.

Flat-foot is common among dancing and gymnastic instructors. Mention of the fact that it is common among dancers is apt to convey the idea that this occupation may cause it because the muscles of the foot are taxed to such a degree. But the fact is that in the average individual, dancer or otherwise, the muscles of the foot are capable of performing their function without pain or inconvenience if their nerve and blood supply are not impaired. While restoration of the arch is greatly aided by special exercises, the real cause of its breaking down is due to an innominate or lumbar lesion. By first setting the lesion, then prescribing exercises, beneficial results are always obtained. Exercise alone, that is, without osteopathic adjustment, will benefit less than 50 per cent of the cases prescribed for. Therefore, to cure flat-foot, that is, the acquired type, the innominate or spinal lesions below the eleventh dorsal vertebra must be adjusted. This done, exercises should be practiced regularly along with, and after, the treatment by osteopathy.

When the arch is falling, before a marked flat-foot condition exists, the person so afflicted feels intense pain in the muscles under the foot. Sometimes the transverse arch alone is growing weak. More frequently the longitudinal arch is at fault, and occasionally, both break down simultaneously. Whether one or both are included, pain is always present, though it moderates periodically, only to return with increased intensity as time goes on. Standing on the toes, or on the external edges of the feet often gives temporary relief.

Arch supports worn inside the shoes, if properly fitted, relieve or moderate the pain, but they never restore a fallen arch to normal. They simply act as props and in no way rebuild the natural structure. They rather tend to increase the weakness present.

To rebuild the arch there are several exercises possible, but only a few that are very good. These should be repeated over and over. In addition to the exercises it always helps to press the fingers into the muscles of the bottom of the foot and give them a thorough kneading, pressing upward as in all kneading. At the same time press the arches into shape by exerting the force on the bones themselves.

1. Patient, sitting, points the toes of the right foot, presses them on the floor, and keeps them dragging firmly on the floor, the heel held as high as possible, as he flexes and extends the knee. (Illus. 382.) This exercise is practiced first with one foot and then the other.

2. Patient, standing, flexes the right knee well out, touches the toes of the right foot against the inside of the left leg, and flexes the knee upward as high as possible, rubbing the toes along the inside of the leg. (Illus. 383.) Repeat with the left foot. This movement taxes the muscles of the arch of the foot to such an extent as to cause pain at times, but it is the kind of pain which indicates that the real work is being done.

3. The patient points the left foot forward, reaching as far as possible with the toes, the foot rotated outward (Illus. 384), and lets the heel down so that the foot is pointed straight outward. This causes a strong tension on the ligaments inside the arch. The left foot is kept in this position on the floor, as the right foot is pointed forward and brought squarely down as the left was, with the toes pointed straight outward. This exercise is kept up in the form of walking, forward and backward. In the backward order the foot is pointed as far back as possible, and the heel is brought down so that the toes point straight out sideways. (Illus. 385.) Then, the other foot is carried backward, etc. This exercise, and the two above have been used with success to develop the arches of a dancing teacher who had congenital flat-foot, and the illustrations for this particular defect were posed for by her.

4. Another form of exercise that is very helpful in developing the arches is to raise the heel and toes of the foot and press down with the ball of it. (Illus. 386.) This exercise forces the arch into position. The idea is to bear down hard with the ball of the foot in a gripping motion, either while sitting or standing, and at the same time lift the heel and toes as high as possible.

5. Rising on the balls of the feet, by lifting the heels and toes of both feet, or walking on the balls of the feet with the heels and toes kept as high as possible, will serve as variations of Exercise 4.

The exercises given above will rebuild the transverse as well as the longitudinal arch, because they tend to strengthen all the muscles under the foot as well as those of the leg whose tendons are distributed under the foot. For special effect upon the transverse arch, when the patient rises on the balls of the feet, as the heels and toes are lifted, he should press outward with the inner metatarso-phalangeal joint (Illus. 387), and press inward with the external metatarso-phalangeal joint. (Illus. 388.) This may be done one foot at a time as the illustrations show, or with both feet, while the heels and toes are kept lifted.

ADHESIVE PLASTER IN FALLEN ARCHES.

Upon feeling pain in the feet most people hasten to procure some kind of arch support to wear inside their shoes. These, if well fitted, usually relieve pain. But mere relief is not, and should not be considered, enough. This kind of relief means that the arches are to remain weak and often even rendered weaker and in time become dependent upon supports in the form of specially made shoes.

In order to achieve permanent cure for fallen arches there are three things necessary. The blood and nerve supply to the feet must be normal or there is sure to be muscular and tendonous weakness that no amount of supporting can replace. With this muscular weakness will occur slight displacements in the bones of the arches of the feet. To merely replace these bones without toning up the muscles controlling them and utilizing a flexible kind of support temporarily will avail little. The question of shoes is important. Shoes must not be so tight as to interfere with free circulation of the blood. Then the nerves which control the sensation, muscular motion and blood supply to the feet must be entirely free from obstruction as they pass down from the lower spine and sacro-iliac region. Only a physician who has made a specialty of the spine can determine and adjust such obstructions and this is not the place to enter into the details of this phase of the subject. The exercises have been explained and it now simply remains to outline the importance and application of the best kind of temporary supports during the re-normalizing course in fallen arches.

Second in importance to the nerve and blood supply must be considered the integrity of the muscles of the feet. These muscles control the flexibility and the action of the feet and they and their tendons control the strength and height of the arches. By wearing shoes that do not interfere with the free play of these muscles and by practicing the special exercises explained above one can restore and preserve perfect arches.

It should be explained that flat-foot in itself does not necessarily mean pain and weakness. In the United States army it was customary to reject any drafted man or applicant for enlistment if he failed to come to the standard test for high arches. The test used to be to place a ruler from the bottom of the inner ankle bone to the large joint of the great toe, (metatarsal), and if the most prominent inside bone of the arch fell below this line it was considered flat-foot or fallen arch. This test obtained for many years. When we entered the World War, however, important exceptions to this rule were noted. For instance, a Southern mountaineer, anxious to enlist, walked one hundred and thirteen miles to the nearest enlistment camp. When he was rejected because the doctors said his flat feet might interfere with his ability to march, he said he was sorry because he had walked all the distance to enlist. The doctors then reconsidered and accepted him. Then later on, when it was found that such renowned athletes as Eddie Collins, the baseball player, and William Johnstone and Maurice McLaughlin, the famous tennis players, all had what the standard proved as flat feet, the army doctors modified the test for flat feet to one of efficiency rather than height of the arch. It is also generally admitted that most savage tribes have what has been considered at least low arches, if not always flat feet. Therefore, a consideration of the ability of the above mentioned athletes to run and of most savages to walk should bring a change of opinion as to the test for flat feet.

If we were to enter into details we would find that the feet have really three important arches. The essential arch, which is made up of three bones, from the heel to about the middle of the foot, is the strongest and the real shock absorber, bearing the weight of the body. Then we have the longitudinal arch, which is from the heel to the metatarsal joints, higher inside than outside, and its chief function is for spring and propulsion. Whether or not the foot is flat, if the tissues composing the arch are elastic and strong, we find the same perfect use noted in the athletes mentioned above. The third important arch is the plantar or anterior arch which has a transverse elevation from the outside to the inside. Besides these three, we find that every bone in the foot is slightly bent with the concavity below and the convexity above, presenting a series of small arches as numerous as the separate bones themselves. The pain and inefficiency may be found in all three important arches but usually in the longitudinal or the transverse, or in both at the same time.

As a temporary help to relieve pain and hasten restoration of the arches no specially made shoes, no matter how well fitted, nor arch supports of any kind can compare to the correct application of strips of adhesive plaster. Strips of adhesive plaster as applied here are only useful and advisable while the spinal adjustment and the exercises are restoring the muscles and other structures to normal. But these are sure to relieve the pain immediately and permanently, and they will not interfere with normal activity of the muscles as all stiff arch supports will do. By the combination of spinal adjustment, exercises and adhesive plaster, the most painful types of broken arches can be restored in from three to seven weeks. There may be exceptions, but they are rare.

Before proceeding to apply the plaster it is best to

tear off the necessary strips. For each foot, tear off two strips about one to one and a half inches wide and fifteen inches long. Tear off two strips of the same width, about eight inches long. Tear off one strip of about half an inch wide and eighteen to twenty inches long. Then tear off two or three strips of half an inch width and long enough to go around the leg for re-inforcements.

With the foot kept at right angles to the leg and the inside edge inverted as high as possible, apply one of the long strips from outside of the ankle bone, across the foot, without using any more pressure than is necessary to cause the plaster to adhere; then, with a hard pull at the height of the arch, stick it along the inside of the shin bone, as shown in (1), Illustration 391. Take one of the shorter tapes, begin at the outside corner of the heel and bring it obliquely forward and inward so as to overlap the first strip at the highest point of the normal arch, where a hard pull is given, and then carry it over the top of the foot, decreasing the strength of the pull as you proceed, around to the outside of the heel. Should there be pain at the anterior, inside edge of the heel, this second strip should be carried straighter upward and around the shin bone from inside outward. The other long strip is then taken and, beginning just back of the little toe, brought obliquely inward along the bottom of the foot to overlap the other two at the high point of the arch, where a hard pull is given and the tape is carried upward along the inside of the leg, slightly backward from the first tape. (2), Illustration 391, shows these three tapes so far. With the foot extended down and the toes held up as high as possible, apply the middle of the long half-inch tape across the ball of the foot. The two ends are crossed over the top of the foot and carried around the ankle, one flap overlapping the other, as shown in (3), Illustration 391. This long tape, properly applied, has the effect of a short shoe in preserving the bow string arch effect, but without the painful experience a short shoe would give. To lift the transverse arch, take the last one-

391

392

inch tape, begin over the little toe joint, carry it inward, across the dorsum of the foot, then down and, while holding the arch in shape by pressing in at the internal and external metatarsal joints, pull it across the bottom, as shown in (4), Illustration 391, then up over the external metatarsal joint and obliquely inward over the top of the foot to the inside of, or around the ankle, as shown in (5), Illustration 391. The two or three strips are then applied around the ankle and leg to keep the vertical strips from lifting off or slipping when the weight is placed on the foot. (6), Illustration 391 shows the job completed.

These supporting tapes are left on for a week or ten days and then renewed if found necessary. Many cases need no more than one taping, proving, of course, that it was a spinal and not a purely foot condition. To facilitate removing the tape hot water or chloroform or naphtha is used. While these tapes are on one can wear ordinary shoes with perfect comfort and freedom. The shoes, of course, should be broad toed, low heeled and with a straight inside line, and flexible at the arch. These tapes will not interfere with bathing. Should the edges roll up, as they sometimes do while bathing, they can be easily smoothed down again.

CORRECTING DEFORMITIES IN TOE JOINTS.

It is a perverse state of mind that regards normal feet as freakish. Yet such is the situation among the majority of people. When one wears a shoe that fits the foot in accord with its natural shape and with a view to its normal function and freedom, most people look askance at the shoes because, being normal, they seem so unusual and ugly. The pointed toe shoes for men and women and the high heel shoes for women have been for several years considered stylish and it seems almost like educating a devotee to fashions all over again to convince him that his corns and bunions and painful arches are not due to the fact that he has feet, but the fact that his shoes do not fit.

Many ask, "What is one to do when everyone wears shoes with pointed toes and shoe clerks urge them upon you?" If we are to get back to normal and regain our bearings so far as locomotion is concerned, the proper procedure is not to have toes removed to fit styles but to compel shoe dealers to sell shoes that will assure healthy feet.

Normal feet have become so rare that to normal minds they now seem a mark of beauty. Of course, even if everyone wore anatomically correct shoes, still would there be variations in the appearances of feet. But the question of beautiful feet is of less importance than healthy, useful and reliable ones. The accompanying picture shows Bobbie Madrecki of Chicago, who is the possessor of beautiful feet. Should any reader, who is afflicted with imperfect feet, wish to acquire normal ones the following suggestions may prove of value.

First in importance in restoring normal feet is to give them normal work. To go barefooted whenever it is convenient would prove one of the best procedures. Next to going barefooted is to wear shoes that allow most freedom to the feet. If the arches are weak one should observe the exercises explained above.

As an aid to restoring normal shape to the toe that is bent down, hammer fashion, take a strip of plaster, about a quarter of an inch in width and four inches in length, begin under the toe, lift it up straight and stick the plaster along the top of the foot to keep it elevated, as shown in (1), Illustration 392. To keep the toe down at proper level after it is straightened, loop another narrow strip of plaster over the middle joint and pull it down to normal level and stick the two ends of the plaster on the bottom of the foot, as shown in (2), Illustration 392.

Where the toes are bunched together and cramped out of shape from wearing too tight or pointed shoes they may be straightened by spreading them apart and the bent ones treated as just explained. To spread toes apart, stick one end of a narrow strip of plaster on the inside of the outermost toe of the group, pull out as far as is necessary, and stick the strip along the edge of the foot. If an adjoining toe has to be pulled out it is done in the same way, the second strip of plaster overlapping the first. This is repeated on each toe, either from the inside or the outside of the foot, until the middle toe of the group, which is usually bent under, is freed from the rest and corrected according to its deformity. When all corrections have been made, to keep the plaster strips from slipping or yielding, circular bands are applied around the foot at the metatarsal area, as shown in (3), Illustration 392. (4), Illustration 392, shows an underview of the same correction.

Bunions are caused by various conditions and are said to occur in savages who never even wore shoes. However, these are rare. The pressure from shoes which are not adapted to normal action of the feet will prove strongly contributory to their existence. To prevent deformities in the internal and external metatarsal joints of the feet the toes of the shoes should not be pointed. The shoes should be broad at the toes and with a straight inside line. If such shoes have always been worn, or if one has gone shoeless and used the feet normally and still has bunions, the cause is higher up than the feet. We should naturally look in the spine for causes.

Given a joint which is swollen and bent inward, if the X-ray does not show the presence of sesamoid bones, the adoption of normal shoes and freedom for the feet plus the proper application of adhesive plaster and cotton pads, will restore the joint to normal. If there are sesamoid bones in the joint, surgery is the only recourse for relief.

To correct a bunion joint deformity by the use of strips of plaster, proceed very much as for the bunched toe deformity explained above. Take a strip of adhesive plaster of about half an inch or slightly less in width and about eight or ten inches in length; begin by sticking the end inside the toe, carry it around the tip of it, place cotton or wool pads in front and behind the swollen joint and carry the plaster over these pads straight to and around the heel. Transverse strips are applied to hold this corrective strip in place, as shown in (5), Illustration 392.

In treating the toes or small joints of the feet the plaster is left on for only one or two days and then the toes are bathed thoroughly and the skin dressed before new ones are applied. Repeated application of these corrective strips in addition to the wearing of normal shoes and giving the feet plenty of activity will in time normalize the feet.

PIGEON-TOES.

This is a condition that can always be corrected in any individual who is able to walk. It is sometimes the result of paralysis in which the external rotators and everters of the feet have been effected. But, even in such cases, persistent effort will correct the defect. One case, that of a woman of 26 years, who had had infantile paralysis in childhood and retained this defect, was cured in less than four months of persistent effort. Another case was that of a five-year-old boy who had a club-foot condition (double equino-varus), that kept him from walking for over two years. No casts or braces were used and nothing was done except to give him corrective gymnastics. In a few weeks he began to walk but in a very ungainly way. His legs were kept spread far apart and the toes turned in so as to make him sway as a duck does in walking. In the course of a little over six months he became as lively as any average boy of his age.

To correct typical pigeon-toes, that is, where the feet simply turn in, it is necessary to strengthen the external rotators of the feet and legs and stretch the internal rotators. In a case resulting from club-foot, where the everters of the feet as well as the external rotators are weak, a few additional exercises are necessary. By practicing daily the following exercises, pigeon-toes can be corrected.

I. Exercises without assistance or resistance.

1. Walking with the feet kept turned outward as far as possible. The patient should walk along the cracks in the floor, or draw chalk lines, and try to place his feet in line with them. (Illus. 389.)

2. Press one foot in front of the other, toes pointing straight sideways, and flex the knees without allowing the feet to rotate. (Illus. 390.)

3. Foot externally rotated, raise the leg forward, carry it sideways and down to position. Keep the knee straight and the foot turned outward as much as possible all through this movement. Repeat with the other leg; and so on, alternately.

4. If the patient has a slight club-foot condition, with pigeon-toes, he should try to walk on the inside edges of the feet, as well as to keep the feet outwardly rotated.

5. In standing position, heels together, toes turned out as much as possible, he should evert the feet, that is, raise the outside edges, over and over.

II. Exercises with resistance.

1. Patient lying on his back, or sitting with the knees extended forward, rotates the feet outward against the operator's resistance. The operator holds at the patient's toes, resists the outward rotation and, when the patient has carried the movement as far as possible, the former forces the feet still farther back to extend the internal rotators.

2. The patient lying or sitting as for Exercise 1, his feet rotated outward and toes pointed downward. As he flexes the ankle upward and outward the operator offers resistance.

3. Patient lying or sitting as for above exercises, his feet rotated outward, and kept so throughout this exercise. As he spreads the legs apart, the operator offers resistance.

4. For club-foot condition, in addition to the above, the patient is lying or sitting and everts the feet against the operator's resistance. When the patient has turned the outside edges of the feet as high as he can, the operator forces them up still further.

EXTERNALLY ROTATED FEET.

This is an uncommon defect but it does exist, and deserves a few words. It is common, and considered normal, for the feet to turn outward slightly, but when they turn out so far that something seems wrong and ungainly to all, it is time to correct them. It is weakening for the feet to turn out too far. In sprinters, coaches often have to correct this defect. Where a race is won by inches, the position of the runner's feet may be the determining factor. If the sprinter's feet are kept straight forward he gets full benefit of his reach in each stride, but, if his feet are turned outward he may lose a fraction of an inch at each stride which rapidly counts up against his chances.

Apart from the competitive aspect of this defect, one whose feet turn out too much loses all springiness of even a normal arch in walking. Such a person cannot stand long walks. He tires easily and all his movements seem ungainly.

This defect is the result of wrong habits in walking, or of congenital maladjustments. It is seldom the result of paralysis in which the internal rotators have been affected. If the muscles are normal and the defect is simply habitual, the patient can easily correct it by persistently walking with the toes held straight forward or turned in. Single and resistive exercises just opposite to those explained for pigeon-toes will have a corrective effect. Every exercise explained under pigeon-toes, except those pertaining especially to club-foot, should be practiced from a reverse aspect.

CHAPTER VII

THE GYMNASTIC TREATMENT OF INGUINAL HERNIA.

There are many forms of hernia, but the inguinal type is the most common and most amenable to treatment.

The term "rupture," so commonly used, is wrong. Rupture means an actual tearing of the peritoneum. In hernia there is seldom a tear, but we find a stretching of the natural openings of the inguinal canal through which the intestines or other tissues protrude. It is interesting to know how the term rupture originated.

R. W. Murray, F. R. C. S., in his book on "Hernia, Its Cause and Treatment," says that Galen (A. D. 131-201), whose knowledge of the body was based upon monkey anatomy, stated that inguinal hernia was "due to a rupture of the peritoneal process, or to a gradual distention of it. In the case of rupture, it was believed that the tear involved the aponeurosis of the abdominal muscles as well as of the peritoneum.

"It is a strong evidence of the master mind of Galen that his anatomical and physiological teaching should have remained unchallenged until Vesalius (1514-1564), after carefully dissecting many human bodies, exposed the numerous errors into which Galen had unavoidably fallen. The awe and reverence for the name of Galen were so great that his statement regarding the rupture of the peritoneum in hernia was generally accepted up to the time of Heller (1708-1777)."

Further on, Dr. Murray says: "Though inguinal hernia is a very common complaint, has wide geographical distribution and a very ancient origin—in fact, it is far from improbable that an inguinal hernia first appeared in one of the children or grandchildren of Adam —we are still far from agreed as to its exact causation, and consequently still further from agreement as to the best way of curing it."

A hernia is a gradual stretching of the tissues and escape of the abdominal contents either into a pre-formed or congenital sac or, as in the common acquired type, by the formation of a sac from the peritoneal lining of the abdomen. Abdominal herniae are named from the part through which they pass, as inguinal, femoral or umbilical. The scrotal or labial herniae are simply the inguinal herniae so developed that the sac and its contents have emerged from the external abdominal ring and entered the scrotum or labia. We may also find the ventral hernia: a protrusion through any part of the anterior abdominal wall except at the umbilicus or above it; the epigastric hernia: a protrusion of peritoneum in the space bounded by the ensiform cartilage, the ribs and the umbilicus; the obturator hernia: a protrusion through the obturator membrane or obturator canal, and felt below the horizontal ramus of the pubes internal to the femoral vessels.

A hernia consists of the sac and its contents. The sac is made up of peritoneum and lining membrane of the abdominal cavity. The sac is divided into the mouth, the neck and body. The mouth is the aperture communicating with the abdominal cavity. The body is the expanded portion. The neck is the constricted part at the abdominal opening.

Hernia of the bladder, caecum and sigmoid flexure may occur without a true hernial sac. The anterior wall of the bladder is not covered by peritoneum and may cause actual protrusion in the inguinal hernia. Protrusion of fairly large size will also drag a part of the bladder covered with peritoneum, when both the bladder and abdominal contents are found. The same condition exists in sigmoid and caecal hernia, except that in these the peritoneum covers the anterior wall of the first and the posterior wall is dragged down without this covering.

The contents of the sac are omentum, intestine, or any movable contents of the abdomen. "In some cases," according to De Garmo, "even a kidney or parts of the liver have been found in the hernial sac."

Herniae are divided clinically into the reducible, irreducible, incarcerated, inflamed and strangulated.

In *reducible inguinal hernia* the contents can be reduced into the abdominal cavity. The acquired sac is always reducible at first. That is, it is free from adhesions. Sooner or later adhesions are formed and render it permanent. The sac then forms a moist serous lining to the inguinal canal.

Irreducible hernia presents the usual symptoms of hernia, but cannot be replaced in the abdomen. A hernia that has been reducible may in time become irreducible because of adhesions, because of the growth of omental fat, or because of the increase in size of the mass. It may result in serious complications because of its prominence, which renders it liable to bruise and thus give pain, or there is always danger of obstruction and strangulation. Irreducible hernia usually requires surgery.

Incarcerated or obstructed means a condition in which there is an obstruction caused by the damming up of feces or undigested food. The fecal current is stopped but the blood flow in the intestinal walls is undisturbed. This condition is most likely to take place in irreducible hernia or umbilical hernia, especially if the patient is constipated. As this condition develops the tumor enlarges and becomes tender and painful. The abdomen may become distended and painful. Soothing procedures are necessary until the bowels are emptied, by first giving an enema, and then castor oil. Surgery is usually necessary to repair this type of hernia.

Inflamed hernia is due to injury of an irreducible hernia. It is a local peritonitis manifesting as a mass that is tender, painful and hot. In inflamed enterocele there is much fluid formed, while in epiplocele the mass becomes hard.   There is constipation, vomiting and usually fever.   The hernia cannot be reduced, and the mass shows impulses on coughing.   Every means possible should be employed to empty the bowels, using enema to first empty below the hernia, then giving castor oil or salts.   Surgery is advisable to prevent strangulation.

Strangulated hernia is a condition in which the blood vessels, whether intestinal or omental, are constricted and blood circulation arrested along fecal obstruction. Strangulated hernia is dangerous to life.   It usually occurs in patients having old inguinal hernia, who lead an active life.   There may occur a slipping out of more intestine or omentum into the inguinal sac and this causes a pressure at the opening or neck of the sac, sufficient to check the blood circulation.   The patient feels sharp colicky pains in the region of the umbilicus soon after this occurs and he rapidly grows weak.   There is much retching and often vomiting.   The pain gradually becomes continuous.   Later the hernia becomes irreducible. It is found larger than usual, tender, painful and the skin above it may be reddened.   There is no impulse upon coughing.

This type of hernia usually results in gangrene with danger of death unless surgery is applied.   Measures should be taken to reduce the condition.   The patient is placed on his back, preferably on an inclined plane with the body higher than the head, the knees bent to relax the abdomen as much as possible.   By gentle manipulation it is frequently possible to reduce this condition. Then, the abdominal walls can be strengthened.   If reduction is impossible, surgery is necessary.

Inguinal herniae are also named according to their contents.   In *enterocele* the sac contains portions of intestine.   In *epiplocele* the sac contains omentum. *Entero-epipocele* is the name applied when the sac contains both intestine and omentum.   A *cystocele* contains a portion of the bladder.

Causes of hernia.   It is most liable to occur in the male.   It occurs at any period of life and sometimes hereditary predisposition seems to exist.   Sometimes a mass of fat forms in the canal before the hernia appears and it seems to have a causative relation to it.   Any strenuous occupation predisposes to hernia.   Weak, flabby abdominal muscles predispose to hernia.   Muscular relaxation from ill-health, or following pregnancy, and wounds or scars following operations, or abscesses may predispose to hernia.   The exciting causes are muscular effort, lifting, strains, jumping, sudden effort to guard in falling, and so on.

When a hernia is forming the person feels a muscular pain in the lower abdomen, which is intensified on sneezing or coughing.   This may be noticed weeks before it is evident that a hernia is present.   If a hernia is suspected, careful examination should be made.   Insert the tip of the little finger in the external ring and ask the patient to cough.   Where a hernia is present, succussion will be detected on coughing.   In a healthy person no more than the tip of the little finger can be inserted in the external ring.   If the top of the index finger can be inserted the aperture is dilated and even if there is no hernia present one may safely be prognosed.   In examining the external ring in a man, invert the skin of the scrotum and carry the finger into the ring.

Reducible hernia.   In reducing a hernia, no instrument surpasses the human hand.   When a hernia is reducible the contents of the sac can be emptied into the abdominal cavity.   But unless the sac can be reduced with the contents out of the inguinal canal into the abdominal cavity, the case is surgical and requires radical treatment.   Most cases are curable by exercise before the sac is adhered.   After the sac is adhered it requires long continued proper use of the abdominal muscles to produce the desired results. Correct use of any muscle tends to make it normal.

The shape of the sac can be felt in the reducible hernia. There is a smooth enlargement at a known hernial opening, larger below than above, which began above and extended downward. It is often possible to feel the neck. In enterocele the enlargement becomes smaller and may disappear altogether on lying down. Straining, lifting, or standing, especially while leaning forward, makes the mass more prominent; cough causes impulse or succussion. The protrusion is elastic and there is a gurgling sound when the mass suddenly disappears on reduction. In epiplocele the mass is less elastic. It is often irregular and compressible and feels doughy. There is little impulse on coughing, and muscular effort or standing has little influence on its size. Percussion gives a dull note and reduction is accomplished slowly and no gurgling sound results.

PALLIATIVE TREATMENT.

The victims of reducible hernia often complain of pain on exertion, of dyspepsia and often, of constipation. It is advisable to eat so as to keep the bowels open, and keep from violent exercises and sudden strains.

The only proper truss is one that does not bore into the opening from outside. All kinds of methods have been applied to hold the viscus in place, but nearly all have had an oval surface which bored into the opening and tended to enlarge it. The standard truss, with its oval or sharp surface, forces into the opening and wrestles with the mass from within which is trying to come out. The result of this wrestling match is never curative. The truss is usually made strong enough and so adjusted as to overcome the pressure of the internal mass. The result of this force either way is to keep the aperture open and permanent. No truss with a conical surface ever acted as more than an artificial support. If a cure results while the standard truss is worn it is in spite of the truss. The only correct truss or support for any inguinal hernia or traumatic rupture of the abdominal wall is a broad stout band, or a band with a flat pad attached to it that exactly fits over and closes the opening from the outside without boring in.   A flat piece of wood about three-eighths of an inch thick whittled out in an oval edge, lined with silk or chamois, and attached to the band will serve properly.   Such an appliance will keep the hernia from bulging, keep the parts normally within the abdomen and give the aperture a chance to close up under exercise.   A proper hernial support can be made by fitting a piece of one to two-inch elastic webbing around the body, bringing it close to the pubes at the front.   Then attach two narrow bands lined with chamois or silk, about one inch apart at the front, pass them between the thighs and attach them at about five inches apart at the back.   With these bands so adjusted that the broad abdominal part fits snugly over the hernial area, attach the flat pad so that it will press at the internal inguinal opening.   (Illus. 393.)   This appliance is to be worn during the day.   While exercising it should be removed.

Treatment.   The gymnastic treatment of inguinal hernia has been used successfully by Dr. Geo. H. Taylor many years ago.   The late Dr. J. W. Seaver, of Yale, contributed a very instructive article to the Yale Medical Journal, February, 1900, 1904, on "The Treatment of Inguinal Hernia in the Young."

In most cases it is advisable to proceed with caution, fitting the exercises to the individual, and regulating their force from gentle to strong as the patient gains.   Our experience has satisfied us that the best way is to proceed progressively from gentle to strong.   Dr. Seaver, whose extended experience enabled him to speak with confidence and authority, allowed even the heaviest gymnastics after the patient had practiced preliminary work for a while.

Dr. Seaver said: "It has been my experience that the patients that are most active and most anxious to take part in athletic work are the ones who repair most rapidly, while men with an aversion to physical activity do not show satisfactory results." Our experience has been such as to corroborate this statement.

The treatment of hernia is in a sense like the treatment for obesity. When the treatment is once made clear, the fact that it requires exertion on the patient's part makes it unfavorable. It is necessary to repeat the need for exercise to the patient, and to insist upon his practicing it daily. Exercise is the only means of reinforcing the musculature of the abdomen. Braces, corsets, props, trusses, never have strengthened anyone. Besides exercise for local development of the abdominal walls, general muscular exercise is advisable. The work outlined in the chapter on home gymnastics should be taken in earnest. Any procedure tending to restore normal, raise the viscera, develop correct carriage, etc., will relieve the pressure upon the abdominal walls and hasten permanent recovery.

It is sometimes advisable to allow the patient to rest a few days or weeks before commencing vigorous exercise. But during this period of rest local kneading and vibration with the proper application of cold water will always prove beneficial.

In the application of exercises, those are best which particularly tax the oblique fibres of the abdominal muscles. The muscle fibres which form the pillars of the internal and external openings are fibres of the oblique and transversalis muscles. There are three layers of muscle: the inner layer is made up of the fibres of the transversalis muscle, the middle layer of the internal oblique, and the external layer of the external oblique muscle. The fibres of the external oblique pass downward from the lower six ribs, and the tendon is inserted at the anterior third of the crest of the ilium. At the pubic crest, between these two points, the muscle is folded upon itself in a tendonous structure that forms the basis of Poupart's ligament. At the lower third of the pubic spine the tendons of the transversalis and internal oblique muscles as well as that of the external, do not coalesce, but leave an arched opening called the external ring. There is a slit-like opening formed by a separation of the horizontal fibres of the transversalis, through which passes the spermatic cord in the male and the round ligament in the female. The passage from the internal to the external ring through which these structures pass, is called the inguinal canal. This canal is formed by the lack of coalescence of the fascia constituting the myolemma of the oblique muscles. It is an oblique canal about an inch and a half in length, directed downward and inward parallel with, and a little above, Poupart's ligament.

Into this canal, by way of the internal ring opening, may pass any free viscus of suitable size. Once in the canal it may pass downward until it is checked at the super-pubic fascia or in the scrotum or vaginal labia. Not infrequently it distends the scrotum and produces a large swelling that hangs down several inches. This form of hernia is known as the indirect or oblique inguinal.

Where the protrusion penetrates some part of the abdominal wall internal to the epigastric artery it is called a direct inguinal, or internal oblique hernia. In this form the protrusion may escape from the abdomen through the fibres of the conjoined tendon or the tendon is gradually distended in front of it so as to form a complete investment for it.

Without further details about forms and names of herniae, let us review briefly the philosophy and application of the gymnastic treatment. It is safe to make the general statement that very seldom do herniae exist in individuals whose abdominal muscles are strong and kept in good tonic condition. We usually find that herniae exist in individuals whose general muscular systems are flabby and weak. The abdominal muscles are relaxed and offer but a weak support to the viscera. The fundamental standing position described in Chapter II explains how these muscles should function. In every case where special exercise is taken to cure hernia, general exercise should also be taken. The reason is obvious.

For local effect the best types of abdominal exercises are performed with a lateral twist of the trunk, with the patient lying on the back, or the legs are drawn up from the sides, having first been placed so as to cause a contraction of the oblique fibres. The exercises described are sufficient to cure any case of hernia that is amenable to exercise. They do not include the entire possible variety, but only a selection of the best and most specific. They are all chosen for their local and specific effects, keeping in mind their general effect upon the organism.

In applying the treatment it is advisable to proceed as follows:

With the patient lying on his back, feet higher than his head:

(1) Reduce the hernia.

(2) Give the necessary osteopathic procedures.

(3) The patient's knees flexed to relax the abdominal muscles, give local kneading and vibration; alternately giving kneading a few minutes, then, vibration a few seconds.

(4) Give the exercises described below. In the beginning give the first five, then, add one at each succeeding treatment until all can be practiced at one session without tiring the patient. When all have been mastered progress by increasing the number of times each movement is repeated, always stopping short of exhaustion.

(5) After exercising give a general manipulation of the abdomen to keep the bowels active. Stimulate the liver by rhythmic pressure, percussion and vibration.

(6) Make sudden applications of cold water or ice bag over the inguinal region to cause contraction before putting on the supporting elastic pad.

As soon as possible urge the patient to lay aside the supporting pad. In a short time the abdominal muscles will be toned up to a degree that will render artificial support unnecessary for hours at a stretch. These periods will increase in length as the tonicity of the muscles is restored. When the patient feels capable he should go without the support, though he should carry it with him to put on in case of need. In a few months, even this precaution will be unnecessary.

While exercising to cure hernia the patient should lie on his back on an inclined table, the feet higher than the head. An incline of 10 or 15 degrees is about right. In this position gravity prevents the intestines from bulging out during the exercises.

1. Patient lying on the back, the legs apart, the arms extended back along the head and the hands grasping the sides of the table. The operator resists as the patient draws the knee of the afflicted side up to his chest. (Illus. 394.) This is repeated a number of times. For the sake of general effect upon the abdominal muscles it is well to flex both knees, with or without resistance.

2. Patient lying on his back, knees bent and apart. The operator offers resistance as the patient brings them together. (Illus. 395.)

3. Patient lying on his back, hands grasping the sides of the table back of his head, he flexes the knees up to his chest and straightens the legs to the left; then, he flexes them again and straightens them to the right, and so on a number of times. This exercise needs no assistance or resistance and particularly affects the oblique muscles of the abdomen.

4. Patient lying on his back, legs far apart, hands grasping the table back of the head. As he elevates the legs he draws the feet together so that they touch at vertical position. As he lowers the legs he gradually spreads them apart again.

5. Reverse leg swimming. The patient is lying on the back, hands grasping the sides of the table beyond the head. He spreads the legs apart, bends the knees

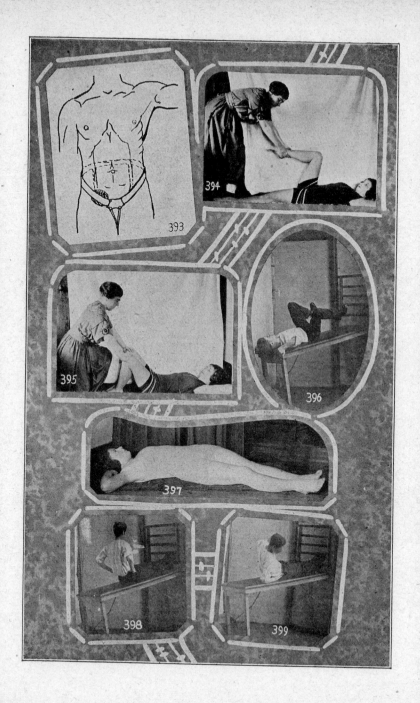

up to the chest as he brings the legs together and then straightens the legs out, while they are close together; he repeats the entire motion a few times; the feet are kept off the table throughout the movement. (Illus. 396.)

6. Circle the knees, keeping the feet off the table. The patient is lying as for above exercises. He flexes the knees up to the chest, carries them out to the side and then downward as he straightens them out, then, continuing in one movement he carries the legs around to the right and gradually flexes the knees as he completes the circle. This is repeated a few times without interruption, then, in reverse order the knees are carried to the right, downward, to the left and up to flexion, and so on. When this circling is done as in the first case, it affects chiefly a right inguinal hernia, and in the second case, a left inguinal, although the movement benefits and strengthens the entire abdominal walls.

7. Lying as for above movements, feet together, the patient elevates the legs and spreads them apart as they go up, bringing them together as they are lowered again.

8. Patient lying as for above movement, he raises the legs to vertical and, keeping them close together, knees straight and feet pointed, lowers them out to the left (Illus. 397), then elevates them to vertical and lowers them to the right, and so on. This is a valuable exercise to strengthen the abdominal walls, elevate the viscera, and reduce the size of the waist. To affect the hernia side especially, the legs are lowered and elevated from the afflicted side most. For instance, supposing there is a left inguinal hernia, the legs may be lowered twice or three times to the left, to once to the right.

9. Patient lying and grasping sides of table as for above exercises, he raises the legs to vertical, keeping the knees straight, toes pointed, and carries them down and outward to the left, then straight down without touching the table, over to the right and upward to vertical again, describing as large a circle as possible with the feet. This circling is done going down to the

right, from vertical position, or in reverse order. It should be repeated several times in either direction in a continuous movement without resting the feet. To affect the hernia side particularly, perform the last half of the circle, that is, the lifting of the legs, to that side, and repeat twice or three times in that direction to once in the opposite.

10. Patient lying, with the hands on the hips, the feet strapped or held down, keeping the head back, he flexes up to sitting position. (Illus. 398.)

This movement, as well as the two following, may be made more difficult by placing the hands at the shoulders, or locking the fingers behind the head, keeping the head in line with the trunk and the elbows well back as the body is flexed upward.

11. The feet held down as for Exercise 10, hands on the hips; to affect a right inguinal hernia, the patient turns the shoulders as far as possible to the left, so as to twist the trunk and place the strain particularly at the right inguinal region. The trunk is kept twisted as it is flexed up a few times. (Illus. 399.)

To affect a left inguinal hernia the trunk is twisted to the right and kept so during the exercise.

12. The feet held down as for the above two exercises, the hands on the hips. The patient flexes the trunk half way up and, holding it there, the head in line with the body, the shoulders well back, he twists to the left and forward, or to the right and forward, a few times. The turning is done opposite to the hernia side. This exercise should be done to both sides, to strengthen the entire abdominal region, but it is best to especially affect the hernia side by turning twice or three times to the opposite, to once on the same side as the hernia.

CHAPTER VIII

LATERAL CURVATURE OF THE SPINE.

A thorough study of the history and treatment of scoliosis would lead us back to the very beginnings of the practice of medicine and would show as much bungling and as many misconceptions of the true nature of the condition as any other phase of healing. The term "scoliosis" preceded the recognition of the deformity itself. The term is derived from a Homeric word which means to bend or twist. We find that Hippocrates first applied the term to designate a lateral form of spinal curve in contradistinction to kyphosis and lordosis.

As happened in so many other departments of medicine, though Hippocrates misunderstood the true nature of scoliosis, his opinions controlled the medical world for centuries. He supposed that a lateral curvature of the spine was due to a dislocation and his method of treatment, of course without success, was similar to his method of treating dislocations. In spinal curvatures his method was to proceed by tying the patient by the feet to a ladder and then have the ladder lifted by huskies and suddenly dropped, thus hoping to cause a straightening of the spine by reducing dislocated vertebrae. Another way was to place the patient on extension and apply pressure to the convexities. This was done by bringing weight with the feet or with a long lever. This pressure was not continued for any great length of time because it was only meant to reduce a supposed dislocation. Among other things, most of them wrong, Hippocrates says: "It is safe for a person to sit upon the hump while extension is being made, and by raising himself to let himself fall down again upon the patient."

Except for a statement by Paul of Egina, 650 A. D., advising that a case of spinal curvature should be bandaged to wooden strips, and another statement—in the spirit of finality that so many physicians of all periods have enjoyed uttering because they seem to think that it is a mark of wisdom to tell a patient that his case is hopeless—by Albukasis, in the twelfth century, that "No one can cure curvature to the side," there was no advance made over Hippocrates for about two thousand years. In the sixteenth century, Ambroise Paré reaffirmed the opinions and methods of Hippocrates and advanced the idea that a padded iron brace might help.

Although the affliction has always been common, little has been written about scoliosis. In his writings, a French physician, Riolan by name, in 1641 deplored the frequent sign of deformities of the spine as well as the posture of the shoulders. He reasoned that the frequent and perhaps the chief cause of scoliosis was the over use of one arm as compared to the other and that the wearing of iron corsets by girls rendered them more prone to the affliction than boys. With all the fine reasoning of the present age, excluding paralysis and rachitic conditions, it is a question whether a better explanation of scoliosis of the occupational type can be advanced.

The first real light upon scoliosis came after a great many autopsies had been performed. The first recorded autopsy was made in 1646, by Hildanus, but little was learned from it. Autopsies have been performed at various times since, but it was not known until the end of the eighteenth century that scoliosis could not be considered in the same light as lordosis or kyphosis. The rotation of the vertebrae to the side of the convexity was then recognized. In 1741, André, who was the founder of the science of modern orthopedics, wrote extensively about scoliosis. The result of his speculation was to recommend corrective apparati such as whalebone corsets and gymnastics as a means of treatment. As he did not understand the true nature of the condition and was not versed in the art of gymnastics, his method was soon shelved.

Although at the end of the eighteenth century the subject of scoliosis began to receive the attention it deserved, the best possible methods of treatment are still undetermined in the minds of most physicians. At the end of the eighteenth and the beginning of the nineteenth century, many books containing theories about the cause of scoliosis appeared and all kinds of corrective apparati were constructed to cure the condition; specially constructed braces, beds, chairs, belts and levers, and all kinds of machines. The types of mechanical correctors were impressive and awe-inspiring; but there never was a device invented of a mechanical nature that accomplished any more than to fix the existing curvature.

Ever since the period just mentioned various mechanical devices have been employed for correcting spinal curvatures. With very few exceptions most of these devices have been rejected as soon as a thorough trial proved their worthlessness. There are not many of these devices in use in this country but in Europe they are employed quite extensively. One would think, from the claims made for them, and from a cursory glance without close analysis, that they should prove efficient. Just why they do not come up to expectations can be readily explained if we consider a few examples of the best of them.

If the reader will look at Illustration 400 he will see what an elaborate and impressive looking machine is presented. The head is in the harness and extended so as to straighten the spine as much as possible. The hips are locked and the pad with the pushing device is applied at the shoulder on the convex side of the curve. The result of applying pressure from the convex side is to cause a natural recoil in the shortened tissues of the concave side of the curvature. Nature always reacts to an external force of this kind by resisting it. The tissues of the concave side are already shortened and do not need the

400

401

what is ↓

↓ what should
do through
patient's own
extension

402

403

404

405

special exercise this mechanical device stimulates. This device could be made effective and the entire mechanical work prove valuable, if the patient were to extend the left arm upward and make an effort to extend it higher, as the weight is rhythmically applied to the shoulder of the convex side. In Illustration 401 we have the same type of a right curvature under treatment and the same kind of mechanical pressure with the same kind of results, only intensified by virtue of the fact that the left hand grasps the bar above and must pull down as the pressure is applied to the convexity of the curve as the base of the machine is tilted. In this particular application of the mechanical force results could be remarkably rapid if only the right arm did the downward pulling and the left arm pushed upward as the base is tilted.

These are two examples which were taken at random from accounts of a score or more of the mechanical devices in use in various cities of Europe. In Boston I once saw such mechanical devices in use and with very few exceptions the same criticisms would apply. It needs little argument to prove the statement that the bad results reported about mechanical gymnastic appliances are due not so much to the failure of mechanics as to the lack of common sense in applying mechanical principles. If the inventors of these machines have knowledge of gymnastics, surely those who use them seem to lack the fundamentals of gymnastic correction. If the principles of gymnastic mechanics were understood the users of mechanical correctors would make no such blunders. In brief, the experimenters who have been honest in their reports confess that the use of mechanical devices has not been very successful. But this is due to wrong applications of these devices. Indeed, many old machines which have been scrapped long ago might prove efficacious if reclaimed and put to use by one who possesses a knowledge of the mechanics of the body.

Let us go back to the history of scoliosis for a brief space of time. In all the early writings on the subject little was said or understood about the muscular relation to spinal posture. As early as 1660, Glisson wrote about the subject and outlined a method of gymnastic treatment. But the results were nil because he did not understand his subject. At about the time of Glisson, the famous Sydenham stated that: "If anyone knew of the values of friction and exercise and could keep his knowledge secret he might easily make a fortune." Just how much Sydenham knew about the subject is doubtful, but there is more truth than fiction in his statement.

Any writer who recommends symmetrical exercise, that is, exercises in which both sides of the body do the same work, such as are explained in Chapter II, for the treatment of lateral curvature of the spine is unreliable and misleading. Such a person does not understand the principles of corrective gymnastics and no matter how efficient he may be in orthopedics or in constructing orthopedic appliances he is no gymnast. It matters not how many cases of scoliosis he may have handled and kept records of, if his tests were conducted with the wrong kind of exercises how can his deductions be taken seriously?

Let us consider some of the present authorities. To give symmetrical work is to fix the curvature, and even though asymmetrical corrective work follows this kind of fixation activity it is counteracted by it. Lovett is wrong in his advice in pages 140 to 147 of his third edition on "Lateral Curvature of the Spine," because these exercises are all of a symmetrical nature. Whether practiced extensively or not they are of a fixing nature. Although his motive is simply to limber the spine, as he states, the absolute law underlying all others is that the body tends to retain the posture it held during activity. The spine is the most important factor in bodily posture and its posture during activity is bound to affect the muscles accordingly. It is because of his experiments in noting his results after this type of work that he misleads all who do not understand the subject and do not go beyond him as an authority on it. Besides Lovett, among the modern authorities most often referred to, Whitman might be mentioned. Nearly all the exercises described in Whitman's latest book on orthopedics designed to correct scoliosis are wrong because, with a few exceptions, they are of the symmetrical nature.

The real start in scientific gymnastics was made by P. H. Ling of Sweden. Ling published his system in 1809. The Swedish government established an institute to teach his system during his lifetime and it still supervises it. Of course Ling made some mistakes, but this can be said of him, when he was wrong he was not far from right, and since most of his assertions have proved the test of the sciences even to our day, it is hard to understand why orthopedists and teachers of gymnastics have been so slow or neglectful in acquiring a better knowledge of his system before proceeding to experiment in their own way or claiming to have discovered a new and hitherto unknown system. Unless one has a working knowledge of scientific gymnastics he is bound to defeat his own purpose by utilizing procedures that not only cannot correct the defect in question but will rather tend to fix or increase it. It is therefore unfair to judge of the possible effects of scientific gymnastics by results obtained from a bungling application of them.

Lovett, who, in the estimation of many, stands highest in the field of spinal curvature treatment, surely proves a lack of complete knowledge of gymnastics. If he understood the importance of gymnastic mechanics and of the effect of posture in exercise he would never recommend symmetrical work. It is because of his mixtures of good and bad that he notes results which cause him to write, p. 134, third edition, "Lateral Curvature of the Spine," "Not only may gymnastics in moderate and severe structural scoliosis fail to do good, but they frequently do serious harm for the following reason: scoliosis of this grade soon results in stiffening of the affected region of the spine. If efficient gymnastics are given, the spine is speedily rendered more flexible and if it is so rendered and not supported at once it will sink into a worse position than before and the curve will be increased." In the last sentence of this quotation, if you prefix the syllable "in" to the word "efficient," the statement will mean just as much and will prove just as fair a test of what Lovett has in mind. Indeed, any kind of gymnastics will tend to limber the spine but at the same time, unless they are specifically corrective, they will prove more injurious than beneficial.

Even in the structural curve where there is no ankylosis of the vertebral bodies proper gymnastics combined with the right appliances will in time overcome the defect. It has been demonstrated over and over that normal function will normalize structure even of bone. Where there is an unbalanced condition of structure of the type found in scoliosis normal function does not mean simply movements common to a normal spine, but rather it means movements that always have the effect of shortening the convexities and extending the concavities. Never should symmetrical exercises be given in any kind of lateral curvature of the spine. Even at the risk of repetition, let it be remembered that a spinal curvature must be considered as the patient's posture while exercising and, according to the gymnastic law that the body always tends to assume the posture it held in activity, and it is clear what symmetrical work will do.

To get back to simple principles and lay the foundation for the correct treatment of scoliosis we must digress for a short time. Any lateral deviation of the spine from the median line, involving several vertebrae, is a scoliosis. Seen from the rear, the spine should be straight. A lateral view should present the normal anterior cervical, posterior dorsal and anterior lumbar curves. These are essential to elasticity and it is a mark of weakness if they do not exist or if they are exaggerated.

Statistics show that left dorsal is most common in

males and right dorsal in females. Why this is true is not so easy to explain as the simple observation of the fact. Another fact: whatever the cause of a curvature, the treatment always follows the same law. Cervical scoliosis is very uncommon. Lumbar scoliosis is not as common as dorsal. In a lumbar curvature we usually find one hip prominent. When a curve has become quite marked there results a secondary or compensatory curve at some other portion of the spine. The secondary curve is the result of nature trying to preserve equilibrium in the body.

Scoliosis may be muscular or osseous in origin. The muscular type is the result of unbalanced muscular action in occupation or play activities and the osseous is due to inequality of growth in the bones or cartilages of the spine. The causes of inequality of growth in the bones may be found in rachitis, osteomalacia or various lesions recognized by the osteopathic school and its imitators. The muscular type is most common and most amenable to proper exercise. The osseous type, as a rule, cannot be materially benefitted in grown persons. In young children, however, by prescribing a bone-forming diet and by having the patients persistently perform proper exercises according to their strength, much can be done.

From the standpoint of mobility and equilibrium, the bones are the most passive tissues in the body. They are held in place by cartilages, ligaments and tendons. The bones, cartilages and ligaments have no power of motion, but they are dependent upon the muscles attached to them. When a bone is out of its normal position it has been displaced by some power not within itself or control, that is, some power in the muscles or outside the body. It, therefore, usually requires a force outside the body to replace the bone. But, to keep it in place the muscles and other tissues around it have to be toned up. Given its normal blood and nerve supply, no power can tone up a region of the body like proper exercise. Unless exercises are used in correcting scoliosis there will be a tendency for it to collapse again. That is why the use of a corrective brace alone, or bone adjustment alone, will not suffice.

The forcible correction by plaster jacket, steel brace, or plaster jacket and bone adjustment combined will not prove sufficient in the majority of cases. The plaster jacket or the brace of any make, used alone, tends to support the spine and relieve the muscles of their work and after the spine has been straightened out, when this artificial support is removed, the flabby muscles prove too weak to hold the trunk erect and there is a falling back to the deformity. *The only correct line of treatment* is to combine the articulating effect of *osteopathy*, the toning up effect of *exercise*, and the use of a *properly adjusted support* that is easily put on or off. With a removable support a patient can practice exercises every day, take osteopathy as often as the case demands and wear the corrective brace between treatments and exercises and even at night to sleep in.

The most suitable brace is made of plaster of Paris and removable. Illustration 402 shows how it looks when finished. Its construction will be explained in detail below. This type of jacket can be put on or off in a few minutes. The exercises, selected to fit the individual case, are practiced every morning and evening and osteopathic adjustment is given at least twice per week. As the spine straightens, the brace is replaced by a more corrective one. Thus we have three forces working: the osteopathic, to correct the bony condition; the gymnastic, to re-establish harmonic relations of the muscles; the gain made by these two forces is preserved by the brace.

To get a clear idea of the gymnastic treatment, let us trace the development of an acquired scoliosis. Uneven muscular action causes an unbalance in the relative stronger and a stretching of the weaker muscles. The strength of the muscles of the spine. As those of one side, usually the right, through work, become stronger than their antagonists, there is a shortening of the stronger and a stretching of the weaker muscles. The common curvature is left dorsal because the muscles of the right side, being stronger, pull the spine over. When the curvature is just becoming apparent the muscles of the concave side are much stronger and thicker than those of the convex. But as time goes on and the curvature increases, the spine becomes bent over so that the muscles on the convex side have to bear the weight of the trunk and thus become hypertrophied while those of the concave side become shortened and, relieved of their work and deprived of normal function, they become flabby and in time may undergo atrophic or fibrous degeneration. That is why we find the tense, enlarged muscles on the convex side of the curvature and the lax tissue on the concave side. Indeed, the concave side muscles sometimes degenerate into nothing more than check bands.

Besides this condition in the muscles we find a more interesting condition in the vertebrae and ribs. As the curvature increases, the vertebral bodies, being so much thicker than the spinous processes, prevent the spine from bending directly to the side. There is a rotation in all the vertebrae included in the curve with the bodies to the side of the convexity where they have most room and the spinous processes to the concave side. Lateral curvature of the spine is always accompanied by the rotation of the vertebral bodies to the convex side and with these must go the ribs which are attached to them. That is why, posteriorly, the ribs bulge out so prominently on the convex side and are so depressed on the concave side. Corresponding to this posterior condition we find the sternum drawn to the side of the convexity and the ribs in front quite prominent on the side of the concavity. (Illus. 403.) The intervertebral disks are also altered as the curvature increases and in extreme cases these are so compressed out of shape as to allow the vertebral bodies to approximate on the concave side and, in rare instances, these ankylose. Total recovery from such an extreme case is impossible even in a child, while total recovery, even in a grown person, is possible in the average case where there is no ankylosis.

There are other causes of scoliosis besides those already mentioned. The above explanation applies in the average individual who is able to get around and work or even take part in athletics. But muscular weakness due to infantile paralysis, malnutrition, and so on, must be considered. The large muscles along the spine are called the *extrinsic,* and the smaller ones which are attached from vertebra to vertebra in short segments and are peculiar to these parts are called *intrinsic.* Persons with weak intrinsic muscles habitually assume bad postures because the spinal column cannot be held firmly in position and thus such weak muscles may be regarded as predisposing if not as exciting causes of scoliosis. As a proof that muscular weakness and not merely unbalanced muscular development may be the cause of scoliosis, if one removes the super-incumbent weight by placing the patient in reclining position or supplying braces that simply support the spine without any special aim at correction, it will often straighten the curve. Removal of the brace, however, will always be followed by a return of the curve unless the muscles have been toned up. When scoliosis is due to infantile paralysis, the same general rule for muscular restoration, explained under the treatment for this ailment, and the laws of corrective gymnastics should be followed. For the person whose spine is weak and bent as a result of muscular weakness general gymnastics are indicated. Indeed, if more attention were paid to scientific gymnastics in the early grades in schools there would be fewer cases of scoliosis.

Another cause of scoliosis is that explained by osteopathy. Scoliosis may follow a twisted or subluxated vertebra or innominate, uneven length of leg or a lesion involving a number of vertebrae due to constant irritation of some internal organ. Where the liver had been sluggish to the extent of producing gall-stones, in one case, marked left curvature from the sixth to the twelfth dorsal was found. Regulating the action of the liver by proper dieting along with osteopathic adjustment was sufficient to produce a correction. Setting a slipped innominate lesion has frequently sufficed to correct slight lumbar curvatures.

The average case is usually a single or C curvature. The advance case almost invariably presents a compensatory curvature and is known as the S curvature. The distribution of weight about the line of gravity in preserving upright equilibrium in the body explains the characteristics of scoliosis. The normal contour of the spine is the result of static conditions and a change of this normal relation in one portion induces a corresponding change from normal elsewhere. A curvature with rotation in the lumbar area will be compensated for by a curve and rotation in the opposite direction in the dorsal region. These curves may divide the spine equally or one may be short and the other long; occasionally three distinct curves may be present.

It is advisable to ascertain which curve is primary and which secondary because the treatment will prove more effective if the primary curve is attended to most. In examining a curvature it facilitates matters to mark the spinous processes. With the spinous processes marked, the patient is placed in the forward lax position, that is, the knees are kept straight and the arms and head hang forward limply as the body is bent from the hips. This position puts the spine on extension and by observing the marked spots one can determine which is primary because the secondary is the one which straightens out most. Another point is that if the dorsal is primary the elevated ribs on the convex side do not flatten out much, whereas when the dorsal is secondary, the ribs flatten out almost to normal. When the primary curve is lumbar there is not much bulging on the convex side here but the muscles are enlarged and tense. There is sometimes a slight rotation of the pelvis accompanying the lumbar curve but this is not necessarily caused by the curvature, rather it may be the cause of the lumbar curve. The dorsal curvature may be so extreme that the spinous processes cannot be palpated or marked and the transverse processes of the convex side of the curve form a line of nodules that may seem like the spinous processes. With the patient standing, if the shoulders are level the curve in the dorsal is compensatory, but if the shoulder on the convex side is higher, the dorsal is primary.

In the correction of spinal curvature there are several things to remember. There are three stages which influence correction: (1) the childhood stage, during which the work is easy and the prognosis very good; (2) the stage of puberty to full growth, when the work is comparatively easy and the prognosis for full recovery good; (3) the quiescent period, in which growth is completed, the bones set and prognosis conditional or very bad. Then, of course, each case has its peculiarities. The exercises must be adapted to the individual's condition and needs. The heart must always be examined carefully because its condition influences the success of the treatment. Many exercises are so strenuous as to be entirely contra-indicated where the heart is weak. The patient's physical condition thus influences the speed or possibility of recovery. There is no case, however slight, which can be cured in a few treatments or adjustments. It usually takes months and frequently years for full recovery and the prospective patient should not be misled into expecting anything different. For results, the patient's co-operation is necessary. He has to do the exercising and his laxity or perseverance will influence the rapidity or slowness of results. If the patient is poorly equipped in muscle, general body upbuilding must accompany the specific corrective procedures.

In correcting spinal curvature, as already stated, nothing equals the combination of osteopathy, medical gymnastics and the adjustable brace. Articulating the vertebrae to gradually alter and reconstruct the intervertebral disks, reducing the lesions to restore proper nervous control of all the organs and, secondarily, their normal functioning, will help. The practice of properly regulated exercises to restore equilibrium and harmony between the antagonistic muscles of the spine is imperative. Lastly, use as an adjunct and temporary necessity the wearing of a corrective jacket between treatments and exercises. These three processes will give results where any one of them alone would fail.

The Abbott method of treating spinal curvature is the best of the fixation type ever devised. There are many points in its favor if one is thinking simply of the correction of the curve without paying special attention to its muscular supports. But it should require little persuasion to prove the advantage of the triple combination just summarized. The Abbott method is still the most popular among orthopedists of old schools and also among many of the osteopaths who have not developed beyond this method of correcting scoliosis. But there really is no excuse for the fixation method of treating spinal curvature by an osteopathic physician. This method interferes with the very kernel of osteopathic practice. No spinal articulation is possible with the fixed jacket, no matter how large the windows. No exercise is possible as long as such a jacket is on, and what gain is achieved after two or more months of fixation can only be retained by carefully selected specific exercises as soon as the jacket is removed. Indeed, if the Abbott method is used, changes in the jacket should be very frequent. In young persons the corrective effect of a jacket is achieved in three or four weeks. Six to eight weeks should certainly be long enough for any jacket and there should be a period of exercise to tone up the muscles before the next is fitted. In adults the jacket may be left on longer than in young people, but surely four to six months is too long for anyone.

At present the writer uses a method which is similar to many that have been used in the past but which has a few distinct advantages over most. In the most advanced methods, as well as those of the past, the aim has been to correct the spinal curvature by applying direct pressure against the rib convexities, not in a manner to rotate the vertebrae back to median line, but, on the contrary, if the pressure is strong enough as usually applied, to rotate them even more pronouncedly to the side of the convexity. Diagram 1, in Illus. 404 shows the direction of pressure as applied by the various methods of forcible correction of scoliosis. The position of the rib articulations with the vertebrae shows what the result of this pressure against the convexities will do. The arrow around the body of the vertebra shows what has already happened and what is increased by such corrective force. What needs to be done is to apply pressure against the front and back convexities by directing the corrective force that way, and not so much from the lateral direction. Diagram 2, Illus. 404, shows by arrow heads the correct angle of force, so as to not only reduce the rib convexities but, at the same time, rotate the vertebrae back to normal. This is entirely in keeping with the anatomical and osteopathic concept and a jacket applied in this way keeps a continuous force in the direction of osteopathic articulation to be explained below.

In order to effectively achieve true correction it is the spine and not the ribs that demands attention. The first step toward this end is taken by lengthening it through extension. The patient is in upright position, the head stretched with about fifty to seventy-five pounds traction, the arms are only held high enough to be out of the way. The hips are secured to prevent too much swaying. A strip of zinc is slipped under the stockinette and a jacket of about half an inch thickness is made. (Illus. 405.) The jacket is built as high up around the shoulders and as low down over the hips as possible. When sufficiently dry, this jacket is slit down the front over the zinc strip, removed and tied with several strings or strips of bandage and allowed to dry thoroughly. When dry it is filled with wet plaster of paris and a torso of the patient is made. The stockinette is sufficient to prevent the newly made torso from sticking to the jacket. It is this torso which affords a better opportunity than the Abbott frame or any other method to make a jacket corrective as one desires. Illus. 406 shows various types of these torsos.

Before proceeding to take off at the convexities and build out at the concavities, take the girth measurements at the chest, the nipples, the waist and the hips. Measure also the distance from the crests of the ilia to the axillae so as to get the correct length of the jacket under the arms. Then measure the distance from the tops of the flexed thighs to the anterior superior spines of the ilia, thus guarding against the chance of making the jacket too long at the front. When the jacket is left too long here it prevents sitting with comfort. In women it is advisable to measure the exact distance from the bottom of the breasts to the anterior superior spines of the ilia in order to allow enough room for the breasts in the finished jacket. Since the original jacket is made with the arms elevated it tends to elevate the breasts higher than normal and when the arms are down the breasts may sag to a degree that might prove painful in a jacket that was not roomy enough.

The torso may be altered according to the needs of the case. It may be increased in length to allow for growth or lengthening out of the torso as the spine straightens. This is shown in Illus. 407. This torso is one of a patient who had a triple curve, namely, a right upper dorsal, left dorsal and upper lumbar, and a right lower lumbar. In a little over four months of treatment and of wearing of the jacket she has grown nearly three inches taller, which means that her spine is straightening out. Illus. 407, 408, 409, 410 and 411 are views of the same torso in various degrees of alteration. Illus. 407 and 408 are a back and side view of the torso. It is

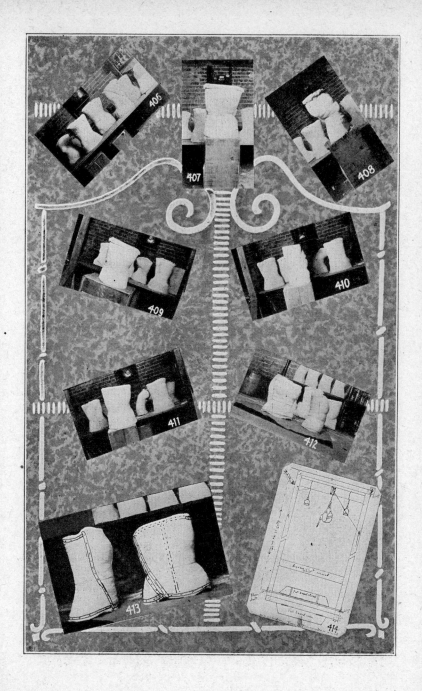

impossible to show all the lines and folds in the skin, but enough of the principal ones appear to make the deformity plain. In the side view the posterior rib convexity and the anterior extremities of the lower ribs are very prominent. Illus. 409 shows how plaster was added to fill the depression at the worst concavity. This was later trimmed down and smoothed with scraper and rasp and about an inch was taken off at the convexities and bulging ribs. Illus. 410 and 411 show the first corrective alteration in order to build a jacket that has proved painfully corrective. The torso in question here shows most of the possibilities of the method and renders it unnecessary to bring in others for various details. However, in Illus. 406 there are dotted lines which show how various alterations have been made.

It is impossible to correct with the lateral pressure method. It is impossible by the Abbott method to establish pressure in the right places for rotating the vertebrae back to normal alignment. But it is entirely possible to so modify a torso as to make the jacket press in from any direction desired. Diagram 2, Illus. 404, shows the correct direction. To render this most effective the torso is trimmed from the back and the front at the convexities as much as from the sides, and to keep the jacket as strong as possible, by building out at the posterior and anterior concavities the jacket will acquire room here that will render windows unnecessary. The finished corrective jacket is slit under the right or left arm, according to the patient's handedness. To assure a firm purchase over the hips the slit is carried obliquely forward at the bottom as shown in Illus. 412. The shoulder on the convex side of the dorsal curve is usually inclined to droop forward. To keep it down and back and also offer firmer pressure against the rib convexity, a strap is attached to the back of the jacket and passed over the shoulder and then secured to the side of the jacket under the arm, as shown in Illus. 402.

For best results this type of a jacket should not be

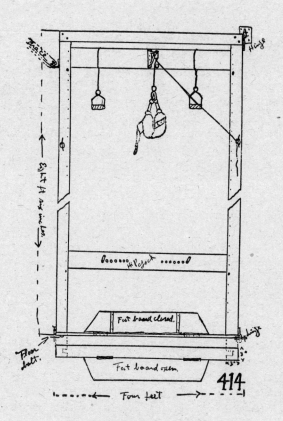

Hinge

Eight ft six inches

Hi Reject

Foot board closed.

Floor bolt.

Hinge

Foot board open.

414

Four feet

worn more than six or eight weeks, when another should replace it. After the first two or three weeks, it should be padded inside where the pressure must be constantly increased at the convexities. It therefore follows that each patient needs frequent changes of jacket. But with this method the out of town patient need not come in each time the new jacket is made. Unless the patient is growing rapidly and the hips are changing, a torso may serve for all the jackets, or at least for a year or more. The corrections are made on the torso and, provided the girths are observed, only one trip to the orthopedist may prove sufficient.

In making the corrective jacket, a piece of stockinette twice the length of the torso is used. The extra length is kept rolled up at the top while the plaster bandages are being wrapped on. When a thickness of about three-eighths of an inch has been reached, the surface is smoothed down and when the plaster is dry enough the lines for trimming are made according to measurement. The jacket is then slit at the side desired, removed and trimmed as gracefully as possible. The appliance maker then rivets on steel strips at the edges of the slit to which buckles are to be secured. Reinforcing strips are riveted around the bottom, the sides and back of the top edge and up the back or sides, according to the strength desired. Illus. 413 shows these steel reinforcements. The dotted lines show the back reinforcements. The stockinette is then sewed on and the buckles and straps attached as desired.

A jacket of this type can be put on or taken off in a few minutes. It is far less expensive than the celluloid or leather brace and although the latter may look prettier they cannot compare to it in usefulness because they are corrective for a no longer period than the plaster kind and their cost is infinitely greater. The jacket is worn during the day, or at night to sleep in, or both day and night. Ambitious patients apply thicker pads at the convexities for night than for day wear. These are pinned into place just before retiring and removed in the morning. Sleeping in a powerfully corrective jacket is difficult at first, but in a few nights this difficulty is overcome.

The apparatus used in making the first fitting is quite simple: Two upright pieces of 3 by 3 inches, hollowed out on the inner side for the cross pieces to slide into. (Illus. 414.) Across the bottom is a board with a hinged extension that allows it to fold up when the apparatus is not in use. Across the top is a strong piece to which is attached a harness hook and from this hook is hung a pulley. To the top piece are also attached handles with a device for adjusting their height. To the rope over the pulley is attached a head harness. The rope at its other end is secured to cleats which are attached to the upright pieces. There are peg holes for pegs to hold the cross pieces at the height desired. On the lower cross piece are peg holes and wooden pegs of about eight-inch lengths to secure the hips while the patient is standing. The entire apparatus is secured to the wall by hinges and to the floor, when open for use, by a floor bolt. At the top or along the upright away from the wall is a hook for a brace from the wall or nearby door frame. If one has a suitable doorway all of the framework could be made permanently secure without the need of hinges or floor bolts.

A word about the osteopathic articulation for spinal curvature. There have been explained and illustrated many ways of applying force to revert the vertebral bodies into front alignment. No method applied with the patient in upright position or while on hands and knees will avail much. The simplest and most effective method is to have the patient in prone lying position. For the lumbar curve, given a right lumbar and left dorsal, place the heel of the right hand on the convexity of the lumbar curve and with the left arm holding under the knees simply bear straight down with the right hand as you swing the legs up and to the right with the left arm. By carrying the legs to the right, more room is created at the left of the lumbar spine and with the pressure from above you apply direct force on the bodies which are already induced to move into alignment by the negative pressure resulting from the bending of the spine against its convexity. For the dorsal left curvature, standing at the patient's left side, have him fold his arms under the face, face turned toward you. Place your left forearm across and under the patient's arms and face, the right hand bearing down on the convexity of the ribs; apply pressure downward as you lift the head and upper body and carry them to the left. The effect of this pressure and swinging the body to the left will be to force the dorsal vertebral bodies into forward alignment. This simple technique applied over and over will prove of positive value, whereas any number of haphazard varieties applied with the patient in positions that lock the spine will only serve to use up the operator's energy without results.

It is needless to present all possible exercises for spinal curvature. We shall limit ourselves to a description of a number of typical exercises with and without apparatus, and then give three typical programs.

In considering the exercises for a single curvature, we must recall the principles of corrective gymnastics. These principles are all that apply here. Now we need to demonstrate a few positions and movements that bring them into play.

For clearness of explanation in considering the exercises for dorsal scoliosis we shall speak of the most common type, the left dorsal. From the muscular standpoint in a left convex curve the muscles of the right side are contracted or shortened and those of the left are extended; weak at first and later hypertrophied as well as hyperextended. The aim of our exercises must be to shorten the muscles of the convex side and lengthen those of the concave. The exercises, therefore, must be such as to cause the right side to be extended and the left side contracted.

The exercises for correcting spinal curvature tend to

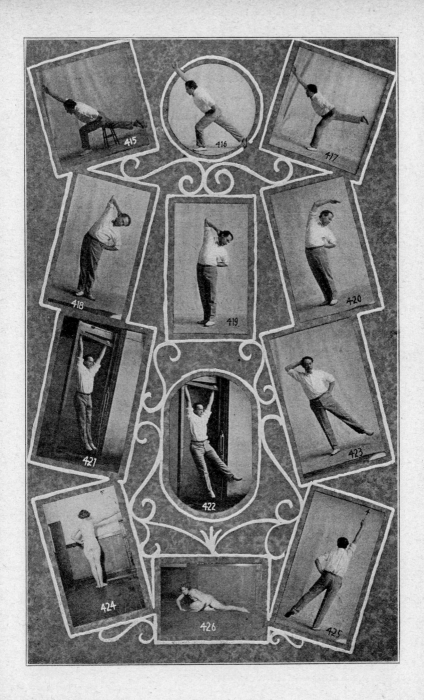

make the hypertrophied muscles of the convex side still larger and to merely extend the already dwindled or atrophied muscles of the concave side. This process must go on until the muscles of the concave side have extended enough to begin performing their duty by antagonizing those of the convex. Then, when balance between the two sides is approximated, the exercises must take on more of a symmetrical nature, such as in the chapter on home gymnastics.

It seems superfluous, yet excusable, to state that the following exercises are to be reversed in case of right dorsal single curvature, or right dorsal and left lumbar double curvature. The point is to always extend the arm or leg on the concave, and flex them on the convex side. The explanation and illustration of each movement should make this clear.

SERIES I.

1. Spring sitting position is one of the most important and effective exercises in lateral curvature. As the illustration (415) shows, the weight of the body is borne by the left buttock resting on the edge of a chair or stool. The left hand grasps the hip, the right arm and right leg are extended, and the body is bent forward until nearly horizontal; from the fingers to the toes should be a straight line, or there might be a slight arching backward of the trunk. In this movement the erectors of the spine are brought into play with the extremities of those on the left brought closer together while the muscles on the right are hyperextended. Spring sitting position is an exercise that is always indicated and advisable in spinal curvature. It should be introduced a few times in each program. It is one of those exercises that is worth several less specific ones done merely for the sake of variety.

2. With the hand on the hip, lunge forward with the left foot, and at the same time extend the right arm upward, pointing as far as possible with the right fingers and toes, gives the same effect as spring sitting, but more forcibly. (Illus. 416.)

3. The same type may be made still more powerful by combining a balance movement with the extension of the right arm and leg. (Illus. 417.) This is called horizontal half-standing position.

SERIES II.

1. Left hand on the hip, right hand behind the head, bend to the left. (Illus. 418.)

2. Left hand on hip, right hand behind the head. Turn the trunk to the left and bend to the left. (Illus. 419.)

3. Left hand on hip, right arm extended upward, turn to the left and bend to the left. (Illus. 420.)

SERIES III.

1. Hang on an incline bar, the right hand higher than the left, reach for the floor as you swing the feet from side to side. (Illus. 421.)

2. Same as 1, except that the legs are held to the left a few seconds at each second or third swing of the feet.

3. Hang with the body bent up to the left; while keeping the left side contracted, abduct and adduct the legs. (Illus. 422.)

SERIES IV.

1. Left hand on the hip, right hand behind the head, elevate the left leg sideways. (Illus. 423.)

2. Left hand on hip, right arm shoulder high at side, palm turned up, elevate the right arm to stretch as you raise the left leg sideways. (Illus. 424.)

3. Left hand on the hip, right arm extended upward, reach upward with the right arm as you raise the left leg sideways. (Illus. 425.)

SERIES V.

1. On hands and knees, bend the left knee under the body, the left elbow outside the knee, the right leg is extended backward and rests against the edge of the table, or is held by the physician. The right hand is

carried around to the left, the arm circling the head, while the trunk is bent to the left. (Illus. 426.)

2. On hands and knees, slightly bend the right elbow so that the trunk is twisted, left side uppermost. Now extend the left leg and arm, and elevate them and the head at the same time, thus causing a contraction of the left spinal muscles. (Illus. 427.)

3. On hands and knees, extend the right leg backward and carry it as far as possible to the left. Carry the right hand over in line with the left and bend the trunk as far as possible to the left. (Illus. 428.)

SERIES VI.

1. Standing with the trunk forward from the hips, the arms bent upward, (1) extend the left arm upward and the right sideways. (2) In one movement, elevate the right and lower the left to shoulder height, reaching up as high as possible with the right. (3) Flex the arms, etc. (Illus. 429.)

2. Arms bent, lunge forward with the left foot. While pointing the right foot backward as far as possible, go through the same arm movement as above. (Illus. 430.)

3. Repeat the same arm movement while in horizontal half-standing position on the left foot. (Illus. 431.)

SERIES VII.

1. Lying on the right side, left arm extended upward, raise the left arm and leg. (Illus. 432.)

2. Bearing the weight on the right arm and side of the right foot, left arm extended, allow the body to sag and elevate the left arm and foot. (Illus. 433.)

3. Bear the weight on the left hand and side of the left foot, right hand on the hip, allow the body to sag and then arch it upward as high as possible. (Illus. 434.)

SERIES VIII.

1. Lying face down, with a weight on the feet, left

hand on the hip, right hand behind the head, arch the trunk upward. (Illus. 435.)

2. Same as one, but when the trunk is arched upward, bend it to the left a few times. (Illus. 436.)

3. Lying face down, with a weight on the feet, arms bent. Arch the trunk upward and go through the same movements as Series VI, Exercise 1. (Illus. 437.)

SERIES IX.

Repeat 1, 2 and 3 of Series III, while pressure is applied at the rib elevation.

In *double curvature* the same general rule holds as in single. For clearness of explanation, let us assume that the S curvature is a left dorsal, as that discussed above, with a right lumbar compensatory. The exercises must be such as to cause an extension of the right dorsal and left lumbar and a contraction of the left dorsal and right lumbar. Therefore, in so far as the dorsal curve is concerned, the parts of the exercises described above, done with the arms and trunk remain the same, but the portions done with the legs are reversed. We shall explain the application by examples, and also add a few that particularly affect the lumbar curve.

SERIES I.

1. Spring sitting is done with the left hand on the hip, the right arm extended upward, the right buttock resting on the edge of a chair, and the left leg extended backward. (Illus. 438.)

2. The left hand on the hip, the right arm extended upward as you lunge with the right foot. Hold this position as you reach with the right arm and left leg. (Illus. 439.)

3. The left hand on the hip, the right arm extended upward, assume horizontal half-standing position on the right foot. (Illus. 440.)

SERIES II.

To effect the lumbar curve, place the right foot on

a book, or block, about 1 inch thick, tense the right lumbar muscles so as to cause an extension of the left lumbar sufficiently to straighten this curve, or force it into the opposite direction. While holding this position with the feet, the upper body goes through the same exercises as in single curvature. (1, 2 and 3, Series II.) (Illus. 441.)

SERIES III.

Hanging on the incline bar, as in Series III for single curvature, except that in each one the right leg is shortened as much as possible without bending the knee. This causes a shortening of the right lumbar and an extension of the left, while hanging on the incline bar, right hand uppermost, will extend the right and shorten the left dorsal muscles. The same rule applies in 1, 2 and 3 of this series. (Illus. 442.)

SERIES IV.

1. Upper body as Series IV for single curvature, right leg is elevated. (Illus. 443.)

Likewise 2 and 3, doing with right foot what was done with the left in single curvature.

SERIES V.

1. With arms, as for single curvature, but right knee is bent under body, the left leg is extended. (Illus. 444.)

2. Place a book on the edge of a stool, sit on the stool resting the left buttock on the book. Have the feet far enough apart to give a firm position, and, without altering the erect posture of the trunk, raise the right buttock to the level of the left. This causes a strong contraction of the right lumbar muscles, and an equal extension of the left. The left hand on the hip, the right behind the head. While keeping the right buttock elevated, turn the trunk to the left and bend diagonally against the bulged portion of the ribs. (Illus. 445.)

3. Using a book on a stool as in No. 2, after setting

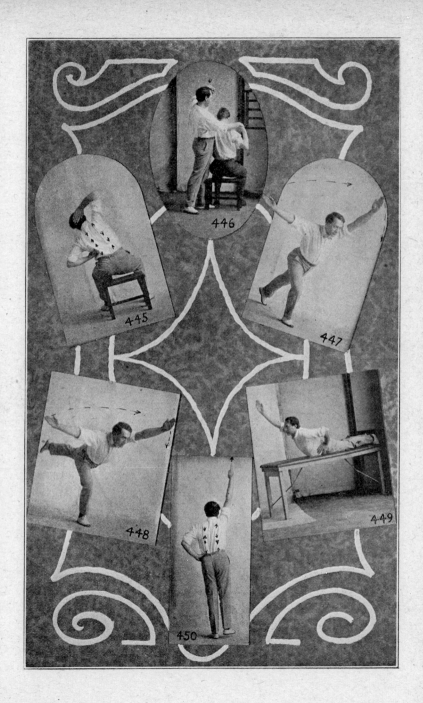

the lumbar spine as erect as possible, the patient endeavors to straighten entire spine by reaching upward with the head. While the patient holds this position, the operator resists as he pulls down with the left and pushes up with the right hand. (Illus. 446.)

SERIES VI.

1. Place a book under the right foot, and fix the lumbar spine as straight as possible; then bend the body forward and practice the arm exercise explained in Series VI, No. 1, for single curvature.

2. Arms bent; lunge forward with the right foot. While pointing the left foot backward as far as possible, repeat the same arm exercise as above. (Illus. 447.)

3. Repeat the same arm exercise as above while in horizontal half-standing position on the right foot. (Illus. 448.)

SERIES VII.

1. Lying face down, with a weight on the feet, the right leg held shorter than the left without bending the knee, the left hand on the hip, the right hand behind the head, arch the trunk upward.

2. Same as above except the right arm is extended upward and kept in line with the ear as the trunk is arched upward. (Illus. 449.)

3. Lying face down with a weight on the feet, right leg shorter than the left without bending the knee, arms bent, arch the body upward and extend the right arm upward as you extend the left sideways. Repeat this arm exercise a few times while holding the trunk arched.

SERIES VIII.

1. Left hand on hip, right arm extended upward, reach upward with the right arm as you elevate the right foot without bending the knee. (Illus. 450.)

2. Patient on stool near stall bar, left hand grasping low rung for steadiness, right arm extended upward as much as possible—under resistance, shorten right leg without bending knee. (Illus. 451.)

3. Patient leaning to the left over pad, right arm over the head, resistive right leg elevation sideways. (Illus. 452.)

SERIES IX.

1. Patient hanging on incline bar, right hand higher than the left. He raises the legs to the left and holds while the right leg is shortened against resistance. (Illus. 453.)

2. Patient hanging on incline bar, right hand higher than the left, convexity of the curvature resting against the pad; give resistive shortening of the right leg without bending the knee. (Illus. 454.)

3. Patient hanging against pad as Exercise 2. The patient shortens his leg, without bending the knee, and keeps it so throughout the exercise. He then abducts the legs against the operator's resistance. (Illus. 455.)

To *correct lumbar curvature,* many of the useful exercises are given under the treatment for double curvature. The part of the work done with the legs is typically corrective of lumbar curvature. Given a right lumbar curve, the upper body may be kept in symmetrical position by having both hands on the hips, or locked behind the head. Or, to emphasize the work, the right hand grasps the hip and the left is locked behind the head or extended upward, while the right leg is elevated sideways, or shortened without bending the knee.

Typical exercises follow:

1. Right hand on the hip, left hand behind the head, raise the right leg sideways.

2. Same position of hands as No. 1, shorten the right leg without bending the knee.

3. Right hand on the hip, reach upward with the left hand as you shorten the right leg without bending the knee.

4. Lying on the left side, raise the right leg, with or without resistance.

5. Hanging on the horizontal bar, resistive right leg abduction. In this movement the left leg is firmly fixed

and only the right is elevated sideways against resistance. (Illus. 456.)

6. Hanging, right leg upward traction against resistance without bending the knee.

7. On hands and knees, bend the right knee under the body, right elbow beside it, extend the left leg backward as far as possible and carry the body over to the right.

8. Lying face down, weight on the feet, right leg held shorter than the left without bending the knee, the right hand on hip, left hand behind the head, arch the body upward and bend it to the right. (Illus. 457.)

9. With the same starting position as No. 8, arch the trunk, carry it to the right, then twist to the right and lower and raise it a few times. (Illus. 458.)

10. Support the body on the left hand and side of the left foot, allow the trunk to sag. While holding this position the patient elevates the right leg against his own resistance. (Illus. 459.)

11. Support the weight on hands and toes, allow the hips to sag, twist the hips to the right and abduct the right leg, with or without resistance. (Illus. 460.)

12. Spring sitting, or horizontal half-standing positions are useful, left arm and leg extended.

In advising a patient to practice the above exercises, the programs are arranged in about the order given. For the first program, Nos. 1 of each series are prescribed. When the patient has mastered these so that they become easy, Nos. 2 are taken as a step in advance, for a second series. Later Nos. 3 are practiced. This rule applies for both single and double curvatures. In single lumbar curvature, a condition which rarely exists without a dorsal compensatory, select the easier movements first and add the harder ones as the patient grows stronger. A constant repetition of these movements, though of limited variety, will bring about best results because of their specific nature. They are the kind of exercises which should be repeated over and over without seeking merely variety.

For results, each movement is to be repeated at least seven times; ten or fifteen times is better. The patient must be made to feel the muscles that are at work and put his entire will power behind each movement. Between exercises he should endeavor to assume and maintain a correct posture of the spine.

The doctor will find that the best method of procedure is to give whatever osteopathic treatment the case requires; then supervise the exercises. Occasionally, examine the brace to see whether it needs readjusting or altering.

If the Abbott method is used, the first program should be practiced for the period elapsing between the first and second jacket. When the second jacket is removed, the patient should repeat the first program a few times and then take up the second. The second is to be repeated until it is so well mastered as to have become easy. By the time the third program can be utilized the average patient will no longer need the Abbott jacket. But the removable jacket should then be utilized, if one is needed.

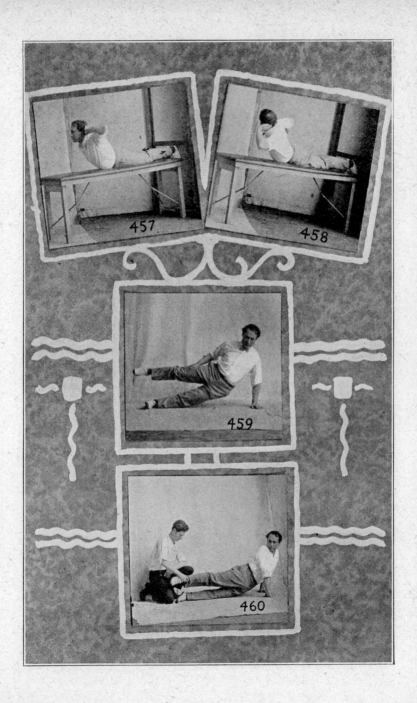

457

458

459

460

CHAPTER IX.

INDIVIDUAL PROGRAMS.

Chapter I explains the principal laws underlying gymnastics. Chapter II gives a number of lessons that meet the needs of the average. Chapter III classifies amusements in a manner to guide one in selecting his play activities. It seems that after having carefully read through those chapters anyone ought to know how to proceed in applying the work, but experience has taught differently. General principles and examples do not seem sufficient. Many want concrete directions. Though they have a fairly clear idea of what to do in given cases, nevertheless they like examples of what has already been done. Chapter VI presents special exercises for various anatomical defects. The following are examples of programs that have been actually arranged for patients.

Every patient is advised to follow the general course of exercises given in Chapter II. But those requiring special attention receive a few minutes as frequently as their case demands. Where children are concerned, the parents or nurse should be instructed in carrying out the home program.

One method is to have a set of forms to fill in according to the individual's needs. In this form may be written the needed exercises, and this is to be added to the regular hygienic gymnastic program. An example of this form is as follows:

CORRECTIVE EXERCISES.

1. Exercises to correct the posture and carriage of the head.

. . . .
. . . .
. . . .

2. Exercises to correct the posture of the shoulders.

. . . .
. . . .
. . . .

3. Exercises to correct posture of the spine.

. . . .
. . . .
. . . .

4. Exercises to correct the defects in the chest.

. . . .
. . . .
. . . .

5. Exercises to correct the legs.

. . . .
. . . .
. . . .

6. Exercises for the ankles and feet.

. . . .
. . . .
. . . .

In the above form prescribe two or three special exercises under whatever defects exist in the patient. Sometimes women or young girls want instructions about how to beautify themselves as well as to improve their health. The following is typical of the most common program:

PROGRAM FOR BEAUTIFYING.

1. Exercises to correct or prevent double chin.

. . . .
. . . .
. . . .

2. Exercises to fill the hollows in the neck.

. . . .
. . . .
. . . .

3. Exercises to reduce the waist.

....

....

....

4. Exercises to reduce the hips and thighs.

....

....

....

The above forms are merely types of what one is called upon to fill out. The selection must be carefully made in prescribing the exercises, and the patient must be impressed with the fact that perseverance is the chief element after the exercises are outlined. Regular periodical repetition of the movements, and holding constantly in mind the ideal aimed at, will bring quickest results.

The above forms are best in cases where patients feel that a specific program is necessary. But, with the majority, the best way is to arrange one program in which the special and general needs are met. This is done by introducing special procedures at appropriate places in a regular day's order.

In applying corrective gymnastics, as in giving treatment, we should attend to the individual, not merely to his drooping head, round shoulders or knock-knees. Therefore a program should be outlined to benefit him generally, as well as to meet his special needs.

In Chapter VI are given enough special procedures for all types of anatomical defects. The present need is to outline home programs for conditions not already covered by preceding chapters, and incidentally, give a clue to making out all types of programs.

SPECIAL PROGRAMS FOR HEART DISTURBANCES.

In disorders of the heart where the bed or office treatment has restored the heart sufficiently to render it safe to practice gymnastics, the following programs are types of what has been actually done with great benefit to the patient. The aim is to gradually rebuild the heart muscle, and the exercises are to be practiced at home every day, morning preferably, besides continuing the treatment explained in Chapter V.

The first program is very mild and the second is moderate. For harder programs the outline on home gymnastics will furnish material. The important point to remember is that a respiratory or vascular expansion exercise is to be introduced at every third or fourth movement.

In a very severe case of mitral incompetence, even with stenosis, or in cases of aortic incompetence, or in combined mitral and aortic valvular lesions, where the patient is confined to his bed, I combine the following programs with osteopathic adjustment. The osteopathic treatment proper takes pre-eminence over any procedures given. If I go into details about the gymnastic procedures and say nothing about the osteopathic ones, it is because osteopathy is specific and varies according to each case, while gymnastics are general and serve merely as an adjunct. But, in order to be of service, an adjunct must be understood and rightly applied. With every program, the osteopathic adjustments are given first and then the gymnastic procedures follow.

A word in explanation of this method of treatment. The osteopathic principle of healing is that after removing the obstructions, nature will accomplish the cure. Any procedure that tends to assist nature after obstructions are removed will hasten recovery. Therefore, by kneading the muscles, and by other procedures that assist to perform the heart's work, the heart itself will have a better chance to reconstruct. As soon as the patient begins to gain strength, easy resistive movements of the extremities are introduced. These are gradually increased in difficulty until the patient is able to exercise himself, when his daily programs are arranged according to the third program below. When the patient has reached the stage where he can exercise safely by himself, the osteopathic treatments and exercises are of course no longer taken together. To make matters clear, in the third program below, I have used the first program of the chapter on home gymnastics with the addition of respiratory exercises. As the patient gains, progression is made according to Chapter II, except that respiratory exercises are introduced in every program as in the one below.

PROGRAM I.

Apply whatever osteopathic procedures the case demands.

1. Ankle and wrist circumduction.
2. Kneading of the arms and legs.
3. Lifting up and back on the shoulders as the patient inhales. As the lifting is released the patient exhales.
4. Hand vibration over the heart area.
5. Kneading of the chest and abdomen.

PROGRAM II.

To be applied when the patient is able to begin the easiest of resistive movements. These are first applied at the small joints of the extremities. Later, the larger joints are exercised and the force is gradually increased. In this treatment I proceed in exactly the order given below. The entire treatment takes from twenty-five to thirty minutes.

1. Whatever osteopathic adjustments the case requires are applied.
2. Patient lying on the back or reclining, give kneading and then circumduction of the left arm, left leg, right arm and right leg, in the order named.
3. Kneading of the chest followed by gentle ulna percussion, or short and light vibration.
4. Lifting of the shoulders with respiration.
5. Manipulation of the abdominal viscera with a view to promoting peristalsis and excretion rather than for its effect upon circulation.

6. Patient lying face down, give kneading of the back, followed by percussion or vibration along the spine.

7. Shoulder lifting with respiration.

8. Resistive movements of the ankles and wrists. The operator offers slight resistance as the patient flexes and extends these.

9. Shoulder lifting with respiration and gentle vibration over the heart area.

In number 8 of this program, the force of resistance is gradually increased as progress is made. As soon as the case warrants it, give easy movements of flexion and extension of the knees and elbows. At first these are hardly resisted, the operator doing little more than guiding. As time goes on and the patient's heart gains strength, more resistance is applied. When the patient is able to sit up, and capable of strong movements of the ankles and wrists and moderate resistive movements of the knees and elbows, introduce movements of the hips and shoulders. Arm and leg rotation, that is, keeping the elbows and knees straight and turning the palms up and down from the shoulder, or the feet outward and inward from the hip, against resistance, with the patient lying on his back, flexing the knee up to his chest, against easy, and later, hard, resistance. Such are types of advanced movements that are to be introduced into the above program as the case demands. The order of procedure never changes. The only change takes place in the strength of the resistive movement.

By the time a patient has reached the stage where resistive movements of the hip and shoulder are possible he can begin with a daily program of home gymnastics. This program should be practiced every day, preferably in the morning. The treatment as outlined in Program II should continue three times, and later, twice a week, for a few weeks after the home gymnastics have begun. Later, the osteopathic procedures and home gymnastics suffice. After the heart is restored, for health and prophylactic reasons, home gymnastics should be continued as a daily habit.

PROGRAM III.
(See Lesson I, Chapter II.)

1. Hands on the hips, head bent backward, lift it to erect posture as you inhale deeply. As the head is flexed backward again, exhale slowly.

2. Turn the head to the left and right alternately.

3. Flex the head to the left and then to the right.

4. Heel elevation.

5. Raise the arms sideways slowly to shoulder height and at the same time breathe in deeply. Lower them slowly as you breathe out.

6. Hands on the hips, feet apart, turn the body to the left and then to the right.

7. (a) Hands on the hips, drop the head back and arch the chest.

(b) Hands on hips, bend forward from the hips.

8. Arm extension forward and upward.

9. Arms at the sides, shoulder high. Keeping the arms straight out from the shoulder, the hands traveling in a circle only as far as the shoulders do, lift the shoulders up and back as you inhale deeply. As you allow the shoulders to settle, exhale slowly.

10. Hands on the hips, (1) rise on the toes, (2) bend the knees half way, (3) stretch the knees and (4) lower the heels.

11. Alternate arm flinging forward-upward, beginning with the left.

12. Repeat Exercise 9 of this program.

13. Hands on the hips, feet apart, bend as far as possible to the left and then to the right.

14. Raise the arms forward-upward, inhaling deeply as they go up. As you lower them, sideways-backward, exhale slowly.

As the reader can see, this program is exactly the same as Lesson I of Chapter II, with the addition of respiratory exercises. This program will serve the average heart patient for a few weeks. Progression in such a case is made by increasing the number of times each movement is repeated. When the program becomes easy, Lesson II may be utilized by adding a respiratory exercise at every third movement, or more frequently, as the case demands. Exercise 9 of the above program is always good for the purpose of filling in a program for a heart patient. It is to this type of illness, what the spring-sitting position is to a spinal curvature.

SPECIAL PROGRAMS FOR CONSUMPTIVES.

Before giving any program in detail let us consider hastily a few prophylactic procedures. Children who inherit the phthisic thorax, or in whose family there has been tuberculosis, should be cared for early in life. Plenty of fresh air, good nourishing food, and corrective gymnastics to deepen and broaden the chest, besides general hygienic gymnastics and outdoor games, are the most important measures to apply. Respiratory exercises to utilize the entire lung tissue and especially the apices of the lungs, should occupy an important place in the daily program. The physical strength should be increased by every means possible.

It must not be forgotten that in pulmonary consumption the lungs are congested and there is always danger of hemorrhage if they are used violently; therefore general chest and breathing exercises are to be employed with great caution at first. Chest percussion, and short vibration, which have the effect of constricting the blood vessels, or preferably, osteopathic procedures that promote peripheral, and decrease thoracic circulation, should be given frequently.

It is seldom advisable and usually unnecessary to send a tubercular patient to a hot, dry climate. The air in one city is as good as another if a patient gets it fresh and in abundance without exposing himself.

When the patient's disease has reached a far advanced stage, little can be done except to make him comfortable. To give active gymnastics or breathing exercises might result in a fatal hemorrhage. Therefore, besides the proper osteopathic procedures, the following program will prove beneficial:

PROGRAM I.

1. The patient lying on the back, his arms out at the sides. Give a general gentle kneading of the arms and legs, chest and abdomen.

2. Lift up and back on the shoulders a few times.

3. Give chest percussion, and gentle vibration.

4. Patient on the side, manipulate the back thoroughly.

5. Rapid circumduction of the hip and ankle joints.

6. Repeat number 2, and let the patient lie or recline easily with his arms out at the side or with the fingers locked behind the head. This procedure is a gentle and safe inducer of activity in the apices of the lungs.

If your patient possesses a strong physique, has good vitality and is receiving the best of care from the standpoint of food, air and cleanliness, there is a chance that he will regain enough strength to derive benefit from the second program. In such a case prognosis is very good and thorough, diligent effort will bear good fruit.

The second program applies to a case that is recovering from a low condition, or to one whose illness is far advanced but not enough to render him helpless. It applies to what used to be known as the second stage of consumption.

Pulmonary consumption used to be generally divided into three stages. The first stage was when the disease was just beginning. There was pain in the chest, the first rales were heard, and the night sweats and daily rising temperature were first experienced, but the patient as yet felt no marked weakness. In the second stage, the disease was marked by more rapid pulse, night sweats and daily rising temperature, and the patient's endurance was very much lessened. An occasional pulmonary hemorrhage of no serious nature may occur at this stage. The third stage was determined by the patient's great weakness, anaemia, emaciation, louder rales, constant coughing and expectoration, and enlarged spleen. At present there is seldom made a division of the disease into stages. There are so many variations to any and all such rules, depending upon the individuals themselves, their environment, the rapid or slow progress of the disease and so on, that the idea of dividing the disease into three stages has become obsolete.

For a patient whose affliction is far advanced, but who is still able to get around the following program will be found very beneficial:

PROGRAM II.

1. Apply whatever osteopathic procedures the case indicates.

2. The patient sitting, hands on the hips, the operator stands behind him and gives him passive shoulder circumduction and respiration. (Illus. 267, Chapter V.)

3. Patient sitting or standing, his fingers locked behind the head, the operator gives ulna percussion of the chest. (Illus. 461.)

4. Patient lying on his back, give rapid circumduction of the hips; first one, then the other.

5. Apply short vibration over the chest, especially at the seat of congestion.

6. Patient sitting, he leans forward, arms out from the shoulders, and, while keeping the body forward, flexes the head backward and at the same time turns the palms upward. (Illus. 462.)

7. Patient reclining, the operator resists as he flexes and extends the ankles.

8. Patient standing, hands on the hips, head turned to the left, he bends it to the left as he inhales. After repeating a few times, he turns the head to the right and bends it to the right at inhalation. This will emphasize the use of the apex of the lung first of the right, then the left. Any of the corrective exercises explained

under one-sided defect in Chapter VI, may be used to advantage here.

9. Patient sitting on a stool, or kneeling, hands on the hips; he turns the trunk to the left and then to the right.

10. Patient reclining, the operator offers resistance as he flexes and extends the knee a few times.

11. Repeat number 2.

12. Patient standing, arms extended upward, hands grasping something, the operator gives chest percussion.

13. Patient advised to lie in an airy place, his body well protected from the cold. He is to lie on his back, preferably with his arms out from the shoulders, or with the fingers locked behind the head.

For the typical consumptive type, the one who is predisposed to tuberculosis of the lungs, as well as the patient who is in the incipient stage of the disease, the following program will be of great value. With plenty of fresh air, good food and other hygienic practices observed, it is sufficient to prevent the disease and restore health in the afflicted.

PROGRAM III.

1. Osteopathic procedures, such as setting and lifting the ribs, adjusting the dorsal spine, promoting peripheral, and reducing pulmonary circulation.

2. Patient sitting, his hands on the hips, trunk inclined forward, he flexes the head and upper trunk backward as he inhales deeply. As the head and trunk are returned to commencing position he exhales. (Illus. 463.)

3. Patient sitting, arms extended upward, the operator stands behind, grasps his hands, and offers resistance as the patient pulls his arms down to flexion. The elbows should be carried straight out from the shoulders as they travel downward. As the arms come down the patient inhales. As they are extended upward slowly, the operator offering no resistance, the patient exhales. (See Illus. 323.)

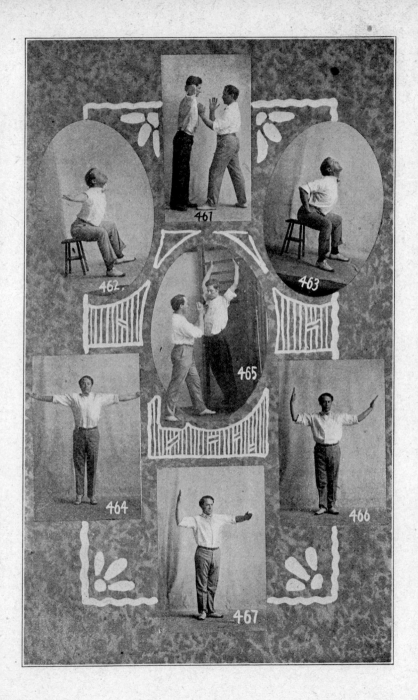

4. Patient kneeling, his fingers locked behind the head. Keeping the elbows well back, head high to keep the chest expanded, he twists the trunk to the left, and then to the right.

5. Patient standing; while inhaling deeply, he elevates the arms sideways to shoulder height and just as they reach shoulder level he suddenly turns the palms forward-upward, and as the palms are turned the heels are lifted. (Illus. 464.) This causes a sudden and great expansion of the apices of the lungs. As the patient exhales slowly, he lowers the heels, turns the palms downward and lowers the arms.

6. Patient lying on the back, arms extended and grasping some heavy object, he elevates the legs alternately or together, according to his strength. (Illus. 85.)

7. Patient takes arch-hanging position and while holding it, the operator gives resistive neck extension. (Illus. 315.)

8. Repeat number 5.

9. Patient standing, arms extended upward, hands grasping stall-bars or trapeze. He rises on the toes and leans the body forward to expand the chest. While the patient holds this position the operator gives percussion of the chest. (Illus. 465.)

10. Fingers locked behind the head, feet apart, the patient bends as far as possible to the left and then to the right.

11. Repeat number 5.

One who is inclined to lung weaknesses of any kind, and especially the typical consumptive type, should be advised to practice the home gymnastics outlined in Chapter II, in addition to all kinds of outdoor activity, according to the individual's strength. To render these programs more specific, at every second or third exercise of these lessons, introduce breathing Exercise Number 5 of Program II, above. In this way the entire set of lessons in Chapter II may be made prophylactic against pulmonary tuberculosis.

SPECIAL PROGRAMS FOR LOCOMOTOR ATAXIA.

Locomotor ataxia is not in itself a disease, but, strictly speaking, it is a symptom of the change going on in those sections of the spinal cord known as the columns of Goll and Burdach. The condition is marked by a loss of control and muscular sense. The muscles themselves show little or no loss in size and strength, but, in the typical case, they show a loss of tone. While the other symptoms, as of the bladder and intestines, and the darting pains, cannot be affected by gymnastic treatment, the muscular condition and control can be greatly benefitted.

One of the most important things to do is to keep the patient's courage up. He must not be allowed to give up hope, but must be impressed with the idea that by persistent and regular effort he can regain control of his muscles. He must re-learn ordinary movements, if they are lost. If he has not lost much of his control he must work to retain his powers and acquire new ones. By acquiring new powers, the simple movements of everyday life are rendered easy and graceful. Therefore, to make walking easy, we teach as many balance movements as possible that require more control than walking. Where there is loss of control of the hands, the same principle holds good with movements of the arms and hands. Of course, in very low cases, where even walking is impossible, and where there is such a poor muscular sense that a patient cannot even carry food to his mouth, the most elementary movements are introduced. It would be impossible to describe in detail every step in progress to be taken in re-developing lost control. Only typical movements and methods can be given.

The ideal in every case is to restore perfect control and muscular sense. This ideal is a condition in which the muscles respond readily to all shades of volition for power, speed, strength, skill and agility. With the patient willing and persistent, this ideal is possible in most cases, if time enough is allowed. Time enough is an unknown quantity, depending upon the patient and his perseverance. Most patients, however, are satisfied if they regain sufficient power of locomotion to get back to work.

To tone up the muscles, to restore strength and to reduce nervousness, it is well to give thorough kneading of the arms, legs and back, and follow this by a few simple resistive movements. Then follow with movements of control.

The following program is by no means intended to be utilized at once. The average patient can stand but very little at each treatment. The outline is simply intended as a suggestion of various steps to follow, but it is the best order in which to introduce progressive steps. Let the patient repeat one or two exercises once or twice a day, according to his strength and skill, and then go on to the next.

A typical locomotor ataxia patient has lost all sense of fatigue; therefore, in giving him exercises it is advisable to watch for signs of it. A very rapid pulse, even as high as 150, and a state of listlessness are signs that enough work has been done for one session.

PROGRAM I.

For a patient who has lost control of his arms and hands.

Always begin by applying whatever osteopathic adjustment the conditions indicate.

1. Give thorough kneading of the arms and shoulders.
2. Give resistive movements of the shoulder joints.

(a) Movements of elevation and depression.

(b) Movements of adduction and abduction. That is, the patient sitting, his arms out from the shoulders, the operator resists slightly as the patient carries them forward and back to position.

(c) Patient sitting, his arms out from the shoulders.

Operator stands behind, holds the patient's hands and resists as the latter turns the palms up and down.

3. (a) Resistive flexion and extension of the elbow joints.

(b) Resistive flexion and extension of the wrists and fingers.

4. (a) Double arm extension sideways.

(b) Double arm extension forward.

(c) Double arm extension upward.

(d) Double arm extension downward.

5. Alternate arm extensions in the four directions given above. The patient extends the left arm sideways; as he flexes the left he extends the right, etc.

6. Arm extensions in bilateral directions.

(a) Left arm upward, palm turned in, right arm sideways, the palm turned down. (1) Bend the arms upward, (2) extend the left upward and the right sideways, (3) bend the arms, (4) extend the right upward and the left sideways, etc.

Following the same count as in (a):

(b) Extend the left forward, palm turned in and the right sideways, palm turned down, changing with count.

(c) Left arm upward, and right forward, changing with count.

(d) Left arm sideways, right arm backward, changing with count.

(e) Left arm forward, right arm backward, changing with count.

(f) Left arm upward, right arm backward, changing with count.

7. (a) Arms sideways, shoulder high, palms down, turn the left palm up (forward-upward). As you turn the left down turn the right up, and so on.

(b) One arm out at the side; while watching it, turn the palm forward, and close your eyes to get the feeling. Turn it down again. Next, without watching, try to turn the palm forward again and hold it.

The operator should vary this exercise by making the

patient turn the palm at various angles. For instance, palm down, have him turn it one-fourth the way upward, then forward, which is half-way upward, then three-fourths the way upward and, finally, completely upward. Have the patient close his eyes and try to stop at various angles. This is to be done first with one hand, then the other.

(c) The patient is made to flex the arm at various angles. The operator may stand before him and flex his arms, and the patient tries to imitate, without watching his own arms.

For instance, the operator begins with his arms at the sides. He turns the palms up and flexes the forearms to right angles. The patient imitates. He then lowers them to an angle of forty-five degrees. He holds one at that angle while he straightens the other, or flexes it again to right angles. Thus one arm is flexed at one angle and the other at another. (Illus. 466.)

He may vary this still more, by flexing both arms at right angles and then, keeping them thus flexed, lower one to horizontal forward position. (Illus. 467.) As he lifts this one, he lowers the other. This same stunt is rendered more difficult by having one elbow at right angles and the other at forty-five degrees.

These are but suggestions of the possibilities in restoring control of the arms. They are capable of all kinds of variations. Our aim is not to exhaust the possibilities, but to make clear the principle.

The chief point to remember is to first make the patient imitate you. Then let him try to do these movements by himself, to command, or from memory, and without watching his movements with the eye, but depending entirely upon his muscular sense.

As a general rule, if a patient acquires skill and control sufficient to perform these movements correctly, his hands and fingers will take care of themselves. But, if special finger work is required, or deemed advisable, one has access to all kinds of devices for the purpose. The following are examples:

(1) Frenkel recommends the use of a perforated board, which is placed before the patient. The holes are numbered and the patient's exercise consists in placing the tip of the index finger of either hand into the hole called for by the operator. Another way is to stick a peg into the hole named.

(2) Have the patient practice drawing vertical and horizontal lines. Later have him draw circles, and then, pictures of various simple objects. Use a large sheet of paper, with a large pencil. The lines should be no less than a foot in length, and the circles over six inches in diameter. The object is to bring in the entire arm and not merely the fingers.

As the patient regains control finer work, requiring more of the wrist and finger action, should be introduced.

One of my patients acquired control by first making a dog-house, and then, after practicing drawing and exercising at a perforated board, regained sufficient skill to make his little daughter a doll-house with all its furnishings, even to wiring it and installing toy electric lights in it.

PROGRAM II.

A series of exercises the ultimate aim of which is to restore walking. The first few are for a patient who is confined to his bed. They are progressively selected and as soon as one is mastered the next should be introduced. All of these exercises are but typical of what one may employ to restore control of the legs.

1. Patient lying on his back in bed.

(a) He flexes first one knee, then the other, drawing the foot lightly over the mattress.

(b) Flexes both knees up together.

(c) Flexes the left knee up. As he straightens the left knee he flexes the right, and so on alternately.

2. Patient lying on his back in bed.

(a) He flexes the left knee up and touches the left

heel to the right knee. He repeats with the right.

(b) He flexes the left knee up, touches the left heel to the right knee and then the middle right shin bone before resting the leg. He repeats with the right.

(c) He flexes the left knee up, touches the right knee with the left heel, straightens the left knee up, flexes it again and touches the middle of the right shin bone with the heel and then lowers the leg. He repeats with the right.

3. Patient lying on his back in bed.

(a) He flexes both knees up, straightens them up and lowers the legs slowly.

(b) He flexes both knees up, straightens them and lowers the legs half-way down, spreads them apart, brings them together again and lowers the legs slowly the rest of the way.

(c) He raises both legs half-way up (knees kept straight), spreads them apart, brings them together again, and lifts them to vertical. As he lowers them he repeats the leg-spreading as described in (b) above.

(d) He raises both legs half-way up, spreads them apart, brings them together and touches the right toes with the left heel, spreads them apart, brings them together again, touches the left toes with the right heel, and, bringing the heels together, raises the legs to vertical.

At first the legs are lowered from this position, without adding to the movement. Later when the patient has gained sufficient strength and control, the legs are spread and heels touched to toes in reverse to the upward movement.

4. Patient lying on his back in bed.

(a) Against the operator's resistance, he flexes one knee up to his chest and extends the leg again. He repeats with the other leg.

(b) Against the operator's resistance, he flexes both knees up to his chest and extends them. The operator grasps at the ankles and resists the movement in each direction.

(c) The patient's knees are flexed, his feet resting squarely on the bed. Against the operator's resistance he spreads the knees apart and draws them together again. The operator grasps outside the patient's knees to oppose as the latter spreads them and he grasps inside as the patient draws them together again.

(d) Patient on his back, knees straight. The operator grasps at the ankles and resists according to the patient's strength as the latter abducts and adducts the legs.

(e) Patient lying on his back, the knees are kept straight and the movement takes place in the hip joint. The operator grasps the patient's toes and offers resistance as the latter rotates the toes outward and brings them together again.

5. To teach the patient to walk again.

(a) If he is unable to bear his weight with the help of his hands grasping a pair of rails about two feet high, arrange the rails overhead so that he can more easily bear his weight in this half-hanging condition. In one case it was necessary to resort to an overhead trolley arrangement. A rail was hung up on which a roller, such as are used for sliding doors, was attached, and from this was suspended a strap that supported the patient from under the arms. For a few weeks he practiced walking back and forth with the aid of this apparatus.

(b) As soon as the patient is able he should practice walking between two rails.

(1) Lines are drawn on the floor at regular intervals, upon which he is to set his toes or heels.

(2) When he has mastered this style of walking, the lines are drawn at irregular distances.

(3) Outlines of the feet are drawn upon the floor, and he is to set his feet squarely and exactly inside these outlines. These are drawn to point straight forward or outward at various angles.

6. As soon as a patient has mastered the above exercises he is to practice walking with crutches and repeat the various exercises explained under 5.

Later he is to try these with one crutch and a cane, and then give up the crutches entirely and practice at first with two and then with one cane.

7. When he is able to stand or walk without any support, exercises such as the following are in order, to be performed without watching the feet any more than is absolutely necessary.

(a) (1) Place the left foot forward about twenty inches, (2) bring it back, (3) Place the right foot forward, (4) bring it back. Repeat a number of times.

(b) (1) Place the left foot sideways about twenty inches, (2) bring it back, (3) Place the right foot sideways, (4) bring it back.

(c) Hands on the hips, rise on the toes. Lower the heels slowly.

(d) (1) Place the left foot forward, (2) rise on the toes, (3) lower the heels, (4) bring the left foot back. Repeat with the right foot forward, and so on.

(e) (1) Place the left foot sideways, (2) rise on the toes, (3) lower the heels, (4) bring the left foot back. Repeat with the right foot, and so on.

The above are typical of the movements indicated in restoring muscular control. When a patient is capable of performing these fairly well he is able to begin with the exercises outlined in the chapter on home gymnastics. Begin with two or three movements of the first lesson. The next day add one or two, and so on, until the entire lesson can be practiced without exhaustion.

All of the movements in Chapter II, especially of the first fourteen lessons, are done in free standing and, therefore, serve as movements of control. Let a patient progress as rapidly as he can in the regular outline.

SPECIAL PROGRAMS FOR INFANTILE PARALYSIS.

After what has been said on infantile paralysis, in

Chapter V, it seems almost superfluous to say any more. But when it comes to instructing mothers, or guardians, on the home treatment of this type of case much time may be saved for the doctor and better results will accrue to the patient if a typical outline is given.

Before describing a hypothetical case and its treatment, a few words about methods of treatment and prognosis might not be amiss. The use of a properly adjusted brace is helpful. It is claimed that many a case has been restored to normal by means of braces alone. This hardly seems possible where there has been extensive destruction of the cells of the anterior horns of the spinal cord. But, in mild cases, the brace alone might suffice. The use of the brace with osteopathy and exercise is the ideal.

There are some braces constructed with elastic attachments that seem to bring quick results, but, as a matter of fact, only aggravate the unbalanced muscular condition. As an instance, a child whose extensor muscles of the legs from the glutei down are the only ones affected, is sometimes fitted with a brace that seems to bring immediate results. Such a brace is made with jointed steel to allow flexion of the hip and knee joints. Steel bands at the waist, back and front of the thighs and legs, furnish anchorage for elastic strips to serve in place of the extensor muscles, thus giving antagonism to the flexors. These elastic strips are attached over the regions of the glutei from a steel band that reaches around the waist to one attached to the thigh steel strips, just below the buttocks. This elastic tissue takes the place of the glutei and extends the hip joint when the flexors of the hip (the psoas-magnus and iliacus) are relaxed. When these muscles contract hard enough to overcome the pull of the elastic bands they flex the hip. Thus by contracting the flexors of the hips the elastic pull is overcome and flexion is produced. When these muscles relax, voluntarily or otherwise, the extension results. The same principle applies at the thigh and leg. Elastic strips are attached to do the work of the depleted extensors and antagonize the flexors.

This principle is wrong because it prevents the possibility of restoring normal muscular control. The elastic bands by antagonizing the flexors really exercise and strengthen them. We, therefore, have a condition in which the weak muscles are kept weak, or made weaker, because they are relieved of their work, and the strong muscles are made stronger by virtue of the fact that they are being constantly exercised.

In cases where one set of muscles is intact and the other only partly paralyzed, elastic strips are sometimes used to assist the weaker set. But, even here, the tendency is to relieve the work of the weaker and antagonize and thus strengthen the stronger muscles. This process, though it enables the appliance maker to sell his goods, and though it may seem like an achievement for the doctor on the case, to say the least, delays progress for the patient.

Elastic strips have no place in proper treatment of infantile paralysis, that is, in so far as they are used to antagonize intact or nearly intact muscles. The proper method of treatment by gymnastics is to apply procedures that tend to temporarily weaken or relax the stronger and gradually strengthen the weakened muscles and thus bring about a state of equilibrium between the antagonists. When equilibrium exists, exercises to strengthen all muscles are in order.

The only brace that can really work in conjunction with osteopathy and exercise is the regulation jointed brace with clasps to lock the joints when necessary. In this brace, if the patient is weak along the spine, a corset brace is added to the leg brace. If a patient is too weak to walk, owing to paralysis of the leg and even the waist muscles, for locomotion all the joints are locked, crutches are used and both legs swing between the crutches. To begin developing control, the brace joint at the hip is unlocked on one side, and the patient makes an effort at each step to control this joint. At every few minutes the movable joint is locked and the other one unlocked, and thus each is exercised alternately. In time, when the thigh muscles have regained strength the knee joints may be unlocked alternately. Later, one hip and the opposite knee, or both hips and one knee are unlocked, according to the patient's ability.

Besides the brace described above, which usually proves sufficient to reinforce the ankle, it is sometimes found necessary to utilize special shoes or ankle braces and artificial arches. These points and others like them are details that the doctor in charge can take care of. It will be found best, however, not to resort to any more artificial supports than are absolutely necessary. Properly applied exercises will develop the weak parts, if there is any possibility of development left, and even though the process is slow in point of time, it is the surest for permanent satisfaction.

Plaster of Paris casts and jackets, and surgical grafting of muscles are methods that are no longer, or at most but very little used. There is really no place for plaster of Paris casts in treating infantile paralysis. Whatever good these can do in correcting deformities may be done far better by rest and exercise. A plaster cast always isolates a part and isolation means weakening in reference to muscles, and the muscles are usually so weak that little isolation is necessary. Muscle grafting is also an ill-advised procedure. The process is to cut strands of unaffected or stronger muscles and graft their loose end into the depleted muscular tissue. It is easily seen that to graft a strand of extensor fibre into a flexor muscle would only lock muscular action if it were successful. If unsuccessful, as this process usually is, the patient is subjected to a great deal of unnecessary pain.

The object in the mind of a surgeon who performs muscle grafting is to stimulate a new growth of muscle cells in the depleted ones. The aim is good, and the work is usually done neatly, but the method and results are wrong. A surgeon who understood the mechanics of exercise would not undertake such a job.

In the first place, the destruction of muscular tissue is not the cause but the result of nerve-cell destruction in the cord. Therefore, even though muscle grafting were a success, still, without proper nerve control, there could be no muscular control. If the grafting of a strand of extensor muscle fibre into a flexor muscle does stimulate new growth here, still, the new flexor muscle fibres are under extensor nerve control, and the best that could possibly result from such an operation would be a locking up of the joint under control of the old and new muscle fibres. In the case instanced, stimulation over the extensor nerve would produce contraction of the fibres under its control and thus the extensor and flexor would contract at the same time. A few so-called successful cases of muscle grafting that have come to me for treatment had immovable ankle joints as a result of such muscle grafting. Such cases cannot be benefitted. If it were possible to perform a second operation to undo the mischief of the first, then the usual process of treatment outlined below might help.

As explained in Chapter V, the aim of the treatment for infantile paralysis is to restore, if possible, the motor cells in the spinal cord. Evolution teaches that our brain and nervous system are the result of necessity. The repeated experiences of lower orders of life gradually gave rise to a central controlling station for the surface activities of the organisms. As we study the different forms of life we find a more and more complex nervous mechanism. In the higher forms, all muscular and organic functioning is under control of distinct nerve cells. The more complex the life of the organism, the greater the number of cells in each group to control special functions. Thus, demand by a functioning part means increase of nerve cells to control this part. So that the law that structure governs function is no truer than that function controls structure.

To exercise the muscles of your arm means better muscles, and to increase the complexity of the arm exercises means a gradual increase of nerve cells controlling it. Therefore, to begin with assistive, then resistive exercises, and later supply exercises of control, will restore a degenerated part, if there are nerve cells left to appeal to. The test for this is whether or not a patient is capable of moving or producing any perceptible contraction in the muscles in question. If he can produce motion in the toes or ankles, or in the fingers and wrists, it is possible in time (and time means months or years), to restore sufficient control to answer a patient's needs, and by persistent self-effort all traces of the ailment may in time disappear.

There is a theory prevalent that infantile paralysis is due to bacterial infection, and some think they have discovered, while others are still seeking, a serum to cure the disease or at least prevent the paralysis that usually follows the acute stage. It is to be hoped that some such discovery will be made soon. But in all the cases coming under my care, diet seems to have played an important part. Without a single exception, in every case that I have treated, or made inquiries about, the patient was partial to, and lived almost entirely upon starches, fats, sugars, and proteins. Vegetables, except the potato, which is also a starch, and, with one or two exceptions, fruits were not relished by this class of patients. It requires coaxing to get such persons to eat vegetables and fruits. In the cases treated, progress has been steadiest and most rapid in those who reduced consumption of meats and starches to a minimum and adopted a diet in which vegetables and fruits predominated. Therefore, diet is of great importance along with other natural procedures.

Given a typical case which shows depletion and almost complete paralysis of the arms and legs, and perhaps a slight weakness of the spinal muscles. Proceed with the treatment somewhat as follows:

1. Give whatever osteopathic adjustment the conditions indicate.

2. Give thorough kneading of the spine, arms and legs, and follow by percussion along the large nerve trunks of the arms and legs.

3. Give assistive, later resistive, and finally single or hygienic exercises.

In the case given above, the exercises are applied in about the following order. Remember that weeks and even months may elapse before a patient has gained sufficiently to progress from the first to the second joint of the affected limb. The first program applies to the arms, the second to the legs, but the first movements of each program are to be used in the same treatment. They are divided for convenience of description.

TYPICAL PROGRAM FOR THE ARMS.

I. The patient on his back or reclining, practices first with one arm, then the other.

1. Have the patient try to raise the arm forward from the shoulder. If he is unable, raise it for him while he is making the mental effort. At first assist, later, resist as far as he can go and assist further to the completion of the movement.

2. The patient tries to raise the arm sideways from the shoulder; if he is unable, raise it for him while he is making the mental effort. Begin resisting his efforts and assisting further as soon as conditions demand it.

3. The patient's arm rests diagonally across his body, instruct him to carry it up and out as far and as high as possible. At first assist, and as soon as the patient has gained sufficient strength and control, offer resistance according to his strength and assist to completion of the movement.

II. The patient lying on his back or reclining.

1. The patient is told to flex and extend his elbow. Assist until he has acquired some control; then resist slightly as far as he can go and assist further.

2. The patient's arm is flexed at the elbow and the forearm held across the body. He is told to keep the elbow flexed and carry the forearm forward and outward from the body. As soon as he has acquired power, resist according to his strength and assist as the case requires, while the patient is making the mental effort.

III. The patient reclining. Clasp his hand and tell him to turn his palm down, then up and out. At first assist, and later resist, according to his strength. Pronation is usually acquired before supination. Therefore, for a time, resistance is greater against the former, but it should not so far exceed resistance to supination as to create an unbalanced condition. When any region seems to progress unevenly, that is, where one set of muscles is restored more rapidly than its antagonists, it is well to guard against developing a deformity. In such a case as this, pay more attention to the naturally weaker movement. This would be done, in this instance, by resisting supination two or three times to pronation once.

2. The patient's arm is held out straight sideways from the shoulder. If he cannot hold it there himself, the operator supports it at the elbow with one hand while he clasps the patient's hand with the other. The patient pronates and supinates the hand against the operator's resistance. In this movement, while the exercise is similar to the last one above, the effect is made more far-reaching by bringing in the shoulder muscles in the pronation and supination.

IV. Patient sitting or reclining.

1. The operator holds his wrist above the joint with one hand and with the other hand he takes hold below the wrist. The patient is told to flex and extend his wrist forward and backward. At first assist and later resist, according to the patient's strength.

2. The operator holding the patient's wrist as for the last exercise. The patient is told to invert and evert,

that is, to flex the wrist from side to side. The operator assists and later resists the movement.

3. The thumbs and fingers are exercised individually or collectively, in the same way as other movable parts. At first assist and later resist, according to patient's strength.

TYPICAL PROGRAM FOR THE LEGS.

I. The patient lying on his back.

1. He is told to flex the hip joint. At first assist and as soon as he acquires ability, resist according to his strength.

2. As soon as possible the patient is to flex both hip joints at once. At first assist and later resist, according to his strength.

II. The patient lying on his back and knees flexed up, heels close to his buttocks.

1. The operator usually has to flex the knees up for the patient and keep them there during the exercise. The patient drops the knees to one side and by twisting the upper body, lifts them up and drops them to the other side. The operator has to assist at first and, later, he offers resistance.

In this exercise it usually occurs that the adductors remain weak longer than the abductors.

2. The patient on his back, knees flexed as for the last exercise. The patient spreads the knees apart and lifts them together again. At first the operator has to assist. Later, according to the patient's strength, he offers resistance.

III. The patient lying face down.

1. He is told to raise one leg at a time off the bed, keeping the knee straight. At first, he needs assistance; the muscles are so depleted that no warning to keep the knee straight is necessary. When he has acquired strength, no assistance is necessary, and he may even stand a little resistance.

2. The patient is told to flex one knee up and extend it. It takes a long time to restore control of the knee,

but, by assistive action, gradually changing to slight resistive movement in each direction, sufficient power is at length acquired to perform a variation of the movement as below.

3. The patient lying face down as before, he is told to flex the left knee. As he extends it, he flexes the right knee, and so on. At first assistance is given and later, resistance is applied according to the patient's strength.

IV. The patient lying on his back.

1. The operator takes hold of his ankles and commands him to spread the legs apart and draw them together again. This movement is done against resistance, or with assistance, as the case demands.

2. The operator takes hold of the patient's toes. The patient is commanded to rotate the toes outward and inward without in the least flexing the knees. This movement brings into play the external and internal rotators of the femur as well as the anterior tibial muscles. The anterior tibial muscles, which are the flexors and external rotators of the ankle, are usually the weaker and need most attention.

3. The patient is told to elevate one leg at a time, keeping the knee straight. While it is coming down the other is elevated. This is in imitation of a walking motion, and for a long time needs the operator's assistance, never his resistance.

4. A somewhat similar exercise to the above is to command the patient to "tread water," that is, he partly flexes the hip and knee and pushes down again against the operator's resistance. As one leg is straightened the other is flexed. The operator offers resistance, or assistance, while holding the patient's feet.

V. The patient lying on his back.

1. The operator commands him to flex and extend his ankles. At first he assists and later resists. The movement is performed first with one ankle at a time,

and later with both together, alternately or simultaneously. The ankle remains weak for a long time.

2. Another exercise of the ankle which supplements the above is for the patient to flex the ankle as he rotates the foot outward. This is done at first with assistance and later with resistance. One ankle is exercised at a time and later, both at once, moving alternately or simultaneously.

3. The patient is told to evert the foot, that is, to turn up the outer edge. The operator assists, and later, resists.

The above outline is very limited when one considers all the movements that are possible to the human body. But these movements are selected as types. According to the patient's specific needs and strength, select from the list of corrective exercises given in Chapter VI, and, as soon as he is capable of performing exercises by himself, utilize those given in Chapter II.

For *paralysis following cerebral hemorrhage,* or for *disability* or *atrophy following fractures* or *other injuries,* the line of treatment explained for infantile paralysis is applicable. This is especially true for cerebral hemorrhage sequelae. All movements are given at first assistive and, as soon as the case warrants it, resistive. Progress is usually quite rapid after a cerebral hemorrhage, that is, if restoration is at all possible, and in comparison to progress in infantile paralysis. In atrophied members following fracture, so much depends upon the amount of destruction caused by the injury that no outline can be given as typical. But the general principle of assistance and then resistance to movements always obtains.

SPECIAL PROGRAM FOR OBESITY.

The question of reducing weight and keeping normal is always one of great interest because many people would like to weigh less, but they do love to eat and hate work or exercise. Nearly all are seeking an easy way, a "royal road" to normal. Few want to pay the price necessary for a normal physique.

People often object to the statement, but it is a fact that we are all lazy by nature, as lazy as we dare be and still get along. Although the statement seems severe, it is a fact that one does not become obese through moderation in eating and practicing regular activity. We are what we are largely through habit. Unless we are possessed of jelly-fish will-power, by a little effort of the will we can stop old habits, acquire new ones, and thereby gain self-control, as well as bodily improvement.

The reason obesity is hard to reduce lies in the obese person himself. He is often obese in will-power as well as in fat. One often hears a fat person say that he has tried all kinds of exercise and dieting and instead of losing he has put on weight. Such a statement is always questionable.

A short time ago a daily newspaper offered a reward for the best letters of not more than a hundred words giving genuine experiences in reducing weight. The editor's skepticism provoked the demand for such letters. Doubtless he had tried to reduce and had failed, of course, after irregular or incomplete effort.

There is no royal road to normal from obesity. In the early days of the automobile it is said that an eastern potentate, advised by his physician to reduce his weight, undertook to do so by making his chauffeur drive his car over rough mountain roads. This method of reducing is as ridiculous and unreasonable as the almost useless vibrating weight-reducer. Massage alone is also a failure. Indeed, few can be *reduced;* but every one can, if he will, *reduce himself.*

The way back to normal is filled with self-denials, sacrifices and hardships to the fatty, chiefly in the form of muscular exertion. First to be considered is the difference between living to eat and eating to live. In Belgium and Germany during the war there were no fat people and many suffered for want of food, yet comparatively few starved to death. Eliminating from the diet those foods which are fattening and retaining only those which are nourishing can only result in improving one's physical and mental being.

Some people are proud of their fat. The fact that most women are ashamed of it might be taken as a proof of a superior type of common sense, but, when one witnesses the numerous silly fads women pursue in the hope of reducing their weight he begins to question the reason for women's dislike of obesity. It can not be a health ideal but only vanity that induces a woman to submit to being rolled and pounded black and blue in "reducing machines." Rolling on the floor, because it uses the oblique abdominal muscles, is a little more sensible, but there are much better ways.

Obesity is really a disease. It represents a form of fatty degeneration of the muscular and nervous tissues. If it is true that function produces structure it is equally true that lack of function induces degeneration of structure. Normal use means tonicity and elasticity of the muscles and normal irritability of the motor nerves. Along with the reduced irritability of the motor nerves there sometimes develops an increased irritability of the sensory nerves. This means that the muscles become poor servants of the brain because the motor nerves are themselves dulled and they have poor instruments, (the muscles), to work with. These facts account for the apparent deliberation, which is only the slowness of inefficiency, and the short endurance of fat people, as well as their sensitiveness to heat and cold. When the motor nerves have been dulled from lack of function and the sensory nerves are allowed to grow more irritable we frequently find extreme nervousness and even crankiness in a fat person. It always seems strange, but all know that it is not uncommon, to find a person who is both fat and cranky.

There is a difference between the naturally "chunky" person who is hard and fat and the watery fat type. It is just as natural for some people to be stout as it is for water to be wet, but such persons are solid and shapely. These people are hard to reduce, because their flesh is hard and even though they perform very long and difficult activities they reduce but little.

The soft, useless, shapeless, impeding type of fat really amounts to an affliction. This kind of fat is due to inactivity and overeating of starches and sweets. The shortest road to normal for such people is to abstain completely from starches and sweets, live upon the following type of menu, and exercise vigorously:

Breakfast—Baked apples or stewed prunes or fresh fruit in season, except bananas.

Lunch—Nuts and raw salads of such vegetables as carrots, onions, celery, cabbage, chopped up to be eaten with a spoon, or tomatoes, lettuce, cucumbers and green peppers, with such dressings as one prefers. Olive oil and lemon juice, with a little horse radish and shirred egg, cottage cheese, tuna fish or salmon, will make a good dressing. Any variety of vegetables, except potato, is good. The above is only a suggestion. Bread should be excluded from this meal.

Dinner—A little lean meat or fish, spinach, chard, dandelions, beet tops, mustard greens, asparagus; or summer squash, cauliflower, stewed onions, carrots or parsley. Bran, graham or gluten bread, or a little dry toast. For drink: water, lemonade, orangeade, grape-fruitade or sweet cider.

If one gets very hungry between meals, fresh fruit is permissible. Such a dietary, combined with proper exercise, will reduce one rapidly to normal. Once reduced, one may again partake of other foods, but in moderation, and exercise must be continued or weight will rapidly increase again.

The importance of exercise in reducing cannot be emphasized too strongly. It is true that one could reduce gradually by the above abstemious diet, even without practicing much exercise, but the results would prove very unsatisfactory, especially if the person in question had a knowledge and appreciation of the ideal physique. When obesity is reduced only by the starvation method, the skin takes on a sagging appearance and the person feels very weak and wrinkly. When exercise fills an important place in the routine of reducing, the fat is gradually replaced by rounded, solid muscles and the shape is improved remarkably. The texture of the skin and the complexion are also benefitted by exercise, while dieting alone makes no material difference in these particulars.

To exercise regularly and correctly will surely normalize the physique and keep it normal as long as the exercises are continued. The main reason for so many failures to reduce, aside from wrong dieting, is the practice of the wrong kind of exercises. The question of making the proper selection is very important. First, let us consider what we mean by the wrong kind of exercise.

There is a common mistake made by writers and teachers of health who do not understand thoroughly the subject of gymnastics or the mechanism of the body. For example, some time ago three of our Chicago newspapers, through their health departments, made the same mistake, all within two days of the same week. The movement in question is that of bending the body forward and touching the floor with the fingers without bending the knees. In each case the claim was made that this movement exercises the muscles of the abdomen. The fact is that this movement accomplishes just the contrary of what is desired. That is, it relaxes the muscles of the abdomen and tones up the muscles of the small of the back chiefly. As the trunk is bent forward, the moment the head and shoulders pass beyond the line of the toes, the weight is entirely controlled by gravity and the muscles of the back assume the entire burden of guiding the trunk downward and lifting it again. The abdominal muscles, which are the ones that need most exercise, play no more than a passive part. They are relaxed to begin with and this movement does not only fail to tone them up but, as the body is bent forward, the bulge of fat and the abdominal contents are bunched together and pressed downward, thus producing a worse sagging than ever. When one considers the fact that all obese persons have sway back, which is in itself a deformity, and that the muscles of the back get all the training, one realizes that this movement, when practiced to the exclusion of all others, as it often is, does more harm than good, for it only increases the sway back and in no wise reduces weight. This is not an arbitrary opinion but it is strictly in keeping with the facts of anatomy.

Another exercise which almost invariably is used as a companion to the above is that of lying on the back and, without the feet being held down, coming up to sitting by stretching the arms or projecting the head forward, or both. While an exercise must be considered primarily from its specific effect it must also be considered from the standpoint of its general reactive effect upon the organism. While this exercise does tax the abdominal muscles, the effect of keeping the head and arms forward in doing it only results in developing drooping head, flat chest and drooping shoulders, thus, at best, removing one defect while producing another. Despite what anyone may say, we are so constituted that no one, unless he possesses abnormally long legs and very heavy feet, can come up to sitting without using his head and arms as just explained. The only correct way to perform this type of exercise is to have the feet held down and to keep the head in line with the body when coming up. Illus. 478 shows the correct position in this movement.

Almost any vigorous form of activity is good to reduce weight, but the most effective type is that which employs, especially, the muscles of the waist and abdomen. The following are among the easier types in the first group. Those of the second group are more severe and they should be added to the first list for daily practice as fast as one can do them without straining too much. Besides all of these exercises, long walks and outdoor games and sports should be enjoyed as frequently as possible. Each movement should be repeated at least ten times to each side. By preserving a good posture of the body throughout the exercises one cultivates grace and normal measurements. Miss Myra Bradford, who posed for the illustrations, is a singer and dancer. She is an experienced gymnast, with a splendid physique, and she performed in an ideal manner.

1. To exercise the muscles of the waist, especially the transverse and oblique abdominals, with the feet apart, arms straight out from the shoulder (and not allowed to come forward in the rotations), twist the trunk as rapidly as possible from side to side. (Illus. 468.)

2. To produce suppleness of the chest, aid respiration and improve bodily carriage, with one foot about two foot lengths in front of the other, toes turned out, arms straight out from the shoulders, arch the upper body backward slowly. (Illus. 469.) As you come up to erect draw in the chin and let the head come up last, puffing out the chest. Study the illustration well, for Miss Bradford performed it perfectly. The waist is kept almost straight and only the upper spine is bent.

3. With the fingers locked behind the head, flex the left knee upward and, without lowering the leg, straighten the knee forward ten times. (Illus. 470.) With the other knee up, repeat. This movement is designed for three purposes: it will tend to relieve the congestion in the small of the back after the backward bending; it will mildly exercise the abdominal muscles, and its chief effect will be to cultivate good equilibrium by requiring balance control.

4. Lying on the back with the fingers locked behind the head, elevate the legs to vertical, the toes pointed (Illus. 471) and lower them slowly many times. This is one of the best types of exercise for the rectus abdominalis muscles.

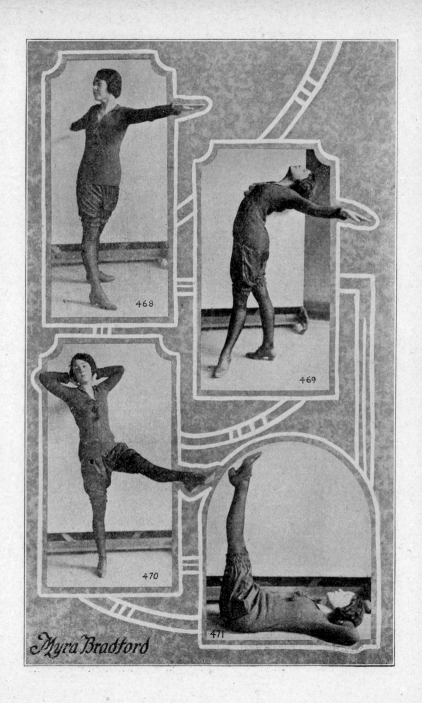

468

469

470

471

Myra Bradford

5. To exercise the muscles of the sides (a group which is very much neglected in everybody), with the feet together, arms extended upward, bend the trunk to each side at least ten times. (Illus. 472.)

6. At the close of every program, no matter how brief or how prolonged, it is always advisable to breathe deeply a few times. An excellent respiratory exercise is to raise the arms forward-upward and inhale deeply as they go up. Lower them sideways-backward as you exhale.

After a few days of the above movements, the following may be introduced, one every few days. Since a certain sequence will work better than a haphazard mixture, we shall indicate the place each new addition should fill in the program.

1. Lying on the back, the fingers locked behind the head, to exercise the abdominal muscles (every group); rotate the knees by flexing them up onto the chest, carrying them to the right (Illus. 473), then straightening them down without touching the floor, bending them as far as possible to the left and up onto the chest again, and so on ten times. Then repeat, circling in the opposite direction.

When introduced into the lesson this exercise should follow number 4, described above.

2. Lying on the back, the fingers locked behind the head, raise the legs to vertical and lower them to the left. (Illus. 474.) Elevate them again and lower them to the right. This movement is especially good for the oblique muscles of the abdomen.

When introduced into the lesson this exercise should follow the last one just described.

3. With the knees bent, place the hands on the floor, fingers in. (Illus. 475.) Kick the feet backward a few times. (Illus. 476.)

4. When the last exercise is mastered, with the feet back, the body kept in a straight line, elevate the legs alternately. (Illus. 477.) To render this more difficult,

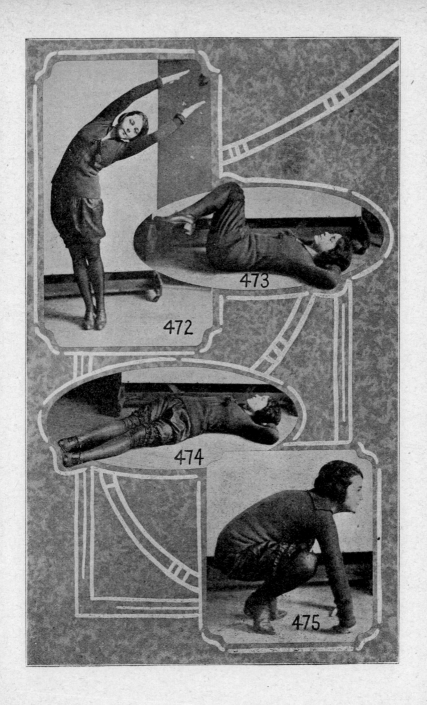

as the feet are sprung back, straighten one leg up, and the other assumes the burden of supporting the weight, as in illustration. Do this alternately.

These last two exercises are especially good to exercise the surface and deeper muscles of the abdomen. They are powerful developers of the abdominal muscles and are also valuable in reducing the hips. When introduced in the lesson they should follow in sequence as given, after the ones described just above.

5. With the feet held down, hands on the hips, keeping the head in line with the body, come up to sitting. (Illus. 478.) This is a very strong movement and an excellent reducer and developer of the abdominal region. Unless the head is kept in line with the body it will produce a drooping head. It can be made more difficult by placing the hands on the shoulders, back of the head, or extended upward. For those who are ambitious for even stronger work, dumbbells of increasing weights can be utilized.

To hold the body at the inclination illustrated and twist from side to side is another way of rendering this movement more complex. The higher the hands are held the more difficult it is rendered.

This movement also, being an abdominal exercise, should follow in sequence, as described.

6. As a step beyond the type of movement described in 3, Illustration 476, turn the body so as to rest the weight onto one hand and the side of the foot. The upper hand is on the hip. (Illus. 479.) Then turn, face downward as in Illustration 476 and turn onto the other side. Hold for a few seconds each side. When this has been mastered, elevate the upper leg a few times before changing sides. This movement is an excellent developer of the side muscles especially, the ones that are usually so weak.

When introduced in the lesson it should follow 5, illustration 5 of the first series.

7. To "limber up" and keep limber and agile, and to

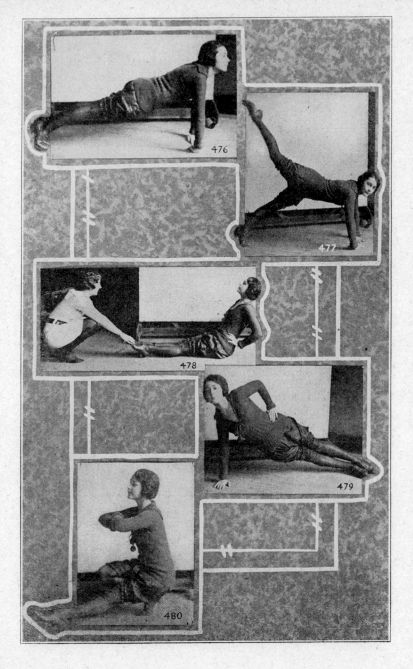

preserve a good leg, thigh and hip development, few exercises can surpass the low down dance. With the arms folded straight in front of the chest, squat down and spring one leg forward and then the other. (Illus. 480.) In learning this exercise, the forward foot may rest on the floor to render balancing easier. Once mastered, however, the extended leg is shot straight forward, off the floor, and brought back as the other is extended.

Following such a strenuous exercise (one that should not be introduced until all the others can be performed without strain), repeat the respiratory exercise explained in 6 of the first series.

ADDING TO ONE'S WEIGHT.

The question is often asked whether it is possible for a slender person to put on flesh. Everyone seems full of advice on reducing, but how about the opposite extreme?

It is more than the common craving for something different that leads the thin person to desire plumpness. There is a mistaken notion held by many people that fat is a sign of good health; that it is a proof of one's improving health if he is rapidly gaining weight. Such is not the case. If one is much under weight as a result of ill health it is a proof of health to regain normal. But the only unquestionable significance of rapidly gaining weight is that a person is well nourished and it bears no other testimony relating to his health. As a matter of fact, beyond the necessary physiological limit, fat is really a form of degeneration of both the nervous and muscular structures and an extreme amount of fat may be regarded as not merely surplus material which may impede freedom of action but something which amounts to disease.

Parents should view with alarm a condition of obesity in their child. It is bad enough to allow one's muscular tissue to degenerate into fat in adult life, but for a child to grow up very fat means that there is no chance for him ever to possess fine fibred muscles. Of the two extremes it is far better and healthier to be thin than fat. The thin person can always feel assured that his muscles are not interfered with, while the fat person can never know what freedom of action means. It is true that we sometimes meet fat persons who seem quite agile and graceful, but what an effort every exertion compels and how breathless every bit of rapid activity makes them. All reliable statistics on the subject prove that the average thin person lives longer than the fat person.

Although slenderness is more desirable than obesity, there is nothing quite equal to the normal. No amount of mental treatment, cajoling or self-resignation to the inevitable can equal normal weight and health. In the last analysis the body's cellular structure is never at a standstill. We are either getting better or worse, improving or degenerating, never holding our own from the metabolic, or cellular growth, standpoint. The test of normality of any tissue or structure is efficiency of function. The secret of efficiency is normal use of every part, never continued disuse or over use. Normal use of the muscles will tend to render them normal in size and power.

Since the muscles are so intimately connected with the rest of the organism and form such a large percentage of the body's structure, exercise is surely one of the most powerful factors in controlling health. The person who is overweight and lazy needs only to reduce the intake of fattening foods and to increase muscular activity. The person who is underweight should exercise every day vigorously for a period of several weeks and thereby create better appetite, digestion and assimilation. Even though a little weight is lost at first the activities should be continued until one reaches a point where he can assimilate more food than formerly. The food, in this case, should consist of milk and cream, butter, potatoes, breads and cereals, sweets, vegetables, in short everything that one relishes provided the meals are balanced from the standpoint of the elements. After the body has acquired the habit of using up more material in its general functions, this habit will remain with it and by skipping activities one or two days per week it will begin to store away some of the surplus materials that it formerly used up. Unless there is some organic weakness, inherited, acquired by abnormal living or as a result of operation, flesh will surely accumulate by this method. Nature always follows the law of supply and demand.

It is not necessary to print a special program here. Any of the programs given in Chapter II, combined with a variety of the play activities referred to in Chapter III will answer.

Reducing the Hips.

Because the body is not put together like a jointed doll, one cannot chop off a part, as it were, and mould it nearer the heart's desire. It is folly to speak of reducing or increasing any part of the body without at the same time affecting some other part. The body is a unit and every gymnastic movement should be selected for its local effect, but not without considering its reactive effect upon the organism as a whole.

But fashion befuddles the heads of its devotees in strange ways. Many in their endeavor to fit the styles, try to add to or subtract from portions of their anatomy with amusing results at times. How well some of us recall the early nineties when bustles and padded hips were in style and big sisters wore them! How often we boys suddenly jumped on for a free ride! Accompanying the bustles and padded hips came the wasp waist. The worst wasp waist in history was that of Catherine de Medici, which is said to have been only thirteen inches. One wonders if that is what affected her mind so as to bring about the bloody massacre of St. Bartholomew's eve, or was her thirteen-inch waist simply another symptom of her general mental condition?

Soon after the last wasp waist and bustle craze, the puff in the sleeves in women's dresses began to run up and down the arms. First there was a puff at the shoulders, then at the elbows and later fullness at the wrists, or between joints. Then came the tight sleeves, then the open sleeves and finally no sleeves at all. Where the sleeves will be next no one pretends to know who is not interested in the dress making trade, where the aim is not symmetry so much as extremes of fashions for the sake of business. The most sensible development in women's dress came with the short skirt and knickers, but now there is the swing back to long skirts even with trains and low neck and no sleeves.

With such silly, kaleidoscopic changes we find girls, usually young girls, worried about the size of some parts of their bodies. It is too bad that there can be no arrangements for "put-on-and-take-off" parts. The most common worry is about the size of the feet. These useful members are never small enough. That is why so many wear shoes several sizes too small and, as a consequence all have to visit the chiropodists regularly. Another method used to camouflage the real size of the feet is the wearing of high heels. Some worry about the size of their ankles and now we find ankle corsets on the market. Others worry about the size of the calf, the thigh, the hips, the waist, the bust, the neck, the chin, wrinkles on the face, but no one has yet expressed a worry about the size of the head or what it contains. What is worn on the head usually determines this.

For the last few years the chief concern of fashion's devotees has been the size of the hips. The styles have resembled a meal bag hung straight down. The only sign of a waist line has been a ribbon or girdle around the hips. To possess a body with the kind of hips these styles demand and which hip corsets have aimed to establish would amount to a deformity. The normal and ideal figure possesses hips that are as large as the girth measurement of the shoulders and when a woman possesses a larger girth measurement of the shoulders than the hips she has a male type of figure and should be an object of pity rather than envy. Nature does not blunder or change her plans every season as modistes do. There is purpose behind every part of one's anatomy and the normal is always beautiful.

The normal woman possesses round hips and all that exercises can do is to normalize the abnormal. If one possesses a surplus amount of fat about the hips exercises will harden the fat into muscle and give the firm, normal contour. If the hips are muscular and large, by virtue of a large bony framework, exercise, except for health, would be a waste of time.

For the person who really has extra fat hips, besides the program for obesity, there are a few special movements that will have an effect on this region. One of the best and simplest of these, if repeated often enough, is the rond-de-jambe of the dancers. In this the leg is raised straight forward, the knee straight, then it is carried out to the side and then back, all the while kept as nearly horizontal as possible with the knee straight and the body kept as erect as possible. From the back elevation the knee is bent slightly as the leg is brought forward to begin the next circle. This exercise is like that used by the French foot boxers. If practiced equally with both legs it will not only reduce the hips to solid muscles but will improve one's agility and nimbleness.

Fencing, most of the vigorous dancing steps, and the leg elevations from lying on the back will affect the hips. Bearing the weight on one hand and the outside of the foot and lifting the upper leg will also have an effect in this direction. Standing with the arms extended upward and then twisting the body to the left and bending until the hands touch the floor, and then coming up to erect and repeating to the right, and so on alternately, will particularly affect the hips.

How to Have a Beautiful Throat.

A defect that is the despair of many young women is a poorly developed throat, chin and collar bone region. Many feel conscious and unhappy every time they wear a garment that does not possess a high collar. It is frequently asked how one can fill the hollows at the base of the neck and develop a smooth throat. There are several exercises that are directly conducive to this end but we must limit ourselves to a few.

Although it is possible to find a well proportioned physique with a poorly developed throat region, it is more common to find that this defect is not a condition in itself but rather an indication of the general lack of tonicity. Few people exercise as frequently as they should and it is largely due to this fact that regional weaknesses and abnormalities exist. Therefore, for lasting results with a special program, one should practice daily a balanced program to affect the entire physique.

The hollows in the neck cannot be obliterated by rubbing in cocoa butter or oils, as many have attempted to do. Nor will pouring in melted paraffin result favorably. There have been all kinds of attempts made to fill these hollows but none can even remotely compare to the results obtained by proper exercises. Real beauty is more than skin deep. Perfection of physique cannot be achieved from the skin inward, but from the center outward, principally through the foods one eats and the activities one performs.

To assure a perfect throat and collar bone region, and to prevent double chin, in addition to general activities the following will prove effective. Refer to Illustration 481.

1. Keeping the shoulders steady, rotate the head slowly to one side and then the other, going as far as you can and then trying to carry the movement farther until you feel a strong pull on the muscles behind and at the sides of the neck. (1.)

2. Beginning with the head rotated, as at the end of the above movement, bend backward, as shown in (2), several times. Repeat with the head turned to the other side. This not only exercises the muscles of the neck but it lifts the upper ribs.

3. Without moving the shoulders, bend the head as far as possible to each side. (3.)

4. Standing with the arms straight forward from the shoulders, palms in (4), fling them upward without moving the head or body. Isolate the action entirely to the arms. As a variation fling the arms upward alternately, putting the force in the upward part of the movement and only lowering the arms to shoulder level each time. (5.)

5. With the arms held straight out from the shoulders, flex the elbows forward (6), and fling the forearms upward with all the force possible, lowering them to the first position again. The elbows should not be allowed to descend as the forearms are flung upward. As a variation, keeping the elbows on line with the shoulders, fling the forearms upward alternately. (See 467.)

The above exercises, if practiced regularly, repeated many times each day, will surely improve the region.

DEVELOPING A NATURAL CORSET.

What was said in the first chapter about respiration is important. That every effort possible to raise the internal organs should be made is clear. It is also important to tone up the muscles of the waist so that they will perform their function of holding up these organs. If one so develops the waist muscles as to assure their normal function he will also render an ideal waist line certain.

Normal function will produce normal structure. There is no substitute in vesture for the natural structure of any part of the body. The corset does not err so much in being ugly as in being unphysiological. To speak of "hygienic corsets," as some advertisements do, is like speaking of hygienic strychnine. Fashion never considers hygiene in its first decrees of styles for women.

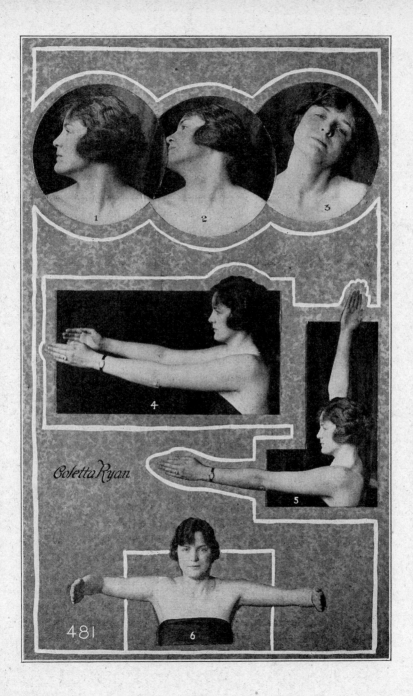

Coletta Ryan

1

2

3

4

5

6

481

The modern corset is made to measure and does not compress the waist as the old styles used to do, but there is not a corset on the market, nor is one conceivable, which does not to some extent limit the freedom of the lower thorax and waist muscles. Even if it does not pinch the waist and does support the viscera, still it is robbing the abdominal muscles of their natural functions and to that extent it is unhygienic. To rob any muscle, or group of muscles, of its chance to perform a natural function is to produce degeneration in its structure. Hygienically and physiologically there is no substitute for the natural.

There are many of the blue law reformers who regard it as a mark of depravity and indecency to go without a corset. Anna Held, the actress, slept in her tight corsets so as not to lose her shape. Her death was the direct result of tight lacing and yet her form was the despair of many women. The corset originated among the Roman prostitutes during the decline of the empire. They wore the corset so as to show a flat abdomen as a proof that they were not pregnant. To hold the attentions of their husbands, in competition with these prostitutes, Roman matrons took up the wearing of corsets. Their rejected corsets were accepted by their servants who wore them in imitation of the great ladies who employed them. From such an origin the corset became a supposed necessity to every woman and finally a mark of Christian virtue. Indeed, at present, the first expression uttered by most reformers when they meet a young girl who goes to dances without a corset is to the effect that such a girl is immoral!

But the corset as such has no bearings whatever on morality except as used by the Romans. It is not physiological and if one develops the muscles of the waist region it will not be necessary. However, if one is too lazy, or if she lacks the graceful waist line even though her muscles are in good tonicity, a corset would improve her shape. If such exercises as the following are practiced daily the right fitted corset will not prove injurious. All the exercises given for obesity and also those explained in relation to the treatment of inguinal hernia are of value in developing the natural corset. The following are specifically recommended. They should each be repeated twenty-five times or more daily.

1. Feet apart, fingers locked behind the head, twist to the right and bend backward. After several repetitions bend forward while the body is still twisted. Repeat from the other side also. (Illus. 482..)

2. Arms extended upward, reach hard as you rise on the toes and walk slowly forward and backward. This taxes the side muscles.

3. Fingers locked behind the head, raise the legs forward, knees straight, alternately, without leaning the body back. (See Illus. 470.)

4. Hands on the hips, keeping the head high, but turning with the body, twist as far as possible to each side.

5. Fingers locked behind the head, the left foot forward, bend to the left as far as possible. With the right foot forward, repeat.

6. Kneeling, knees apart, fingers locked behind the head, twist the body from side to side.

7. With the arms straight from the shoulders bend forward and, keeping the body bent, twist the trunk and touch the floor first with one hand and then the other. (Illus. 483.)

8. Feet apart, arms bent, extend the arms as you bend one knee and touch the floor to one side, then the other. (Illus. 484.)

9. Feet apart, arms out from the shoulders, keeping the arms in line with the shoulders, twist the body around as rapidly as possible. (See Illus. 200.)

EXERCISE WHILE TRAVELLING.

An expert swimmer once swam two miles with his hands and feet tied. Some one remarked that such a feat would be good training for dressing in a Pullman berth.

To mention exercising in a Pullman berth may sound ridiculous, but it is possible to practice a variety of exercises that will prove sufficient to keep one fit and alert physically while on a train for several days. On a long journey by rail one always feels "logy" and restless. Having to sit for so many hours each day is apt to spoil one's appetite, to develop constipation and to ruin a perfectly good disposition. Spending hours in the smoking car, playing cards, or reading are not good remedies for these symptoms. The short stretches and walks indulged in by a few while the train makes short stops prove to be teasers rather than relievers. However, it is possible to preserve a sweet disposition and suffer no inconveniences if one will observe a few simple rules.

The first thing to attend to is the diet. No matter how much exercise is practiced, if the diet is not correct trouble and discomfort will probably follow. One has to be more particular about food while under the forced inactivity of travelling. Besides the usual eggs, meats, fish or fowl, one should make a special effort to get plenty of prunes, figs, apples, oranges and other fruit of a distinctly laxative nature and plenty of raw vegetables. Lettuce, celery, cucumbers and tomatoes are usually procurable on dining cars. If one's purse cannot stand both the meat and vegetable elements it would be better to eat the vegetable foods with milk. Milk and cream should replace the usual tea and coffee.

To assure a good appetite and freedom from disagreeable symptoms the day should begin with a series of exercises before getting up. As it is not practical to exercise on a train after one is up, it is best to do this in one's berth. There are varied exercises which can be practiced in the berth to reach every part of the body.

To obtain the greatest benefit from the exercises, have the window of the berth open, lie on top of the bed covers so as to have perfect freedom, relax thoroughly and breathe deeply a few times, raising the ribs at inha-

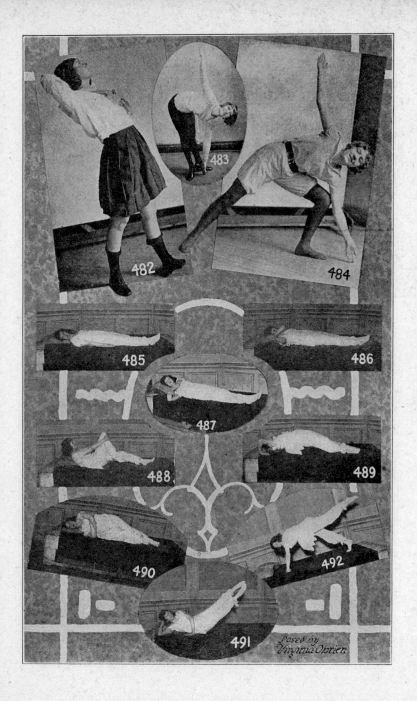

482   483   484   485   486   487   488   489   490   491   492

Posed by
Virginia O'Brien

lation.   Repeat each exercise twenty-five to fifty times to each side.

1. While lying on the back, twist the head as far as possible from side to side.   (Illustration 485.)

2. Raise the knees and, while keeping the feet off the bed, go through a running motion.   Keep this up as long as you feel disposed before stopping, and then repeat again.   Following this running exercise practice a few deep breaths again.

3. With the left hand beside the body, bear down upon it with the right hand as you lift it up to and beyond the head.   After repeating it a number of times, reverse the hold and lift the right against resistance.   (Illustration 486.)   This exercise will tax the muscles behind the shoulders.

4. To expand the chest through making the back shoulder muscles stronger, lock the fingers and resist as you first pull one hand out to one side and then the other.   (Illustration 487.)

5. Bear against the knees with the hands as you bend the knees up to the chest.

6. Lock the fingers over the left knee and press hard with the knee against the hands.   Later repeat with the right knee.   (Illustration 488.)   This exercise will benefit the back muscles as well as promote bowel action.

7. Lying on the back, arms out to each side, without touching the bed, circle the knees in as wide a circle as possible, first in the left, and then the right direction. (See Illustration 473.)   This exercise will help the abdominal muscles.

8. Carry the arms up and back of the head, press the palms flat beside the ears.   By pushing hard with the head and the hands, arch the body up from the heels to the head.   (Illustration 489.)   Repeat this arching up several times.   This exercise will tone up the entire back muscles.

9. To help the side muscles, lying on one side, elevate the hips, bearing the weight from the shoulder and the

side of the foot. (Illustration 490.) Repeat many times and then turn and repeat on the other side.

10. Lying on the side, elevate the legs as high as possible, first from one side and then the other. (Illustration 491.)

11. Bearing the weight on hands and toes, kick the feet forward and back. To make it harder, as you kick the feet back, let one assume the weight as the other is held up in the air. (Illustration 492.) Repeat this several times, changing feet each time.

12. Lying on the stomach, elevate the head and the feet as high as possible, so as to arch the body up. Keep the arms bent as you twist the head from side to side, or practice arms swimming while holding the head high.

End the program by practicing deep breathing again.

Stretching and Relaxing Exercises for the Muscle-Bound.

Many people, when they decide that exercise is good for them, are easily attracted by the flagrant advertisements in periodicals in which the "Professors" with foreign names guarantee to "enlarge your arm one inch in one month or money refunded." These "Professors" (always spelled with a capital "P") usually claim to have discovered an entirely new system, or rediscovered an old, ancient and forgotten one. The basis of their methods is usually a form of tensing or resistance muscular work, or graduated weight lifting, that develops a hard, stiff and tight muscular condition. The ardent enthusiast who follows such advice is certain to increase his muscle bulk in a short time, but it is a question whether the ultimate results will satisfy him.

The kind of muscles that one develops by this work will only last as long as the exercises are continued. Such muscles are to be approved more for their bulk than their quality. One has to exercise merely to keep them up. Instead of being of much service to the brain, the brain must be of service to them.

The type of physique that these muscles furnish is a poor tool to the brain. Instead of responding to all shades of volition, such muscles are only fit to perform the type of work of the exercises. The individual who possesses such a physique always holds himself as if he were under a strain. His muscles are tense and rounded out like a dime museum freak on exhibition. When one is conscious of such a physique he is constantly feeling his own arms, chest, or legs, to sense the elevations of flesh. In other words, pride in the possession of muscle bulk makes itself manifest by the possessor's deportment as well as by his stiff, posing attitudes. There are a number of women who use tensing and dumbbell exercises and they show it by their mannish, dumpy appearance.

It is easier to change a stiff, muscle-bound individual into a graceful and agile one, than to build substantial muscle onto a flabby, loose-jointed person. The former has foundation to work on, and perseverance in correct exercises will surely bring about desired results. But it is always difficult to build muscle on one who is weak, delicate, or lazy by nature.

A muscle-bound condition is usually the result of one's occupation. Those who exercise hard enough to develop such a condition are few compared to the number of clumsy, large-muscled men who acquire their stiffness from hard labor. But, of those likely to undertake procedures that will counterbalance their muscle-bound condition few will be recruited from the army of toilers. Therefore, the following outline takes into consideration primarily the person who exercised himself into such a condition, although about the same general outline applies to the case of a hard laborer.

1. To learn to relax well, lie on your back and make yourself as limp as a rag. Relax the muscles from the toes up. This method of relaxing will not only limber up stiff muscles, but, when one finds it difficult to get to sleep, it will prove valuable in conjunction with, and following vascular expansion of the legs. This procedure is

best mastered by closing one's eyes and concentrating on the region that is being relaxed. Begin with the toes. Imagine them so limp that they are hanging down like the tips of a withered plant. Next, allow the ankle to drop from limpness. Next, feel the muscles of the legs, from the ankles to the knees, become so soft that they seem to hang like water-bags from the bones. Next, get the same feeling in reference to the muscles of the thighs and hips. Then, feel the spine loosen up and apparently drop onto the mattress segment by segment. Next, allow the fingers, wrists, forearm, and upper arm to relax as you did the legs. And last, the neck and head feel as limp as the rest of the body.

2. Another procedure is to stand or kneel on a mattress and suddenly relax the muscles so that you drop down like a balloon collapsing.

3. Lying on the back, arms extended, reach with the fingers and toes as far as possible.

4. Practice light club swinging, fencing, tennis and any of the games or dances that require agility and nimbleness.

For a daily program, besides the above general procedures, the following outline will prove of service:

1. Arms bent, extend them upward slowly, reaching as high as possible and rising on the toes as you inhale deeply. Slowly flex the arms and lower the heels as you exhale.

2. Arms bent. As you lunge sideways-forward with the left foot, extend the left arm upward and the right downward along the right thigh. In the lunge allow the rear heel to leave the floor, keeping only the toes of the right foot down. In this position, reach and stretch the left arm and right leg to the utmost. Repeat the movement, lunging to the right with the right arm extended upward and the left downward. (Illus. 493.)

3. (a) Arms extended upward, feet apart, bend the arms, head and upper body backward, without holding the breath. (Illus. 494.)

(b) Arms extended upward, bend forward as far as possible without bending the knees. Reach the floor if possible. (Illus. 146.)

4. Hang on a horizontal bar or trapeze, make the body as limp as possible and reach the floor. While hanging, swing the feet from side to side and at every swing try to feel so limp that the feet seem to descend lower and lower.

5. Arms extended upward, rise on the toes and reach upward. While reaching, keep your balance steadily as you alternately flex the knees to right angle. (Illus. 495.)

6. Arms extended upward, raise the left leg backward and at the same time bend the trunk forward until the entire body, from fingers to toes, is in a horizontal position with the extremities slightly arching upward. While holding this position reach with the fingers and toes. Repeat with the right leg elevated backward. (Illus. 167.)

7. Fling the arms forward-upward as you lunge forward with the left foot, and as you bring the foot back bring the arms down to the sides in a sideways-backward sweep. Repeat with a lunge with the right foot. The arm motion should be a continuous one, forward-upward and sideways-backward to the sides, while the lunging foot travels forward and then back immediately, only stopping long enough at the lunge to complete the movement without having to introduce ungainly efforts.

8. Practice high kicking, or hitch-kick.

9. Arms held straight out from the shoulders, feet apart, twist the trunk rapidly from side to side.

10. Arms extended upward, feet apart, bend first to one side and then the other, curling the further arm over the head.

11. Practice the "low-down dance." (See Exercise V, Lesson XIX.) Or, holding a stick with both hands, jump forward and backward over it without losing hold of it.

12. Repeat Exercise Number 1 of this program.

ANTAGONISTIC EXERCISES FOR THE FLABBY-MUSCLED LOOSE-JOINTED INDIVIDUAL.

A person who has never worked hard, exercised or played games to any extent cannot have firm, well-rounded muscles. This may not always show in his appearance because, in these days of padded tailoring, the scrawny and the robust may be given the same outline. But the facial expression will disclose weaknesses that tailoring can never conceal. The physical incapacities of the individual are also apparent in his bearing, motions, voice, and lack of aggressiveness. Even politeness in a weakling seems less good manners than policy. It serves him as a method of self-defense. A strong, virile person feels more pity and contempt than respect for a weakling.

Good muscle and a submissive or subservient will cannot exist in the same individual. One cure for cowardice is physical training. The strong personality has a solid physical foundation.

The normal body is at least forty-two per cent muscle. The quality of this muscle tissue is an index to the mind and will of its possessor.

A weak-willed individual may be repaired and rendered strong by exercise. To be effective this exercise must be persisted in. For a weak-willed person to become persevering means that he must utilize, and acquire by utilizing, powers that in themselves amount to virtues. Patience, perseverance, concentration and self-sacrifice are all necessary to achievement in physical development. Therefore, when a weakling is really improving himself physically, his work has a manifold reactive effect upon his mental power.

The best kind of work for a flabby muscular condition is of a tensing, antagonistic type. When firmness and sufficient bulk have been acquired it is proper to change from the type of work outlined below to the kind outlined in Chapter II.

As already stated in discussing the program for muscle-bound individuals, most exploiters of physical culture teach a type of work that tends to tense and add bulk to the muscles. Therefore one need never be at a loss for that kind of exercise. But such work is never really adapted to the needs of anyone except the flabby-muscled person. And for his purpose its need is only temporary.

As explained in Chapter I, exercising a part will tend to render it normal. The quality of effort required to perform the exercise will develop that same quality in the muscles. Therefore any procedures that require tensing of the muscles will give tone to flabby muscles.

To keep within bounds of danger it is best for the individual to resist his own movements by opposing one arm or leg against the other.

1. Close the fists and, pressing the knuckles against each other, move the arms up and down or from side to side.

2. Lock the fingers and, while pulling outward on the hands, move them up and down or from side to side.

3. Press the palms of the hands firmly against each other and, keeping the elbows straight, move the arms vertically and then horizontally as fast as possible without shifting the position of the hands.

4. Keeping the left elbow close to the body flex the arm a few times against resistance offered by the right hand. The right hand clasps the left firmly and keeps up a resistance as the left forearm moves up and down. Practice this exercise with the right arm, resisting with the left.

5. Grasp a wand or stick, holding it behind the head, the hands at a little more than shoulder width apart. Move the wand from side to side by flexing one arm as the other extends. For about ten counts apply the force inward; that is, push one hand against the other.

6. With the hands in the same position as in Number 5, move the wand from side to side while applying the

force outwardly, that is, pull hard, one hand against the other.

7. The wand held in front of the shoulders, push the hands inward against each other as you move the wand from side to side.

8. The wand as in Number 7, pull outwardly on the hands as you move the wand from side to side.

9. The wand held in front of the thighs, hands about as far apart as for the above exercises, keeping the elbows straight all through the exercise, move the wand in a sweeping motion up to the left, then down and up to the right. Apply the force inward, pushing one hand against the other for about ten counts, and then, repeat the motion while pulling outward on the hands, thus applying the force outward.

10. The wand held back of the thighs, elbows kept straight, move the wand as far as possible up to the left and right corresponding to Exercise 9; first applying the force inward and then outward.

11. The arms extended upward, the wand held with the hands far enough apart so that when one arm is lowered to shoulder height the other is vertical, keeping the elbows straight and pushing inward on the wand, carry the wand down the left, then up, and down the right. Repeat the same movement while pulling outward on the wand. The effect of this exercise can be increased by bending the trunk sideways to the side at which the wand is lowered.

12. Take a rope or strap, about three feet in length. Hold one end in each hand and place one foot over the center of it. Flex the arms up and extend them as high as possible above shoulder height while offering resistance with the lifted foot. Repeat a number of times and then exercise with the other foot.

13. Flex one knee up behind and loop the rope around the instep. The ends of the rope held in the hands, extend the arms upward against the resistance of the leg. Repeat with the other leg.

Resistive exercises with a rope, wand, or merely with one arm or leg against the other, are capable of many variations. The pupil will easily evolve new movements. As one tries those suggested above many others suggest themselves.

Another method of developing firm muscles is to exercise with spring or elastic exercises. The old style chest weights, while very useful for all-around purposes, do not equal the elastic or spring exerciser for specific development of tense muscle. It is useless to do more than mention this form of exercising because every spring or elastic exerciser of good or medium quality has a chart or handbook of instructions accompanying it.

Besides the above suggestions another good plan for developing firm and unyielding muscles is for two persons to resist each other's movements by following the outline given above; or by making the work more playful, as hand-wrestling, stick-wrestling, turning wrists, locked-finger-wrestling, or lifting chairs by their bottom rung. Hand- and stick-wrestling have been explained. Turning wrists, consists of opponents sitting at opposite sides of a narrow table, resting their right elbows on the table, clasping hands and each trying to twist and bend the other's wrist and forearm to the table. The elbows must not be lifted off the table. This exercise should be practiced with either hand. Locked-finger-wrestling consists in opponents standing facing each other with arms extended upward, palms facing and opponents' fingers crossed. The object of this exercise is to force your opponent to his knees by bending his wrists backward. It will develop strong fingers and forearm muscles. To lift a chair by the bottom rung is to grasp firmly with one hand the lower front rung and lift the chair in its upright position. The tendency is for the chair to drop backward unless the hand grips tightly enough. All exercises or games of this kind will develop muscular tenacity.

CORRECTING SPECIAL DEFECTS IN CONJUNCTION WITH A
GENERAL HYGIENIC PROGRAM.

One is frequently called upon to arrange an outline of exercises for a patient who cannot take regular treatment, or follow out a progressive course of lessons. Out of city patients who are only in town for a few days are the ones likely to make such a demand. The most interesting case that ever applied to me for such advice was given the program below, which is introduced here as typical. For a patient with different defects the corrective procedures must be selected to fit his needs, but the same general principles are followed.

The patient, a 15-year-old boy, presented round and narrow shoulders, narrow chest with an upper right rib depression resulting from pleurisy, a slight left dorsal scoliosis, and flabby abdominal muscles with an inclination to sway back. His general muscular condition was very flabby.

The problem was to select a number of exercises and arrange them as nearly as possible according to the Swedish day's order. The following program was made up and the patient was instructed to continue special work as long as his case demanded. When the corrections were made he was to discontinue special work and take up symmetrical work of the kind outlined in Chapter II. His parents were instructed to write me as soon as any defect seemed corrected and I would then advise what to do next.

1. Raise the arms sideways-upward while inhaling deeply, and at the same time rotate the trunk to the right. As you lower the arms, sideways-backward, rotate the trunk forward and breathe out slowly. The trunk is rotated twice to the right to once to the left. The effect of rotation to the right is to expand the right upper chest more than the left, and the movement has a corrective effect on the depressed ribs. The elevation of the arms sideways-upward tends to produce lateral expansion of the chest and thus correct the narrow chest condition.

2. Alternate double arm extension sideways with left arm sideways and right arm upward. In four counts this movement is performed as follows: (1) Arms are bent forward, (2) they are extended sideways forcibly, (3) they are flexed, (4) they are extended with the left going sideways as in (2) and the right upward.

The effect of forcible extension sideways is to broaden the shoulders and chest; combining the left sideways with the right upward is corrective of the left dorsal curvature.

3. Head rotation to the left and right. When the head is turned to the left bend it sideways-backward to elevate the right upper ribs.

4. (a) With the head turned to the left, fingers locked behind the head, keeping the elbows well back, bend the head and upper spine backward a few times.

The head turned to the left combined with backward flexion, tends to elevate the right ribs more than the left. The backward flexion in itself elevates all the ribs and supplies the chest. Keeping the elbows back in this movement reacts by correcting the round shoulders.

(b) For the purpose of relieving congestion of the back after any backward flexion one should always follow by bending the trunk forward. Therefore, in this case, to render this movement corrective of the spinal curvature as well as relieving of the congestion, place the left hand on the hip and the right behind the head, as you flex forward from the hips a few times.

5. (a) Hang on a slightly inclined bar or trapeze, with the hands as far apart as possible, right hand higher than left, and flex the arms to pull the body up a few times. Keep the elbows well out to the sides instead of close to the body.

(b) If unable to pull the body up to arm flexion, or in addition to it, hang with the arms as far apart as possible, right hand higher than the left, and flex one or both knees up to the chest a few times.

(c) Whenever you have the chance, play hang-tag, climb trees, or exercise on travelling rings.

The purpose of keeping the hands far apart is to produce lateral expansion of the chest and shoulders. The same reason applies for keeping the elbows to the sides at arm flexion as well as to correct the round shoulders. Knee upward flexion tends to strengthen the abdominal muscles and also correct lordosis.

6. Arms sideways, shoulder high, palms turned up. Elevate them to vertical as you raise the legs sideways alternately.

Besides being a balance movement this exercise has a broadening effect on the chest.

7. Arms flexed forward, fling them sideways forcibly as you lunge forward, first with the left and then with the right foot.

The chief effect of this exercise is to expand the chest and correct the round shoulders.

8. Running out of doors, or rope-skipping, to get up a good circulation and a demand for oxygen; thus reacting on the lungs by causing rapid respiration.

9. Arms bent, flex the trunk forward from the hips. While holding this position, in one motion, extend the left arm upward and the right sideways at the same time. The right palm is turned upward. Continuing the motion, elevate the right arm to vertical as you lower the left to horizontal and flex the arms again. Repeat a few times always to the same side.

The effect of this movement is corrective of the spinal curvature. Performed while the body is stooped forward with the head kept high, it is corrective of the round shoulders.

10. Lie on the back, arms resting on the floor back of the head. Elevate the legs to vertical a few times. Later, elevate them and lower them to one side; elevate them again and lower them to the other side, and so on. Various forms of leg elevations or movements may be introduced for variety.

The effect of this form of exercise is to strengthen the abdominal muscles, and thus support the viscera and correct sway back.

11. Standing with the feet apart, left hand on the hip, right hand behind the head, twist the trunk to the left and then to the right. When the trunk is turned to the left, bend the head and upper body to the left slightly.

The effect of this movement is to develop the transverse and oblique muscles of the abdomen, and thus strengthen nature's corset. By keeping the right hand back of the head while the left is on the hip, and especially by bending the upper spine to the left when the body is turned to the left, the right spinal muscles are extended more than the left and the movement is thus rendered corrective of the spinal curvature.

12. Arms held sideways at shoulder height, the feet apart. The right palm is turned upward while the left is kept downward. The trunk is bent to the left and then to the right alternately. As it is bent to the left the right arm is elevated and curled over the head; at the same time the head is turned to the left and bent slightly backward as it bends sideways with the trunk. As the body bends to the right the right arm is lowered to a line with the shoulder and the left arm is kept in line with the left shoulder while the head is simply bent sideways with the trunk, without being rotated to the right.

The general effect of this movement is on the side and waist muscles. It taxes the lumbar muscles, and the lateral fibres of the oblique abdominal muscles. It tends to broaden the waist and the chest. Lifting the right arm over the head as the trunk bends to the right, is corrective of the spinal curvature. Turning the head to the left, and bending it slightly backward as the trunk bends to the left is corrective of the right upper rib depression.

The physiological effect of sideways bending is to hasten portal circulation and, thereby, assimilation. As the trunk bends to the right the liver is compressed, thus forcing the blood out of it, and at the same time the portal veins and their branches are extended and their paths straightened, thus reducing the friction of the blood on the walls of the vessels and easing its flow. As the trunk bends to the left the portal veins and their branches are slightly compressed, thus forcing the blood out of them, and at the same time the liver is expanded and its capacity increased and the blood is sucked into it. This entire process, by hastening portal circulation, keeps up a rapid exchange of blood in the intestinal region and thus aids digestion.

13. Practice antagonistic exercises or various exercises with an elastic or spring exerciser.

Details are not necessary here because the program preceding this one can be referred to for suggestions. Just such exercises as are given there were explained to the pupil for whom this program was made out.

14. Practice various forms of jumping; upward, forward, sideways. Upward jump with arms and legs flung sideways particularly applies. (See Chapter II for various jumps.)

15. Repeat Exercise 1 of this program.

At the end of three months the boy's parents wrote that his spinal curvature was corrected. They were advised to omit those portions of the exercises that particularly applied to this defect. Thus the work was performed symmetrically, that is, the same movements were done to each side. But the head positions and movements corrective of the right upper rib depression were continued. It took over nine months to correct the rib defect. But the general musculature still lacked tone and the exercises on an elastic exerciser were continued. After over a year and a half of this program, the pupil was given an outline corresponding to those in Chapter II.

A FEW EXERCISES TO ARTICULATE AND LIMBER THE SPINE.

Every osteopath has had to treat patients whose spine was so rigid that it seemed almost hopeless to limber it enough to yield to treatment without hurting the patient. For such cases it is helpful to prescribe a few exercises that can be practiced at home daily to limber the spine. The following have been used with success. They are all exercises that occur at some time or other in a hygienic gymnastic program, but they will stand repetition in a group by themselves:

1. Arms extended upward, bend forward, touching the fingers to the floor if possible, without bending the knees. As you erect the trunk, keeping the spine limber, carry the arms backward and bend the head and trunk backward slightly. This is to be repeated several times.

2. Standing with the arms extended upward, twist the trunk to the left and bend forward, in relation to the shoulders, until the hands nearly or quite touch the floor. In coming up from this movement, still keeping the body turned, carry the arms and upper body back and then, forward and down again. Repeat a few times and then practice the movement with the body turned to the right.

3. Lock the fingers behind the head, the elbows forward, forearms close to the sides of the face. Twist the trunk to the left and bend as far as possible forward (in relation to the way the shoulders are facing), and to the left, at the same time pulling hard on the head to limber the upper dorsal spine. Repeat with the trunk turned to the right.

4. Standing with the feet apart, arms straight out from the shoulders. Make the spine as limp as possible while still preserving an erect position, and rapidly twist the trunk from side to side. The head should turn as far as possible so that one can see around further than to the rear and thus give the entire spine a longitudinal twist.

5. Standing with the feet apart, arms extended upward, bend as far as possible to the left, carrying the head as far as possible to the left and curling the right arm over the head. Bend to the right in the same way. Keep the spine limp in this exercise in order to get all the lateral bend possible.

6. Arms straight out from the shoulders, heels together, bend forward from the hips and, keeping the body bent and the arms straight from the shoulders, twist the trunk to the right so that the left arm will point directly at the floor while the right arm is straight upward. (Illus. 483.)   In this position reach for the floor, touching it between the feet, or, if possible, outside the right foot. Still keeping the body bent forward, twist it to the left and reach for the floor with the right hand, and so on.

7. Hanging on a horizontal bar, the spine as limp as possible, swing the legs from side to side, reaching for the floor with the feet. While simply hanging limp, with vibration applied along the spine, much relaxation is produced.

Occupational Gymnastics.

This term is used as expressive of gymnastics for harmonious development that are designed to counteract the evil influences of one's occupation. All occupations have some influence upon the health, be it good or bad. Many in themselves have an evil influence. Most forms of toil may be made to improve health through their effects upon the muscular system.

Whatever one's occupation may be, even though the entire muscular system is used, the exertion usually consists of a repetition of the same general motions. Thus all toil tends to produce one-sided development. To counteract this tendency one must vary his work, or make it bilateral, or practice some kind of exercise to counteract its one-sidedness.

For perfect health the body must be in perfect adjustment, each part with all the others, and if the daily occupation is such as to completely bring some portion out of co-operation with the rest, or to compress it and interfere with its normal functioning, deformity will result.

The principle in corrective gymnastics illustrates what happens in one-sided work. If one set of muscles is weak, its force is overbalanced by the muscles pulling in the opposite direction and the parts depending upon support and posture become deformed or diseased. The shortened flexor muscles of the arm in oarsmen or wrestlers show a condition produced by over contraction of these muscles and a neglect of their antagonists, the extensors. Dr. Sargent cites an example of swimmers who begin in childhood and continue frequent swimming to advanced life and thus acquire a broad, flat hand which better serves as a propeller in water.

The abnormalities which it is possible to develop by one-sided muscular exertion give us a clue as to how they may be counteracted. It is needless to reiterate the principles of corrective gymnastics; therefore we shall limit ourselves to a few concrete examples.

Shoveling dirt is a healthy form of toil from the muscular standpoint. The fibres of the deltoid and trapezius muscles that lift the shoulder up and back, on the side of the forward hand, the flexors of the arm and the forearm muscles that flex the fingers, the extensors of the back and legs, and the rotators of the entire trunk are brought into forcible action. The extensor muscles of the rear arm, that is, the one at the handle, are used more than its flexors. It has been said with good reason that this form of toil is one of the most healthful. When not overdone it ranks with the old style form of hay pitching. But the shovel user always has a favorite side. Usually, if one is right-handed, the left hand grips the shovel along the shaft and the right hand holds the grip. The shovel is thus lifted toward, and sometimes above, the left shoulder, and the body is at the same time twisted to the left. To counteract the one-sidedness that may result from this the shovel should be carried as much with the right hand forward, left hand back, and lifted to the right, as it is to the left. Whether this is done by timing oneself or counting the lifts matters little, so that each side is taxed equally. This would render shoveling a complete developer of the large and strong muscles.

But, for perfect physical development, it should be counteracted by light work preferably in the form of play. Shoveling is a slow and hard form of toil and produces slow, labored, clumsy movements, because it develops a muscle-bound condition. Relaxing exercises, free-standing home gymnastics, stretching exercises and games should be indulged in at every opportunity. Opportunities are abundant at present with the increasing number of playgrounds.

What is said about shoveling applies with equal force and little variation in pitching hay, swinging the sledge, chopping, hoeing and whatever other occupations require lifting or striking. Whatever the motion is, the opposite should be done to balance the effect of the effort and any game or corrective procedure that is indicated should be supplemented for the sake of health and physique.

It is needless to enumerate every form of toil in which the corrective principles may be applied, for the plan of procedure to counteract any abnormal development is plain.

The details I have stressed as necessary to develop a perfect physique may frequently seem trifling, but remember Michael Angelo's statement to one of his visitors. Michael Angelo had been working a long time at a piece of sculpture which to his frequent visitor had seemed finished for many days. The visitor wondered why the sculptor kept puttering away at it, touching it here, then there, and then all over again, never seeming quite satisfied with it, so he asked why the sculptor wasted so much time on trifles which no beholder could ever discover. Angelo, who was too thorough to ever turn out a piece of work short of perfection, answered: "It is true that these are mere trifles, but trifles make perfection and perfection is no trifle."

APPENDIX

For the benefit of teachers of gymnastics who wish to make use of the movements described in Chapter II, the commands are given below. The descriptions of the movements alone do not suggest the best commands and unless one has made a study of Swedish gymnastics he is liable to confuse his pupils with inexact commands. Every teacher of gymnastics has some method of arranging his pupils for class work and we will not take up space for such explanations. The commands are given for the movements in the order they come in the lessons. A dash precedes and an exclamation point follows the words that are to be emphasized. The commands are given only once, or for one side. Since each movement is to be repeated at least three times to either side for developing effect, the reader will understand that a repetition of the same commands with the side indicated will suffice. If the hands, arms or feet are left out of fundamental position after a movement has been repeated a sufficient number of times, the command "Position!" should be given.

LESSON I.

1. "Head to the left (r)—turn! Forward—turn!"
2. "Head to the left (r)—bend! Upward—Stretch!"
3. "Hips—firm! Heels—lift! Heels—sink!"
4. "Arm elevation sideways with respiration—one! Two!"
5. "Hips—firm! Left foot sideways—place! Trunk to the left (r)—turn! Forward—turn! etc. Position!"
6. (a) "Hips—firm! Trunk backward—bend! Upward—stretch!" (b) "Trunk forward—bend! Upward—stretch! Position!"
7. "Arm extension upward and forward, in four counts—one! Two! Three! Four! etc. Position!"
8. "Hips—firm! Heels—lift! Knees—bend! Knees—stretch! Heels—sink! Position!"
9. "Alternate arm flinging forward-upward, beginning with the left—one! Two! etc. Position!"
10. "Hips—firm! Left foot sideways—place! Trunk to the left (r)—bend! Upward—stretch! etc. Position!"
11. "Arm elevation forward-upward with respiration—one! Two!"

LESSON II.

1. "Head backward—bend! Upward—stretch!"
2. "Heels—lift! Sink!"
3. "Arms upward—bend! Arm extension sideways with respiration—one! Two! Position!"
4. "Prepare to jump—one! Two! Three! Four!"
5. "Hips—firm! Left (r) foot forward—place! Trunk to the left (r)—turn! Trunk forward—turn!"
6. As Lesson I.

7. "Arm extension sideways and backward—one! Two! Three! Four!"

8. "Hips—firm! Left (r) leg backward—lift! Sink!"

9. "Arms upward—stretch! Heels—lift! Upward—reach! Lowering the heels slowly—position!"

10. "Prepare to run! (This means to bend the forearms along the chest, fingers curled upward, and at the same time rise on the toes.) In place—run! Halt! Or, in place—walk! In a gymnasium class it should be: 'Double quick—march!' after 'Prepare to run!'"

11. "Arms sideways—lift! Palms upward—turn! Turn them down again! Repeat with count—one! Two!"

12. "Lie on your back! Arms upward—stretch! Left (r) knee upward—bend! Upward—stretch! Leg sink!" To bring the pupils to position: "Place the hands under the small of the back—push against the floor as you come up to sitting. Cross the legs and spring up to—position!"

13. "Hips—firm! Trunk to the left (r)—bend! Upward—stretch!"

14. "Upward jump—one! Two! Three! Four! Five!"

15. "Arms forward—bend! Arm flinging sideways slowly with respiration—one! Two! Position!"

Lesson III.

1. "Hips—firm! Left foot sideways—place! Heels—lift! Sink! The same—one! Two! etc. Position!"

2. "Arms upward—bend! Alternate extension upward, beginning with the left—one! Two! etc. Position!"

3. As Exercise 14, Lesson II.

4. (a) "Hips—firm! Left foot sideways—place! Trunk to the left (r)—turn! Keeping it turned, trunk backward—bend! Upward—stretch! etc. Trunk forward—turn!"

(b) Going on from (a), "Trunk forward—bend! Upward—stretch! etc. Position!"

5. "Hips—firm! Feet—close! Left (r) foot forward—place! Heels—lift! Sink! etc. Position!"

6. "Arms forward—bend! Arm flinging sideways forcibly—one! Two!"

7. "Prepare to run. In place—run! Halt! (See Exercise 10, Lesson II.) Position!"

8. "Hips—firm! Trunk half-forward—bend! Head to the left (r)—turn! Forward—turn! etc. Trunk upward—stretch! Position!"

9. "Lie on your back! Arms upward—stretch! Left (r) leg upward—lift! Sink!" (Back to position as Exercise 12, Lesson II.)

10. "Hips—firm! Feet—close! Trunk to the left (r)—bend! Upward—stretch! etc. Position!"

11. "Hips—firm! Heels—lift! Stride jump—begin—one! Two! etc. Stop! Heels—sink! Position!"

12. "Arm elevation sideways-upward, with respiration—one! Two! etc."

Lesson IV.

1. "Hips—firm! Left (r) foot sideways-forward—place! Change feet—one! Two! etc."

2. "Arms upward—bend! Arm extension sideways slowly with

the palms turned up, inhaling as they go out—one! Two! Position!"

3. "Prepare to jump—one! Two! Three! Four!"

4. (a) "Hips—firm! Trunk to the left (r)—turn! Keeping it turned, trunk backward—bend! Upward—stretch!" etc.

(b) "Trunk forward—bend! Upward—stretch! etc. Position!"

5. "Arms upward—bend! Trunk to the left (r)—turn! Arm extension sideways—one! Two! etc. Trunk forward—turn! Position!"

6. "Hips—firm! Alternate heel and toe elevation—one! Two! etc. Position!"

7. "Arms upward—bend! Arm extension sideways forcibly, palms turned up—one! Two! etc. Position!"

8. (As Exercise 10, Lesson II.)

9. "Arms sideways—lift! Trunk half-forward—bend! Head to the left (r)—turn! Head forward—turn! etc. Trunk upward—stretch! Position!"

10. "Heels—lift! Knees—bend! Place the hands on the floor, fingers inward, elbows inside the knees. Feet backward—place! Feet forward—place! etc. Position!"

11. "Hips—firm! Left (r) foot forward—place! Trunk to the left (r)—bend! Upward—stretch! etc. Position!"

12. "Forward jump—one! Two! Three! Four! Five!"

13. "Arm elevation sideways slowly with heel elevation and respiration—one! Two!"

Lesson V.

1. "Arms upward—bend! Alternate arm extension sideways, palms turned up, beginning with the left—one! Two! etc. Position!"

2. "Prepare to jump—one! Two! Three! Four!"

3. "Arms sideways—lift! Palms upward—turn! Arm elevation with heel elevation and respiration—one! Two! etc. Position!"

4. "Hips—firm! Feet—close! Left (r) foot forward—place! Trunk to the left (r)—turn! Forward—turn! etc. Position!"

5. (a) "Arms sideways—lift! Left (r) foot sideways-forward—place! Trunk to the left (r)—turn! Keeping it turned, trunk backward—bend! Upward—stretch! etc. Trunk forward—turn! Position!" (b) "In one movement, left foot sideways place and arm upward—stretch! Trunk forward—bend! Upward—stretch! Position!"

6. "Arms upward—bend! Trunk to the left (r)—turn! Arm extension upward—one! Two! etc. Position!"

7. "Hips—firm! Heels—lift! Head to the left (r)—turn! Forward—turn! etc. Heels—sink! Position!"

8. "Double arm flinging forward-upward—one! Two!"

9. "Prepare to run! In place—run!" Or, "Double quick—march! Halt! Position!"

10. "Arms sideways—lift! Trunk half-forward—bend! Palm turning forward-upward—one! Two! etc. Trunk upward—stretch! Position!"

11. (As Exercise 10, Lesson IV.)

12. "Hips—firm! Feet—close! Left (r) foot forward—place! Trunk to the left (r)—bend! Upward—stretch! etc. Change feet—one! Two! etc. Position!"

13. "With 90 degree turn to the left (r), upward jump—one! Two! Three! Four! Five!"

14. "Arm elevation forward-upward with heel elevation and respiration—one! Two!"

LESSON VI.

1. "Arm elevation sideways-upward with heel elevation and respiration—one! Two!"

2. "Arms forward—bend! Arm swimming—one! Two! Three! etc. Position!"

3. "Prepare to jump—one! Two! Three! Four!"

4. "Feet—close! Arms sideways—lift! Trunk to the left (r) —turn! Forward—turn! etc. Position!"

5. (a) "Feet—close! Arms sideways—lift! Left (r) foot forward—place! Trunk backward—bend! Upward—stretch! etc. Position!" (b) [As (b), Exercise 5, Lesson V.]

6. "Arms upward—bend! Trunk to the left (r)—turn! Arm extension upward and forward—one! Two! Three! Four! etc. Trunk to the right—turn! etc. Trunk forward—turn! Position!"

7. "Arms sideways—lift! Heels—lift! Head to the left (r) turn! Forward—turn! etc. Heels—sink! Position!"

8. "Left arm upward and right arm sideways stretch—one! Two! Change arms—one! Two! etc. Position!"

9. (As Exercise 9, Lesson V.)

10. "Arms sideways—lift! Trunk half-forward—bend! Palm turning forward-upward—one! Two! etc. Trunk upward—stretch! Position!"

11. (As Exercise 11, Lesson V.)

12. "Hips—firm! Left foot sideways—place! Trunk to the left (r)—turn! Trunk to the left (r)—bend! Upward—stretch! etc. Trunk forward—turn! Position!"

13. "Sideways jump—one! Two! Three! Four! Five!"

14. "Arms forward—bend! Fling them sideways slowly, as you place the left (r) foot forward and breathe in—one! Two! Right foot forward, three! Four! etc. Position!"

LESSON VII.

1. "Arm elevation forward-upward with heel elevation and respiration—one! Two!"

2. "Hips—firm! Feet—close! Alternate foot placing forward with heel elevation, beginning with the left—one! Two! Three! Four! Five! Six! Seven! Eight! etc. Position!"

3. "Arms upward—bend! Arm extension sideways, palms turned up—one! Two! etc. Position!"

4. "Arms sideways—lift! Trunk to the left (r)—turn! Forward—turn! etc. Position!"

5. (a) "Arms sideways—lift! Left foot sideways—place! Trunk backward—bend! Upward—stretch!" etc. (b) (Continuing with the feet apart.) "Arms upward—stretch! Trunk forward—bend! Upward—stretch! etc. Position!"

6. "Neck—firm! Heels—lift! Sink! etc. Position!"

7. "Arms forward—bend! Trunk half-forward—bend! Arm flinging sideways—one! Two! etc. Trunk upward—stretch! Position!"

8. "Prepare to run! Double quick—march! Halt! Position!"

(The running in class work is only one of the maneuvers of marching.)

9. "Arms upward—bend! Trunk half-forward—bend! Arm extension sideways and backward—one! Two! Three! Four! etc. Trunk upward—stretch! Position!"

10. "Stoop-fall position—one! Two! Head to the left (r)—turn! To the right (left)—turn! etc. Position—one! Two!"

11. "Hips—firm! Left (r) foot forward—place! Trunk to the left (r)—turn! Trunk to the left—bend! Upward—stretch! Trunk forward—turn! Change feet—one! Two!" [Repeat to the right (left).] Position!"

12. "Arms upward—bend! Trunk to the left (r)—turn! Arm extension sideways and upward—one! Two! Three! Four! etc. Trunk forward—turn! Position!"

13. "Hips—firm! Left (r) foot forward—place! Heels—lift! Change feet jumping, begin—one! Two! etc. Stop! Heels—sink! Position!"

14. "Arms upward—bend! Feet—close! Trunk to the left (r)—turn! Arm extension sideways slowly, palms turned up, with respiration—one! Two! Trunk forward—turn! Position!"

Lesson VIII.

1. "Arms forward—bend! Feet—close! Trunk to the left (r)—turn! Arm flinging sideways slowly, with respiration—one! Two! Trunk forward—turn! Position!"

2. "Hips—firm! Left (r) foot crosswise-forward—place! Heels—lift! Sink! etc. Change feet—one! Two! Heels—lift! Sink! Position!"

3. "Arms sideways—lift! Palm turning upward—one! Two! Position!"

4. "Arms sideways—lift! Left (r) foot sideways-forward—place! Trunk to the left (r)—turn! Forward—turn! Change feet—one! Two! etc. Position!"

5. (a) "Right hand on the hip, left arm upward stretch—one! (Both arms bend upward)—two! (The left arm goes up while the right grasps the hip.) Right foot forward—place! Trunk backward—bend! Upward—stretch! Change arms and feet—one! Two! etc. Position!"

(b) "Arms upward—stretch! Trunk forward—bend! Upward—stretch! Position!"

6. "Arms upward—bend! Trunk to the left (r)—turn! Arm extension sideways and backward—one! Two! Three! Four! Trunk forward—turn! Position!"

7. "Neck—firm! Left foot sideways—place! Heels—lift! Sink! Position!"

8. "Arms forward—lift! Arms flinging sideways—one! Two! Position!"

9. (As above for running.)

10. "Arms forward—bend! Trunk half-forward—bend! Arms swimming—one! Two! Three! Trunk upward—stretch! Position!"

11. "Lie on your back. Neck—firm! Grasp! Knees upward—bend! Knees upward—stretch! Slowly, legs sink! Position! One! Two!" (See Exercise 12, Lesson II.)

12. "Hips—firm! Left (r) foot sideways-forward—place!

Trunk to the left—turn! Trunk to the left (r)—bend! **Upward**—stretch! Change feet—one! Two! etc. Position!"

13. "Arms flung sideways, upward jump—one! Two! Three! Four! Five!"

14. "Arms forward—bend! Trunk to the left (r)—turn! Arm flinging sideways slowly with respiration—one! Two! Trunk forward—turn! Position!"

LESSON IX.

1. "Arms forward—bend! Arm flinging sideways slowly with respiration—one! Two! Position!"

2. "Arms upward—bend! Left (r) arm upward and right (l) arm sideways—stretch! Change arms—one! Two! etc. Position!"

3. "Prepare to jump—one! Two! Three! Four!"

4. "Arms sideways—lift! Left (r) foot forward—place! Trunk to the left (r)—turn! Forward—turn! etc. Change feet—one!

5. (a) "Left foot sideways—place! Left (r) arm upward stretch and right (l) hand hip firm—one! Two! Trunk to the left (r)—turn! Trunk backward—bend! Upward—stretch! etc. Trunk forward—turn! Change arms—one! Two! Trunk to the right (l)—turn! etc. Position!"

(b) As (b), Exercise 5, Lesson VIII.

6. "Arms upward—bend! Trunk to the left (r)—turn! Arm extension forward and upward—one! Two! Three! Four! etc. Position!"

7. "Neck—firm! Feet—close! Left (r) foot forward—place! Heels—lift! Sink! etc. Change feet—one! Two! etc. Position!"

8. "Arms sideways—lift! Arms flinging forward—one! Two! Position!"

9. As given above for running.

10. "Arms upward—bend! Trunk half-forward—bend! Left arm upward and right arm sideways—stretch! Change arms—one! Two! etc. Arms—bend! Trunk upward—stretch! Position!"

11. "Lie on your back! Neck—firm!" The rest is as for Exercise 9, Lesson VIII.

12. "Hips—firm! Trunk to the left (r)—turn! Trunk to the left (r)—bend! Upward—stretch! Trunk to the right—turn! etc. Forward—turn! Position!"

13. "Arms and legs flung sideways, upward jump—one! Two! Three! Four! Five!"

14. "Feet—close! Trunk to the left (r) turn! Arm elevation forward-upward with respiration—one! Two!"

LESSON X.

1. "Arms upward—bend! Arm extension sideways slowly, palms turned up, with respiration—one! Two! Position!"

2. "Hips—firm! Heels—lift! Head rotation to the left and right—one! Two! Heels—sink! Position!"

3. "Hips—firm! Left foot sideways-forward—lunge! Change feet—one! Two! etc. Position!"

4. "Feet—close! Arms sideways—lift! Left foot forward—place! Trunk to the left—turn! Forward—turn! Change feet—one! Two! etc. Forward—turn! Position!"

5. (a) "Arms upward—bend! Trunk backward—bend! **Arm**

extension sideways—one! Two! etc. Trunk upward—stretch! Position!" (b) As (b), Exercise 5, Lesson VIII.

6. "Arms upward—bend! Trunk to the left (r)—turn! Arm extension forward and sideways—one! Two! Three! Four! etc. Position!"

7. "Hips—firm! Heel elevation and knee flexion to sitting position—one! Two! Three! Four! Position!"

8. "Arms upward—bend! Trunk half-forward—bend! Arms forward—stretch! Arms flinging upward—one! Two! etc. Arms —bend! Trunk upward—stretch! Position!"

9. As for running in above lessons.

10. "Arms upward—bend! Left foot sideways—place! Trunk half-forward—bend!" Remainder of command as Exercise 10, Lesson IX.

11. "Stoop fall position—one! Two! Foot placing forward and backward—one! Two! etc. Position—one! Two!"

12. "Hips—firm! Feet—close! Trunk to the left (r)—turn! Trunk to the left (r)—bend! etc. Trunk to the right (l)—turn! etc. Trunk forward—turn! Position!"

13. "Half-step forward jump—one! Two! Three! Four!"

14. "Feet—close! Trunk to the left (r)—turn! Arm elevation sideways-upward with respiration—one! Two!"

LESSON XI.

1. "Arms sideways—lift! Palms upward—turn! Arm elevation with respiration—one! Two! Position!"

2. As Exercise 1, Lesson I.

3. "Hips—firm! Left foot forward—lunge! Change feet— one! Two! etc. Position!"

4. "Feet—close! Arms sideways—lift! Left (r) foot forward—place! Trunk to the left (r)—turn! Forward—turn! etc. Change feet—one! Two! etc. Position!"

5. "Arms upward—bend! Left foot sideways—place!" The rest like Exercise 5, Lesson X.

6. "Left foot sideways—place! Trunk to the left (r)—turn! Arm extension forward, upward, sideways and backward—one! Two! Three! Four! Five! Six! Seven! Eight! etc. Trunk to the right (l)—turn! Repeat with count—etc. Trunk forward— turn! Position!"

7. "Arms upward—stretch! Heels—lift! Reach upward! Arms bend and heels sink! etc. Position!"

8. "Arms sideways—lift! Trunk half-forward—bend! Arm flinging forward and sideways—one! Two! etc. Trunk upward— stretch! Position!"

9. As for running in above lessons.

10. "Arms upward—bend! Trunk half-forward—bend! Alternate arm extension sideways, palm turned up, beginning with the left—one! Two! etc. Trunk upward—stretch! Position!"

11. "Hips—firm! Heels—lift! Knees—bend; Kneel! Trunk backward—incline! Upward—stretch! etc. Sit back on the heels and spring up to—Position!"

12. "Hips—firm! Left foot sideways—lift! Grasp! (At stallbars the foot is hooked between two rungs.) Trunk to the right— bend! Upward—stretch! Left foot—sink! About—face! Right foot sideways—lift! etc. Position!"

13. "Hips—firm! Heels—lift! Hop forward—begin! Stop! Heels—sink! Position!"

14. "Arms sideways—lift! Arm circumduction with respiration —one! Two! etc. Position!"

Lesson XII.

1. "Arm elevation forward-upward. with respiration—one! Two!"

2. "Alternate arm flinging forward-upward, beginning with the left—one! Two! etc. Position!"

3. "Hips—firm! Feet—close! Left foot forward—lunge! Change feet—one! Two! etc. Position!"

4. "Arms sideways—lift! Heels—lift! Knees—bend! Kneel! Trunk to the left—turn! To the right—turn! etc. Forward— turn! Sit back on the heels and spring up to—Position!"

5. (a) "Arms upward—stretch! Left foot forward—place! Trunk backward—bend! Upward—stretch! Change feet—one! Two! etc. Position!"

(b) As given above.

6. "Arms upward—bend! Left foot forward—place! Trunk to the left—turn! Arm extension sideways—one! Two! Trunk forward—turn! Change feet—one! Two! Trunk to the right— turn! etc. Position!"

7. "Feet close! Arms upward—stretch! Heels—lift! Reach! Heels—sink! Position!"

8. "Arms sideways—lift! Arms half-forward—bend! Arm flinging upward—one! Two! etc. Position!"

9. As given above.

10. "Arms upward—stretch! Trunk half-forward—bend! Arm extension upward—one! Two! Trunk upward—stretch! Position!"

11. "Lie on your back! Neck—firm! Left leg upward—lift! Sink! Right leg—lift! Sink! etc. Place the hands under the small of the back. Push up to—sitting! Cross the legs and spring up to—Position!"

12. "Left arm upward, stretch, and right hand hip—firm! Trunk to the right—bend! Upward—stretch! Change arms—one! Two! etc. Position!"

13. "Hips—firm! Left leg backward—lift! Heel—lift! Toe hopping—begin! Stop! Heel—sink! Change feet—one! Two! etc. Position!"

14. "Arms forward—bend! Trunk to the left—turn! Arm flinging sideways slowly with respiration—one! Two! etc. Trunk to the right—turn! etc. Position!"

Lesson XIII.

"Arm elevation sideways with knee flexion and respiration —one! Two!"

2. "Arms sideways—lift! Arms flinging forward—one! Two! Position!"

3. "Prepare to jump—one! Two! Three! Four!"

4. "Neck—firm! Left foot sideways—place! Trunk to the left—turn! Forward—turn! To the right—turn! Forward— turn! Position!"

5. (a) "Feet—close! Arms upward—stretch! Left foot for-

ward—place! Trunk backward—bend! Upward—stretch! etc. Change feet—one! Two! etc. Position!"

(b) "Arms upward—stretch! Trunk to the left—turn! Trunk forward—bend! Upward—stretch! Trunk to the right—turn! etc. Position!"

6. "Arms upward—bend! Feet—close! Left (r) foot forward—place! Trunk to the left (r)—turn! Arm extension upward—one! Two! etc. Trunk forward—turn! Change feet—one! Two! etc. Position!"

7. "Feet—close! Arms upward—stretch! Left foot forward—place! Heels—lift! Sink! etc. Change feet—one! Two! etc. Position!"

8. "Arms upward—bend! Left foot sideways—place! Trunk half-forward—bend! Arm extension upward—one! Two! etc. Trunk upward—stretch! Position!"

9. As given for running in above lessons.

10. "Arms upward—stretch! Trunk half-forward—bend! Arm elevation—one! Two! Trunk upward—stretch! Position!"

11. "Hips—firm! One the left—kneel! Trunk backward—incline! Upward—stretch! etc. Change knees—one! Two! etc. Position!"

12. "Right hand hip firm and left arm upward stretch—one! Two! Trunk to the right—bend! Upward—stretch! Change arms—one! Two! etc. Position!"

13. "One hundred and eighty degrees turn, upward jump—one! Two! Three! Four! Five!"

14. "Left foot sideways—place! Trunk to the left—turn! Arm elevation sideways with respiration—one! Two! Trunk to the right—turn! etc. Trunk forward—turn! Position!"

Lesson XIV.

1. "Arm sideways—lift! Palms upward—turn! Arm elevation with knee flexion and respiration—one! Two! Position!"

2. "Hips—firm! Alternate foot placing forward with heel elevation, beginning with the left—one! Two! Three! Four! Five! Six! Seven! Eight! Position!"

3. "Left arm upward and right arm sideways—stretch! Right palm upward—turn! Arm elevation—one! Two! Position!"

4. "Neck—firm! Heels—lift! Knees—bend! Kneel! Trunk to the left—turn! To the right—turn! etc. Forward—turn! Sit back on the heels and spring up to—Position!"

5. (a) "Left foot sideways—place! Arm upward—stretch! Trunk to the left—turn! Trunk backward—bend! Upward—turn!"

(b) Continuing from (a), "Trunk to the left—turn! Trunk forward-downward—bend! Upward—stretch! etc. To the right—turn! etc. Trunk forward—turn! Position!"

6. "Arms upward—bend! Feet—close! Left foot forward—place! Trunk to the left—turn! Arm extension sideways—one! Two! etc. Trunk forward—turn! Change feet—one! Two! Trunk to the right—turn! etc. Trunk forward—turn! Position!"

7. "Hips—firm! Left foot forward—place! Heel elevation and knee flexion—one! Two! Three! Four! Change feet—one! Two! etc. Position!"

8. "Left foot sideways—place! Arms upward—bend! Trunk

half-forward—bend! Arms forward—stretch! Arm flinging sideways—one! Two! Arms—bend! Trunk upward—stretch! Position!"

9. As given in above lessons for running.

10. "Arms upward—bend! Trunk half-forward—bend! Left arm upward, right arm sideways, palm turned up—stretch! Arm elevation—one! Two! Arms—bend! Trunk upward—stretch! Position!"

11. Pupils facing stall-bars or facing each other in two lines. Command is given to one line. "Sit on the floor! Feet—grasp! Trunk backward—stretch! Upward—bend! etc. Cross the feet and spring up to—Position!"

12. "Feet close! Left hand hip firm and right arm upward—stretch! Left foot forward—place! Trunk to the left—bend! Upward—stretch! etc. Change arms and feet—one! Two! etc. Position!"

13. "Hips—firm! Left foot sideways—place! Heels—lift! Heel-striking stride jump—one! Two! etc. Heels sink! Position!"

14. "Arms upward—bend! Left foot sideways—place! Trunk to the left (r)—turn! Arm extension sideways, palms turned up, with respiration—one! Two! Trunk forward—turn! Position!"

LESSON XV.

1. "Head backward—bend! Upward—stretch! Head to the left—bend! Upward—stretch! To the right—bend! Upward—stretch!"

2. "Heels—lift! Sink!"

3. "Arms upward—bend! Arm extension upward with lunging forward alternately, first with the left foot, and then the right—one! Two! Three! Four! etc. Position!"

4. "Prepare to jump—one! Two! Three! Four!"

5. "Arm elevation sideways-upward with heel elevation and respiration—one! Two!"

I. (a) Class lined up back to wall or stall-bars, or in double line, rear line to support. "Arms upward—stretch! Trunk backward—bend! Grasp! Heels—lift! Sink! etc. Upward—stretch! Position!"

(b) "Left foot sideways—place! Arms upward—stretch! Trunk forward-downward—bend! Upward—stretch! Position!"

II. Pupils facing bars. "Under grasp—grasp! Arms bend! Stretch! etc. Position!"

III. (a) "Hips—firm! Leg circling beginning with the left—one! (Raise the leg forward.) Two! (Circle it and bring it forward at "one!" etc.) Change feet—one! Two! etc. Position!"

(b) "Hips—firm! Left foot crosswise-forward—place! Heel elevation and knee flexion—one! Two! Three! Four! etc. Change feet—one! Two! etc. Position!"

IV. (a) "Arms forward—lift! Arm flinging sideways—one! Two! Position!"

(b) "Arms sideways—lift! Arms half-forward—bend! Arm flinging upward—one! Two! etc. Position!"

V. As explained in above lessons for running.

VI. "Arms upward—bend! Trunk half-forward—bend! Arm extension upward slowly—one! Two! Trunk upward—stretch! Position!"

VII. "Stoop fall position—one! Two! Alternate leg elevation beginning with the left—one! Two! Three! Four! Feet forward —place! Position!"

VIII. "Arms upward—stretch! Left foot forward—place! Trunk to the left—turn! Forward—turn! etc. Change feet—one! Two! etc. Position!"

IX. "Side-fall position on the left hand—one! Two! Three! Leg elevation—one! Two! etc. Change hands—one! Two! etc. Forward—turn! Feet forward—place! Position!"

X. "Arms upward—stretch! Heels—lift! Slow walking forward—one! Two! etc. Backward—one! Two! etc. Heels—sink! Position!"

XI. (a) (Class lined in single file and take turns running and walking as teacher directs.)

(b) "Twice upward jump—one! Two! Three! Four! Five! Six!"

XII. "Arms forward—bend! Arm flinging sideways slowly with slow marching forward, beginning with the left foot—one! Two! etc. About—face! The same, beginning with the right foot— one! Two! Position!"

Lesson XVI.

1. "Neck—firm! Heels—lift! Sink! Position!"

2. "Arms forward—bend! Arm flinging sideways with lunging forward beginning with the left—one! Two! Three! Four! Position!"

3. (As given above.)

4. "Arms upward—bend. Arm extension sideways, palms turned up—one! Two! Position!"

5. "Arm elevation forward-upward with respiration—one! Two!"

I. (a) "Arms upward—stretch! Trunk backward—bend! Grasp! Left knee upward—bend! Stretch! Right knee—bend! Stretch! Trunk upward—stretch!"

(b) [Continuing from (a).] "Trunk forward-downward— bend! Upward—stretch! Position!"

II. (a) Class in single file, take turns at travelling rings.

(b) Class facing horizontal bar, chest high. "Over grasp— grasp! Feet forward—place! Arms—bend! Stretch! Position!"

III. "Neck—firm! Heels—lift! Left leg backward—lift! Sink! Right leg—lift! Sink! etc. Heels—sink! Position!"

IV. "Arms upward—stretch! Trunk half-forward—bend! Lower the arms forward. Arms upward—fling! Lower them again. The same with count—one! Two! etc. Trunk upward— stretch! Position!"

V. For running, as given above. "Hips—firm! Heels—lift! Knees—bend! Sit! Hopping forward—start! Stop! Knees— stretch! Heels—sink! Position!"

VI. "Lie face down. Feet—grasp! Arms upward—bend! Trunk upward—bend! Arm extension sideways, palms turned up —one! Two! Trunk—sink! Place the hands on the floor, fingers turned inward. Arms—stretch! Feet forward—place! Position!"

VII. "Hips—firm! Heels—lift! Knees—bend! Kneel! Trunk backward—incline! Upward—stretch! Sit back on the heels and spring up to—position!"

VIII. "Neck—firm! Feet—close! Left foot forward—place! Trunk to the left—turn! Forward—turn! etc. Change feet—one! Two! etc. Position!"

IX. "Arms upward—stretch! Trunk to the left—bend! Upward—stretch! To the right—bend! Upward—stretch! Position!"

X. "Over grasp—grasp! Knees upward—bend! Alternate knee extension forward, beginning with the left—one! Two! etc. Knees downward—stretch! Position!"

XI. "Jump to opposite sides, first to the right—one! Two! Three! Four! Five! Six!"

XII. "Arm elevation sideways-upward with heel elevation and respiration—one! Two!"

Lesson XVII.

1. "Heels—lift! Sink!"

2. "Hips—firm! Alternate leg elevation sideways, beginning with the left—one! Two! Three! Four! Position!"

3. "Arms forward—bend! Arm flinging sideways with alternate lunging forward, beginning with the left—one! Two! Three! Four! Position!"

4. "Arm elevation sideways with palm turning upward, heel elevation and respiration—one! Two!"

I. (a) "Arms upward—stretch! Trunk backward—bend! Travel downward—one! Two! etc. Travel up again—one! Two! etc. Trunk upward—stretch! Position!"

(b) "Arms upward—stretch! Left foot forward—place! Trunk forward-downward—bend! Upward—stretch! Change feet —one! Two! etc. Position!"

II. "Over grasp—grasp! Feet forward—place! Feet backward—place! etc. Position!"

III. "Arms sideways—lift! Palms upward—turn. Arm elevation with heel elevation and leg elevation sideways, beginning with the left—one! Two! Three! Four! Position!"

IV. "Hips—firm! Left foot sideways-forward—lunge! Arms forward—lift! Arm flinging sideways—one! Two! etc. Hips—firm! Change feet—one! Two! (The same arm movement.) Hips—firm! Position!"

V. As given above for running.

VI. "Lie face down. Feet—grasp! Arms upward—bend! Trunk upward—bend! Arm extension upward—one! Two! etc. Trunk—sink! Place the hands on the floor, fingers inward. Push up to stoop fall. Feet forward—place! Position!"

VII. From the above movement, instead of coming to stoop fall the pupils might be commanded to: "Turn over! Neck—firm! Legs upward—lift! Sink! etc. Place the hands under the small of the back. Push up to—sitting! Cross the legs and spring up to —position!"

VIII. "Feet—close! Arms upward—stretch! Left foot forward—place! Trunk to the left—turn! Forward—turn! Change feet—one! Two! etc. Position!"

IX. "Arms upward—bend! Left foot sideways—place! Trunk flexion alternately to the left and then to the right, with arm extension—one! Two! Three! Four! Position!"

X. Pupil at the parallel bars. "Balance hang—hang! Arms—bend! Stretch! etc. Position!"

XI. Class in line to follow in turn as directed.

XII. "Arms forward—bend! Arm flinging sideways slowly, with half-step sideways-forward and respiration—one! Two! Position!"

Lesson XVIII.

1. "Arm elevation sideways with heel elevation and respiration—one! Two!"

2. "Hips—firm! Left leg backward—lift! Sink! Right leg—lift! Sink! Position!"

3. "Left arm upward, right arm sideways—stretch! Change arms—one! Two! etc. Left arm upward, right forward—one! Two! etc. Left arm sideways, right arm forward—one! Two! etc. Position!"

4. As given in preceding lessons.

I. (a) and (b) as in preceding lesson.

II. Class in line taking turns to do as commanded.

III. "Hips—firm! Horizontal half-standing position on the left foot. Right leg backward—lift! Arch the body from head to foot! Right leg—sink! Left leg backward—lift! etc. Position!"

IV. "Arm flinging forward-upward with lunging forward alternately, beginning with the left foot—one! Two!"

V. As given above for running.

VI. "Lie face down. Feet—grasp! Neck—firm! Trunk upward—bend! Forward—sink!"

VII. Continuing from the above: "Place the hands on the floor, fingers inward. Push up to stoop fall! Feet through the hands—place! Feet backward—place! etc. Feet forward—place! Position!"

VIII. "Arms sideways—lift! Left foot sideways—place! Rapid trunk rotation to the left and right—one! Two! etc. Trunk forward—turn! Position!"

IX. "Side fall position on the left hand—one! Two! Three! Right arm upward—stretch! Arm and leg elevation—one! Two! etc. Change sides—one! Two! Left arm upward—stretch! etc. Trunk forward—turn! Feet forward—place! Position!"

X. "Over-grasp—grasp! Legs forward—lift! Sink! Position!"

XI. "Ninety degrees turning to the left, upward jump—start! Stop! The same to the right—start! Stop! Position!"

XII. "Arms sideways—lift! Palms upward—turn! Arm elevation with heel elevation and respiration—one! Two! Position!"

Lesson XIX.

1. "Arm elevation forward-upward with respiration—one! Two!"

2. "Hips—firm! Left leg sideways—lift! Sink! Right leg—lift! Sink! Position!"

3. "Arm swimming—one! (At one the arms are bent forward.) Two! Three! (Two and three are run together as the arms are carried forward and sideways.) Position!"

4. As Exercise 3, Lesson XVIII.

I. (a) "Arms upward—bend! Trunk backward—bend! Arm extension sideways—one! Two! Trunk upward—stretch! Position!"

(b) "Arms upward—stretch! Trunk forward-downward—bend! Touch the floor! Upward—stretch! Position!"

II. At the teacher's discretion.

III. "Arms forward—bend! Horizontal half-standing position on the left foot. Right leg backward—lift! Arm swimming—one!

Two! Three! etc. Right leg—sink! Left leg backward—lift! etc. Sink! Position!"

IV. "Hips—firm! Left foot sideways-forward—lunge! Trunk to the left—turn! Arms forward—lift! Arm flinging sideways—one! Two! etc. Hips—firm! Trunk forward—turn! Change feet—one! Two! etc. Position!"

V. Running as explained above. Low down dance. "Arms forward—lift! Heels—lift! Knees—bend! Right knee forward—stretch! Change feet jumping—start! Stop! Knees—stretch! Heels—sink! Position!"

VI. "Arms upward—bend! Horizontal half-standing position on the left foot right leg backward—lift! Arms sideways—stretch! Palms upward—turn! Arm elevation—one! Two! Arms—bend! Right leg—sink! Left leg backward—lift! etc. Left leg—sink! Position!"

VII. "Stoop fall position—one! Two! Left leg—lift! Arms—bend! Stretch! Left leg—sink! Right leg—lift! etc. Feet forward—place! Position!"

VIII. "Feet—close! Arms sideways—lift! Trunk rotation rapidly to the left and right—one! Two! etc. Trunk forward—turn! Position!"

IX. (a) "Hips—firm! Trunk flexion sideways with opposite leg elevation, first to the left—one! Two! Position!"

(b) "Right (l) foot sideways and arms sideways—lift! Trunk flexion to the left (r)—one! Two! etc. Position!"

X. "Balance hang—hang! Horizontal lever trunk forward—bend! Legs in line with the body. Trunk upward—stretch! Position! or, 'Spring off!' "

XI. (a) At teacher's discretion.

(b) "Sideways-forward jump, first to the left—one! Two! Three! Four!"

XII. "Arm elevation forward-upward with trunk rotation and heel elevation, first to the left—one! Two! Three! Four!"

Lesson XX.

1. "Head to the left—turn! Forward—turn! To the right—turn! etc. Head backward—bend! Upward—stretch!"

2. "Arms upward—stretch! Left foot sideways—place! Heel elevation and knee flexion—one! Two! Three! Four! Position!"

3. "Arms upward—bend! Left arm upward, right arm downward, stretch, and left foot sideways-forward—lunge! Change arms and feet—one! Two! etc. Position!"

4. "Arm elevation forward-upward with heel elevation and respiration—one! Two!"

I. (a) "Neck—firm! Left foot sideways—place! Trunk to the left—turn! Trunk backward—bend! Upward—stretch! etc. Trunk to the right—turn! etc. Trunk forward—turn! Position!"

(b) "Arms upward—stretch! Trunk to the left—turn! Trunk forward-downward—bend! Upward—stretch! Trunk to the right—turn! etc. Trunk forward—turn! Position!"

(a)' "Arms upward—stretch! Left foot sideways—place! Trunk backward—bend! Place the hands on the floor! Upward—stretch! Position!"

(b)' "Arms upward—stretch! Trunk forward-downward—bend! Touch the palms to the floor! Trunk upward—stretch!"

II. "Over grasp—grasp! Legs forward—lift! Leg abduction

—one! Two! Arms—bend! Leg abduction—one! Two! Arms —stretch! etc. Legs—sink! Position!"

III. (a) "Neck—firm! Heels—lift! Left knee forward— bend! Stretch! Right knee—bend! Stretch! etc. Heels—sink! Position!"

(b) "Arms upward—stretch! Horizontal half-standing position on the left foot right leg backward—lift! Right leg sink, arms forward—reach, and right leg forward—lift! Left knee—bend! Stretch! Right leg backward—lift, with arms upward—stretch! etc., as before. Change feet—one! Two! Left leg backward— lift! etc. Position!"

IV. "Arm flinging forward-upward with long lunge forward— lunge! Arm flinging with change of feet forward—one! Two! etc. Position!"

V. As explained above, in Exercise 5, Lesson XIX.

VI. "Lie face down! Feet—grasp! Arms upward—stretch! Trunk upward—bend! Arm elevation—one! Two! etc. Place the hands on the floor, fingers inward and push up to stoop fall. Feet forward—place! Position!"

VII. (a) "Arms upward—stretch! Left leg forward—lift! Grasp! Trunk backward—bend! Upward—stretch! Change feet —one! Two! etc. Position!"

(b) "Reverse stoop fall!" Or, "On the hands—stand!"

VIII. "Arms upward—stretch! Rapid trunk rotation to the left and right—one! Two! etc. Position!"

IX. "Feet sideways place and arms sideways—stretch! To the left—wheel! To the right—wheel! etc. Position!"

X. "Balance hang—hang! Horizontal lever on the left hand, right arm upward stretch and trunk forward—bend! Legs and arm in line with the body! Trunk upward—stretch! Change arms —one! Two! etc. Spring off to—position!"

XI. "Lie on your back! Prepare to spring up. Legs over head bend and hands on the floor—place! Spring up to—position!"

XII. "Stepping out with the left (r) foot, hitch kick—one! Two! Three!"

XIII. "Arm elevation sideways with palm rotation, heel elevation and respiration—one! Two!"

INDEX